Nova Scotia, *Digby to Cape Breton Island*

Including the Bras d'Or Lakes

A CRUISING GUIDE TO

Nova Scotia
Digby to Cape Breton Island

Peter Loveridge

Including
the Bras d'Or Lakes

PHYLLIS BLADES/ATLANTIC STOCK

INTERNATIONAL MARINE · Camden, Maine   McGraw-Hill Ryerson · Toronto/Montréal

International Marine/
Ragged Mountain Press

A Division of The **McGraw·Hill** *Companies*

10   9   8   7   6   5   4   3   2   1

Library of Congress Cataloging-in-Publication Data
Loveridge, Peter.
     A cruising guide to Nova Scotia : Digby to Cape
Breton Island, including the Bras d'Or lakes / Peter
Loveridge.
          p.   cm.
     Includes bibliographical references and index.
     ISBN 0-07-038808-3 (hardcover : alk. paper)
     1. Pilot guides—Nova Scotia.   I. Title.
VK986.L68   1997
623.89'29716—dc20   96-43313
                                                    CIP

*Questions regarding the content of this book should be
addressed to:*
INTERNATIONAL MARINE
P.O. Box 220
Camden, ME 04843
207-236-4837

*In Canada, questions regarding the ordering of this book
should be addressed to:*
MCGRAW-HILL RYERSON
Order Service Department
300 Water Street
Whitby, Ontario L1N 9B6
Phone: 1-800-565-5758
Fax: 1-800-463-5885

*In the U.S.A., questions regarding the ordering of this book
should be addressed to:*
THE MCGRAW-HILL COMPANIES
Customer Service Department
P.O. Box 547
Blacklick, OH 43004
Retail customers: 1-800-262-4729
Bookstores: 1-800-722-4726

A Cruising Guide to Nova Scotia is printed on acid-free
paper.

Printed by R.R. Donnelley, Crawfordsville, IN
Design by John Reinhardt
Production and page layout by Janet S. Robbins and
     Mary Ann Hensel
Edited by John Kettlewell, John Vigor, Tom McCarthy
Approach and harbor sketches by the author. Running
head maps by Paul Mirto.

For Heather, my love and constant companion in good times and adversity, both of which we have experienced to the full, and to our children, Jonathan, Sarah, and Lennox, who in maturity have come to appreciate the wonderful experiences of cruising this coast.

—PETER LOVERIDGE

Contents

Bay of Fundy

Port Wade
Digby
Annapolis Royal

Petit Passage

Brier I.

St. Mary's Bay

Kejimkujik
Lake

Bridgewater

Lake
Rossignol

Liverpool Hr.

Port Moulton

Yarmouth

Shelburne Hr.

Lockeport Hr.

Region 1

Pubnico Hr.

Seal I.
Baccaro Pt.
Cape
Sable I.

Barrington Passage

Region 2

LaHave River
LaHave Is.
Port Medway

Chester Hr.
Mahone Hr.
Mahone Bay
Lunenburg Hr.

Region 3

Bedford Basin
Head Hr.
Hubbards Cove
St. Margrets
Bay

Pennant Pt.

Halifax
Osborne Hd.

Region 4

Liscomb
Necum Teuch Hr.
Sheet Hr.
Popes Hr.
Ship Hr.
Bea

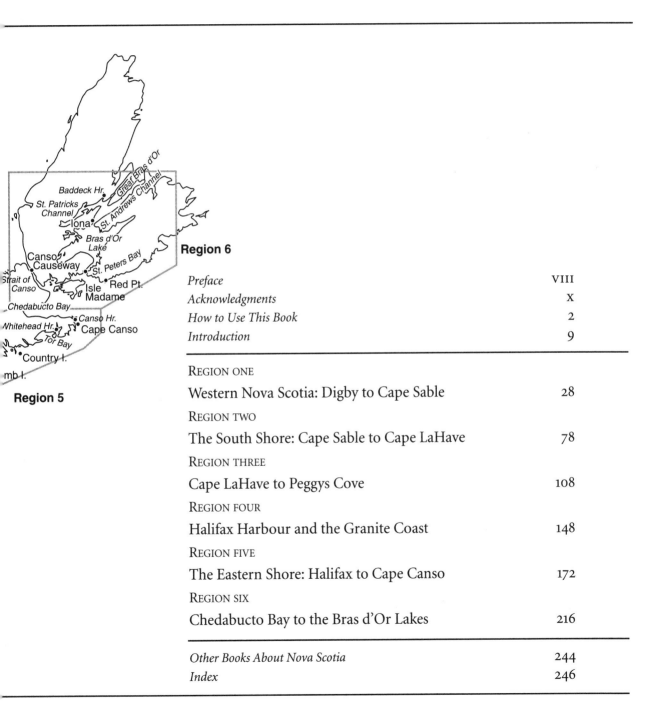

Baddeck Hr.
St. Patricks Channel
Great Bras d'Or
St. Andrews Channel
Iona
Bras d'Or Lake
Canso Causeway
St. Peters Bay
Strait of Canso
Isle Madame
Red Pt.
Chedabucto Bay
Canso Hr.
Whitehead Hr.
Cape Canso
Tor Bay
Country I.
mb I.

Region 5

Region 6

Preface	VIII
Acknowledgments	X
How to Use This Book	2
Introduction	9

REGION ONE

Western Nova Scotia: Digby to Cape Sable 28

REGION TWO

The South Shore: Cape Sable to Cape LaHave 78

REGION THREE

Cape LaHave to Peggys Cove 108

REGION FOUR

Halifax Harbour and the Granite Coast 148

REGION FIVE

The Eastern Shore: Halifax to Cape Canso 172

REGION SIX

Chedabucto Bay to the Bras d'Or Lakes 216

Other Books About Nova Scotia 244
Index 246

Preface

When I read other cruising guides, I am sometimes a little jealous. To produce them, there seems to be an army of helpers, and no end of helpful government departments and the like. Living in rural Nova Scotia, while always a challenge and sometimes a delight, removes one from much of this assistance, and it was with some trepidation that I started this project. Had I known what was involved—given that my day job does not usually allow me much free time—this project might have remained in my chart table as a series of hand-drawn charts in a loose-leaf folder.

I settled in Nova Scotia over twenty years ago, and in those days there were no guides of this type, or at least none available to me. I did, however, manage to visit virtually all the harbors in this book without that "local knowledge" beloved of official pilot books, but never to be found when you need it. During this process, I kept careful track of courses and bearings, in the hope that I could make an entry a second time, or at least, not run aground again on the same rock. The charts, drawings, and other navigational information that I collected were eagerly photocopied wherever I went, eventually resulting in this book.

I spent a great deal of this time on small, marginally outfitted boats, with cramped and poorly lit chart tables. Particularly when we were going to windward, such boats forced me to use every inshore passage and harbor of refuge, rather than motor-sail to windward ten miles offshore—the common practice of those with handier vessels than mine. My slow, and in many ways inadequate, vessels led to my visiting many more harbors than most cruisers did. Virtually none of my cruising has been done with more than a double-handed crew, though Heather and I are now getting quite efficient at this type of existence. Throughout the writing of this book, I have kept in mind the thought that the reader might be tired, cold, hungry, seasick, and apprehensive. I have been in all these states myself, sometimes all at the same time, so my major effort has been to try to clarify the pilotage. You cannot begin to experience a place unless you make its harbor safely, so I hope this type of priority will be helpful. All this has led to a book of rather a personal nature, and my tastes may not be the same as yours. I have also expressed my opinions as truthfully as I can, rather than acting as an agent of propaganda for the Department of Tourism. I realize that this will not find me favor everywhere I go. I have also drawn the sketches, and rarely under ideal conditions; but I hope they will give a reasonable representation of the harbors described. Any imperfections are all my own.

Those of us who live in Nova Scotia are used to the quirks of the place, and it could be that those of you "from away" might find the pace of business here somewhat frustrating. I know, for example, that on most of the eastern seaboard of the U.S.A. you can order a part from a mail-order catalogue on Monday, have it shipped by UPS or some similar organization, and receive it on Tuesday, if you pay the going rate. No such thing will happen here, regardless of any cajoling, expense, or outright bribery. It recently took me four months to get a V-belt and an impeller for my engine. Every business in the province has to deal with this sort of problem, so service may not be quite the same as it is in a U.S. metropolis.

Regarding this as part of the charm of the place, and easing your schedule somewhat, will be better for your blood pressure. Cruising from marina to marina, with telephone and power hook-up every night, is not possible anywhere in the province. Even simpler things, such as buying groceries or beer, can be a challenging experience. There may be times in the book when I have forgotten to emphasize this, so please accept my apologies.

Another quirk is language. American, Canadian, and "English" English are, despite outward similarity, quite different in spelling, grammar, and style—a fact that is only too apparent when you use computer programs to check them. I was born in England, but I'm now an assimilated Canadian, so I get confused myself, which may account for some eccentricities in the wording.

One of my favorite memories, and one that sustained me in the long nights of writing this work, is a comment from my friend Albert mentioned in the acknowledgements. Albert is an Acadian whose ancestors settled in the province in 1653. Roughly translated from his unprintable original was the comment: "Mais . . . (deleted) . . . Peter, it goes right to my soul that I have to admit that the best parts of Nouvelle Ecosse were shown to me by a . . . (deleted) . . . Brit."

I hope this book will be just as inspiring to those of you exploring our province. There will, perhaps, be some of you who feel, as I do, that the coast of Nova Scotia is the finest accessible cruising ground in North America. Nova Scotia has five thousand miles of shoreline, and any guide, especially when done singlehanded, is bound to become gradually outdated, or to be missing something altogether. Please send any corrections or additions to me, care of International Marine, P.O. Box 220, Camden, ME 04843.

Acknowledgments

I would like to sincerely thank the following people who have helped and encouraged me during the long nights I've spent producing this book.

First, my wife, Heather, who not only put up with the constant mess I created while building and maintaining old (and lately not-so-old) boats, but who has tolerated even greater disorder as I have worked on this book every night for eighteen months, remaining remarkably composed and encouraging.

To Wayne and Sherrill Bower, of the yacht *Teelok,* out of Maryland, who first suggested that my handwritten notes would be worth making into a book.

To Bill Shellenberger, author of *Cruising the Chesapeake: A Gunkholer's Guide,* whose advice guided me to International Marine.

To our friends and constant cruising companions of the last ten years, Albert and Myrna d'Entremont, of the yacht *Tiptoe,* out of West Pubnico, Nova Scotia, who have never failed in their belief that this would be the most comprehensive cruising guide to Nova Scotia ever printed.

To John Kettlewell and the staff of International Marine, who have turned my idle musings into reality.

I would also like to thank Cathy d'Entremont of the Western Regional Library, and Alice Newell of the Medical Records Department of the Yarmouth Regional Hospital for invaluable logistic support.

There is, however, another group of people I would like to thank—though many of them are no longer around to receive thanks in person—and to whom this book is dedicated. I refer to my predecessors in cruising the coast of Nova Scotia, the fishermen of western Nova Scotia of the first part of this century, many of whom made long voyages, as far away as Cape North or the Grand Banks, often in winter, and occasionally in open boats as small as thirty feet whose sole motive power was a make-and-break engine or a converted car engine. Aids to navigation in that era consisted of a compass and a lead line, and I will never be able to equal those sailors as a navigator. Those few remaining, all in their eighties by now, will, I hope, be pleased to know that this is my attempt to maintain and record their tradition. It is always humbling to me, as I enter a tricky harbor in thick fog with the help of the latest electronic wizardry, that one of these fellows did it sixty years ago by sniffing the wind and listening to the sea gulls.

PETER LOVERIDGE
Lower Argyle, Nova Scotia
November 1996

Nova Scotia, *Digby to Cape Breton Island*

Including the Bras d'Or Lakes

How to Use This Book

Harbors and Anchorages

I have visited by boat almost every harbor mentioned in this guide. The few I have not will be clearly indicated. I have cruised the area extensively for nearly 20 years, and there is little of interest to cruising sailors that's missing from these pages.

If there is a bias, it is toward greater detail and attention to small, tricky passages than to large commercial harbors. This, of course, relates to the navigational difficulties of the place, and I hope my bias will prove more useful to the practical sailor.

Please remember that I may have missed an uncharted rock by 10 feet—and you may not. Some of the surveys on even the most up-to-date charts were done in the nineteenth century and undoubtedly do not show all the hazards. Every guide like this should be used as an aid. None is a substitute for looking where you are going, and doing the things that prudent navigators do.

Especially do not attempt tricky inshore passages in thick weather relying implicitly on loran or GPS. You will hit something. Neither the electronic aid, nor the precision of the chart datum has the accuracy needed to make some of the inshore passages. Do not rely on a radio direction finder (RDF) to enter any harbor.

The order of anchorages is basically west-to-east, as this is the most common route for cruising the province.

Where possible, I give all relevant information about restaurants, stores, boatyards, and so on. Please bear in mind, though, that Nova Scotia's Atlantic coastline is over five thousand miles long, and I can't visit it all every year. For example, a store that's there one year may not be there the next. That's one of the realities of running small businesses in Nova Scotia, and it is likely I will miss a few of these enterprises. In addition, I live quite far away from the urban centers of the province, and not being a city person, don't know the most fashionable bars and restaurants. As I presume no one makes the effort to go to Nova Scotia for its nightlife, perhaps this doesn't matter much. I received no favor from the places I mention, and most of them wouldn't know me from a hole in the ground.

One of my frustrations with the existing guides to the province is that historical information is often more prominent than navigational information. This tends to be most apparent when you have a 30-knot wind at your back, visibility is 50 feet, and you're trying to enter some rockbound harbor with the sound of breaking surf ahead of you.

I have tried to concentrate more on the needs of the cruiser than the historian, and perhaps these pages provide less information relating to the province's museums and cultural activities than do some other guides. Please accept my apologies for this. For those of you interested in such things, the Nova Scotia Department of Tourism produces a number of publications, updated more or less every year, that are available in just about every hotel, restaurant, or tourist information center.

In rural areas of the province, local people are almost invariably delighted to talk to visitors about their communities, and this is by far the best way to learn a little of their way of life.

Beauty and Interest Ratings

It is impossible to be strictly objective in rating a particular anchorage, but the following are the criteria I have used:

★★★★★   An outstandingly beautiful place, one of my favorites. Not to be missed.

★★★★   Very attractive, well worth a visit.

★★★   Attractive or interesting, but perhaps other factors, such as ease of provisioning, and the like, are more relevant to the rating.

★★   Nothing specially attractive, or there may be disadvantages.

★   Use only for shelter from bad weather.

Protection Ratings

The categories listed are:

5   Excellent shelter, good chance of surviving a hurricane.

4   Good protection for most summer conditions. You can sleep soundly at night and leave the boat unattended for a day or two.

3   Exposed to a few directions. All right for overnight anchorage in usual prevailing winds, but unwise to leave the boat unattended for more than a few hours.

2   Protection in settled conditions only. Overnight anchorage only in good weather, and unwise to leave boat unattended.

1   No protection, approach only in fine and settled conditions.

Incidentally, most of the larger government wharves provide the highest degree of shelter. Thousands of boats here spend every winter in the water facing storms with winds over 70 knots. Very few boats are damaged at such wharves during these storms, and most wharves provide excellent protection, if less than aesthetic scenery.

Ease of Access Ratings

Not all Nova Scotia anchorages are easy access for strangers (some aren't for locals, either), so I have used the following rating system:

A   A relatively easy and safe harbor to enter under all conditions. I would have no difficulty at night, and relatively little difficulty in fog, when it would be possible to enter with GPS or loran only. Please bear in mind that entering a harbor in thick fog is not an easy matter under any circumstances, and there is really nothing that gives you more peace of mind than radar.

B   All right under clear conditions, by day or night, but requiring serious thought in thick weather, strong onshore winds, or the like.

C   These are places I think carefully about in anything but the clearest conditions. Some of these places I would not attempt at night or thick fog, despite now having both radar and night-vision glasses. Probably better not attempted by strangers in these conditions.

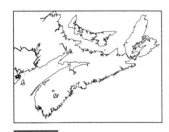

Facilities

Generally, facilities are few and cannot be relied on from one year to the next. Moorings and alongside docking are available in so few places that I mention them specifically in the text. The facilities listed are:

🍴 Restaurant within walking distance.

🛒 Groceries within walking distance.

🧊 Ice. Many grocery stores have cube ice, but block ice is hard to find.

⛽ Fuel—both diesel and gas.

🫧 Laundromat.

🔧 Boat repair facility of some sort. Very few will have yachts as their primary interest.

🚰 Water on tap, by hose. There are very few places in the province outside Halifax where unrestricted fresh water is available.

🚿 Showers available.

Charts

The sketch charts in this book are all drawn with true north at the top. They are not intended to be used for taking bearings or measuring distances, but simply to add clarity to the government charts, with which they should be used. If there is a latitude and longitude on my chart it is generally safe to approach the area using an electronic positioning system such as loran or GPS. If there is no grid, it is not safe, and approach should be visual or with radar.

All bearings in this book are magnetic and are noted as "mag." on my charts, all distances in nautical miles or yards, and all depths in feet, rather than in fathoms and feet. Where it would be useful, metric measurements are given in parentheses. Miles and knots are not converted, since the nautical mile equals one minute of latitude and is in universal use by navigators. Yards are not converted either, but for the purposes of this book they may be presumed to be meters. I long ago came to the conclusion that every mathematical calculation used in navigation had a capacity for error that would usually manifest itself at the worst possible time. For this reason I have tried to keep things consistent, in recognition of the realities of small boat navigation, which include such things as the fold in the chart cutting off the compass roses, poor lighting, and the like.

Official charts, depending on the date of publication, may have soundings in meters or, on the older charts, fathoms. Any black-and-white government chart will use fathoms, or fathoms and feet. This, as you can imagine, can cause trouble, as running into water marked 1.5 on a metric chart (which you took to be fathoms) will cause a big thump on many boats. At the time of writing, most U.S. charts are still in fathoms and feet, but are due to be changed to meters in the future.

The conversion table below is accurate enough for most navigation.

I refer exclusively to Canadian charts in this book, though U.S. Defense Mapping Agency (DMA) charts cover most of the province.

In many ways, the older Canadian charts are to be preferred, as they show more detail, have a larger scale, and for many inshore regions give a clearer depiction of the rocks and hazards. They will not show loran lines, and the buoys will not be correctly numbered, and may not be shown at all. The same can be said about the U.S. charts.

Given the Canadian Coast Guard's penchant for changing the numbering and positioning of buoys, seemingly without rhyme or reason, there

Fathoms	1	2	3	4	5	6	7	8	9	10	11	12	13	14	15	16
Feet	6	12	18	24	30	36	42	48	54	60	66	72	78	84	90	96
Meters	2	3.8	5.4	7.2	9	11	13	15	16	18	20	22	24	26	27	29

is absolutely no guarantee that even the latest chart will be correct. There is no easy solution to this problem, but the bottom line is this: since the rocks don't move about a lot, don't throw your old charts out.

Other Useful Navigational Publications

The following publications are available from the Canadian Hydrographic Service:

Canadian Tide and Current Tables, Volume 1. It is essential to have this on board.

List of Lights, Atlantic Coast (TP 395E, latest edition). This is handy if you have outdated charts, but is frequently out of date itself.

Atlas of Tidal Currents, Bay of Fundy and Gulf of Maine.

Sailing Directions, Nova Scotia (Atlantic Coast) and Bay of Fundy. This is oriented toward big ships and is of limited use to small craft, though it has some nice pictures, particularly of harbors in Cape Breton.

If all else fails, all charts and navigational publications can be ordered directly from Ottawa. The phone may be answered in an incomprehensible mixture of French and English, but—provided the person in Ottawa is not having a bad day—if you plug away you will make yourself understood. All these people, including the government, accept payment by credit cards issued by Visa and MasterCard. This is the address:

Hydrographic Chart Distribution Office
Department of Fisheries and Oceans
1675 Russell Road, P.O. Box 8080
Ottawa, Ontario, K1G 3H6
Tel: (613) 998-4931; Fax: (613) 998-1217
e-mail: chart__sales@chshq.dfo.ca
INTERNET Web side: http://www.chsq.dfo.ca

I have found the following chart agents in Nova Scotia satisfactory:

Gabriel Aero-Marine Instruments, Ltd. Tel: (902) 425-5030 or (800) 561-5030. Fax: (902) 492-1220.

South Shore Marine. Tel: (902) 275-3711. Fax: (902) 275-2416.

The Yacht Shop. Tel: (902) 634-4331. Fax: (902) 634-8358.

Not all agents have all charts. Gabriel's usually has the largest stock. I strongly advise your getting all the charts you need before you set off, as there is no guarantee that you will be able to find a missing chart for any out-of-the-way area once you get here. If you buy the charts before entering Canada, you will also be spared the loathed 7 percent GST (Goods and Services Tax—or "Gouge and Screw Tax," depending on your view) and the provincial sales tax, another 11 percent.

These chart agents in the United States carry good stocks of Canadian charts:

Bluewater Books and Charts, Fort Lauderdale, Florida. Tel: (800) 942-2583. Fax: (954) 763-6533.

Landfall Navigation, Greenwich, Connecticut. Tel: (203) 661-3176. Fax: (203) 661-9613.

Armchair Sailor, Newport, Rhode Island. Tel: (800) 292-4278. Fax: (401) 847-1219.

Chase Leavitt, Portland, Maine. Tel: (800) 638-8906. Fax: (207) 772-0297.

Recommended Charts

Unless otherwise noted, all the chart numbers in this book refer to Canadian Hydrographic Service (CHS) charts. If a chart number is bold, I consider it essential. You can manage without the others.

Nova Scotia Approaches

NOS 13260 Bay of Fundy to Cape Cod.

NOS 13009 Gulf of Maine and Georges Bank.

4003 Cape Breton to Cape Cod.

4011 Approaches to the Bay of Fundy.

Note: At least one of the charts listed above is essential, in addition to chart 4011, if you are departing south of Mount Desert Island.

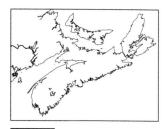

Nova Scotia Coast

4012 Yarmouth to Halifax.
4013 Halifax to Sydney.

Note: You can get by without these if you don't mind shuffling the larger-scale charts.

West of Cape Sable

4340 Grand Manan. This chart is essential if you are visiting Grand Manan.

4342, 4124 Harbors on Grand Manan. Not essential.

4396 Annapolis Basin. You can probably get by with 4011 or 4012 if you are just visiting Digby.

4118 St. Marys Bay. Essential to visit any harbor in this area, unless you have 4323 or 4324.

4323, 4324 Obsolete charts of St. Marys Bay. Works of art worth framing. Still quite usable.

4243 Tusket Islands to Cape St. Marys. Essential to enter any harbor in this area.

4245 Yarmouth Harbour. Not essential if you have 4243.

4244 Wedgeport and vicinity. Essential to enter any harbor in this area unless you have 4326.

4326 Pubnico to Yarmouth. Obsolete. Newer chart is better.

4330 Cape Sable to Seal Island. Obsolete. Best chart of the Seal Islands.

4242 Cape Sable to Tusket Islands. Essential to enter any harbor in this area.

4210 Cape Sable to Pubnico Harbour. This is the best chart for West Head and the Cockerwit Passage, but you can do without it if you have 4242.

4216 Cape Sable to Pubnico. Obsolete, but still useful if you have it.

4230 Little Hope Island to Cape St. Marys. Lack of inshore detail severely limits this otherwise useful chart. Not advisable to enter any harbor using this chart, but it is good for coasting.

Cape Sable to Halifax

4241 Lockeport to Cape Sable. Essential to enter any harbor in this area.

4215 Cape Negro to Cape Sable. Obsolete, but has better detail than the new chart.

4214 Lockeport to Cape Negro. Obsolete, but has better detail than the new chart.

4213 Little Hope Island to Lockeport. Obsolete, but has better detail than the new chart.

4212 Western Head to Little Hope Island. Also obsolete, but hang on to it.

4209 Shelburne and Lockeport Harbours. Nice chart, but not essential.

4240 Liverpool to Lockeport. Essential unless you have the old series of charts.

4379 Liverpool Bay. Not required. I don't have it.

4211 Cape LaHave to Liverpool. Essential for Port Medway. You can probably get into Liverpool with small-scale chart 4012 if the weather is clear. Entry is straightforward with chart 4240.

4384 Pearl Island to Cape LaHave. Essential for all harbors in this area.

4394 LaHave River—East Ironbound Island to Riverport. Nice to have if you are visiting the LaHave Islands, but not essential.

4391, 4395 LaHave River. Not required. I don't have them.

4320 Egg Island to West Ironbound Island. This goes all the way from Cape LaHave to Ship Harbour, and is tempting to use, but the scale is a little too small for use in any but clear conditions. DMA chart 14083 is almost identical.

4328 Lunenburg Bay. Not required if you are just visiting Lunenburg, but essential for the smaller places such as Cross Island.

4381 Mahone Bay. Essential unless you want to take a chance with 4320.

4386 St. Margarets Bay. Essential.

4385 Osborne Head to Betty Island. Essential for Rogues Roost and Terence Bay. Includes Halifax Harbour, but this is best shown on chart 4237.

4318 Obsolete, but a handy chart of the Sambro area, which is better shown than on chart 4237.

4237 Approaches to Halifax Harbour. Essential if you don't have chart 4385.

4201, 4202, 4203 Plans of Halifax Harbour and Bedford Basin. Not essential.

Halifax to Canso

4326 Taylors Head to Shut-In Island. Essential to enter any harbor in this region, but suffers from a small scale. Many of the smaller anchorages are not apparent on this chart. If you have any of the old charts listed below, they are in many ways preferable for exploring the inshore waters.

4347 Charles Island to Osborne Head. Obsolete. An 1853 survey makes it of historical interest. Still usable if you don't have chart 4326.

4352 Ship Harbour. Obsolete, but a fine chart. Better detail than chart 4326 if you are gunkholing.

4353 Popes Head to Charles Island. Another of Captain Bayfield's 1854 surveys. Again, better detail of the inside passages.

4289 Sheet Harbour to Popes Harbour. Obsolete, a 1960 survey. Much better than 4326 for details of the inside passages.

4361 Sheet Harbour. Obsolete, Captain Bayfield's original survey.

4227 Country Harbour to Ship Harbour. Small-scale chart, not much use for coasting, not essential.

4235 Barren Island to Taylors Head. Essential if you don't have the old large-scale charts. Better detail than 4326, though it is the same scale.

4364 Beaver Harbour. Obsolete, surveyed by Captain Orlebar in 1857. A work of art. Better detail than 4326.

4355 Necum Teuch. Obsolete. Better detail than 4326.

4234 Country Island to Barren Island. Essential for this area if you don't have the old charts. Better detail than the others in this series.

4356 Liscomb and Marie Joseph Harbours. Obsolete. Surveyed by Captain Bayfield. Another work of art, much to be preferred to the new chart.

4321 Cape Canso to Liscomb Island. You can use this chart to enter Country Harbour, New Harbour, and possibly Whitehaven. Don't use it to enter Canso.

4233 Cape Canso to Country Harbour. Essential if you don't have the old large-scale charts and want to visit the harbors in this area.

4285 Port Bickerton to Liscomb Island. Obsolete, but clearer than 4234 and larger scale.

4284 Country Island to Port Bickerton. Obsolete, but clearer than 4234 and better detail.

4283 Berry Head to Country Island. Obsolete. Not essential.

4282 White Head Island to Berry Head. Obsolete. Better than 4233.

4280 Approaches to Canso. Obsolete. Better than 4233. You can use this to get into Canso if you don't have chart 4281.

4281 Canso Harbour and Inner Approaches. You need this if you are visiting Canso and don't have 4280. Not essential if you are just passing through to Cape Breton.

Canso to Baddeck

4335 Strait of Canso and Approaches. Essential.

4307 Canso Harbour to Strait of Canso. Not essential

4308 St. Peters Bay to Strait of Canso. Not essential, but handy if you are going to Isle Madame.

4275 St. Peters Bay. Desirable, as it is the only chart with the approach buoys to the St. Peters Canal on it.

4279 Bras d'Or Lake. Essential, though rather a small scale.

4278 Great Bras d'Or. Essential, larger scale than chart 4279.

4277 Great Bras d'Or, St. Andrews Channel. Not essential unless you are exiting the lakes to the north.

This means, unfortunately, that you need 20 charts for an extensive cruise of the province if you enter at Yarmouth; 17 if you enter at Shelburne; and 23 if you go via Grand Manan. This represents a cost of $400 (Canadian) plus postage for

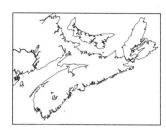

the 20 charts if you order them direct from Ottawa (the cheapest way for non-residents). Long ago I came to the conclusion that a few extra charts cost less than a new boat, a state of mind no doubt brought on by entering a strange harbor on a dirty night with too small a scale chart.

If you want to use U.S. DMA charts, and take a chance with the buoyage not being correct, the following cover the province. For some years they have been based on the Canadian surveys and use the same database as Canadian charts.

14061 Grand Manan. Same as 4340.

14062 Yarmouth to Three Islands.

14066 Lockeport to Yarmouth. The scale is rather small for entering most harbors.

14081 Port Medway to Lockeport.

14083 Egg Island to West Ironbound. Same as 4320.

14086 Mahone Bay. Same as 4381.

14087 Osborne Head to Betty Island. Same as 4385.

14090 Approaches to Halifax Harbour. Same as 4237.

14093 Taylors Head to Shut-In Island. Same as 4236.

14115 Country Island to Egg Island.

14100 Country Island to Barren Island. Same as 4234.

14105 Cape Canso to Liscomb Island. Same as 4321.

14110 Strait of Canso and Approaches. Same as 4335.

14135 St. Peters Bay. Same as 4275.

14134 Bras d'Or Lake. Same as 4279.

14133 Great Bras d'Or. Same as 4278.

Slightly fewer DMA charts are needed, but at the expense of smaller scale and loss of inshore detail.

Introduction

A voyage to Nova Scotia can be a daunting prospect, as getting home from Nova Scotia to the more populated places on the East Coast of the United States can involve a beat of over 500 miles to windward. The Bras d'Or Lakes are more than 400 miles from my home near Yarmouth, Nova Scotia, and even this voyage is not undertaken lightly in the sort of boats I have owned. My first boat was a converted fishing vessel with no electronics and an engine that gave a speed of 3 knots on a good day. The next one was a classic (though old) 30-footer with a diesel inboard and up-to-date electronics: a depth-sounder, loran, and a rudimentary radar set. My latest vessel is a plastic one, molded from boat number two, and actually has a reliable engine and real radar. Nonetheless, I did make a voyage out to the lakes and back with boat number one during a four-week vacation. More recently, a friend accompanied us on a trip to Cape Breton with a family including three small children, in a modest 26-footer with an outboard auxiliary. This should demonstrate that you don't need a new 50-foot Hinkley for a satisfactory trip here; though undoubtedly such a vessel would be a nice way to do it.

I have tried to consider what makes Nova Scotia different, and why one should make the extra effort to get here. One of the reasons would be the lack of development of the coastline. The eastern shore, for example, is almost deserted. You can sail for a week without seeing another boat, and for a day without seeing a sign of human habitation. I have never been charged anything for lying to my own gear, and only once or twice in 20 years have I been charged for tying up to a government wharf.

I never worry that there may be no room to anchor by the time I get to a harbor. That simply doesn't happen. Even during an event like Chester Race Week there is always room handy somewhere. I have never seen more than 20 people on any beach in the province, and most of the time, you and your crew will be the only ones there.

Another reason would be shore access. Every Nova Scotian has an unfettered right of access to uncultivated land anywhere. This means that all beaches, offshore islands, and the like, have unrestricted public access unless the land is cultivated or is obviously a lawn or a garden. Access for activities such as "studying the fauna and flora" are specifically mentioned in legislation, as are angling and hunting. The latter causes not a few problems for local landowners. To prevent hunting on a property you have to post signs every 50 feet around the boundary of the property. There is therefore no place in Nova Scotia where signs can legally state "Private Beach—Keep Off" or anything similar, so such signs are never seen. Most rural Nova Scotians consider it their God-given right to hunt, camp, or drive all-terrain vehicles (ATVs) wherever and whenever they please, and the fencing off of a piece of land by an absentee landlord counts almost as an act of war.

It is often said that "Nova Scotia now is like Maine was 40 years ago." In some ways, yes, but in western Nova Scotia, at least, this illusion will vanish the moment you set foot on a wharf. Maine has never had fishermen whose average incomes were over $100,000 a year, and certainly not 40 years ago. But this is the normal state of affairs west of Shelburne. If you want to see vibrant, prosperous fishing communities, western Nova Scotia is the only place on the eastern seaboard

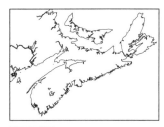

where you are likely to do so. It will be an eye-opener for those of you from an urban environment.

A final reason for making a special effort to visit Nova Scotia could be the sheer number of harbors and anchorages. There are more good anchorages within a day's sail of my house than in the entire eastern Caribbean. Nova Scotia has 5,000 miles of shoreline, most of it undeveloped, thousands of offshore islands, and so many anchorages that one person could never experience them all.

The very characteristics making Nova Scotia an attractive destination do, however, carry a small price. The lack of development requires more self-reliance on your part. You should be able to do your own simple boat, rigging, and engine repairs, as there will likely be no one else to do it for you. You should have a reasonable knowledge of piloting in areas of considerable tidal streams, especially west of Shelburne. You need to have ship's stores of such quantity that you don't need to go to a store every second day. You will find Nova Scotians universally friendly and helpful, but they will wonder what the hell you are doing on the water if you can't replace a V-belt or a fuel filter.

While many areas in the United States provide overnight delivery for things such as spare parts, Canada Post takes a week to send a letter from Halifax to Yarmouth. So bring that essential spare part with you. In the words of the advertisement for a popular charge card—"Don't leave home without it" unless you want a lot of frustration. Our economic system, which encourages trade with central Canada, and results in our paying high prices for indifferent service, isn't overly popular with us either.

In this introduction, I will try to give some insight into conditions here that may be different from what you are used to.

Getting Here

These are often-used courses, and the distances they cover:

START AND DESTINATION	COURSE (°MAGNETIC)	DISTANCE (NAUTICAL MILES)
Cape Cod to Brazil Rock (southeast of Cape Sable)	090°	220
Cape Cod to Yarmouth	080°	200
Cape Elizabeth to 15 miles south of Cape Sable	114°	200
Cape Elizabeth to Yarmouth	100°	190
Mount Desert Rock to 15 miles south of Cape Sable	130°	115
Mount Desert Rock to Yarmouth	126°	86
North Head, Grand Manan, to Yarmouth direct	184°	60
North Head, Grand Manan, to Yarmouth via Grand Passage	170° 190°	34, then 34
Bermuda to Cape Sable	013°	675

Miscellaneous Tips

The choice of route is very individual, but a husband-and-wife team in a relatively small boat may find the direct crossing from Cape Cod a little arduous, given the high density of fishing boats, the prevalence of fog, and the large ships in this area. It may be even more so on the way back, unless conditions are ideal.

A departure from Cape Elizabeth is a little shorter, but is still likely to require two nights at sea unless your boat is fast, or conditions ideal.

Departure from Mount Desert Rock has a lot to commend it, as the trip can almost always be done in 24 hours. With the prevailing southwesterlies, the boat is on a reach, which is usually the most comfortable way to travel. I use this route going to Maine, as Mount Desert can be reached in a southwesterly with the sheets just started, and without having to tack.

Using the routes from Mount Desert or Cape Elizabeth to Yarmouth will put you on the same route as the daily summer ferries. This has the disadvantage of a risk of collision, but on the other hand, the reassurance that you are on course. If you use the Mount Desert route going back to Maine, it is best to leave Yarmouth, or the Tusket Islands, just before high water. The ebb will give you a push to windward, and by the next flood you will be 30 miles from the coast of Nova Scotia and out of the region of strong tides.

If Cape Sable is your departure point from Nova Scotia, try to get there at low water. The flood will hurry you along to Yarmouth, and you will then be in the best position for crossing the Bay of Fundy.

Going via Grand Manan has the advantage of being able to do the entire passage in daylight. I think this advantage is more apparent than real, as wind conditions on summer nights tend to be more stable, and are often lighter (see the weather section). Perhaps I have always been plagued with such slow boats that I always arrive in a strange port at night.

The easiest way to enter Grand Manan is to go up the Grand Manan Channel, on the west side of the island, round Northern Head and Swallow-tail, then dock in the village of North Head. Keep clear of the rock off Net Point. The cliffs on the western side of Grand Manan are 200 or 300 feet high, very bold and clear, and this route is well lit, presenting no great problem at night. Avoid the southeast coast of Grand Manan. It is an area full of rocks and serious tiderips.

North Head Harbour is just past the ferry dock, and has a long floating dock, which makes tying up in the 24-foot (7-m) tidal range somewhat easier. It is quite crowded with fishing boats, and most of these fellows tend to get under way at 0400. It makes departure easier for the boat you're tied up to if you run your own warps to the wharf, as well as to the other boat. This may save you from being woken at some hideous hour. There is a Customs Office at North Head.

Departure from Grand Manan should take into account the tide. Offshore, it turns a half-hour after high water (further reference should be made to the tide tables). Brier Island, 30 miles away, can almost certainly be made on the ebb, and it might be possible to get as far as Yarmouth (60 miles) without too much adverse tide. This will, however, in the prevailing winds be a wind-against-tide situation, which in the Bay of Fundy can be a truly horrible experience if either are strong. This has more effect on smaller boats, the very ones that might be tempted to break up long days at sea by this route. It is conceivable that a run of bad weather could keep you in port here for a week. There are a number of other harbors on Grand Manan, and it is an interesting place to visit, but you should be aware of the prevalence of fog and the continuous need to monitor the strong tides.

Weather

Weather forecasts are available on the continuous VHF bands, most of the province being covered. There are a few gaps in the eastern shore, especially in harbor (so you don't know what awaits you when you get out). Local radio stations also broadcast weather forecasts of variable quality. In the west, fishing is the main industry, and private forecasts are geared to this. They are often better than the official ones. Around Halifax and the eastern shore, this is not the case.

There appear to be a number of failings with the forecasts, however, and to avoid endless frustration you should be aware of these problems and the local weather patterns. There is an informative booklet called the *East Coast Marine Weather Manual* (Ministry of Supply and Services, # En 56-81/1989E; ISBN 0-662-16934-4) that explains some of the limitations of the forecasting system. The major fault is that the regional center, Halifax, does not appear to be able to collate actual conditions around the province, so that while the sequence of weather patterns is usually correct, the timing is hopelessly wrong. A common occurrence, for example, is a cold front coming through from west to east, the actual conditions in Yarmouth being those of a brisk, gusty northwesterly, while

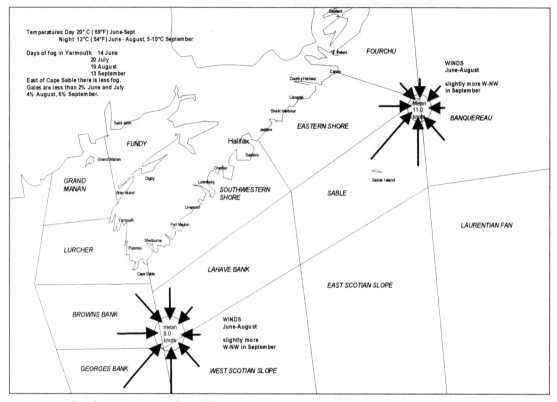

Marine weather forecast areas and wind directions.

the forecast calls for light southerlies and fog. Another problem is that at weekends, there seems to be nobody looking out of the window, so forecasts are often out of sync with the real conditions. Canada's government services are now subject to major budget cuts, and we certainly expect the quality of forecasts to worsen.

The following are common weather patterns in summer.

Fog

This is the biggest menace on this coast. It is why almost any local boat bigger than a dinghy has loran or GPS and radar. Fog here really is thicker than almost anywhere else, and visibility often is less than 50 feet. Under these conditions, the minimum working range of your radar is of much more practical use than the maximum range. In addition, dense fog may be accompa-

nied by winds of up to 40 knots, and a common occurrence is what is locally known as a "fog breeze," where a 30-knot southwesterly wind is accompanied by thick, drippy fog.

While there are many articles written in yachting magazines about predicting fog, in Nova Scotia they are not much use, as fog can appear at any time. There are some conditions, however, that make fog a virtual certainty:

- When a sustained wind starts blowing from the east, fog is almost certain to form within 12 hours.
- If islands loom up and show mirages, an easterly wind will start blowing by the next day, and it will bring fog.
- If you breathe out through your mouth and you can see your breath, fog is lurking nearby.
- Fog is densest early in the morning, and often lightens up in the afternoon. This means the

best time to make a landfall is about 2 P.M. to 4 P.M., local time.

- East of Cape Sable there is usually a band of better visibility close inshore, and it is usually clearer in a harbor.
- Peninsulas or islands that stick out a lot, such as capes Sable, Canso, and Sambro, tend to have more fog than usual.
- When a cold front goes through, and the wind comes from the northwest, the fog will usually depart, sometimes to linger as an offshore bank.
- If it is clear, and the wind is from the west through north, it would be most unusual for fog to form.
- In many harbors, fog will go a little offshore with the ebb, and come in again with the flood.

This all means that any cruise in the province is bound to involve at least some fog, and you should be as prepared for it as possible. My experience is that our weather patterns have changed over the last few years and we now have less fog than we used to.

Frontal Systems

Warm Fronts. An approaching warm front will start with rising easterly winds. If they are northeasterly, the storm center will pass to the south of you. In the summer, northeasterly winds are not common. The storm center will be fairly close and quite intense. Gales and even storm-force winds can occur under these conditions, and it is best to be circumspect about putting to sea with a falling barometer and rising northeasterly winds. Most depressions track north of the province in summer, and their warm fronts are associated with a slowly falling barometer and southeasterly winds whose strength will depend on the intensity and distance of the storm center. Approaching warm fronts always bring fog.

No boat cruising the province should be without a barometer. The following table of barometer readings will help you predict wind strength.

6 mb fall in 3 hours—30 knot wind within 6 hours
10 mb fall in 3 hours—40 knot wind within 6 hours
15 mb fall in 3 hours—50 knot wind within 6 hours

When the front has passed, the wind will shift to the southwest or west and will often drop, sometimes leaving an awful slop. The fog may lighten or lift.

Cold Fronts. Cold fronts bring west-to-north-westerly winds. There is usually no warning of the wind strength from the barometer, as the winds are blowing at full tilt before it starts to rise. Winds are gusty, especially in the entrances of harbors, with maximum gusts being twice the speed of the sustained winds, or higher. From May to August, this kind of wind does not usually blow for more than 12 hours, though in September we can get days of sustained 30-knot westerlies.

Stable Summer Weather

The wind is light, or calm at night, and by about 10 A.M. it starts blowing from the southeast. Within an hour or so it goes to due south. By afternoon, southwesterlies are well established and can get up to 25 knots, and occasionally 30 knots, especially close to land. By 6 P.M. the wind drops and veers to northwest, to become calm again by dusk. This means if you are going east, and want to sail, there is no point in being up at the crack of dawn. On the other hand, if you are going west, and don't want your teeth shaken out, get up early, or travel at night under power.

Hurricanes

Yes, hurricanes do occur in Nova Scotia, every second or third year, and most frequently in August. As the cold water of the Labrador Current cannot sustain tropical storms, they begin to die out once they leave the Gulf Stream. But, remember, the stream is only 100 miles off the coast, and

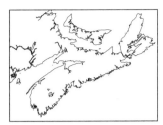

winds in excess of 60 knots may reach land.

Hurricanes are usually well tracked by forecasters, but the notice you get is quite brief. A storm centered off Cape Hatteras will not be mentioned at all, and there will be minimal information about anything south of Cape Cod. As this is only 12 to 36 hours' traveling time for your average hurricane, this can be a little disturbing. If I am making an overnight passage, or going to an area where harbors are not well sheltered, I listen to the tropical storm information just after the hour on shortwave radio station WWV, which can usually be picked up well on 10 or 15 MHz. You can also get the U.S. National Hurricane Center's Atlantic forecast by phone on (305) 229-4483.

If the barometer is above 1020 mb, these storms will usually skirt around the area. Hurricanes, unlike winter storms, are very localized, so it can be blowing a screecher, say in Yarmouth, but be light in Halifax. I have never seen one of these storms that wasn't preceded by a big swell at 10- to 30-second intervals, giving at least 24 hours' notice.

Without exception, every winter brings two or three extra-tropical cyclones with winds exceeding 70 knots. Most large government wharves provide adequate shelter for such storms, provided all boats are made fast properly.

Temperatures

Daytime summer temperatures are usually between 65°F and 80°F (20°C to 28°C) from June to August, and about 10°F (6°C) lower in September, October, and May. It is an uncommon night at sea when one does not need a thick sweater, and cabin heaters are always useful.

Equipment Required to Cruise Nova Scotia

A Good Engine

As one who didn't have a reliable engine for years, I can only say that possession of such a beast makes a cruise enjoyable, rather than an ordeal. I have rowed a heavy boat the entire length of Halifax Harbour, and taken five days to get to Yarmouth from Portland. While cruising in areas such as the eastern Caribbean may not require auxiliary power, cruising in Nova Scotia, with tight, rockbound harbors, and exceedingly variable winds, is constant frustration without one. You should carry the more obvious spare parts such as V-belts, filters, impellers for water pumps, and the like. You are most unlikely to find these stocked by local agents.

A Decent Dinghy

There are very few commercial marinas in the province, and every natural anchorage requires a tender to get ashore. In some harbors (Lunenburg comes immediately to mind) it can be dangerous to row ashore if your tender is too small. I have towed a rigid tender back and forth to Maine and all up and down this coast, but some of you may prefer an inflatable.

Adequate Anchors

Decent anchoring systems are an absolute necessity. I don't think any one type works any better than another, but they should be big enough. Many anchorages have a lot of kelp on the bottom, and light anchors will not penetrate it. "Big" means at least 25 pounds (11 kg) on even the smallest boat. Some thought should also be given to hauling it up. Pulling up a 35-pound (16-kg) anchor when the tide is doing 3 knots past the boat is almost impossible without a windlass, or a hefty crew.

Hefty Fenders and Lines

Most government docks are faced by 8-inch square posts, but some are not faced at all. Big fenders, at least 12 inches (30 cm) in diameter are required. Most visiting boats have fenders that are too small. A fender board is also helpful.

West of Cape Sable, the tidal range is in excess of 12 feet (3.7 m), so long lines are needed to tie up to a dock. In places where the tidal range is over 10 feet (3 m), you will be all over the place unless you rig spring lines, so you should have at least four lines, each twice as long as your boat.

Effective Insect Screens

Nova Scotia has plenty of pestiferous flying and biting insects, though they usually only come out at dusk and dawn. They are slightly less troublesome, on the whole, than they are in Maine or New Brunswick, and are not known to carry disease.

Ticks are common in the western part of the province, but have not yet been shown to carry Lyme disease, though all the necessities for its transmission are present.

Workmanlike Anchor Lights

While I try to state where riding lights *must* be shown, no one has ever lost a boat by putting one up when it wasn't legally necessary. In a recent lawsuit, the judge held that a yacht not showing a light (just off the Lunenburg Yacht Club) was partly responsible for damages and injuries sustained by the passenger in a high-speed runabout with an impaired driver that hit the yacht and sank.

Mast-top anchor lights in crowded anchorages are sometimes confused with stars, and in such circumstances, a riding light lower in the rigging might be preferable. You certainly don't need a riding light when you're tied up to a wharf, though, unless you are the sixth boat out, and obstructing the fairway.

Electronic Navigational Aids

Loran. Almost every local boat uses loran because its readings are highly reproducible. Thus, you can return to within 100 feet (30 m) of a previously recorded position. But the absolute accuracy can be almost a mile out from charted positions. Some of this can be compensated for by noting the errors alongside a known position such as a buoy. Don't depend on this, though, as the buoy may not be in its charted position either. I do not advise entering corrections into your loran unless you intend to remain in the area, as this may make your loran position worse when you move more than 10 miles or so. The 5930 XY chains are the preferred stations, though east of Halifax 5930 XZ may occasionally be better.

GPS. The satellite-based Global Positioning System (GPS) is inherently more accurate than loran, but Selective Availability (a deliberate and random downgrading of the system's capabilities by U.S. military authorities) reduces the accuracy to 300 feet (100 m) or more. GPS on its own does not provide sufficient accuracy to enter many harbors safely.

Radar. A radar set is the single most valuable navigational aid in these waters, though there are a few cautions associated with it. Many objects on the water are marked with radar reflectors, and their echoes can be very confusing if a proper plot is not kept. I have cruised everywhere in this guide using only a Whistler (Ranger) set but having recently acquired a small liquid crystal display (LCD) display set, I have to say it makes traveling in thick fog, while not quite a pleasure, so much easier that I could almost do without all the other stuff. Passage inshore, at night, in thick fog, without radar is something to be avoided at all costs.

Radio Direction Finders. Although the RDF system is nearly obsolete, I keep on the boat an old Seafix RDF set with an internal battery, in case I have a total electrical failure. RDF stations are gradually being withdrawn. There are

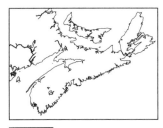

still enough stations in the area round Cape Sable, however, to form a useful backup system on this dangerous stretch of coast. Details of individual beacons are given in the text.

Communications

VHF Coast Radio Stations. There is generally good coverage everywhere along the coast, provided you are one or two miles offshore, from Yarmouth (VAU), Halifax (VCS), or Sydney (VCO). These are government stations operated by the Coast Guard. Repeaters along the coast extend the range of the stations. If you're east of Liverpool, call Halifax. If you're east of Country Harbour, call Sydney.

Channel 16 is the calling channel for coast radio stations. As all these stations handle a lot of commercial traffic, there could be a long wait to get a call through. In harbors, there are occasional gaps in reception, especially around Mahone Bay and many places east of Halifax. This can cause difficulties with the continuous weather channels. Coverage in the Bras d'Or Lakes is very spotty and cannot be relied on. There are no commercial marine radiotelephone services in Nova Scotia.

Cellular Phones. Coverage for cellular phones is quite good west of Halifax, but almost nonexistent east of the city until you get to Canso. Where coverage is available, it is a lot more convenient than trying to place a call through one of the Coast Guard stations.

Provisions

Fuel. Diesel and gasoline are available at most wharves, but it's sometimes difficult to get your tanks filled because of the taxation problem. Suppliers are licensed to sell fuel to commercial fishermen free of taxes or duties. Every so often they must make a declaration that their fuel is "to be

used solely in the commercial fishery." Cash, no receipts, and no questions will usually solve the problem. Otherwise, these are the only places where one can fill up:

Baddeck
Dundee
Halifax—yacht clubs
LaHave—the LaHave Bakery, the LaHave Yacht Club
Liscomb—Liscomb Lodge
Lockeport
Lunenburg—Scotia Trawler
Mahone Bay—the marina
St. Margarets Bay—the marina
St. Peters—Lions Club Marina

It's advisable to carry a 5-gallon (20-liter) can, so that if all else fails you can get fuel from a service station. When you're east of Halifax, especially, be aware that this is a sparsely populated area where you can sail for two days without seeing a house. Always top up your tanks when you get a chance.

Propane. Propane gas can be had at most large Irving service stations, though few of them are handy to a wharf.

Kerosene. A few Irving service stations carry kerosene. Small quantities may be available at Canadian Tire stores.

Stove Alcohol. Anyone who cruises with an alcohol stove in this part of the world had better have big tanks. Canadian Tire stores usually carry something called methyl hydrate (methanol) which will work.

Compressed Natural Gas (CNG). I have never found any place in the province where this is sold, let alone somewhere handy to a boat.

Water. There are not many places with piped water, partly because of the problems of freezing in the winter. In addition to the fueling places mentioned above, you can get water at Yarmouth, the Shelburne Yacht Club, and Sheet Harbour.

Dry summers may limit the supply at some of these places.

Food. Places where the local supermarkets are not a day's hike from your boat include Digby, Yarmouth, Shelburne, Lockeport, Liverpool, Bridgewater (at the top of the river), Lunenburg, Mahone Bay town, Chester Basin, Halifax (the Maritime Museum berths), and Bedford.

If a local taxi is available, the process is easier, but on the Eastern Shore, the only supermarkets are in Sheet Harbour or Canso. At Liscomb Lodge, the marina manager will sometimes lend you a truck. St. Peters or Baddeck in Cape Breton also have supermarkets. I have found the selection better in St. Peters, but in both places the stores will deliver to your boat.

In each section of this book I mention the locations of the nearest stores, but please bear in mind that operating a store in rural Nova Scotia is an enterprise with a high failure rate, and if it is there one year it might not be the next.

Ice. Block ice is hard to find. If you find some, it is as well to get as many blocks as your icebox can hold. The more usual ice chips can be found in any supermarket. The ice that fish plants produce, and that is loaded on to fishing boats, is a fine, flaky, stuff that really isn't useful for ice boxes. I make my own blocks (in 3-liter plastic pop bottles) and these will usually freeze hard if left in a commercial freezer for 24 hours. You may find a fish plant or small store willing to do this for you, particularly for a small consideration. I find that beer and wine stays at an acceptable temperature in the bilge because sea temperatures rarely exceed 50°F (10°C) unless you are in the Bras d'Or Lakes.

Garbage. There are distressingly few places where you can deposit garbage on or around wharves, though this situation has improved slightly over the years. If you find a place to dump garbage, use it while you can. I try to reduce the amount of stuff that ends up in landfills by separating out the biodegradable material and dumping it over-

board offshore. This may not be politically correct, but is probably less damaging to the environment than putting it in a landfill. I suspect the same may be true for cans and bottles, given the lack of accessible recycling programs. But never dump plastic of any kind at sea. There are harbors totally blighted by the fishermen's habit (only just now dying) of dumping overboard anything they don't want. It may be *your* cooling water intake that gets plugged by one of those darned plastic bait bags.

Marine Sanitation Devices. Don't worry about MSD enforcement here. There are no regulations, and certainly no pump-out sites, except at Baddeck. Given that the entire population of the Halifax-Dartmouth region dumps all its sewage, untreated, into Halifax Harbour (despite having paid pollution abatement taxes and supported a highly paid board for over five years) I don't experience a great sense of guilt about the little I produce.

Tides

Visitors often are caught unawares by the strength of the tidal streams, which in places run faster than any experienced on the east coast of the United States. The range of the tide here also is greater.

Tidal streams (sometimes referred to as currents) have to be allowed for anywhere west of Shelburne, where they run at a maximum of about 1 knot. They increase to about 3 knots and higher west of Cape Sable. Tidal streams east of Shelburne, except in a very few restricted places, run at no more than 0.5 knot.

In addition to the tidal effect, the Labrador Current sets southwest at about 6 to 10 miles a day. None of these streams is particularly well charted and all are affected by the wind. There is a general inshore set in all large bays. For this reason, when steering between headlands, I always steer a few degrees offshore from the theoretically correct course.

Tidal Ranges

Strong southeasterly winds raise the level of high and low tide. They also cause the flood to start early and turn late. This effect can produce a surge 3 feet (1 m) higher than the predicted tide and cause at least an hour's delay in the turn of the tide. Northwesterly winds have an opposite, but lesser effect, and are unlikely to affect water levels by more than 1 foot (30 cm).

The datum for Canadian charts is Lowest Normal Tide. Lowest Normal Tide is the same as the lowest predicted tide or the lowest astronomical tide. It is therefore very unlikely that in summer the depth of the water will ever be less than the charted sounding.

Some American charts, on the other hand, may use Mean Lower Low Water (MLLW) as the datum level. What all this means is that west of Shelburne there can at certain times of the month be 3 feet (1 m) less water than is actually shown on some charts. Whatever chart you use, be sure to check the datum level. And check again when you change to another chart.

Tidal ranges (the difference in height between high tide and low tide) are about 8 feet (2.4 m) east of Cape Sable, rising to 16 feet (4.8 m) at Yarmouth. It is not safe to navigate in this area without a copy of the *Canadian Tide and Current Tables, Vol. 1*. This is widely distributed and available in most small communities in the province.

In the absence of better information, you may assume that high tide arrives one hour earlier in Yarmouth than it does in Saint John, New Bruns-

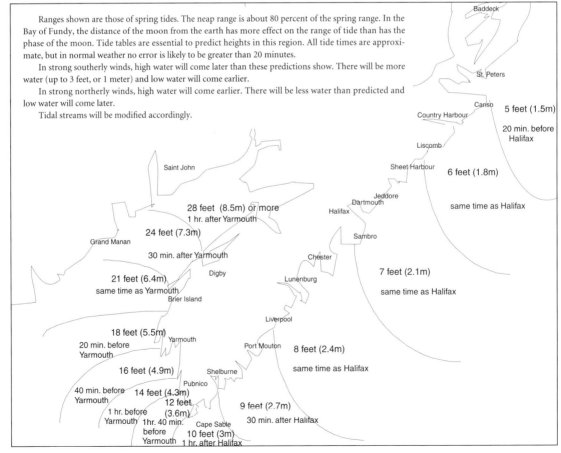

Tidal ranges and times.

wick, and two hours earlier than it does in Boston, Massachusetts. The whole coast from Shelburne to Canso has high water at nearly the same time, roughly two-and-a-half hours before Yarmouth.

Tidal Streams

The accompanying charts (see page 20) may help, as may *An Atlas of Tidal Currents of the Gulf of Maine and Bay of Fundy* (Canadian Hydrographic Service, 1981). Please remember that the latter is a computer prediction and the observations on which it is based are actually quite limited.

For those of you who find it too testing an experience to figure out tidal vectors while trying to navigate a short-handed vessel in thick fog, the table below may help.

Corrections to the vessel's course are in degrees and should be made upstream—that is, the boat's bow should be turned toward the current. All speeds are in knots.

Buoyage

Nova Scotia uses the IALA "B" system with red and green lateral buoys or spars ("red right returning") and a few yellow-and-black cardinal buoys. In the last few years there has been exten-

sive renumbering of buoys, so that now, for example, when you come across a red buoy in the murk it will have "N2" on it instead of "Cape Sable." This is supposed to be progress.

Canadian buoys look different from those in the U.S. The term "nun" is not used—if you ask about one, you will be directed to the rectory. Nova Scotians refer to all unlit, non-spar buoys as cans, whether they are red or green. When there is a symbol on a chart that looks like a nun, it represents a low, red, conical buoy with no cylindrical base. these are found in very few places east of Cape Sable.

Green cans look like their U.S. counterparts. East of Cape Sable almost all unlit buoys are spars, whether red or green. The tops of red spars are cone shaped, but this is hard to distinguish from more than 50 yards off. In this area the charts may show some other buoy shape, but this is almost always incorrect. Spars do not need to be removed when the winter ice arrives, and are becoming the preferred style because of this. West of Cape Sable there isn't a lot of winter ice, and some cans remain.

Lighted buoys are invariably flat cans with a latticework tower on top. Some may have a distinctive topmark. Cardinal buoys have a similar shape, but with a higher tower and double topmarks.

The orientation of buoyage is entering from

Stream on bow, or quarter, at approximately 45 degrees

Speed of Tidal Stream	Boat Speed in Knots					
	2	3	4	5	6	8
0.5	10°	7°	5°	4°	3°	2°
1.0	20°	13°	10°	8°	6°	5°
1.5	32°	20°	15°	12°	10°	7°
2.0	45°	28°	20°	16°	14°	10°
2.5		36°	26°	20°	17°	12°
3.0		45°	32°	25°	20°	15°
4.0			45°	33°	28°	20°

Stream on beam

Speed of Tidal Stream	Boat Speed in Knots					
	2	3	4	5	6	8
0.5	15°	10°	8°	6°	5°	4°
1.0	30°	20°	15°	12°	10°	8°
1.5	37°	30°	23°	18°	15°	12°
2.0		38°	30°	23°	20°	15°
2.5			37°	30°	25°	18°
3.0			45°	38°	30°	22°
4.0				48°	38°	30°

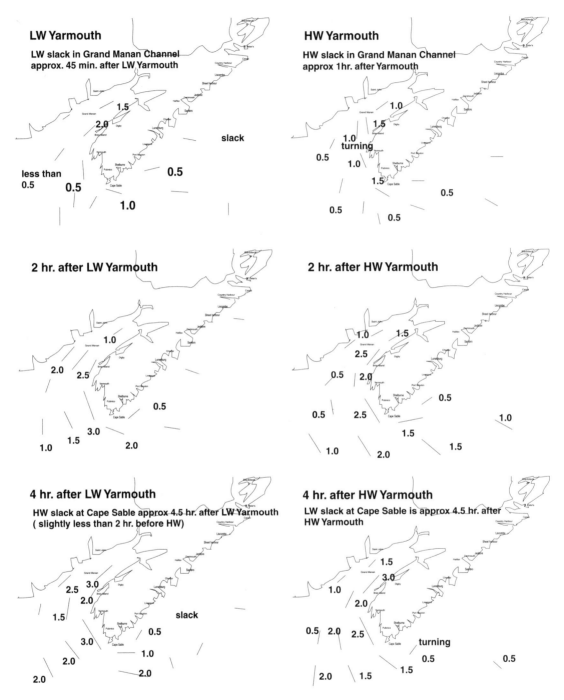

LW Yarmouth

LW slack in Grand Manan Channel
approx. 45 min. after LW Yarmouth

1.5
2.0
slack
less than
0.5
0.5   0.5
1.0

HW Yarmouth

HW slack in Grand Manan Channel
approx 1hr. after Yarmouth

1.0
1.5
1.0
turning
0.5
1.0
1.5
0.5
0.5
0.5

2 hr. after LW Yarmouth

1.0
2.0   2.5
0.5
3.0
1.0   1.5   2.0

2 hr. after HW Yarmouth

1.0   1.5
2.5
0.5   2.0
0.5
0.5   2.5
1.0
1.5
1.0   2.0   1.5

4 hr. after LW Yarmouth

HW slack at Cape Sable approx 4.5 hr. after LW Yarmouth
(slightly less than 2 hr. before HW)

2.5   3.0
2.0
1.5
3.0
slack
0.5
1.0
2.0
2.0
2.0

4 hr. after HW Yarmouth

LW slack at Cape Sable is approx 4.5 hr. after
HW Yarmouth

1.5
3.0
1.0
2.0
0.5   2.0   2.5
turning
0.5   0.5
2.0   1.5   1.5

All directions are approximate. Times of high water and low water in harbors are usually different from the times of reversal of the streams outside.
High water at Yarmouth comes 40 minutes after the stream outside turns to the ebb. For more accurate predictions, the tide tables must be consulted.
There are many quirks of the tidal streams inshore that cannot be shown on this chart.

Tidal streams.

seaward or going with the flood tide. These are not necessarily the same thing, so the chart should always be checked. Round the backs of islands, and so forth, the buoyage can get quite idiosyncratic.

Unlit starboard-hand marks are red, have conical tops, and even numbers.

Unlit port-hand marks are green, have flat tops, and odd numbers. A buoy marked as black on an older chart will, in reality, be green.

Fairway buoys have red-and-white vertical stripes, show a white flashing light—one short flash and one long flash (letter A in Morse code)—and have letters only as identification. Cardinal buoys generally mark isolated dangers and are various configurations of yellow and black. It is easier to identify them from their topmarks.

Cardinal buoys and bifurcation marks also will have letters only as identification.

As far as offshore buoys are concerned, the orientation of the flood stream is clockwise: southwesterly along the coast of Nova Scotia from Cape Breton to Cape Sable, then northwesterly toward the upper Bay of Fundy. Thus when you're heading in a clockwise direction around Nova Scotia, the buoys are red on the right.

Medical Facilities

There are major hospitals in Yarmouth, Bridgewater, Halifax, and Dartmouth. At the time of writing, there are smaller hospitals at Digby, Shelburne, Liverpool, Lunenburg, Sheet Harbour, Sherbrooke, Canso, and Baddeck.

There are, in addition, physicians in Meteghan, Argyle, Pubnico, Barrington, Lockeport, Chester, Hubbards, Arichat, and St. Peters.

But be aware that in the rural areas services are limited. Non-emergency facilities may not be available. You can expect a long wait in any emergency department unless you have a life-threatening problem. A crisis in rural health care, prevalent throughout North America, but particularly acute here, may even mean that emergency services are not available at all.

If you're visiting from the U.S. or any other foreign country, expect to pay with cash or a credit card unless your health insurance carrier has made special arrangements in Nova Scotia.

It should be obvious by now that a certain degree of self-reliance is essential.

Search and Rescue

Use VHF Channel 16 for emergency calls. The airwaves are not cluttered with idle chit-chat, and a swift response is likely.

There are lifeboats at Westport, Clark's Harbour, Port Mouton, Sambro, and Port Bickerton. There are also three vessels at sea most of the time whose nominal base is Dartmouth. There is a federal government helicopter stationed in Yarmouth, but it is restricted to visual flight rules. Thus it may well be grounded when you need it. There is an air–sea rescue squadron at Greenwood. Port Mouton station is currently threatened with closure due to budgetary restraints.

The rescue coordination center is in Halifax, and they will do the best they can with what they have if you have a real emergency. They will not look quite so kindly on calls for assistance from sailboats that have run out of fuel and so forth, and may send you a large bill for towing.

Local fishermen who break down usually get towed in by one of their colleagues, at least until the lifeboat shows up. West of Shelburne you may find a fisherman willing to give you a tow. East of Halifax you will be unlikely to see anyone. Very few fishermen know how to tow sailing vessels, and they might have an eye on salvage.

Channel 16 is the usual way of communicating with the lifeboat. Helicopters and the lifeboats sometimes talk to each other on channel 19. This may not be the same channel 19 as in the U.S. The rescue coordination center or the coast radio station will designate a working channel, and their instructions should be followed implicitly.

Incidentally, the Sea King helicopters used in this province for search-and-rescue sorties are 35 years old. Think about that very carefully before calling one out.

21

Customs

There are customs posts at the following ports of entry (all area codes are 902):

Yarmouth	742-0880
Shelburne	875-2324
Liverpool	324-3268
Lunenburg	634-4401
Halifax	426-2071—or call Halifax Traffic on VHF Channel 16 and ask for instructions about where to clear customs.

A cellular phone will make some of this calling easier, of course.

You may think you can enter at Baddeck, but if you come through the St. Peters Canal, the lockmaster will want to see your cruising permit, which you won't have. This will cause difficulty. You can, at least theoretically, enter at Baddeck if you are coming from the north, through the Great Bras d'Or Channel.

The entire network of ports of entry is in the process of change because of government cutbacks. By the time this book is in print, all the regional offices will be closed. The procedure will then be to call the customs by phone. The above numbers will still be in operation. A cruising permit number will then be issued over the phone. There will be random checks and inspections by either the customs or the Royal Canadian Mounted Police (RCMP). When this system is in place, it would obviously make sense to contact the customs by phone as soon as you are in range.

You will not need to check in after you have received the cruising permit number, and you don't need to check out. There will, in any case, be no-one to check in with. If you check in at Grand Manan, you don't need to bother with the customs again; however, this office too, may be closed as a result of budget cuts.

The accepted procedure prior to these cutbacks is to tie up or anchor. Then the captain *only* should go ashore to find the customs official. If you need to anchor for the night in a place that is not a port of entry, there are usually no problems as long as clearance is made when an entry port is reached. While technically no one is allowed ashore in this instance, I have never heard of anyone being arrested.

If you can't find a customs official and are in a small port, and want to follow the letter of the law (though no Nova Scotian would dream of such a thing, at least where the Customs Department is concerned), call the RCMP. To save a lot of hassle and bureaucratic tomfoolery, tell them you entered this port through stress of weather, and would now like to know what procedure to follow.

Customs officials work office hours, so any clearance requested outside those hours can result in overtime charges. There is no charge for clearing a boat during normal office hours in a port of entry. You will be given a cruising permit good for six months and won't have to bother with the customs again. Telephone clearance will obviously cause some changes, but certainly has the potential for less irritation.

There are limits on the amounts of alcohol and tobacco that can be imported, but no one will hassle you about normal ship's provisions. If you wish to leave a boat in Nova Scotia for more than six months there is a singularly unpopular impost called the Goods and Services Tax (GST), which at 7 percent, plus import duties of 12 percent, could become expensive. The easiest way to avoid this is to get a boatyard to do some work on the boat (repainting the bottom, for instance). This will allow at least one extra season before the federal government's leeches get you.

As you might surmise, customs is responsible for collecting a number of little-loved government taxes, such as GST and duties on imported products. They are therefore not held in the highest regard by Nova Scotians.

Nova Scotia is a popular destination for drug runners. This means the coast is more closely monitored than you might think. Suspicious behavior will probably be noticed. Even small amounts of recreational drugs will cause the boat to be impounded and the crew arrested. Handguns are prohibited and should be declared on entry. You are unlikely to need firearms for self-protection in Nova Scotia, but if you feel you need to carry them while you're traveling to Nova Scotia, bring a shotgun or a rifle. These weapons are permitted if you have some sort of documentation. A U.S. hunting license or gun registration will do. If you are in a state that doesn't require such things, you must get some sort of federal permit. You cannot get one here.

Banking

There are banks in almost every community of any size along the coast. Attempting to get money from a check drawn on an American bank can be a trying experience, but now most banks have money machines, compatible with all the major cards. Money machines are also found in many shopping malls.

When I get money out of one of those things it always bothers me that they can ascertain the state of my overdraft at the speed of light—and this in such backward places that you sometimes wonder if they even have running water in their homes. But I suppose this is progress. It certainly beats waiting a half-hour in line.

Visa is accepted everywhere and MasterCard almost everywhere. American Express, Diner's Club, and the like are recognized in fewer places, especially outside major tourist areas. U.S. dollars are also accepted almost everywhere, but you may not get the best deal on the exchange rate. The best exchange rate is obtained by using a card in one of the aforementioned infernal machines. Exchange rates are quite variable, but for the last few years have been in the range $1.00 U.S. = $1.30–$1.40 Canadian.

Fishing Vessels

Nova Scotia has, or at least had, one of the world's most productive fisheries. As fishing vessels are found here in great numbers at all times of the year, it is as well to be able to recognize the commonest types, if for no other reason than being

able to keep clear of their gear. The following list is not exhaustive, but gives the most common types and their areas of greatest concentration.

Lobster Boats

Lobster fishing west of Halifax Harbour takes place in winter, and the season ends on May 31. To the east of Halifax, it ends in June or July. Unless you are here early in the season, you are unlikely to come across lobster pots, which will be a relief to those of you used to Maine. Many of these boats are used for hand-lining or gill netting in the summer. When hand-lining, boats are usually anchored. East of Cape Sable, most of these boats have a small riding sail at the stern to keep them steadier while handling the gear. These riding sails are not often seen west of Cape Sable. The highest concentration of these boats is within 30 miles of Cape Sable, though they can be found anywhere. Another area where there are a lot is in the vicinity of the LaHave Islands. There are not many east of Halifax.

Gill nets are a curse, as they are difficult to see in the day, and impossible to see at night. You are not likely to encounter many east of Halifax, but between Lunenburg and Cape Sable there are a lot.

Most lobster boats are between 30 and 44 feet (9 and 13 m) long. The larger size is the maximum allowed by the Department of Fisheries. The bigger boats are found largely in the western part of the province. Almost all of them have radar and other similar electronic gear.

Longliners

A longline (known locally as a trawl) is about 500 to 1,000 feet (150 to 300 m) long, and each end has an anchor that almost always is marked by a long pole with a radar reflector. They are found in pairs, a useful thing to remember when you are trying to sort out a whole load of targets on your radar. The line, with hundreds of baited hooks, lies on the bottom, and the only things going to the surface are the anchor lines at each end, so it is most unlikely you will get fouled up in one;

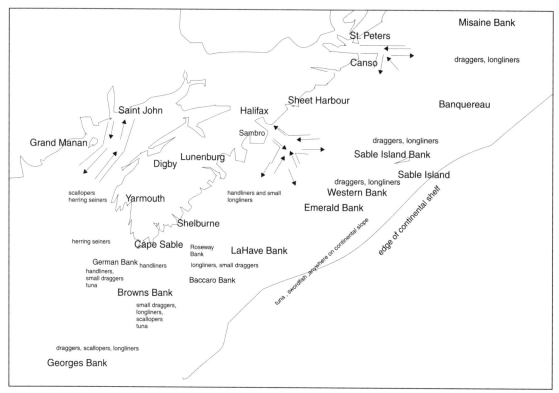

Fishing and separation zones.

though if you have no radar, you can easily run into one of the poles. It is unlikely that such a collision will damage a well-found boat.

Longlines can be found anywhere, including on the banks 100 or more miles offshore, but they are most commonly found between Cape Sable and Canso. There are very few in inshore waters west of Cape Sable, but many on Browns and Georges Banks. Longliners tend to be bigger than lobster boats and can be up to 70 feet (21 m) long. A popular size is 65 feet (20 m). They can be distinguished by a chute at the stern. Most of them have riding sails. They can't move while handling gear, but otherwise are not a great hazard.

Swordfish and Tuna Boats

If you see something that looks like a longliner, but with a long pulpit at the bow and a high crow's-nest, it's probably a swordfish or tuna boat. Some tuna boats are smaller, more the size of lobster boats. These are found in the western part of

the province, usually well offshore, out as far as the Gulf Stream. Most tuna are caught by longlines in this part of the world, and most swordfish by spearing from the pulpit, though there is considerable overlap. You may come across this activity if you cross Georges or Browns Bank. As an individual tuna can be worth $10,000, you will not be thanked if you get in the way.

Draggers

Draggers come in sizes large and small, and are found mostly on the offshore banks. The big ones are not supposed to fish within 50 miles of the shore, though this is sometimes ignored if the captain thinks he can get away with it. While dragging, maneuverability is severely restricted and the only thing the dragger can do to avoid a collision is stop. This will cause a major foul-up with the nets, and much cursing. The trawl extends about 1,000 to 2,000 feet (300 to 600 m) astern and you should not cut too close astern if the net is out.

Most draggers will make 2 to 4 knots while actually dragging, and if you see one of these boats going this slow you should be aware that her nets are probably extended. I have had a number of near-misses with the bigger boats of this ilk, which, I suspect, put to sea from their home ports while most of the crew are recovering from hangovers, and perhaps are not as attentive as they should be. Most of the inshore fleet have had similar experiences, and every once in a while there is a collision. I would advise giving these boats a wide berth, fishing or not, even if you have the right of way.

On Georges, Browns, and German Banks, some small draggers may be operating pair trawls. They will be steaming slowly on parallel courses, with each boat attached to one arm of the trawl. It is inadvisable (to say the least) to pass between them. The international collision regulations prescribe all sorts of navigation lights and shapes for boats engaged in this activity, but I have never seen any of them shown correctly.

Dragging goes on day and night. Bright deck lights obscure almost any navigation lights. If you are confused, consider calling on channel 16 or whatever channel there seems to be a lot of gab on. All these fellows have dual watch or multiple radios set to different channels.

Scallopers. These are draggers modified to fish for shellfish, with a big chain being dragged instead of the more familiar otter trawl. They are found only in western Nova Scotia, most commonly on Georges and Browns Banks, but the smaller ones may be found anywhere in the Bay of Fundy. The base of the smaller ones is Digby. They are side trawlers, and the wheelhouse is aft. If anything, they are even less maneuverable than other draggers while fishing. Most have an overall length of between 45 and 120 feet (14 and 36 m).

Herring Seiners

A herring seine is a big circular net deployed from the seiner by a small powerboat, and extending about a quarter of a mile. Massive hydraulic winches tighten up the net, and the unfortunate fish are pumped into the hold. Not only are these boats incapable of movement while this is going on, there are usually a whole group together, extending over several square miles.

Herring travel in enormous schools at high speed, and these boats, mostly 120 feet (36 m) or so long, charge all over the place trying to find and encircle the fish. This activity almost always takes place at night, and is certainly not stopped by thick fog. Getting mixed up in the seining fleet with no radar on a foggy night could be a terrifying experience, and should be avoided like the plague. If you come across a whole fleet of fishing boats showing deck lights, looking like a small town on the water, this is probably what is going on. Scanning the VHF channels should give you some information, as these fellows talk all the time. Asking for the best way to take you clear of the fleet may get you out of the worst of the close encounters.

This type of fishing usually takes place west of Cape Sable, around German Bank, Trinity Ledge, and deeper into the Bay of Fundy, but is occasionally found farther afield. Between July and September, it would be most unusual to find this fleet more than 50 miles from its summer base in Yarmouth.

In connection with this fishery, large factory vessels for over-the-side sales to Russia and Poland are often found anchored northwest of Yarmouth and in Lobster Bay. You can usually hear or smell them before you hit them.

Aquaculture Facilities

Aquaculture pens are a hazard in protected bays and anchorages. They come in a variety of shapes and sizes, and I will mention in the text where I have found them, but their locations vary greatly. Some of my charts indicate their locations with the abbreviation "aq." They are not supposed to interfere with navigation, though often they do. It is usually possible to get around these things in daylight, but they can be a menace in the dark. Most tanks with fish in them need at least 30 feet

(10 m) of water at low tide, so it is rare that they obstruct a whole anchorage.

Having ruined the traditional ground fishery with mismanagement, the Department of Fisheries and Oceans is now encouraging aquaculture as a substitute. This means that grants, tax breaks, low-interest loans, and the like will be available, and so you may come across these sites in the most unlikely places. They are all supposed to be marked with radar reflectors and (in high traffic areas) lights, but this is often not done. They are easy enough to avoid by day, but can be a hell of a nuisance at night.

It was, of course, overcapacity encouraged by government incentives that caused most of the problems in the traditional fishery, but bureaucrats in this department seem incapable of learning from experience, and their assistance in these ventures may turn out to be the kiss of death.

Traffic Separation Zones

Vessel Traffic Services (VTS) zones are established in the Bay of Fundy, between Digby and Grand Manan, in the approaches to Halifax Harbour, and off Canso. Vessels shorter than 45 feet (13.7 m) do not have to report and are not obliged to follow the separation zones, but must give way to a large vessel correctly traversing them. All the zones have lanes in the "keep-to-starboard" mode. VHF Channels 12 and 14 are monitored. It is handy to listen to these channels while crossing a zone. Halifax Traffic, Channel 14 outside the harbor, is very helpful in thick conditions.

A Note on Names

Place names in this guide have been changed to agree with those on the charts and official government publications as much as possible. These are often not the names that local people use, and they may vary from one chart series to another. This makes the placement of apostrophes and the like somewhat eccentric and not always grammatically correct. Our bilingual official languages policy has unfortunately bred a generation of civil servants semiliterate in both languages, but to avoid endless confusion I have used their spelling, whether correct or not.

Western Nova Scotia: *Digby to Cape Sable*

Digby Gut, Digby

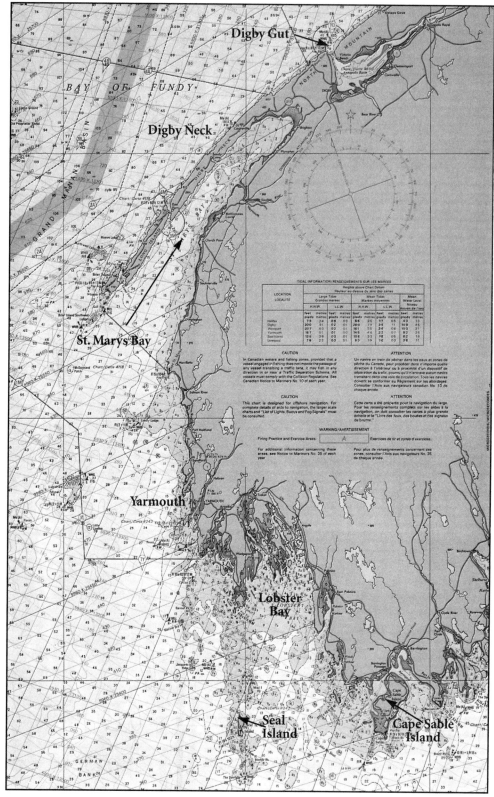

Based on CHS Chart 4012. Not to be used for navigation.

After entering or clearing at Yarmouth, most cruisers hurry through western Nova Scotia, deterred by its strong tidal streams, high traffic densities, and the prevalence of fog. Those of us who live here feel these cruisers are missing one of the more interesting areas of the province, ranging from the historic settlement of Annapolis Royal, to the remoteness of Seal Island. Yarmouth is a major port of entry, with an international airport and a ferry, and is unlikely to be affected by government cutbacks, unlike some of the smaller ports.

The Annapolis Basin

Charts: 4011, **4012, 4396**

Note that charts 4011 and 4012 are small-scale charts and should not be used for entering any harbor in this area except possibly Digby. Entering Digby in clear weather with one of these charts is probably all right, but in fog things might get a little tense. Chart 4396 is a large-scale chart of the Annapolis Basin and is essential if you are going anywhere in the basin other than Digby.

Digby ★★★

Digby Gut is hard to see from seaward until you are right on top of it, though it can be identified by a dip in the hills.

Approaches. From fairway buoy "V" steer 186°M. While the shore is quite steep-to, there tend to be eddies close inshore that could be disturbing. The tidal stream in the entrance is fierce, about 5 knots at springs. The tide turns here about an hour after it does in Yarmouth, and entry is much more comfortable with the incoming tide. Entry can be made in any weather condition, as there is plenty of water. Strong wind-against-tide conditions (particularly an ebb tide against a northwesterly gale) can make

for extremely rough water, but you are not likely to be overwhelmed.

When you pass the ferry terminal, come to about 198°M to aim for the town wharf. In rough conditions, the water is marginally smoother on the east side of the first part of the entrance than on the west side past the ferry terminal. There is a minimum depth of 22 feet (6.7 m) in the buoyed channel, and it slopes off fairly gradually to the east. The rise and fall of the tide is 30 feet (10 m) at springs, 22 feet (6.7 m) at neaps—a major consideration when tying up at wharves or anchoring. If you have never seen such a range, you will also be tested going up and down ladders at wharves higher than the average house.

There is a ferry to Saint John, New Brunswick, that makes several trips daily. The terminal is on the west side of the Gut, just where it expands into the Annapolis Basin. There is room only for the ferry to tie up at the terminal, so don't head there. It is hard to dock the ferry in strong easterly winds, and in these circumstances it should be given plenty of room.

Anchorage, Dockage. The town wharf is the headquarters of the Digby scallop fleet. It is crowded and there are so many strings going everywhere that tying up is difficult. There is a float at the end of the inside wharf that may be vacant, but it is unwise to leave the boat unattended. It is possible to anchor just to the south of the dock, where the locals have their moorings. This is totally exposed to the east, with a fetch of over 10 miles, and makes for a horribly uncomfortable experience.

The new marina is just southwest of the government wharf, and sheltered by it. Its position makes its berths much preferable to the alternatives. At this time, there is water available, but no fuel or showers.

Ashore. One of the advantages of Digby as a port is that the town center is extremely compact, and everything is available without walking more than three blocks. There are half-a-dozen restaurants, all the usual stores, and the Liquor Commission is

31

only a short walk to the north of the dock. Digby had a reputation for being a rowdy place on a Saturday night, but the new development may improve this. I haven't been overly disturbed here myself.

If you are interested in an upmarket experience, Digby Pines resort hotel is about a mile to the northwest, just under the big green water tower. It has an excellent restaurant and the best Sunday brunch I have had anywhere (for about $18). Reservations might be advisable if you have a big crew. There is a championship 18-hole golf course at this establishment, one of the best in the province.

Annapolis Royal ★★★ BY BOAT

Chart: 4396

Annapolis was the site of Champlain's second settlement (the first being on an island on the Saint John River in New Brunswick). The site, just north of Goat Island, and originally occupied in 1605, has been reconstructed and is now a national park.

Approaches. Annapolis Royal is at the head of navigation of the Annapolis River, the preferred channel being to the west of Goat Island. The strength of the tide, the lack of a good landing place, and the thickness of the mud make it a rather difficult journey by boat, and I can't conceive of going here to provision. It is, however, an interesting place to visit by land.

Ashore. French settlement in Nova Scotia was never really accepted by New Englanders, and the original habitation was burned to the ground in 1613. Ownership changed hands several times during the rest of the seventeenth century, but the Treaty of Utrecht in 1713 finally established Eng-

land as the colonial power. Annapolis then became the provincial capital, to be replaced by Halifax in 1749. Not surprisingly, Annapolis is a pleasant town, with many historic buildings.

Bear River ★★★

NO FACILITIES

Chart: 4396

This harbor is a fairly good anchorage, though the approach is difficult at low water. You cannot go under the bridges, so anchor just north of them. There are a few local boats moored here. Bear River is one of the arts and crafts centers of the province, and there is also another resort, the Mountain Gap Inn, and a provincial park a mile or so to the west.

Digby Neck and St. Marys Bay

Charts: **4118, 4243,** 4323, 4324

Cruising in this area is not for everyone. The coastline is more intimidating than most of the rest of the province, and there are long stretches without harbors of refuge. Almost all of the harbors are exposed to the northwest, and because of refraction, even southwesterly winds tend to cause swell in the entrances. The tidal streams are really strong, exceeding 7 knots in a few places, and thick fog is prevalent. Many harbors are inaccessible at low tide.

If you are passing outside Brier Island, give it at least 5 miles' clearance. The area is full of horrible tiderips. None of the harbors on the mainland side of St. Marys Bay, or from Cape St. Marys to Yarmouth, is safe to enter in northerly gales. One of my neighbor's sons and two members of his crew were lost when their 44-foot (13-m) fishing boat tried to run into Port Maitland in a northwesterly gale on Christmas Eve, 1992.

I have not mentioned in this area most harbors

where it is necessary to take the ground at low water, though there are a number that determined gunkholers might like to explore.

Apart from Digby, where a few hardy souls keep their boats, this area is rarely visited by cruising yachts and you are almost certain to be the only one in any harbor. Although getting into many of these harbors can be a test, once inside you will find shelter from almost anything the weather can produce. There are hundreds of fishing boats based in this area, all of them operate year round, and significant damage to a boat tied up to a wharf is a rare thing indeed.

Gullivers Cove, Centreville (Trout Cove), and Whale Cove

★★   NO FACILITIES

Charts: 4118, 4110

Going west from Digby, there are small harbors at Gullivers Cove, Centreville (which may be marked Trout Cove on your chart), and Whale Cove. Centreville has a sizable population of fishing boats, but is not sheltered unless you can tie to the wharf, and drying out becomes problematic.

Approaches. Gullivers and Whale Coves are open to the northwest, but could be used to wait out a tide. I wouldn't enter either at night or in bad visibility, as fish weirs are occasionally erected at these places. The coast is otherwise steep-to and free of obstructions.

Petit Passage and Tiverton

Chart: 4118

This the most direct route from Digby to Yarmouth, and would be straightforward were it not for the strength of the tidal stream (more than 7 knots at springs). The tide turns about 30 minutes after high or low water at Yarmouth, and about 30 minutes before local high or low waters. There is only a few minutes of slack water. The exact time of low-water slack is 1 hour 3 minutes before low water at St. John, and high-water slack is exactly 1 hour before high water at St. John.

The passage runs more or less north-and-south, but because the tide goes faster than most yachts, you have to adjust your heading to keep out of the rips at each end. The western side is rather smoother, but is still a lumpy passage even in a flat calm. There is also a car ferry to avoid. This is not a place for the faint-hearted, nor a good place to be without a reliable engine or radar. I would never try this at night or in fog. Strong wind-against-tide conditions here are really dangerous and can sink you.

About halfway through the passage, on the western side, lies the settlement of Tiverton, where the navigable channel narrows to little more than 200 yards (200 meters). There is a ferry terminal at Tiverton, and although this is officially a prohibited anchorage, it is possible to anchor (albeit uneasily, with a big anchor and the minimum scope you think you can get away with) among the moorings just south of the ter-

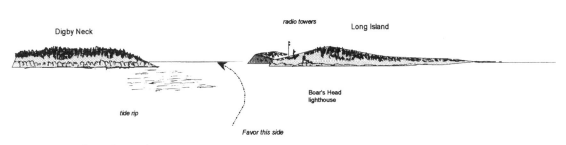

Petit Passage from the north.

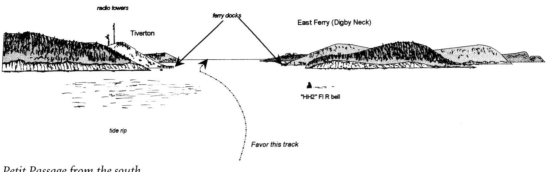

Petit Passage from the south.

minal. Both ferries stand by on Channel 14, so call them if you think there will be any difficulty getting around them.

Grand Passage

Chart: 4118

When approaching Grand Passage from the north, beware of the extensive tiderips off and between Northwest Ledge and Moores Rock, some 3 miles northwest of North Point. These can be avoided if you keep no more than 1 mile off Long Island. Grand Passage runs approximately north-and-south, and the tide also runs hard, 6 knots at springs, turning a few minutes before it does in Petit Passage. There are also inshore eddies, as there are in Petit Passage, but it is generally smoother. The western side of the passage must be favored as there are half-tide rocks and ledges obstructing the eastern side. The main channel is to the west, between Peter Island and Brier Island, not the much wider channel to the east of Peter Island. The preferred channel actually looks too narrow, but in fact it is unobstructed and deep.

Westport ★★★★ ⬛2 ⬛C

🍽 🛒 ▣

Chart: 4118

Westport, in Grand Passage, affords better anchorage than does Tiverton, but it is still very much exposed to the northwest.

On February 2, 1976, western Nova Scotia was assaulted by an intense extra-tropical cyclone, whose center passed right over Westport. The wind reached a sustained velocity of 134 knots, the highest wind speed ever recorded in the province. There was a storm surge of about 6 feet over the high-water spring level and much of Westport's waterfront was flattened.

Anchorage, Dockage. The anchorage is just to the south of the ferry dock, among the local moorings. It's tempting to pick up a vacant mooring, but its owner is likely to return at some hideous hour of the morning. Tying to a wharf is also possible, but finding a space—and the 20-foot (6-m) rise and fall of the tide—make this somewhat of a chore.

Ashore. Westport, where Joshua Slocum spent his childhood, has had a resurgence of its tourist industry in the last few years. Brier Island, on which it is located, is a gathering place for one of the Atlantic Ocean's very few humpback whale populations, and about 100 of these mammals gather here in August and September, attracted by the same schools of herring that attract the seiners. Whale watching has now become big business. Brier Island is also a major flyway for all sorts of migrating birds throughout the year.

There are scenic walks all over the island, though it is really a day's hike to get to one end from the other. Naturally, these attractions have drawn more tourists, though the type that come after these gentle pleasures tend to be of the less offensive variety.

There are now some quite nice restaurants and inns on the island, a grocery store, and even a bank. Brier Island is still a remote place, however, as you will find if you try to drive to Digby. It requires a major effort to accomplish the 40-mile trip in less than two hours. There is a Coast Guard lifeboat at Westport.

Freeport ★★★★

Chart: 4118

Freeport, on Long Island across Grand Passage from Westport, is somewhat larger but less developed. Local boats tie up in Northeast Cove, which mostly dries out at low water. A ferry crosses every half hour between Freeport and Westport, and needs to be given a good berth. Similarly, it is not a place for the faint-hearted, those with unreliable engines, or at night, or in thick fog, unless you have radar.

East Sandy Cove ★★★★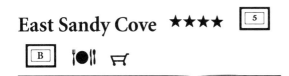

Chart: 4118

Going clockwise around St. Marys Bay, East Sandy Cove is the first non-drying harbor north of Petit Passage. It is by far the best harbor in the bay.

Approaches. Entry is simple: Follow the buoys going between the two big headlands. The line of high ground will be seen to have a big dip in it on the approach. At low water, entry might be difficult at night.

The channel is buoyed, and if you stray far from it at low water you will run aground. Though it is called Sandy Cove, it is mostly mud. The best place to make fast is at the northernmost wharf. On the inside, there is about 7 feet (2.1 m), and on the outside about 9 feet (2.7 m) at low-water springs. It is home to about 20 small draggers, and you will have to tie alongside one. Especially if you can get the inside berth, nothing could bother you in here. There is no room to anchor, though, unless you want to dry out at low water.

Ashore. Sandy cove is a very pretty little community, and there is a restaurant, Ye Old Village Inn, a take-out, and a grocery store within easy walking distance of the wharf. If you have the energy, take the little road leading west. After going up and down a big hill, you will come to West Sandy Cove, which does indeed have the red sand characteristic of this area as well as a delightful crescent beach that usually is deserted.

Weymouth ★★

NO FACILITIES

Chart: 4118

Weymouth Harbour is almost opposite Sandy Cove, but the town of Weymouth is a long walk (at least two miles) from the wharf.

Approaches. From the fairway buoy, steer about 130°M, which will put you just to port of the conspicuous water tower. On the starboard side going in there is a flashing white light (4 seconds) on a concrete tower set on a small island. The channel is to port of this tower as you go in, marked with spars, and very narrow. Be aware that the tide goes out of here like water down a drain.

35

Anchorage, Dockage. You can moor at the end of the large government wharf, which has about 7 feet (2.1 m) of water at low-water springs, but it is an uneasy berth because of the tidal currents. The root of the wharf dries out. Anchoring is just possible (in about 6 feet, or 1.8 m, at low-water springs) just a little farther in from the wharf, and before the bridge. Incidentally, I have not seen the clearance of this bridge mentioned on any chart. It looks to be about 35 feet (10.6 m) at high water, but I know it has snagged the upperworks of small draggers, and I wouldn't advise passage in a sailboat.

l'Acadie

Chart: 4118

Going south from Weymouth, you come to the Acadian shore (called the French shore, or *Pars-en-haut,* by locals). This is the center of Acadian culture in Nova Scotia, with a French language university at Pointe d'Eglise. Massive churches reflect the power of the priesthood in the first part of this century, a power that is now somewhat in decline. Relations between the vast majority of Acadians and the English-speaking segments of the population are generally good, with much intermarriage.

Unfortunately, political relations, as in other parts of Canada, are a little more troubled. Some Acadians from the academic and politically active communities decry what they label "assimilation," and lobby for "homogenous" Acadian institutions such as schools, local councils, and the like. The "English" in the region, the majority of whose ancestors came as refugees from the American War of Independence, the Highland clearances, or the potato famines in Ireland, are unsympathetic to the idea of special treatment for Acadians to atone for the sins of the colonial power 230 years ago. These tensions occasionally result in a climate somewhat lacking in contentment and harmony. Baser members of the political classes occasionally exploit this tension, as they do in other places, and with the usual results.

Everyone here *can* speak English, but a few *won't.* Similarly, if you speak French to someone in an English-speaking community, you may receive blank looks or hostility. In general, there will not be much of a problem using English around most wharves, stores, and restaurants.

Saulnierville ★

NO FACILITIES

Chart: 4118

Saulnierville is partly protected by a large breakwater, but is open to the northwest. There is about 8 feet (2.4 m) at the end of the breakwater at low-water springs.

Approaches. You can approach easily from just about anywhere to seaward. Once inside, you will have to tie alongside a fishing boat. There is a large fish-processing plant, but no other facilities.

Meteghan River ★★

Chart: 4118

This is the site of the A.F. Theriault shipyard, the largest repair facility in the region. They can handle anything up to about 120 feet (36 m). The harbor dries at low water, however. Any vessel with a draft of less than 8 feet (2.4 m) can probably get in after half-tide. Larger vessels (drawing up to 12 feet, or 3.6 m) are worked on here, but much attention is paid to the tide tables.

There is a tavern here, but you'd have to have a mighty thirst as an inducement to visit this harbor if you didn't need the services of the shipyard.

Meteghan ★★

Chart: 4118

Meteghan, the center of French culture in Nova Scotia, has the largest wharf in the immediate area. The harbor has received massive support from the government, and the breakwater would probably survive a hit from a small nuclear bomb.

Approaches. There is considerable shoal water extending north of the wharf. Thus, when entering, keep on, or slightly to the south of, a line from the outside buoy, "HC2," to the breakwater, which has a flashing red light and a foghorn. This is a course of about 122°M from the buoy, but—as with all harbors in this region—the tide runs across the track, so careful note should be made that you remain on the correct approach. The harbor is rather crowded, and the head of the basin, including the small floating dock, dries at low water. Turn to port immediately upon entry and moor alongside the northern wharf.

Ashore. The wharf is close to the commercial center of the municipality of Clare. (It has always intrigued me that the center of the French culture in the province should have so many Irish names.) A number of grocery stores, pharmacies, banks, and the like are within walking distance, as are a couple of restaurants and the local outlet of the Liquor Commission.

Other Harbors in St. Marys Bay

There are a few other small harbors in the bay, but they all dry at low water, are of little scenic attraction, and are of little use to most deep-draft yachts.

Cape St. Marys ★★★

Chart: 4243

The harbor at Cape St. Marys is a pretty little place that offers reasonable shelter unless it is blowing a screecher from the southeast. Chart 4243 shows a large-scale inset of the harbor.

Approaches. When approaching this harbor, give the rip to the south of the cape a wide berth. If you're coming from the north, keep at least 1 mile off the cape, and go south of the fairway buoy before you turn into the bay. If you're coming from the south, keep the fairway buoy well to port.

There is only 3 feet (0.9 m) at low-water springs at the ends of the wharves, but during most days in summer there will usually be more than 5 feet at LW. It is, however, not a suitable place if you draw 7 feet (2 m).

Ashore. To the south is the two-mile stretch of Maivillette Beach Provincial Park, a beautiful and sparsely visited white sand beach, whose only drawback is the frigid water.

There is a quite acceptable restaurant handy to the wharf, and two boatyards capable of handling most boats of 50 feet (15 m) or less.

Cape St. Marys to Yarmouth

Southwest of Cape St. Marys, at distances of 6 and 15 miles respectively, are Trinity Ledge and Lurcher Shoal. Trinity Ledge has a drying rock, Lurcher Shoal a minimum depth of 7 feet (2 m). Both have horrible tiderips, and the herring seining fleet is often active around Trinity Ledge. Both areas should be given a wide berth.

If you have an old copy of chart 4324, it shows the inshore waters better than the new chart

4243. While the tidal range is not quite as high as that in the Annapolis Basin, streams are just as strong, and constant attention to your track is required, especially if visibility is restricted.

Note: The small harbors between Cape St. Marys and Yarmouth are all protected by artificial breakwaters, but offer marginal facilities at low water, especially for boats drawing more than 5 feet (1.5 m). They should absolutely never be attempted in strong westerlies.

Port Maitland ★★★

Chart: 4243

Port Maitland, little more than 6 miles south of Cape St. Marys, is once again in the territory of *les anglais.* The harbor offers about 6 feet (1.8 m) of water at low-water springs on the south side of the wharf, right next to the skeleton tower with the green light on it. If there is a big swell outside, there is a little one inside, so the berth is rather uneasy. The inner harbor dries.

Approaches. Entry is not advisable with an onshore wind of any strength, nor with less water than half-tide except in the calmest of conditions. People fish out of here all winter, but they must be made of sterner stuff than I am. There are no dangers in the approach, which can be made from any reasonable direction, but there always seems to be a swell in the entrance, which is dangerous on occasion.

Ashore. About a mile from the wharf, along the only road, you come to a restaurant and bakery.

Sandford ★★★

NO FACILITIES

Chart: 4243

Sandford is about 4 miles south of Port Maitland and has a sectored red, white, and green light (2-second isophase) leading to the entrance. The center of the white sector lies on an incoming heading of 154°M. There is about 5 feet (1.5 m) inside the wharf at low-water springs, though this is not at all apparent from the chart. There is an inner basin that dries, guarded by a small, picturesque drawbridge much painted by local artists. If you can find a space alongside the wharf, you should be safe from anything but a major storm from the north.

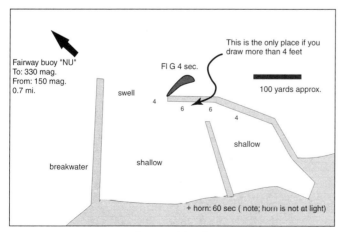

Port Maitland.

Chegoggin ★★★ ☐3 ☐B

NO FACILITIES

Chart: 4243

Chegoggin is the final harbor on this coast before you get to Yarmouth. As the harbor entrance is sheltered from the northwest by Chegoggin Point, it is a little easier to enter in adverse conditions, and there is more water in the approach—about 10 feet (3 m) at low-water springs. Nevertheless, I would still recommend not attempting it in an onshore wind of more than 15 knots.

Approaches. Approach with the end of the wharf bearing about 044°M. This is right on the 31130 line on the 5930-Y loran chain, which is what all the fishermen use. As this is the most accessible harbor between Cape St. Marys and Yarmouth, you can expect it to be crowded, but if you draw 6 feet (1.8 m) or less, there is usually room to tie up alongside a fishing boat, many of which will not be in use in the summer. Yachts are rarely seen in any of the harbors along this stretch, so you can expect to be the center of attention.

Chegoggin to Yarmouth

Charts: 4243, 4245

The Department of Fisheries and Oceans (DFO) *Sailing Directions* warn that Chegoggin Point and Cape Forchu, 3 miles to the south, look very similar on short-range radar. If you mistake one for the other, you can expect to be in serious difficulty in short order, so if it is not clear which you are looking at, check your position with another device.

Cape Forchu marks the entrance to Yarmouth Harbour. Cape Forchu light is somewhat obscured from the west and you may not see it if you are close inshore.

Motor yachts with adventurous captains might be able to cut under the fixed bridge at Yarmouth Bar to enter Yarmouth Harbour without going round Cape Forchu. There is 7 feet (2.1 m) overhead clearance at high-water springs, which translates to about 15 feet (4.5 m) at half-tide, when there is 6 feet (1.8 m) of water in the channel. Local fishing boats often use this shortcut, but the tide goes through here like a drain, and without chart 4245 and local knowledge I can't really recommend it.

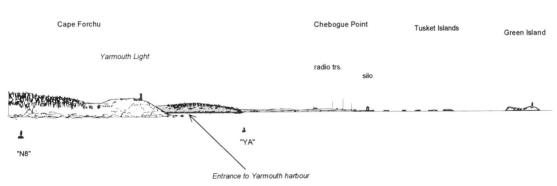

Approaching Yarmouth from the west—five miles out.

Yarmouth to Little River

Charts: **4243**, 4244, **4245**

Yarmouth is the major commercial center of western Nova Scotia, and though much reduced from its heyday in the nineteenth century, it is still a busy port. Many cruisers arriving from Maine will choose to clear customs here, though if there is fog, and you have no radar, this can be a testing, if not dangerous, experience. This is a place where running aground in bad weather can easily cause the loss of the vessel. If you need to enter port, for provisions or clearing customs, and are uncertain of your position or ability to navigate in thick weather, go to Shelburne, which is much safer. Entering any harbor in this area is not advisable using the small-scale charts, though you can make do without the plan of Yarmouth Harbour (4245) in most conditions.

Yarmouth Harbour ★★★

Charts: **4243, 4245**

Yarmouth serves quite a large population, and most services are available here, though some may take more tracking down than you might think. Marine services are geared to the local fishing industry, one of the most prosperous in the world, so there will be no trouble fixing engines, electronics, refrigeration systems, and the like. There might, however, be some problem fixing sailing gear.

Approaches. From the west, Cape Forchu can be safely approached on any heading from 030°M to 120°M. Be careful not to be set too far to the east, especially in thick weather. The tide sets northwest on the flood and southeast on the ebb. This is right across your track while entering, and can run at up to 4 knots, which will cause difficulties if you are not aware of it.

The tide turns about 40 minutes earlier outside the harbor than it does inside. The tidal streams in the Bay of Fundy also tend to drive you north of your track, so that you can easily end up north of Cape Forchu without realizing it. This, of course, was more of a hazard in the days before electronic position-fixing systems were available.

Yarmouth is safe to enter at any state of the tide and in any strength of wind, though it can get lumpy if a southwesterly gale is blowing against the ebb.

Fog is the main danger. The entrance is quite narrow and there are rocks on either side. The west side is marginally safer in this respect.

Do not enter this harbor in fog using loran or GPS as your sole navigation aid. There is a radio beacon at the airport (QI, on 206 kHz), but I do not recommend it be used for entering this harbor. Be especially careful of the Hens and Chickens Rocks, on the starboard side going in. Every year someone runs up on them.

Large vessels, ferries, draggers, and so forth use this harbor on a constant basis. Farther up the harbor, there is very little room in the dredged channel when the ferries are coming in and out. In addition, ahead of these vessels there is an unusual shallow-water effect that sucks water into the center of the channel, right into the big ship's path. The most dangerous place is about 500 yards either side of Bunker Island, where the oil tanks are situated. Shipping movements can be ascertained by calling Fundy Traffic on Channel 12 or 14.

To enter the harbor, follow the buoyed channel. The course inside the harbor is 020°M to Bunker Island, then 052°M to the public wharf. The spars that mark the edge are unlit, and about 12 feet (3.6 m) tall. It makes a hell of a bang if you hit one in the dark. They are metal and have radar reflectors.

Anchorage, Dockage. There is a reasonably quiet anchorage just north of Ships Stern and west of Sollows Rock. There are no facilities. As

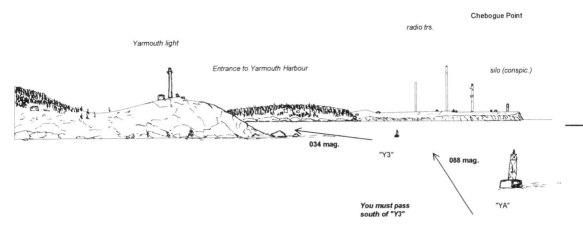

Approaches to Yarmouth from the west—two miles out.

you go farther in, past Bunker Island, you may come across a number of scallop draggers anchored on the starboard side. They are usually between 40 feet and 55 feet (12 m and 17 m) in length, and may not be showing lights.

The buoyed channel leads straight to the town wharves, which will lie on your starboard side. There is very little water outside the buoyed channel, and you will certainly run aground if you stray far from it.

At the head of the harbor, on the port side, just east of small, cormorant-infested Doctors Island, the town has laid about 8 moorings for visitors. The weights were originally concrete planters supposed to make the main street more attractive, but they got in everybody's way and took up parking space. These blocks weigh several tons each, and are not likely to drag, but their polypropylene mooring warps are of uncertain durability.

After totally neglecting the waterfront for over a century, the Town Fathers finally awoke to the concept that visiting yachts could be a source of income. Accordingly, there is now a small floating dock at the north end of the public wharves. It usually has a vacant space and is reasonably well sheltered, though the water can be a bit lumpy in a strong northwesterly. There is a small bandstand close by.

Fresh water is available, but fuel has to be delivered by truck. Yarmouth Harbour still has a considerable amount of pollution, and a lot of it seems to collect in this corner, but as the town no longer dumps its sewage directly into the harbor, it is improving in this respect. In the unlikely event that the floating dock is full, you can tie up alongside a fishing boat inside one of the other government wharves. There is constant activity, however, and it is inadvisable to leave the boat unattended. In 1996, a bunch of rowdy native fishermen made this an unpleasant spot. This might change.

Ashore. The customs office—(902) 742-0880—is by the ferry terminal at the south end of the docks. The captain of your boat should go directly to the customs office before anyone else is allowed ashore.

The two ferries are in daily operation in the summer (departing at 1000 and 1500) so there should be a customs official around most of the day. If you get in late at night and the crew wants to go ashore to eat, I doubt that any federal civil servant is going to get excited enough to arrest you.

Most services are available in Yarmouth, but like most small towns in Nova Scotia, the main shopping centers are on the outskirts. In this case, the main malls are on Starr's Road—north on Main Street, then turn right. It is about a mile, but taxis in Yarmouth are cheap. I personally don't find any of the downtown restaurants inspiring, but Joshua's, on the waterfront, provides good snacks.

The Nova Scotia government has the quaint idea that it is less corrupt than the Mafia, and so

41

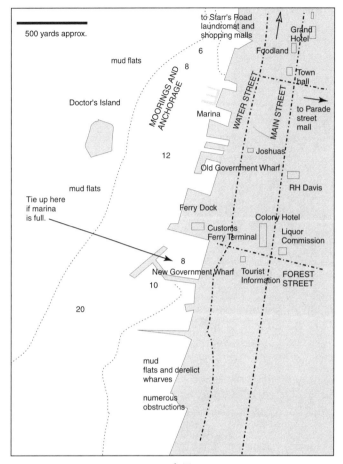

Yarmouth Town.

the first mall on Starr's Road, is a good place for an economical hearty meal. If you seek more sophistication (and a drinkable wine list) you'll find the Austrian Inn, Wagner's, Harris's, and the Manor Inn (in that order) to the north on Route 1, several miles from town.

Because a 19 percent government tax is added to everything on a restaurant menu, including the already heavily taxed booze, visitors will experience wallet shock. We don't like it either.

R.H. Davis, on Main Street, is the store that sold Joshua Slocum the famous alarm clock that he serviced by boiling in oil. They are still in the clock business, and are also chart agents. Most local charts are usually in stock.

Fresh fish is sold at Wade Nickerson's fish market at the north end of Main Street and at the supermarkets and the "Surf and Turf" on Starrs Road.

For boat repairs, contact Darren Cottreau at (902) 742-4134 or West Nova Marine at (902) 742-8595.

controls all sales of alcoholic beverages through the sinister-sounding Nova Scotia Liquor Commission. The nearest outlet is one block due east of the ferry terminal. Those of you accustomed to free enterprise will find the prices outrageous and the service indifferent.

The nearest laundromat is at the north end of Water Street, about a half-mile from the dock. There is another one on Parade Street, a little farther away.

The nearest tavern is the Clipper Ship, just opposite the liquor store. It used to be a place where the natives got quite restless, but I am told it is now more sedate. We certainly admit to the Emergency Department fewer walking wounded from this establishment than we used to. Grizzled foredeck hands may find it to their taste.

Arthur's, in the Red Knight tavern opposite

Yarmouth's Past. In 1880 Yarmouth was, by measure of the shipping tonnage handled, the fourth busiest port in the world. I have to wonder how this came about. It is difficult, even now, to beat out of this harbor against the prevailing wind, and it's hard to imagine how square-riggers managed at all. The Yarmouth County Museum, on Collins Street, three blocks east of R.H. Davis, details much of the maritime history of the region. Unfortunately, the twentieth century has not been so fruitful, and the last decade has seen a decline in the town's major industries.

Things to Do. History buffs will be interested to visit the Yarmouth County Museum, whose curator has crossed the Atlantic in a square-rigger, and the Nova Scotia Firefighters' Museum, on

Main Street next to the jail, which also shows nationally circulated historical exhibits (at least those not axed by budget cuts). There are frequent performances at the Yarmouth County Arts Centre about a half-mile east on Parade Street, past the high school, and there is nightly dinner theater at the Grand Hotel during the summer.

Passage East of Yarmouth

Charts: **4242, 4243**, 4244

The quickest and most sheltered route if you're heading east from Yarmouth (rounding Cape Sable, for example) is to pass Chebogue Point inside Roaring Bull Rock, take Schooner Passage, and then proceed toward Cape Sable.

Courses and distances are as follows:

From mid-channel in Yarmouth Harbour entrance to Chebogue Point bell buoy "E," steer 182°M for 3.6 miles.

Keep about 0.4 mile off Chebogue Point. This course leads inside the Roaring Bull, a drying rock 1.8 miles northwest of the point.

From Chebogue Point, steer 165°M for 4.6 miles to buoy "NSH," the outer bell buoy leading to Schooner Passage. Pass though Schooner Passage steering approximately 176°M.

There are two hazardous rocks just off the southern entrance to Schooner Passage, the Old Man and the Old Woman, to the west and east, respectively, of your track. Both are marked by buoys, but there are no sound signals. Keeping Owls Head (at the northern tip of Owls Head Island) in sight and separated from Johns Island leads you clear of both these rocks.

Then, from buoy "T1" (Old Man) to buoy "N2" (Cape Sable), the course is 160°M for 21 miles. Eight miles along this course from buoy "T1," whistle buoy "P" (Pubnico) appears 1 mile to port.

The course to Pubnico Point from buoy "NS4" (Peases Island) is 120°M for 9.8 miles.

From buoy "NS4" to "TT" (Old Woman, south cardinal) the course is 104°M for 2 miles, and from there to Argyle it is 078°M for approximately 10 miles, depending on your route.

I would have serious reservations about doing these passages in fog without radar. If visibility is a half-mile or more it should be all right under otherwise favorable conditions, that is, not blowing a gale, and with the wind free. The area is well lit, and there should be no problems for experienced navigators at night, if it is clear.

Assuming you can get out of Yarmouth Harbour, but do not have radar and are relying on GPS or loran, the following route is probably the safest:

From mid-channel, Yarmouth Harbour entrance, to "Y2" (Roaring Bull bell buoy) steer 214°M for 2.2 miles.

From "Y2," steer 175°M for 10 miles to bell buoy "NSC" (west of Outer Bald Tusket Island). On this leg, Green Island lies to starboard after about 4 miles and you should be able to hear the horn.

From "NSC," steer 152°M for 22 miles to buoy "N2" (Cape Sable Whistle).

This route gives at least one mile clearance from any rock, which should be enough to compensate for any unforeseen error in an electronic navigation system. There is a large tiderip south of the Tusket Islands on this route, which is unavoidable.

For either of these passages, departing at the right stage of the tide is critical. The flood, flowing northwest, starts 2 hours earlier at Cape Sable than at Yarmouth, giving only 4 hours of favorable tide. It is best to leave Yarmouth 2 hours before local high water. You will spend a short time bucking the tide while you get out of the harbor, but it is not strong here (at least compared to the current at Cape Sable) and it will be falling off. If you don't get to Cape Sable before the new flood starts, you will spend a long time looking at it while your teeth are shaken out and buckets of green water crash over your deck, most often in a wind-against-tide situation.

From points farther west it is best to go well south of Seal Island, preferably at least 1 mile

43

south of Blonde Rock whistle buoy ("N4"). The area between Blonde Rock (named after a ship that hit it and sank) and the south point of Seal Island is poorly charted and extremely dangerous, every rock being named after a shipwreck.

The passage between Seal and Mud Island (locally called The Hospital) is unencumbered by rocks but extremely rough due to the strong tide. A 20-knot northwesterly wind blowing over a spring flood here will raise a 15-foot (4.5-m) sea, which might better be left to local fishermen to experience. Avoid going close to Rip Point on the north side of Seal Island. I have been pooped there when the wind was blowing only 20 knots.

The passage between Flat Island and Soldiers Ledge is shallow, irregular, and charted from an 1851 survey. It is rougher here than it is at The Hospital. The deepest, and marginally smoother, water lies about a half-mile off Flat Island, going northeast. I don't recommend it in anything of a wind, though.

Chebogue River ★★★★ 4

 C NO FACILITIES

Chart: 4243

This undeveloped harbor is just east of Yarmouth. It has two entrances, the west entrance being very much easier for strangers. The tides run hard across the entrances, which makes navigation difficult if visibility is poor.

Approaches. Green Island, some 2.5 miles southwest of the entrance, is conspicuous, high, and grassy. It has a lighthouse and a fog signal. From the north point of this island, a course of 052°M will bring you just west of Crawleys Island, a large wooded island in the middle of the harbor entrance.

There is always a current running here, so make sure the bearing of Green Island astern remains 232°M. This is the safest way to enter the river, but there is a rock, Chebogue Ledge, just to port on this bearing, and a more extensive rock pile, Reef Ledge, just to starboard.

If you're coming from farther north, for example from Yarmouth, it is sometimes easier to run along Chebogue Point—a low, grassy cliff with a conspicuous grain silo and radio towers on it—to bell buoy "E" 200 yards south of the point. The current runs at about 4 knots off the point, so you'll make slow progress if it's adverse.

There are no good leading marks for the east entrance, and the passage involves keeping about 60 feet (18 m) to the west of Reef Island, on a heading of about 022°M going in, until you are about 300 yards north of the island, by which time the green spar "EA5" should be visible. Alter course to leave it close on your port side. Reef Island, like many of the smaller islands in this area, is a drumlin, a glacial gravel deposit, and is a distinct shape. This particular one is grassy, with no trees.

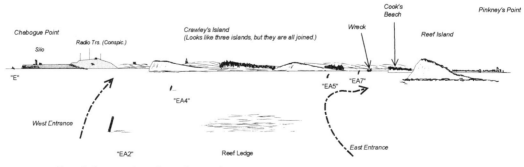

44

Entrance to the Chebogue River from the southeast.

This is not a good place to be in thick weather unless you are absolutely certain of your position. Without radar, I would not enter this harbor at night. There is only 5 feet (1.5 m) in the east entrance at low-water springs, and it is very rough in wind-over-tide conditions. The west entrance is deeper, but can be awful with a fresh onshore wind and an ebb tide. The spars can be difficult to see, or pick up on radar, in anything of a sea. Once you're inside, though, the entire river is well sheltered.

Anchorage, Moorings. On the northwest corner of Crawleys Island is a mooring used by local sailors. There is a shingle beach here where clams are quite plentiful. In this river they are unlikely to be contaminated. This is a quiet overnight anchorage. The mooring itself is substantial but the maintenance of the tackle is suspect. If you can't find the mooring, or don't like the look of it, the holding ground is good.

Flying insects can be pestiferous here, so screens on cabin doors and portlights are essential at dusk.

Upper Reaches of Chebogue River

Chart: 4243

The spars are right on the edge of the channel, which is quite narrow. The banks are mud flats in most places in the river itself. The spars may be moved from time to time if the channel changes, so they may not be exactly as shown on 4243. Be cautious when approaching "E3" and "E8." They always look as if they are out of position, but they are not, and going on the wrong side will result in grounding.

The black-and-yellow cardinal spar "EB" marks a long spit that extends from the northeast corner of the group of islands joined to Crawleys Island at low water. It causes considerable confusion. If you are in the west channel, keep it on your starboard side, and in the east

channel on your port side, while going upstream. Do not cut across from "AE9" to "E8" or you will run aground even at high water.

Just east of "EB" is the wreck of an old wooden scalloper, which was washed up here in an extra-tropical cyclone on February 2, 1976. It is still quite conspicuous, though it will not last forever.

Town Point

The spars continue to Town Point, north of Clements Island, where there is a small wharf. This is quite a busy place, even in the summer, and it is unwise to leave an unattended boat here. There is also a long-simmering dispute between native and non-native lobster fishermen. The regular lobster fishing season is from November to May. This means that if you are offered fresh lobsters from a small boat in summer, they have been caught illegally. Aboriginal fishermen maintain they have the right, under a 1752 treaty, to catch lobsters whenever they please, and do whatever they like with them. As there are limited quotas for the non-native fishery, the going rate for a license is about $100,000. Tempers are short in this respect. Boats have been burned to the waterline, and a few people have been shot at.

Openly buying lobsters out of season from other than a registered dealer could further inflame the situation. It is unlikely that any visitor would be a direct target in this confrontation, but you should be aware of the possibility of getting caught in the cross-fire.

Town Point is the landing site of the earliest settlers of Yarmouth County from New England, and the nearby graveyard has some very old headstones.

The river continues above Town Point for several miles, but is not marked. It is easiest to go up on a new, rising tide that has not yet covered the extensive grassy banks on each side. At high tide, the water looks a half mile across, but the channel is only 100 yards (100 m) wide.

45

Anchorage. About 2 miles above Town Point there is a big mound on the starboard side, locally called the Ponderosa. Just round the bend in the river are the moorings of the members of the Chebogue River Aquatic Club. There is a small-boat launching ramp here, and it is possible to put a deep-draft boat alongside to work on the bottom.

Anchoring is possible anywhere along this stretch of the river, or there may be a vacant mooring. The tidal current is strong here, and may be disturbing if you are not used to it. The easiest way to anchor in this situation, I have found, is with a single big anchor. Mooring with two anchors results in endless twisting of the rodes as the tide changes.

There is at least 8 feet (2.4 m) of water all the way up the river to the highest of the club moorings. The tidal range is about 12 feet (3.6 m) at neaps and 14 feet (4.3 m) at springs, with the tidal stream running at 2 to 3 knots.

The river can be navigated at high water as far as Arcadia, about 2 miles past the club's moorings. Except for the most adventurous, however, it is best done in a dinghy.

Ashore. There are few fancy yachts here, but the members of the aquatic club are friendly, and will tell you how to get supplies and other essentials. Indeed, they will usually offer you rides to Yarmouth. There is a small grocery store, a service station, and a post office at Arcadia. Yarmouth International Airport, a rather overblown description of our regional facility, is about 2 miles from the aquatic club.

Pinkneys Point and Little River Harbour ★★

Chart: 4244

These anchorages are on the west and east side of the Little River, the next inlet east of the Chebogue River.

Approaches. Entry is straightforward. The bell buoy at the mouth of the river bears 092°M, distant 4 miles from Green Island, or 010°M, distant 2.1 miles from Candlebox. The entrance is sheltered from all except westerly winds, and the tidal streams are not as strong here as at the Chebogue River, so there is rarely any difficulty entering. Both harbors have lighted marks. It is possible to find Pinkneys Point in fog without radar, if you can hear the bell.

Pinkneys Point

Pinkneys Point is a busy fishing community and you will almost certainly have to tie up alongside a fishing boat. It is usually possible to find one under repair that won't be departing at 0300. If there is no ice on board these fishing boats (check the gray insulated boxes on deck), it is a fairly safe

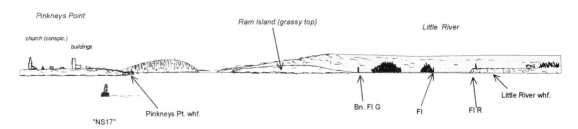

Pinkney's Point and Little River Harbour.

bet that they won't be leaving before you get up. If your boat draws less than 6 feet (1.8 m), you won't have a problem anywhere in this harbor, but check the depth and the tide tables if you draw more.

There is fuel at Pinkneys Point—ask at the fish plant how to get it, and offer cash. There is a store a mile up the road to Yarmouth. There are no other facilities.

Little River Harbour

Little River Harbour is quieter, and there may well be a berth alongside the public wharf. There is a depth of about 6 feet (1.8 m) at low-water springs at the outer end, but most low waters during the summer will be at least 1 foot (30 cm) higher than this. It is possible to anchor just northwest of this wharf if preferred, but be aware of the two drying rocks to the north, which are visible at anything below half-tide.

Green Island

Grass-covered Green Island lies about 3.5 miles west-southwest of Pinkneys Point. It runs north and south for about a third of a mile, and has reefs and extensive shallows off the south end. There is a landing place on the northeast side: a prospect only on a flat calm day, for the truly adventurous.

Schooner Passage and The Tusket Islands

Chart: 4244

The Tusket Islands are a group of some 20 islands just east of Pinkneys Point. While they support only a handful of year-round inhabitants, there are numerous camps on Deep Cove, Ellenwoods, Johns, and Harris Islands. They are busy during fishing seasons, and there is always someone about.

The islands are less inhabited now than they once were, probably because the advent of larger and more powerful inshore fishing vessels—most are now 40 feet (12 m) or bigger, and capable of 10 knots or more—has made it less advantageous to have a base near the fishing grounds. Nonetheless, as this is the center of quite possibly the most productive lobster ground in the world, there are still numerous fishermen's wharves. (There are no female commercial licence holders in this part of the world at this time.) As the lobster season is from November to May, there is always vacant docking space, saving visiting yachts the sometimes difficult task of anchoring in this area of strong tidal streams.

Forty years ago, there was a major sport fishery for bluefin tuna in this area, and the ruins of buildings constructed for the sport are still evident. There is still a tuna fishery, but the fish now only rarely come into inshore waters, and they are caught by longlines or trolling 50 miles offshore.

The islands have been inhabited for well over 150 years, and at one time there were 200 inhabitants, canning factories, and a school. Some of

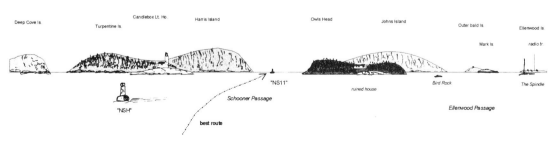

Schooner Passage from the northwest.

the islands were settled with people from Wedgeport, and others from Cape Sable Island. The fact that the first group were French-speaking and Catholic, and the latter were English-speaking and Protestant, has led to some interesting mixtures. For those interested in such things, Big Tusket and Harris Island are French islands; Johns and Ellenwoods are English. Deep Cove is mixed. You thought Canadian politics dull, eh? Some of this vanishing lifestyle is detailed in a recent book, *Life on the Tusket Islands,* by Caroline B. Norwood. (Norwood Publishing, P.O. Box 1192, Westport, Nova Scotia, BOV 1HO.)

This is a very scenic area, and there is nowhere else in the province quite like it. Those of you who have cruised the Maine coast may find it somewhat reminiscent of Matinicus, but it is much more sheltered.

You should not transit this area without chart 4244. The small-scale charts, and the U.S. charts of the area, do not show the numerous hazards.

Schooner Passage ★★★★★

    NO FACILITIES

Schooner Passage is the most commonly used channel to transit this area, and it is the quickest and most sheltered way to go east from Yarmouth.

Approaches. A course of 160°M from Chebogue Point bell buoy "E," distant 4.5 miles, leads to Schooner Passage's west entrance bell buoy "NSH." The tide runs almost directly along this bearing, and in either direction (340°M going west, 160°M going east) you will not deviate much from your track.

If you approach the passage from the north end of Green Island, the course is 132°M for 3.8 miles. If you have a favorable current, you will find yourself being deviated to the south. A course correction of about 15 degrees to port

will usually suffice to keep you on this track. If greater accuracy is required, see the table in the Introduction.

Unless you have a particularly large and powerful vessel, bucking the tide in this area is inadvisable. Sailing against wind and tide, unless your boat can do more than 10 knots, is impossible.

If you are unfamiliar with the area, the safest approach at night is from Green Island. If you keep Green Island light dead astern, and Candlebox Island light dead ahead, you will not hit anything.

From the west, follow the buoys until Candlebox lighthouse is abeam to port, then come to 173°M. If you draw more than 6 feet (1.8 m), and are within an hour of low water, keep about 20 yards (20 m) to the west side of buoy "NSF." This is the non-preferred channel, but there is at least 10 feet (3 m) at low-water springs. If you pass too close to the correct side, you may hit the rock at dead low water if you draw more than 6 feet (1.8 m).

The southern end of Schooner Passage is narrow, and this is where the tide runs hardest—about 5 knots at springs. The buoys heel over with the tide, have a big bow wave, and wiggle around quite a bit. It is essential to keep the boat moving, and not to get too close to them. I often sail through here, but my crew becomes agitated if the engine is not immediately available. Anyone going through here for the first time, or at any time if visibility is poor, should at least have the engine running.

There are large rocks at the southern end of Peases Island, which are not indicated on chart 4244. They look like teeth, and are just waiting to sink themselves into the bottom of your boat. Similar fangs are present on Peases Island Ledge. You must pass on the correct (west) side of the two red conical buoys "NS8" and "NS6."

There is an eddy on the flood that sets you strongly on to the rocks at the south end of Peases Island. To avoid this, I pass close to the *east* of buoy "NS4," and then head up to keep "NS6" about 20 yards (20 m) to starboard when going north.

The ebb sets straight out, and you don't have to worry about this when going east with it. Close

Peases Is.   Ellenwoods Is.   Johns Island   Owls Head   Candlebox   Harris Island   Turpentine Island   Big Tusket Island

SCHOONER PASSAGE AND THE TUSKET ISLANDS

Dangerous rocks at south end of Peases Is.

"NS4"

"NS6"

"NS8"

Bn R

The Spindle Fl R

This is the safest route.

Peases Island ledge (dries 2 ft.)

Alternative route in good conditions.

Schooner Passage from the southeast.

to the islands there is often a back-eddy, which can make docking a long-keeled boat a rather interesting experience. Local fishermen use these eddies to buck the tide. I can only recommend this if you have a really reliable engine. The tide also forms whirlpools which can turn you round backwards if you don't have enough way on.

Neither GPS nor loran is accurate enough for you to attempt this passage in thick fog without radar. It might be conceivable to do it if you have differential GPS, or have the on-site (as opposed to charted) positions of the buoys as waypoints in your loran. You could, of course, meet at the narrowest point a 120-foot (36-m) herring seiner coming the other way—which might call for a stiff drink and prompt a firm resolve to buy a radar set at the next port.

There are fog signals at the lighthouses at each end of the passage, but their highly directional horns point out to sea, so you cannot reliably hear either when you are in the passage. This passage may look a little intimidating at night, but I have done it often and it is straightforward enough if there is no fog.

The southern end of the passage can be rough in southerly gales with an ebb tide. A local 40-foot (12-m) fishing boat capsized here a few years ago with loss of life.

Anchorage, Dockage. Anchoring is possible in Deep Cove, Ellenwoods Channel, and the southeast corner of Turpentine Island, which is the quietest. At the other places, the tide tends to swirl you about. It is possible to tie up at a wharf almost anywhere, but I favor either Deep Cove or Harris Island.

Deep Cove Island ★★★★★

4		B	NO FACILITIES

Chart: 4244

Tie up at the southernmost wharf, on the outside. There is 8 feet (2.4 m) of water here at low-water springs. This is the largest wharf and it has small buildings on its end. It is also possible to pick up a vacant mooring or to anchor, though the water is deep and there are often tidal eddies. Good fenders are essential when tying up. The maximum rise and fall of tide is about 15 feet (4.6 m), so use long warps.

Deep Cove Island has only a few trees, so it is possible to walk all over, and there are spectacular views from the top. There is a somewhat sandy beach inside the wharves. As this is a working island there is all sorts of debris from the fishing industry, so it is inadvisable to walk barefoot. One of the reasons why Deep Cove Island is one of my favorite places is the almost complete absence of biting insects at any time of the day or night.

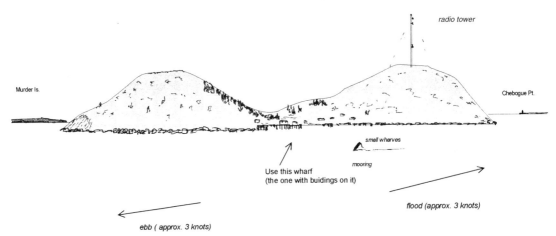

Deep Cove Island from the southeast.

Shelter is excellent from most directions except southeast, and even then nothing short of a hurricane is going to bother you if you have big fenders.

Harris Island ★★★★ 5 C

NO FACILITIES

Tie up at any convenient wharf. The outer ends are deep enough for all normal boats. Shelter is excellent. In an extra-tropical cyclone in 1976, when the wind speed was over 100 knots for two days, there was minimal damage here. There are numerous fishermen's cottages on the east side where the wharves are. Anchoring is not practical as the channel is narrow and the tide strong. Though it doesn't look so from the chart, it is possible for a boat with a draft of less than 5 feet (1.5 m) to circumnavigate the island at any state of the tide.

Approaches (when approaching from Schooner Passage). Give the southern end of Harris Island a wide berth as there is a shoal spit extending about 20 yards (20 m) to the south. In Schooner Passage, coming from the north, pass about halfway between the end of the island and the conical buoy "NS8," going east. Don't turn up into the channel until you can clearly see the first wharves.

It is possible to skirt the southern end of the passage by passing close to the two beacons on the south end of Big Tusket Island (see illustration). This looks quite intimidating, but local fishermen use it all the time.

Turpentine Island ★★★★

 4 C NO FACILITIES

Chart: 4244

Anchor just past the spar buoy "NU9" and as near to the wharf as you can. There are a couple of unmarked and uncharted rocks off the end of the wharf that I have hit on occasion. There is a small sandy beach here.

Ellenwoods Island ★★★ 3

 B NO FACILITIES

Chart: 4244

There is less of a tidal stream in Ellenwoods Channel than there is in Schooner Passage, though the channel is not as well marked as the passage. Favor the west side of the channel, as there are unmarked drying rocks extending a long way out from the west side of Owls Head. It is possible to anchor halfway down the eastern side of Ellenwoods Island, though it is open to the south. Ellenwoods has no trees and it is possible to walk all over it. There is a sandy beach by the anchorage.

Johns Island ★★ 3 B

NO FACILITIES

Chart: 4244

Tie up at the large wharf with buildings on it on the eastern side. Tidal currents run hard here and form swirls. I have found this an uncomfortable place to lie alongside.

Peases Island ★★★ 2 B

NO FACILITIES

Chart: 4244

On a quiet day it is possible to anchor in the bight on the east side of this island, though at low-water springs you might touch ground. There is good walking, and, on a clear day, beautiful views all the way to Seal Island.

Wedgeport ★★★★

5 NEW WHARF   4 TUNA WHARF

A NEW WHARF   C TUNA WHARF

Chart: 4244

Wedgeport is one of the few places along this coast where the first language of the majority of the inhabitants is French. Everyone here, however, speaks English as well, and there will be no language problems. The local French dialect

contains a number of eighteenth century expressions, numerous English words and syntax, and sounds quite unlike anything else. Every village, too, has its own patois—to confuse visitors who think they speak French.

Approaches. There are two wharves, one on the east, and one on the west of the peninsula. The eastern one, New Wharf, is bigger and easier to approach—just follow the buoys in. In order, from the east end of Schooner Passage, they are "T3," "T7," "TA," "TA3," and "TA5."

To the western wharf, the Tuna Wharf, there are a number of channels, but the best-marked one lies west of Snipe Island. On the final approach, there are two lighted beacons on the eastern edge of the channel, and at the last one, make a sharp turn to starboard to come to the wharf.

The last portion of the channel is marked by stakes, whose placement is sometimes a little eccentric, so do not rely on them absolutely. The channel here is narrow, with extensive mud flats on either side. It is easier to arrive when the flats are not totally covered.

Wedgeport has been favored mightily by the federal government and has about a dozen light-buoys marking the area. The only difficulty you'll experience while getting in here at night is deciding which one is which.

There is a passage north of Big Tusket Island, which greatly reduces the distance between Little River and Wedgeport. It is called Hells Gate, not without reason. It is not that clearly marked for strangers and I cannot recommend it, though local fishermen use it at half-tide or more.

Anchorage, Dockage. There are no good anchorages in Wedgeport, but there is always room to tie up at one of the wharves.

Ashore. There is a branch of the Royal Bank, a credit union, a co-op with a large grocery department, a number of boatbuilders, and a marine supply store, A. L. Leblanc—telephone (902) 663-2516; fax 902-663-2694—that supplies most of the boatbuilders in western Nova Scotia. It carries

51

a large supply of hardware for the fishing industry, so can be relied on for engine parts, rope, plumbing, pumps, and so forth. The store will deliver almost anywhere within one or two days.

There is a small restaurant at the Tuna Wharf. Apart from this, most of the facilities are a fair hike from the wharves, but you will often find someone to give you a ride. Just about anyone you see at a wharf in this part of the province will give you directions.

Seal Island, Mud Island, and Flat Island

Charts: **4242, 4230,** 4330

This is a group of islands south of the Tusket Islands. The three mentioned above have anchorages, but the other two in the group have no satisfactory landing places, except for skiffs in the calmest of conditions.

Visiting these islands is not for the fainthearted. There is no really protected anchorage, the tide runs very hard, there are numerous unmarked rocks, and running for shelter if the weather turns bad involves traversing tiderips that could overwhelm a small vessel. No one without local knowledge should visit these islands without chart 4242. If you have an old copy of obsolete 4330, don't throw it out. It has much better detail than the newer charts.

The islands are quite remote, the largest, Seal Island, being 15 miles from the mainland. It is difficult, with the usual strength of the tide, to visit the islands as a day sail, so a trip here involves overnight anchorage in an open roadstead, unless you go to Flat Island and dry out. I never sleep soundly anchored anywhere here, and constant attention to the state of the weather is essential. Seal Island was continuously inhabited year-round from about 1840 to 1986, and is certainly a fascinating place to visit if the weather is stable.

Seal Island ★★★★

NO FACILITIES

Charts: **4242,** 4230, 4330

Seal Island at one time had 80 inhabitants, and some of my older patients were born on the island. The church, on the east side, is still standing, and so is a fairly substantial house owned by Mrs. Hamilton, now deceased, who was the last permanent resident of the island. The church is still used occasionally—a wedding was held there in 1995.

The island is shaped roughly like a figure eight. The north and south ends are joined by a low-lying marsh. The lighthouse on the southern end is high and conspicuous in clear weather. There is a radio beacon at the lighthouse, broadcasting Morse code H (. . . .) on 322 kHz. The marsh abuts on to two sandy coves, on the west and east sides of the island.

A conspicuous wreck, locally believed to be that of a drug runner, is neatly aground on the east side beach. It appeared on a dirty night in the early spring of 1988, without any trace ever being found of the crew, who are now probably back in Colombia.

Approaches. The courses and distances to steer on various approaches are as follows:

From Green Island: 180°M, 17 miles.
From West Head (Cape Sable Island): 280°M, 15 miles.
From Pubnico Point: 235°M, 14 miles.
From Schooner Passage: Roughly southeast, 13 miles. A direct course cannot be steered because of intervening islands and rocks.

It is much easier to approach from the east than from the west. If you do approach from the west, keep Seal Island light bearing 160°M, or greater, to avoid Limbs Limb, which is covered at high water. Devils Limb, to the south, always shows. Stay well southwest of a line from Soldiers Ledge whistle buoy ("NS") and Noddy Island to avoid Black Ledge.

Do not go anywhere near the southern tip of Seal Island. It is an extremely dangerous area of poorly charted rocks and continuously breaking seas, not at all well indicated as such on chart 4242. You should also keep at least a half-mile off Race Point, the northern tip of Seal Island, if at all possible, though going too close is more likely to scare you than sink you, which is not the case at the southern end.

This is not a good place to be at night or in thick weather, with or without radar, unless you really know what you are doing.

The tide runs hard around the northern points of these islands, and because the streams have a few quirks, the tide might not be doing quite what you imagine. A copy of an older chart should help.

Anchorage, Dockage. There is a wharf on the west side (in what is called Crowell Cove on the chart) where local inhabitants haul their boats out in foul weather. There are some substantial moorings in this cove, large enough to hold any normal cruising boat. The boats operated by the local fishermen are usually about 42 feet (13 m) overall, and displace 10 to 15 tons.

The west side cove also offers marginally more shelter than the chart suggests, and can be used with winds of no more than 25 knots from the southwest. It is much to be preferred to anchoring on the east side, but is, of course, completely open to the northwest. The holding ground is mostly hard sand, and quite good—if you don't snag a rock or a big piece of kelp.

Tempted as you might be, don't ever try to ride out an easterly gale in the west cove. All easterly storms have a good chance of veering to the northwest and intensifying.

You can tie your dinghy up at the slipway, but be sure to allow for the rise of tide. Some care is required, as the timbers of the slip are round, slippery, and quite far apart. You are a long way from an ambulance if you fall through and break a vital part of your carcass. If you don't feel athletic enough to chance it, drag your dinghy up the beach immediately to the north of the slip. When

the winds are in the east, there is not much swell or tidal current.

The east side cove is sheltered from westerly winds (anything from due south through west to due north) but there is a swell here all the time. I don't sleep well at anchor anywhere at Seal Island, but it's almost impossible to get any rest at all in the east side cove unless it has been flat calm for a week. A new wharf on the east side was destroyed in an easterly cyclonic storm in March, 1993.

Theoretically, it would be possible to ride out a northwesterly gale in this east-side anchorage if all else failed—but there wouldn't be a thing left standing on your shelves, your crew would likely be as sick as dogs, and you would have seaweed all over your deck.

Ashore. A path leads from the east side south to the lighthouse, past the church and Mrs. Hamilton's house. The old lifeboat is drawn up on the grass here. If you walk a little farther past the light to the east, just beyond the whirling tiderip off the south point, there is a little clearing with three gravestones commemorating three unidentified women from an 1861 shipwreck. This path circles back to the east-side beach, but is quite hard going past this point. There is a similar, though more modern, gravestone at the church. There are quite possibly another 100 unmarked graves from shipwrecks at various sites around the island.

Another path, a much wider one, runs northwest from the church to the settlement of West Side, where the fishermen who stay here during various fishing seasons have their cottages.

It is possible to walk around the northern part of the island, though the going is somewhat harder. The last lighthouse keeper left here in 1992, but in summer quite a few people from Cape Sable Island move here to get some peace, so there are usually at least a few people on the island during the cruising season.

Because hundreds of shipwrecks had occurred around this island, the original settlers arrived in about 1840 to maintain the lighthouse. Settlement peaked in the first part of this century, and has been declining since 1950.

Although it is possible to fish year-round here, as there is never any sea ice, new, larger boats have made such a lifestyle obsolete, and now there are only a half dozen fishermen using the island as a base for the winter lobster fishery.

In days long past, it was customary to row a dory the 16 miles from Seal Island to Clark's Harbour, on Cape Sable Island, for weekend entertainment and a night ashore. Given the usual state of sea and tide around these parts, and given the likelihood that not many of these dories even had a compass on board, this is something that truly astonishes me.

There are rabbits behind almost every tree on Seal Island. There are numerous sheep, and a multitude of different types of bird. Visiting birders are also quite common on the island.

All the islands in this group were visited occasionally by the aboriginal inhabitants of the province, though I am not aware of any permanent habitation.

Most of Seal Island is privately owned, but absentee landlords in this part of the world are only tolerated if they don't interfere with the customary lifestyle of the inhabitants; that is, hunting, fishing, and driving all-terrain vehicles. In addition, there is a common-law right in the province to travel to any watercourse over any private property. All land below the high-water mark is publicly owned, with free right of passage. This means that you have the right to land on and walk around virtually any offshore island, or any piece of coastline for that matter. It would be irresponsible, however, to start a brush fire by carelessness or leave an area littered with plastic bags.

Ashore. No visit to Seal Island is complete without a walk to the church and the lighthouse. The church is never locked, and seems to attract tourists even in February, so feel free to sign the visitors' book. The beach on the east side consists of the finest white sand, and almost certainly you will be the only ones on it. There are times when I have anchored here and it has been too rough to row ashore in safety, however.

I have always found Seal Island a rather special sort of place, despite the difficulty of getting there and the indifferent anchorage. If I were superstitious, I might think it was because of its hundreds of ghosts.

Mud Island ★★★

NO FACILITIES

Charts: **4242,** 4320, 4330

Mud Island is thickly wooded and is difficult to walk over, except at the northern end. It is known as the burial site of the "petrified woman," whose body, according to local legend, has been exposed and reburied at various times since the 1850s. No one knows the origin of this possibly aboriginal body, or where it is now.

Anchorage. There is a reasonably good anchorage off the northwest cove of Mud Island. There are also substantial fishing-boat moorings here, which can certainly be used if they're vacant. Hard sand makes for good holding ground in the cove.

The moorings may be occupied during the week as this is a popular spot for "Irish mossing," the gathering of a certain pink seaweed, which can be surprisingly profitable. A fishing vessel of about 40 feet (12 m) is used as the base for this operation, the actual harvesting being done with a hand rake from an outboard-powered skiff. Enormous loads of seaweed can be seen being towed to the processing plants, or being dried on various wharves. Young fellows with strong backs can make $1,000 a week doing this work, and are often seen around the islands at low water.

Irish moss is the source of a group of chemicals called "carragens." These are widely used as stabilizers in emulsions and various food products, such as cosmetics, beer, and ice cream. I think this is the only place in North America where it grows, though other sites include Norway, Chile, and the Philippines.

Flat Island ★★★

NO FACILITIES

Chart: 4242

Flat Island is lower than the other islands, and from more than 2 miles away only its buildings are visible. This looks a little odd, and makes it instantly recognizable. The small harbor on the north end of the island has a substantial wharf that dries at low water. A boat with a draft of 5 feet (1.5 m) can get in at half-tide or more.

Approaches. Make toward the head of the wharf on a course of 180°M (true south). About 30 yards from the wharf, just to starboard of this track, is an unmarked rock, and you should veer slightly to port (to the east) to miss it. If the tide is not high enough for you to enter, there is a good anchorage along the line of approach; alternatively, you could use one of the moorings. Make sure it *is* a mooring, and not the "buoy" that marks the rock on the port side of the approach line—it's usually a polystyrene lobster pot buoy.

The wharf is protected on the eastern side by a shingle spit and a small rocky islet where a particularly aggressive tern colony nests in spring. They don't like your invading their territory at all, and let you know it.

The shingle bar may be subject to change in severe easterly storms. We have had some real screechers in the last couple of years, so this harbor should be used with a certain degree of caution.

The harbor itself is quite sheltered, except in easterly gales, if your boat can dry out tied to the wharf. It is probably the one place in this island group where you will get a decent night's sleep.

There are no trees of any size on Flat Island, but there are many sheep, and, on the northwestern beach, many attractive multicolored pebbles.

Lobster Bay

Charts: **4244,** 4326

Lobster Bay extends from Wedgeport to Pubnico Point. It is deeply indented and contains nearly 100 islands separated by numerous channels. I have lived here for 20 years, but still have not visited every creek and anchorage. Were there less tide, it would be as developed as Mahone Bay, but most of the islands remain devoid of summer homes, and are deserted apart from the odd hunting camp.

I am not a wildlife expert, but there is extensive bird life, including the largest osprey colony in the province,

---

Map text:

Enter on course 180 mag. to end of wharf

Keep well clear north of this islet.

to Argyle (Whitehead lt. ho.) 054 mag. 11mi.

to "NS" (Soldiers Ledge whistle buoy) 305 mag. 3.6 mi.

rocky islet with tern colony

15

moorings

awash at LW not marked

12

normal LW mark

usually marked

shingle bar

Beach is subject to change in storm conditions and may break through in easterly storms.

100 yards approx.

10

depths at mean HW

wharf

8

sand

Tie up here and be prepared to take the ground.

shingle

large shed

houses

Flat Island.

and virtually every kind of duck that inhabits eastern North America. Visiting boats are not often seen, and you can reckon that most anchorages will be deserted.

During the lobster season, from the end of November to the end of May, over 300 boats will be fishing in these waters, and the average catch will easily exceed $100,000 per boat over that period. This comes as a surprise to most visitors, and, for that matter, to most Canadians. In the more prosperous fishing communities of this district, most houses have two new vehicles, ATVs, speedboats, and the like, and many of the houses would be in the half-million-dollar price bracket were they in Halifax.

As most of the fishermen here are at least as wealthy as the average yacht owner, you won't experience the awkward feeling that occurs when you bring an expensive boat into a dirt-poor community. Most of the local people, moreover, will be interested in where you've come from and where you're going, and will give you every assistance. I think you'll find this the normal state of affairs until you get past Lunenburg, when, in polite terms, a more urban mindset takes over.

Local fishermen have, over the years, become masters at manipulating the tax and income-support programs, so that this area enjoys some of the highest mean family incomes in the entire country—and, at the same time, one of the highest registered unemployment rates.

Outside the islands, that is, south of Gull Island, there are few hazards, apart from the Old Man and Old Woman rocks guarding the southern entrance to Schooner Passage. The tide is not strong, either, being less than 1 knot until you get east of Pubnico Point.

Incidentally, note that chart 4244 is essential for navigating this area. In a pinch, obsolete chart 4326 will do, but none of the smaller-scale charts is safe.

The Tusket River ★★

 C   NO FACILITIES

Chart: 4244

The Tusket River is the longest river in western Nova Scotia, and can be traversed by canoe for almost 40 miles from its mouth. In a larger vessel, I have found it a disappointment. The lower reaches of the river are almost a half-mile wide, and there is little shelter. There are beacons as far as Squires Island, but no other marks, and the upper reaches are encumbered with rocks and mud flats subject to frequent change. The tides run at 2 to 3 knots.

A hundred years ago, many large vessels were built and launched at Tusket, ships of 100 feet (30 m) and more in overall length, and with drafts of 12 feet (3.6 m), so at some time it must have been possible to go up this river, but it is certainly difficult now.

Indian Sluice Bay ★★★

 C   NO FACILITIES

Chart: 4244

Indian Sluice Bay, which joins the Tusket River just above Wedgeport, has recently been marked with navigation aids, and even lit. At the head of navigation for boats with masts, the Surettes Island bridge, there is a wharf and a launching ramp. It's not called the sluice for nothing, and the tide boils under this bridge at about 6 knots during spring tides. Shelter is indifferent here unless you tie up at the wharf, and that involves getting close to the bridge, which will cause white knuckles unless you have a reliable engine capable of driving your boat at 6 knots or more. You will, however, become one of a very small band of gunkholers to have penetrated to this point.

Ashore. In Tusket, about 4 miles north, there is a grocery store and a good restaurant, called the Flying Dutchman, which is owned by a yachtsman. There are a number of service stations and car dealers, a laundromat, the oldest courthouse in Canada—now turned into a museum—and the seat of our local government, although it's doubtful whether the latter can truly be considered an asset.

Morris Island and Vicinity

★★★★ [4] [C] NO FACILITIES

Chart: 4244

You can approach this area from the west by going either south or north of Gull Island. It's easier to go south. Gull Island Bar extends a long way north of the island, and many of my neighbors have hit it at one time or other. There are three cardinal buoys north of Gull Island, and you should certainly pass between the two westernmost ones. From there, there is a clear passage north, along the west side of Wilson Island, to the Tusket River. It is possible to anchor off the east side of Wilson Island, but it is open to the southeast, and there are better anchorages nearby.

The Tittle ★★★ [4] [C]

NO FACILITIES

Chart: 4244

There is good anchorage at The Tittle. Approach between Jones Island and the beacon on Nickersons Rock, heading about 350°M with Whitehead Island light directly astern. In westerly winds there is some swell in the entrance, but it flattens out as soon as you pass Bar Island. Favor the east side until the green beacon is abeam, avoiding the 4-foot (1.2-m) patch in mid-channel. The chart says the beacon has a green flashing light, but the last time I was there, the beacon itself had a serious list and I couldn't see a light.

Then keep slightly to the west of mid-channel. Chart 4244 is somewhat mistaken in this area when it denotes a "Crazy Island." It appears to be a drying rock, not an island. There is a red beacon, just west of this rock, that you should leave to starboard. Ahead, there is a spit that sticks out southeast from the wharf, so swing over to the east again to avoid it. The channel continues all the way to the Morris Island bridge, but is unmarked and tortuous above St. Helena Island.

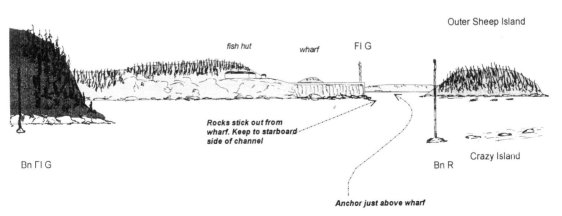

Bar Island
(50 ft. high)

fish hut wharf Fl G Outer Sheep Island

Rocks stick out from
wharf. Keep to starboard
side of channel

Bn Fl G Bn R Crazy Island

Anchor just above wharf

The Tittle.

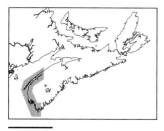

Anchorage. There is good anchorage above the wharf, sheltered all around. The only drawback is that the flying insects are numerous here. There are no facilities, and the nearest house is about 3 miles up a dirt road.

Morris Island ★★★

NO FACILITIES

Chart: 4244

There is a small wharf at the southeastern end of Morris Island at Muise Head. Unfortunately, there is not usually room to tie up there, but anchorage to the east or west of the moorings is good.

Approaches. Coming from the west, either pass south of Jones Ledge (the spar is difficult to see) or about 50 yards south of the end of the island itself. On the latter course, keep the northern end of The Thrum (which has a few straggly trees on it) in line with the southern end of Lears Island, which is tall, with a grassy top. There's a summer home being built on Lears Island, and if it survives the gales of winter it should certainly be conspicuous, though perhaps reminiscent of Prince Charles' comments about monstrous carbuncles. The Thrum has a long drying spit extending north of it that shouldn't be confused with the island. The mark you need is where the beach dips. This will keep you clear of Jones Ledge.

Anchorage. Before you come to Morris Island, there is a nice anchorage in the bight between Jones and Etoile islands. There is only 4 feet (1.2 m) of water at low-water springs but the bottom is soft and the holding ground good. A boat with a draft of 5 feet (1.5 m) or less would not be likely to have any trouble if the height of the tide in the Yarmouth section of the tide tables is less than 14 feet (4.3 m). When the charted height of the tide in Yarmouth is less than 14 feet, it is a neap tide, and there is MORE water than usual at low tide (usually at least 4 feet more). This anchorage is open to the southeast, but is otherwise satisfactory.

As you pass farther north, keep to the west side of the channel. A bar sticks out from Hog Island much farther than shown on the chart. In fact it comes almost halfway across the channel. The wind, particularly the westerly wind, sometimes funnels through here in fearsome gusts.

At the end of Morris Island there is a rock just off the end of the wharf, usually with some sort of mark on it. The last time I passed, it was a buoy in the form of a whale's tail. There's another rock on a line between the end of the wharf and the next

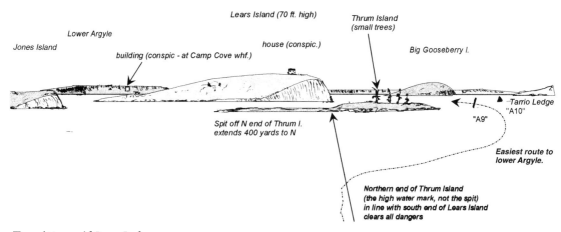

Transit to avoid Jones Ledge.

point to the northeast. I occasionally anchor in the bight called Horse Creek, just far enough in to be out of the current, but not enough to go aground. This is a well-sheltered spot.

Above The Sluice, the river becomes a large bay, and although it is completely enclosed, its very size makes it less than sheltered. Passage as far as Fox Island and Roberts Anchorage is not a big problem, but there are lots of shallow spots farther up the bay. Shallow-draft vessels can get as far as Abrams River.

There are no facilities of any sort in this area, and most of the anchorages will be completely deserted except for wildlife. Some of the smaller passages between the islands are marked by stakes, but I would advise you not to rely on them too much.

The Abuptic (Argyle) River

★★★★   5   B   🍽️   🔧

Chart: 4244

To clear up any confusion about names, the oldest title for this river is the Abuptic River. This is an English corruption of the Mi'kmaq name for the place, one translation of which is "Where the rivers meet the sea." The government calls it the Argyle River. On old charts it may be called the East River.

Approaches. From seaward, the easiest approach is from the Abbots Harbour fairway buoy "A," on a heading of 022°M. This takes you straight to the end of the breakwater at Lower Argyle. This looks intimidating on the chart, but I have done it hundreds of times, often in fog or at night. There is little tidal set on this course, on either the ebb or the flood.

On this approach, Whitehead Breaker is about 400 yards to port. There is 2 feet (60 cm) over it at low-water springs, so you're unlikely to hit it unless it's within 2 hours of low water. Ram Island is the next hazard, about 100 yards to starboard. It is a high island, easy to see in any reasonable visibility, day or night. There is a 10-foot (3-m) shoal just to the west of Ram Island but this should not be a problem to any but the largest vessel. There are two drying rocks off the northwest end of Ram Island that are not shown on chart 4244, about 60 yards off the shore. There are similar uncharted rocks, closer in, off the northwest corner of Big Gooseberry Island. From here to the wharf, the going is straightforward.

The buoyed channel passes close east of Whitehead Island, where there is a lighthouse and a fog signal, then north to Tarrio Ledge, a nasty bunch of teeth on which I once ran aground. Then the

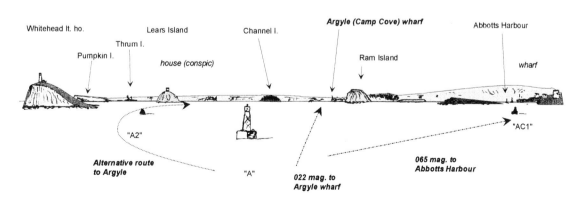

Approaches to the Argyle River.

Keep an eye on your chart and heading as many of the islands have the same profile

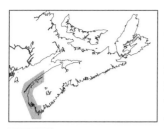

channel leads roughly north-east to the wharf. This is all right in clear weather, but none of the marks is lit, and most of them are small spars that make indifferent radar targets.

If you're coming from Jones Island, be sure to pass north of "NE14," which marks a very long spit running south to Lears Island, then by any convenient course that avoids the charted but unmarked rocks 200 yards south of Birch Island, another lump I have managed to fetch up on. You should be aware that, for some reason, the seas never seem to break over the hazardous rocks in this area, so you cannot rely on seeing white water to avoid them.

Anchorages in the Argyle River and Sound

Big Gooseberry Island

In the cove on the northeast side of this island is a rather nice beach of fine gravel. I often anchor here on quiet summer nights, as there are few flying bugs around. There are not many trees, and a good view may be had from the top of the island.

Argyle Sound

This is the most protected anchorage outside the river itself. Enter between Frost Island Ledge and Morton Neck, just south of the large house on the hill, going 090°M. Avoid the rocks on the ledge by keeping 30 yards or so south of Morton Neck until you can clearly see all the way down the sound, when you can turn south.

Anchor east of the small shingle beach on the northern part of Frost Island, in about 8 feet (2.5 m) at low-water springs. The holding ground here is excellent, I once rode out a major winter storm here on a single 25-pound CQR anchor.

There may be a little slop in a southerly gale, but the flats at the southern end of the sound break up most of the sea.

Camp Cove Wharf
(Argyle Wharf)

The wharf at Lower Argyle is reasonably well protected, especially inside the enclosed area. There is a substantial floating dock just inside the breakwater, where I usually keep my boat. This is sheltered from all but serious northwest gales. I have kept my boat afloat in here all winter on occasion.

Ashore. Gas, diesel, and water are available from the fishermen's co-op, but you will need your own hose for water. There is also electricity at the end of the floating dock. Engine repairs of all types are available from Paul d'Entremont Marine—(902) 762-3301. All types of metal work on boats can be done by R. & N. d'Entremont Fabrication, Ltd.—(902) 762-2779.

There are three boatbuilders in the immediate vicinity. The one with the most experience of yachts is Doug Murphy—(902) 643-2932. All these people will come to the wharf to do boat repairs. There is a grocery store 2 miles away in Pubnico Head, and a small snack bar at the wharf. My house is the second one south of the breakwater, with the sailboat windvane. I'd be quite happy to show anyone around.

The Argyle River

To go up the river, pass either side of Nanny Island. The west side is deeper, but don't go too close to shore. There is a rock about 50 yards east of the small beach on the northeast corner of Nanny Island with about 3 feet (90 cm) over it at extreme low-water springs. We have all hit it on occasion. There is a bar going across the channel from Nanny Island to the mainland with about 6 feet (1.8 m) at low-water springs. Your depth sounder may indicate less than this, as the bar is full of eel grass, which may register on the sounder. I have never run aground here.

Just north of Nanny Island on the mainland is a breakwater and a resort that opened in 1995, Ye Olde Argyler—(902) 643-2500. There are moorings, and the resort has laundry, a restaurant, and accommodation. This anchorage is sheltered from everything but gales from due south. A vehicle is available for visiting yachts.

Higher Reaches of the Argyle River

Going farther upriver, pass between Globe Island and Rankins Island. There is a small islet with a hut on it just southeast of Globe Island, unnamed on the chart but known to locals as Clam Island. This whole area is full of drying mud flats, so keep about 30 yards from Rankins Island, where there is at least 12 feet (3.6 m). It is possible to anchor in the northeast cove of Rankins Island, but to get into the sheltered part it is necessary to anchor close to the bank—and a change of wind can put you ashore.

A somewhat better anchorage, mentioned in the old books, is in the bight northeast of the passage between the Board Islands. This passage has only about 2 feet (60 cm) at low-water springs, so it is a little tricky to sail between the islands, though chart 4326 might tempt you to think you can. West of Rankins Island, all the way to Morris Island, is a mass of unmarked reefs that even the locals avoid.

The channel passes farther north between a high, wooded peninsula and Eagle Island. When you get this far, you will see an imposing house just to starboard. It is the Ardnamurchan Club, built by a family of Americans as a summer home in about 1908. Their descendants still use it.

The channel splits just above the club, and close to the Ardnamurchan side there is an excellent anchorage just above an old wharf and a dirt road. The current swirls a little here, but it is secluded and absolutely protected. It is used as a hurricane hole by the locals.

It is possible to proceed a little farther up this channel, leaving a small islet to port, to enter a pond called The Dumbbells. Seventy years ago, this was much used as a winter anchorage by local fishing schooners.

The main arm of the channel veers a little to the northwest, between Ryders Island and Harts Island. Be careful to avoid the rock off the southern end of Harts Island. Anchorage is good in the first part of Glenwood Bay, just east of High Head.

The channel continues just south of the little islet with trees on it, and then it rounds Mackinnons Neck. It is possible to reach the bridge at Argyle Head, but the channel writhes and is unmarked. The bridge, until about 40 years ago, was a swing bridge, and many large ships were built and launched at the head of the river, about 2 miles farther up from this point. There are no facilities here, but numerous ospreys and great blue herons.

Argyle is an English-speaking community sandwiched between two larger French-speaking ones, which on occasion makes the natives restless. There is a certain rivalry between the communities, usually (though not always) good-natured. This rivalry often manifests itself at the annual community festival, held at the end of July, and generally regarded as the most enjoyable and best-attended festival in western Nova Scotia.

Mindful of the need for a distinct symbol to unite the community, a competition was held at the school to design a community flag. The winning design, a green-and-white St. George's cross on a blue background, is widely flown, even on local boats. Interestingly, the designer of the flag was born in Ethiopia.

The half-dozen or so visiting boats that tie up here every year are viewed with interest by the locals, and crews are often invited into homes, driven around to see the sights, or lent vehicles.

Abbotts Harbour and Ledge Harbour ★★

Chart: 4244

These two small harbors lie some 7 miles northwest of Pubnico Point.

Abbotts Harbour is a busy place. It houses one of the largest herring plants in Nova Scotia, just up the hill from the wharf. Vessels unload at all hours of the day and night, and about 20 smaller fishing vessels lie on moorings.

Ledge Harbour is open to the south, but has a small wharf on which there may be room to tie up.

Approaches to Abbotts Harbour. Take a course of 070°M from bell buoy "A." There is a fixed green light on the mainland, but it doesn't look very green at night and it tends to get lost in the glare of other shore lights. Entrance buoy "AC1" is forgiving of passage on the wrong side, but that's still inadvisable. Leave it to port. You can exit Abbotts Harbour to the north, where there are depths of about 8 feet (2.4 m) at low-water springs.

Anchorage. Be aware that in commercial ports such as Abbotts Harbour, every ladder could be covered with a slippery and hazardous mixture of fish parts and oil. There is usually no room to anchor, but it might be possible to tie up inside the wharf.

Ashore. About a mile down the road is the Liquor Commission, a good restaurant (the Red Cap), a pharmacy, and a small grocery store.

Approaches to Ledge Harbour. This harbor lies about 2 miles south of Abbotts Harbour and bears 096°M from the fairway buoy "A." There is a green flashing buoy at its entrance.

Do not pass between this buoy and the island because there is a long spit on which you will run aground. If you're coming up from Pubnico Point, be mindful of two small islets (The Brothers) that are unlit and make indifferent radar targets. On one of these islets is the only breeding colony of the roseate tern on the eastern seaboard.

Anchorage. Ledge Harbour looks like indifferent shelter. One of my friends, however, keeps his boat there on a mooring all summer, and he has had to move it only for hurricane warnings. If there is no room to tie up at the wharf, the best shelter is as far past the wharf as you think you can get. You cannot sail out of this harbor to the north because there is a rocky bar that just covers at high water.

Pubnico Harbour

Charts: 4210, 4242, 4320, 4236, 4330, 4012

The entrance to Pubnico Harbour is straightforward. There are no dangers in the approach, apart from Johns Island and Johns Island Ledge, 2 miles to the south. While the entrance is narrow, it is easy to find, and can be entered at any state of tide or wind. The main channel is deep, nearly 40 feet (12 m) all the way in, making Pubnico Harbour a useful port of refuge. It is by far the easiest port to enter on this coast in severe storm conditions. I have never had any serious concerns about entering this harbor at night or in thick fog, although a good lookout must be kept for fishing boats.

Approaches. The entrance bears 120°M from the Tusket Islands; 055°M from Seal Island; 056°M from Pubnico whistle buoy "P;" and 028°M from Johns Ledge bell buoy "ND4." The harbor can be entered in virtually any state of wind or tide. The church in West Pubnico has a tall spire and looks isolated. The church in East Pubnico is more of a tower, and is surrounded by buildings. Both churches are conspicuous, as is a cellular-phone tower in East Pubnico showing bright flashing red lights at night. A conspicuous water tower is located in East Pubnico, about 1 mile inshore.

A course of 060°M from the entrance bell buoy "P1" leads to the lighthouse at Beach Point. This lighthouse has a good fog signal and can almost always be heard. The shore here is steep-to and can be approached almost within spitting distance. Beach Point is a large barachois harbor with a break in the northeast corner. Local fishermen use it to lay up and work on their boats. Although it is possible to get a boat with a draft of 6 feet (1.8 m) or more in here at half-tide, the entrance changes often in storms, so I cannot give directions. Barachois harbours are formed by storm, wave, and tidal action on a shingle spit. A spit gradually extends downstream from the direction of the strongest forces, to enclose, over a few thousand years, a sort of pond. Wave and tidal action may knock a few holes in this spit, or it may not have completely enclosed the pond, allowing access to the sheltered enclosure. There are a lot of these in Nova Scotia.

After you've passed the light at Beach Point, alter course to about 030°M, to the green can buoy. On the port hand are the drying rocks of Pubnico Ledge, and quite close to the can buoy is a drying rock. This rock, amazingly, was missed by the multitude of civil servants who surveyed this harbor. I'm sure the local fishermen knew of its existence, but it wasn't put on a chart until I told the authorities about it in 1979.

Lower East Pubnico ★★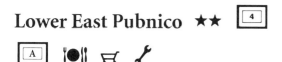

Charts: **4210**, 4242

A few hundred yards north of Beach Point light, on the starboard hand, is the Lower East Pubnico wharf. This used to be a miserable thing, but has recently been extended, and now provides quite good shelter. Moor on the south side, inside the "L." You will have to tie alongside a fishing boat, but it is somewhat quieter here than it is at the main wharf at Dennis Point, on the west side of

the harbor. There are few facilities here, but there is a restaurant, Gwen's Diner, about 1 mile north of the wharf, and a grocery store, about 2 miles in the same direction. The post office is almost at the head of the wharf. A boatyard with a slip capable of taking anything up to about 80 feet (24 m) in length is about 1 mile farther to the north.

Dennis Point Wharf ★★★★

Charts: **4210**, 4242

Approaches. A course due north from the green can buoy "P5" brings you to the main Pubnico wharf at Dennis Point. Just outside the wharf there is a rock with about 2 feet (60 cm) over it at low-water springs. This is marked by a green spar at the southern end (which causes endless confusion) and a north cardinal at the other end. The rock itself lies close south of the cardinal buoy. To get to the wharf, pass well to the west of the green spar, *that is, on what seems to be the wrong side,* and keep close to the wharves.

Anchorage, Dockage. Dennis Point is an enormous structure on which the federal government has lavished tens of millions of dollars. As there is nearly 2,000 feet (610 m) of wharf space, it is usually possible to find a spot to tie up here. There are almost 100 fishing boats based here, and when you look at all these vessels, most less than 10 years old and stacked full of every variety of high-tech electronics not always found even on the most luxurious of yachts, you may come to the realization that (to paraphrase Mark Twain) reports about the death of the East Coast fishery have been greatly exaggerated. The fish-processing plants are busy day and night—which is one of the drawbacks of this place if you want peace and quiet.

Above Dennis Point, the channel is rather narrow at low water, rather featureless, and unmarked, though the adventurous could get as far as Pubnico Head, some 4 miles farther up.

63

If you would rather anchor, there is a good spot just north of the wharf, sheltered from all directions except north through east. I should warn you, though, that the natives view as slightly cracked anyone who would rather anchor than tie up to a wharf.

The northern basin is slightly less busy and is where the smaller boats tie up. It is usually possible to moor alongside one under repair. If you're in doubt, ask anyone at the wharf.

Gasoline and diesel are piped to the wharf, and it may be possible to get them piped into your tanks. Water is more of a problem. If you have a large vessel, Paul's Water Service—(902) 762-2785—will deliver you a truckload for $30 (1995 price), though this may be overkill for a 30-footer.

Ashore. West Pubnico is a community of nearly 2,000 people, and many services are available, though at a little distance from the wharf. If you take the road running north from the wharf, turn right when you reach the main road. The co-op is not far along the main road, and has an excellent grocery and hardware store. Somewhat farther in the same direction is another grocery store, an excellent restaurant called the Red Cap—(902) 762-2112—the liquor store, a large pharmacy, and a bakery, among other things.

There are several boatbuilders, but Camille d'Eon—(902) 762-2326—has the most experience with yachts. For other boat-related services, see the Argyle section.

The local inhabitants are interested in visiting yachts, and give them a warm reception. You will almost certainly find someone to give you a ride to the local stores, and so on. About a dozen yachts a year visit this harbor, so you are unlikely to overwhelm the community.

This is the center of the Acadian culture on this coast, and some three-quarters of the inhabitants speak French as their first language, though almost everybody is fluent in English as well. The real heart of the Acadian culture is down-home hospitality, rather than lobbying for language rights, so visiting boats can be assured of having a good time here. That also counts for most harbors on this stretch of coast.

Albert and Myrna d'Entremont—(902) 762-2064—offer a consulting service for visiting yachts. They are also on the Internet (nyis @ atcon.com), demonstrating that advanced technology has arrived even here.

There is a small museum at the north end of the community. Laurent d'Entremont, one of the experts on local history and culture, offers tours in a restored Model-T Ford. He can be reached at the museum or at the Red Cap restaurant. If you want something really different, try the country-and-western music at the Fire Department every Wednesday night.

At the head of the harbor is the only 18-hole golf course in this part of the province. Visiting golfers are welcome, as they are at all rural courses in the province, and equipment—power carts and the like—may be rented.

You will see another unusual flag flying in this community. It looks like a French flag with a yellow star on the hoist. This is the Acadian flag, adopted at a congress at Memramcook, New Brunswick, in 1895.

The Cockerwit Passage and Vicinity

Charts: **4210, 4242,** 4330, 4216

Running southeast from Pubnico, the Cockerwit Passage extends to Shag Harbour. If you're heading east, and if you didn't stop at Seal Island, this will be your first experience of Shelburne County. It could be enlightening for those of you from a more urban environment.

The inhabitants of this area, by and large, are rugged, hard-driving individualists, who work and party with equal vigor. Fishing here is a year-round occupation, which means going to Georges Bank and Sable Island, or the Grand Banks of Newfoundland, in February, usually in a boat of 65 feet (20 m) or smaller. This will almost certainly be the last place on the continent to be converted to political correctness, and if you address a fisherman as a "fisherperson" or a "fisher," you will be looked upon as if you had two heads.

Not surprisingly, the natives occasionally get restless. The last criminal prosecution for piracy in Canada took place right here in 1983. Yes, 1983.

Local fishermen decided that the fisheries regulations were being enforced in a less than even-handed manner, and decided to take direct action. Department of Fisheries patrol boats were ambushed and burnt to the waterline. Their crews were lucky to escape drowning. Many in the community tacitly approved of this extreme action, believing, as they do with deep conviction, in the manifest incompetence of the Department of Fisheries.

A few years earlier, a Fisheries Department helicopter was shot down because it was interfering with duck hunting.

Now this is not, by any stretch of the imagination, a poor fishing community. In fact, it could fairly be nominated for the richest fishery in the world. I have known fishermen with a personal income of more than a half million dollars in a good year. You will get a warm welcome in any of these communities as long as you aren't a fisheries official or a tax collector.

Passage from Pubnico and the Tusket Islands to the East

If you don't want to dodge the rocks in the Cockerwit Passage when proceeding from Lobster Bay or Pubnico Harbour, go to Johns Island bell buoy, "ND4," whence a course of 170°M will bring you to Cape Sable whistle buoy, "N2." The tide does not set you too much either side of this track unless you are bucking it, when you will be set to port and toward Bon Portage Island (Outer

Island). Duck Island, which has a radar reflector on it, is quite close to this track and you should beware of being set on to it.

Having passed "N2," alter course to 108°M. When you hear Cape Sable horn clearly astern of you, come on to a course of about 075°M toward LaTour fairway buoy "JA," and points east. If the tide is turning to flood shortly after you round Cape Sable, your course should be about 085°M, rather than 075°M, to allow for the onshore set of the current. This will keep you out of the worst of the rips around the cape. It's not necessary to go all the way out to Brazil Rock. No local skipper would dream of it. It is impossible, however, to miss the rip at Shag Harbour, a fact to bear in mind when planning dinner on this passage.

If you're going east, there's not much point in taking the inside passage around Cape Sable Island, unless you are coming from Stoddart Island or Clark's Harbour. For details, see the later section on Cape Sable Island.

Approaching this area from Schooner Passage, Seal Island, or Blonde Rock is straightforward enough, though it will be a rare day when there isn't some lumpy water, even in a flat calm.

Incidentally, do not pass inside (north) of Blonde Rock. It's named after one of His Majesty's warships that was lost doing just this.

If you're heading west, give Cape Sable a wide berth, unless you are using the inside passage, and take departure from buoy "N2." It's almost always possible to hear its whistle 2 or 3 miles downwind. For further details, see the Cape Sable section.

The Cockerwit Passage

Chart: 4210

The Cockerwit Passage runs about northwest-southeast from Pubnico to Woods Harbour. The tidal stream is very brisk here: The buoys heel over at an impressive angle and raise a good-size bow wave. On one of my trips through here,

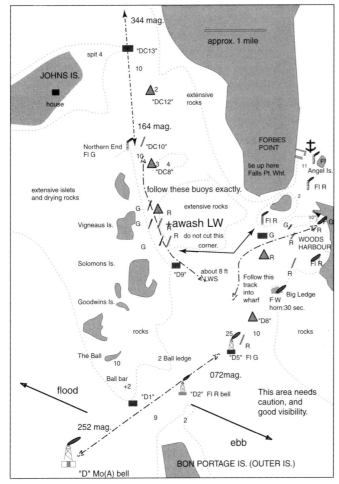

The Cockerwit Passage.

Map labels (from the chart figure):

344 mag.

"DC13"

approx. 1 mile

spit 4

JOHNS IS.

10

house

2
"DC12"

extensive rocks

164 mag.

FORBES POINT

Northern End Fl G

"DC10"

tie up here Falls Pt. Whf.

11   Fl
Angel Is.

10   3   4
"DC8"

Fl R

follow these buoys exactly.

extensive islets and drying rocks

extensive rocks

2

G   R
awash LW

10   Fl G

Vigneaus Is.   G

R do not cut this corner.

G   WOODS HARBOUR

Solomons Is.   G

R

R   Fl R

about 8 ft
LWS

"D9"

Follow this track into wharf

R

Goodwins Is.

F W
horn:30 sec.   Big Ledge

rocks

rocks

"D8"

25   10

The Ball   10

2 Ball ledge

R
"D5" Fl G

Ball bar
+2

072mag.

flood

"D1"   "D2" Fl R bell

This area needs caution, and good visibility.

252 mag.

9   2

ebb

BON PORTAGE IS. (OUTER IS.)

"D" Mo(A) bell

running south before a strong northwesterly wind, and with a spring ebb hurrying us along, I hit one of the rocks at full speed. I thought the keel was going to fall off.

It is essential to keep to the buoys, which are not marked correctly on my edition of chart 4210. It is a little easier to make this passage going north from Woods Harbour, rather than coming south from Pubnico. It is also advisable to ask one of the fishermen in Woods Harbour if your chart is correct. This cannot be done in Pubnico, as few fishermen based there use this passage. If the Coast Guard leaves the buoy numbers and positions alone for a while, my chart will remain correct.

From the north, leave the green can buoy

"DC13" (on the end of the long spit from Johns Island) on your starboard side. Steer 164°M toward a flashing green light on a small skeleton tower at Northern End Ledge. Pass between the tower and the red spar buoy. There is a red spar buoy on your port hand, halfway along, which marks a rock with only 2 feet (60 cm) over it. From the tower, veer a little to starboard, leaving another red spar on your port side. If you go on the wrong side of this one you will hit something.

Then comes the tricky part! There are three pairs of spar buoys, red to port and green to starboard, and you must pass between each pair. The middle pair are just to the west of the rock that I hit, and the channel is only 20 yards across at this point. After passing the last pair, you can aim for Big Ledge, a rock with a small lighthouse on it, and then, without cutting the corner, turn for Woods Harbour, or head for points south.

There is not really anywhere to anchor here. In the 1970s, Johns Island was inhabited by an American couple who tried homesteading, and the house is still standing, but it offers no anchorage in anything but a flat calm. My father-in-law tows a 100-foot (30-m) barge, with a draft of 6 feet (1.8 m), through here at all states of the tide in any sort of weather conditions, but going through here at night may create more excitement than you need.

If there is more than a half-tide of water, you have a lot more margin for error. The best conditions under which to try this passage for the first time, going toward Pubnico, would be to leave Stoddart Island or Woods Harbour at half-tide, in reasonably calm weather, and with good visibility. Without radar, I would not attempt this passage at night or in fog under any circumstances, and I would give it a lot of thought even if so equipped. Do not even think of doing it with GPS alone.

Woods Harbour ★★★

Charts: **4210,** 4242

Yachts are rarely seen in Woods Harbour, so if you have a vessel of any size, you will be quite an attraction. This is a prosperous fishing community of about 2,000 people, with two grocery stores and a couple of small restaurants quite handy to the wharf.

There are three approaches to Woods Harbour, the first being the Cockerwit Passage described above. Here are the other two:

Bon Portage Approach. This approach, used by all the local boats, lies north of Bon Portage Island. This is shown as Outer Island on the chart, though no one who lives here calls it that. As you approach from the southwest, you'll find the entrance is well buoyed, but the spits stick out a lot farther than you think. The spit on Ball Bar, to port, has a nasty pointy rock within spitting distance of the green can buoy "D1." The tidal currents here run hard and in a manner that strangers find very disconcerting. For example, take careful note that the flood runs northwest and *out* of the harbor, while the ebb runs east-southeast and *into* it.

When crossing this bar, it is important to remember this, and to keep on the direct line between the two bell buoys "D" and "D2." The course is 072°M going in, and 252°M coming out. Because of the tide, it is difficult to keep on the direct line, and you must keep track of your drift, unless you are fortunate enough to be crossing the bar at slack tide, which occurs 1 hour 30 minutes before slack at Yarmouth.

There is about 8 feet (2.4 m) over the bar at low-water springs, which makes it rough in a brisk southwesterly with a flood tide. I towed one of my friends over this bar once, as the choppy seas kept exposing the propeller of his outboard motor. This was neither a pleasant, nor a particularly safe, experience.

Having crossed the bar, and having kept the red bell buoy "D2" close (and I mean close) to starboard, come to about 150°M to pass close to buoy "D5." Beware of Ball Ledge on your port hand.

Southern End Approach. By far the easiest approach is from the south, rounding Southern End at Bon Portage (Outer Island) at any convenient distance, and entering the more sheltered waters of The Sound without getting into shallow water or a tiderip. The rocks extend at least a quarter-mile southeast of Southern End lighthouse, so do not cut this corner too close.

This all sounds rather forbidding, but the last time I entered here it was midnight, in thick fog, with visibility less than 50 feet (15 m), and dead low water. I hit one of the spars, but was otherwise unscathed. I have to admit I did buy a real radar set after that experience.

Dockage. The best wharf to head for is the northernmost one, and unless your draft is over 7 feet (2.1 m), come to about 020°M after you've passed "D5," and give Big Ledge a clearance of about 200 yards. Then veer to starboard, toward the end of the wharf, which has a fixed green light on it. Keep to port of the last spar, "DD6." You will have to tie up alongside a fishing boat.

Ashore. If you are a city dweller and have not experienced really fresh fish, this is one of the places to try it. You can probably get whole fresh fish at most times of the year from one of the fish plants if you want to cook it yourself. After living here for so long, I am a little reluctant to order fish in an urban restaurant. I have experienced the real thing, and you don't always get it.

Dixon's Boatbuilders—(902) 723-2878—is the biggest boatyard on this part of the coast and can handle virtually any repairs if your vessel is less than 100 feet (30 m) long.

Forbes Point

★★★ 

NO FACILITIES

Chart: 4210

If you are looking for peace and quiet, Forbes Point may be more to your liking than Woods Harbour. It is just to the north of the harbor, but there is a large shoal patch, with 2 feet (60 cm) over it, right in the middle of the channel. Local boats go either side of it, but visitors may find it easier to pass about 50 yards west of the Woods Harbour upper wharf, looking out for the drying rock (it dries 10 feet, or 3 meters) just at the head of the wharf, and heading for the northernmost tower with the flashing red light, which must be passed on your starboard side. There is a bar here, also with 2 feet over it, locally called The Falls. Although the local boats, most of which draw less than 4 feet (1.2 m) go over this bar at almost any state of the tide, it is advisable to wait until 2 hours or more after low water. There is a quiet and sheltered anchorage just north of the wharf, with about 10 feet (3 m) at low-water springs. The tide runs here at about 2 knots.

Bon Portage Island
(Outer Island) ★★★

  NO FACILITIES

Charts: **4210**, 4242

It is possible, on a fine day, to anchor just off the slipway on the eastern side of the island. Bon Portage is a nature reserve, owned largely by Acadia University. It is a pleasant walk to the unmanned lighthouse. This is not a place, however, to spend the night, as a big slop will rapidly build up if the wind comes to the northwest.

Stoddart Island ★★★

B NO FACILITIES

Charts: **4210**, 4242

A course of 044°M from bell buoy "ND2," off Bon Portage Island (Outer Island), gives you safe clearance from the light, and brings you to the entrance buoy, "NC4."

Anchorage. Anchorage is as far in between the islands as you dare. I usually anchor just off the north side of Stoddart Island, level with the green spar "NC7." There is about 8 feet (2.4 m) here at low water. This is not a bad stop if you are going east and are too late for the tide round Cape Sable, or are going west, and run out of a favorable tide after rounding it. It is a little exposed to northwesterly gales, and open to the east. There is, however little tidal current in the anchorage.

I was once anchored here because I missed the tide for the cape, and the weather forecast was for 25-knot southerlies. The wind actually blew 60 knots from the east. I was hanging on a single anchor 25 feet from the rocks, and couldn't reach the foredeck because there was a foot of green water over it every two seconds. With no windlass, it was impossible to raise the anchor, and it blew a screecher all night. This at least demonstrates that the holding ground is excellent—but I'd give this place a miss if the wind is due east. As local boats sometimes go out of here at night (which you might find difficult to believe) a riding light is essential.

The chart indicates a buoyed channel to the east of Inner Island, and I guess some of the 30 fishing boats based in Shag Harbour use it occasionally, but most of them go out through the mess of rocks labeled on the chart as Bear Point Thrums. This looks even worse in real life than it does on the chart, if such a thing is possible, and I don't recommend it.

The adventurous among you might like to try the channel inside Inner Island, which has the

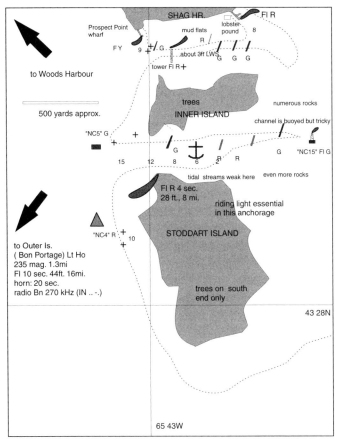

Stoddart Island and Shag Harbour.

merit that its edges are soft mud. You should be aware that the orientation of the buoys changes midway along the channel, just to make it more interesting. This is much easier in the dinghy.

Ashore. There is a store, a couple of fish plants, and a small museum in Shag Harbour. At Stoddart Island there are no facilities, though walking is easy, as there are few trees.

Some years back, at the end of the wacky 60s, one of our politicians proposed the establishment of not one, but 10, nuclear power plants on Stoddart Island. The plan was to sell the power via an undersea cable to the USA. If you anchor here and enjoy the unspoiled surroundings, you might like to contemplate the abomination it could have been. Of course, the natives around here (who once shot down a government helicopter for interfering with their duck hunting) probably

would have laid waste to the House of Assembly, had this proposal been approved.

Cape Sable Island

Charts: **4210, 4241, 4242, 4230,** 4330, 4215, 4216

Originally described by Champlain on his first voyage, Cape Sable Island, known locally as Cape Island, is a densely populated community of nearly 4,000 people. It is the home of the Cape Island boat, the workhorse of eastern Canada's inshore fishing fleet, a design that was first built by Frebert Atkinson and William Kenney in 1907. Mr. Atkinson's grandson is still making boats at the same site, though since the early 1970s they've been made of what L. Francis Herreshoff described as "frozen snot." One of my most treasured possessions is a half-model of one of these boats, given to me by Mr. Kenney's granddaughter, now a vigorous lady of 80.

The island is quite large, being 7 miles from north to south. It is dumbbell-shaped, and the southern shore is fairly well sheltered by a series of small islands and sandbars.

Cape Sable itself is on one of the fringing islands and rather inaccessible because of rough water and many intervening channels. In the mid-1950s, a causeway was built to connect Cape Sable Island to the mainland. This has no opening for boats, so going east or west requires that you round the cape, a good contender for the title of the roughest water in Nova Scotia.

The chart warns that the coastline is liable to change after severe storm conditions, but I think this more applicable to the inner banks, rather than to any major coastal features. The causeway has created a nice little anchorage at North East Point (on the northern end of the island), but

also caused Hawk Channel to fill in, so it is now scarcely passable in a skiff.

There is a net migration of sand and pebbles down the coast in this region, sweeping counterclockwise round Barrington Bay and then south to the cape. Prior to the causeway, the sand was flushed out through Barrington Passage, but now it gets flushed through the little channels between Cape Sable and the Hawk, filling them in. This has not been formally studied yet (though it would make a good Ph.D. thesis for someone), but years ago, a study was made on the migration of pebbles on the coast of East Anglia, where a similar phenomenon takes place. Radioactive pebbles were tracked over a period of years, demonstrating migration from the Wash to the Thames estuary, a distance of about 120 miles. Some of the pebbles moved as much as ten miles a year.

The sand dunes constituting Cape Sable have changed considerably over the years. Charts of the nineteenth century describe the Ratcliffe Hills as 50 to 80 feet (15 to 25 m) high. The 1950 edition I have of chart 4330 gives them as 29 feet (8.8 m) high. Now, according to the latest chart, they hardly touch 20 feet (6 m).

Tidal streams run hard off Cape Sable. The bottom is shallow and irregular a long way out, making for exceedingly rough wind-over-tide conditions. For further details see the later section on rounding the cape.

Harbors on the west side of the island, counterclockwise from North East Point, are: Newellton, West Head, Clark's Harbour, and Swim Point. On the east side, counterclockwise from Cape Sable: South Side, Stoney Island, and North East Point. These latter harbors on the east side are described later in this book in the South Shore region, as Cape Sable forms a natural (and formidable) boundary.

Note: The best chart for the west side of the island is 4210, while 4241 is best for the east side—though 4215 and 4216 show more detail and should not be thrown out. Charts 4242 and 4330 will serve for the west side in a pinch, but 4230 should not be used to enter any harbor on Cape Sable Island.

West Head ★★

NO FACILITIES

Charts: **4210,** 4242, 4230

This is by far the easiest harbor to enter if you're coming from the west, and it is the only one on the west side of Cape Sable Island that should be attempted in storm conditions from the southwest.

Approaches. You may approach from anywhere between Bon Portage Island (Outer Island) and Green Island (which has a radar reflector on it), keeping clear of the reefs that encumber the entrance to Clark's Harbour. There are no real dangers in the approaches for any boat with a draft of less than 10 feet (3 m).

Dockage. West Head has a large breakwater, which should be rounded, after which you can tie up to one of the inner wharves. Like most harbors on this coast, this is a busy place, and the outside wharves are used by large seiners, longliners, and draggers. The inner wharves, however, are less congested and may even have free spaces. Once you're in here, you're sheltered from almost anything. The fog horn is about 200 yards south of the end of the breakwater, which can be disconcerting if you are trying to enter in fog without radar.

Fuel and ice may be available from the fish plants. There are no other facilities here, but the town of Clark's Harbour is about a mile down the road. Turn right at the end of the wharf road.

The Archaeleus Smith museum, detailing much of the history of the island, is about a mile north of the West Head wharf.

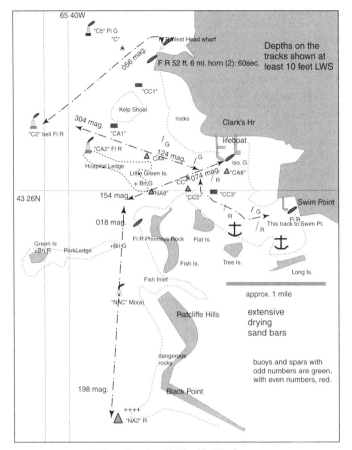

West Head and Clark's Harbour.

Newellton

Newellton, just over a mile north of West Head harbor, has a similar, though smaller, wharf. A beacon with a flashing red light marks a drying rock in the entrance. Keep close to the breakwater, as a shoal patch extends to within 20 yards of its end. I have never stayed here as I have always found enough room at West Head. The rest of the bay is not well sheltered from the prevailing westerly winds.

Clark's Harbour ★★★

Chart: 4210

Clark's Harbour is a colorful and prosperous place, the inhabitants having their own version of the English language, which might sound a little strange to visiting cruisers. A few years ago, after he'd toured Nova Scotia, some yuppified professor of modern languages was quoted on radio as saying that regional accents were dying out. Because of television, he added, we would all end up speaking the insipid language of Toronto—or some such nonsense. He obviously never got to Clark's Harbour. Here alone, there are three distinct dialects on the island.

Politics around here is equally colorful, with public figures seeking election going under such names on the ballot as "Raving Ronnie." Unfortunately, after a little matter of issuing death threats to the local RCMP, Ravin' Ron is no longer eligible for public office.

Approaches. Even at the best of times, Clark's Harbour is a little tricky to approach. That's not to say it can't be attempted by strangers in clear conditions, although intricate pilotage is required.

At night, or worse, in thick fog, I would think very hard about trying to enter. Not all the buoys are shown on all the charts, and they are subject to change without notice, so that pilotage can get very confusing in fog, with or without radar.

Not without reason, there is a lifeboat station here.

There are two approaches to Clark's Harbour, from the south through Doctors Channel, and from the northwest by way of bell buoy "C2." The latter is the safest approach coming from the

west. If you have rounded Cape Sable by the inshore passage from the east, Doctors Channel is quite straightforward, provided that the weather is clear, and that you don't draw more than 6 feet (1.8 m). Local fishing boats use it all the time, at any state of tide or wind. If you should use it after coming from the southwest, bear in mind that the track from whistle buoy "N2" to buoy "NA2" runs very close to a really nasty set of rocks, Southwest Ledge, Pinnacle Rock, and Cape Ledge. The ebb tide will try to set you right on these rocks with a velocity approaching 4 knots.

A few years ago, a tug towing a scrapped 10,000-ton natural gas tanker didn't follow this advice. The derelict grounded on these rocks. As it was November, conditions were so bad that it took months to get it refloated. The natives got to calling it the world's biggest duck blind and thought it would be a permanent fixture. Eventually, however, the tanker came free and was towed away.

Approaches to Clark's Harbour via Doctor's Channel. From "NA2," steer 018°M. Don't come too close to Black Point as there are a number of drying rocks there. There is usually broken water marking them, however, and the sound is generally intimidating.

You can pass fairway buoy "NAC" close on either side, but leave the green beacon on Pork Ledge a good distance to port as there is a 4-foot (1.2-m) shoal that sticks out for about 80 yards. Ahead, leave the flashing red beacon on Phinneys Rock a similar distance to starboard. You are out of the worst of the tide here and it runs along your course, flooding north. I have always thought Fish Inlet would make an interesting anchorage in good weather, but I have never had the fortune to be here at the right time.

Keep on 018°M until the point of Northern End bears 150°M or greater, then turn to pass midway between the green beacon on Little

Green Island and red buoy (may be a spar) "NA8." From here a course of 074°M takes you right to the end of the breakwater. If you keep the breakwater dead ahead and Little Green Island beacon dead astern, you won't hit anything, and you don't have to worry too much about the spars, except "CA6" and "CA8," which should be left to starboard.

Approaches to Clark's Harbour via the Western Approach. From bell buoy "C2," on the northern side of Hospital Reef, follow the buoys in on a course of approximately 124°M. The flood will carry you a little to port, and the ebb to starboard. When you get to buoy "CA5," you can veer to port to come to the end of the breakwater.

Neither of the approaches outlined above leaves much margin for error, but at least 50 boats use this harbor regularly—including the Coast Guard lifeboat *CG Clark's Harbour,* which goes out in fouler weather than any summer visitor would like to contemplate.

Dockage. When you're inside the harbor, tie up anywhere convenient, except alongside the lifeboat. The rise and fall of tide here is about 10 feet (3 m) at springs and 7 feet (2.1 m) at neaps.

Ashore. The grocery store, bank, and post office lie handy to the end of the wharf, but you must remember that Barrington, not Clark's Harbour, is the commercial center of the district, so selection here is limited.

But Clark's Harbour is the center of the local boatbuilding industry and there are at least four boatbuilders within walking distance of the wharf. Previously mentioned Bruce Atkinson—(902) 745-2109—or Sea Pride Boat Works—(902) 745-3110—have the most experience with yachts.

Swims Point ★★★

Chart: 4210

Swims Point lies about three-quarters of a mile south-southeast of Clark's Harbour, and you'll find it somewhat quieter. Follow the buoys exactly, from "CC" to "CC5," because the shore between Clark's Harbour and Swims Point is foul with all manner of rocks.

Anchorage. The best anchorage is between Flat Island (Round Island on the old charts) and Tree Island (which, naturally, has no trees), just southwest of "CC6" in about 8 feet (2.4 m) at low-water springs. Alternatively, you can anchor southeast of Swims Point wharf, off Long Island, which is better in easterly winds.

In both these anchorages, however, beware of the ledge with 1 foot (30 cm) over it, southeast of "CC6." Shelter is indifferent here, as the islands are low, and at high water the fetch is extensive. By way of compensation, there is a certain bleak and austere beauty to this place that only the adventurous are privileged to experience.

Ashore. A short walk south of Swims Point wharf brings you to Geneva's, a licensed restaurant that is quite acceptable.

Rounding Cape Sable

Charts: 4210, 4241, 4242, 4230

I have rounded this headland some 40 times, which I guess is as much as anyone who is not a professional mariner. It is never something I undertake lightly. Cape Sable is regarded by Nova Scotia yachtsmen as the local equivalent of Cape Horn. This reputation is well-deserved.

One of the local legends concerns a colorful fishing captain from Clark's Harbour. One February, he was bringing his fully loaded longliner back from a trip, trying to outrun a severe winter storm. But by the time he was in sight of Cape Sable, the wind was blowing over 100 knots from the northeast, and icing was so bad that the boat was in imminent danger of capsize. He turned her around to run before the wind—no trifling task in the conditions—and bore off to the south. By the time the storm blew itself out, he was only 100 miles from Bermuda.

Others were not so fortunate. In 1993, the *Atlantic Conveyor,* a bulk carrier nearly 1,000 feet (300 m) long, was lost with all hands about 30 miles off the cape in full view of television cameras, but under conditions in which our elderly search-and-rescue helicopters could not fly. The *Cape Aspy,* a 120-foot (36-m) scallop

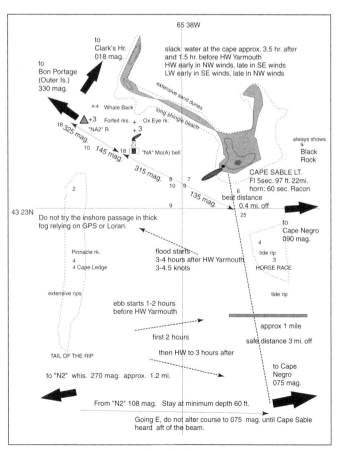

Cape Sable.

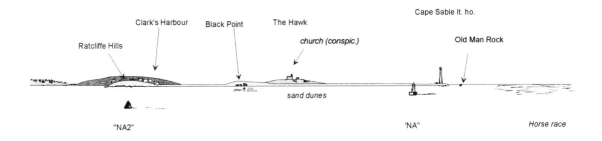

Cape Sable from about two miles to the west.

From any greater distance, Cape Sable light appears detached from the land.

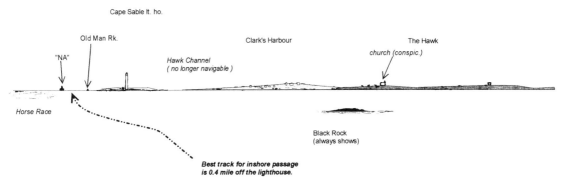

Cape Sable from about two miles to the east.

dragger, sank the same year with the loss of half the crew in much the same place, because of icing and leaks from unsecured hatch covers.

While summer weather is not likely to bring forth icing, severe storms are far from unknown, and this is no place to be with a backing wind and falling barometer. Never forget the old warning: "There at sea, with backing wind and falling glass, soundly sleeps a careless ass."

Tidal streams at Cape Sable run at about 4 knots at springs, and the bottom is shallow and irregular for about 5 miles out. In addition, around the cape there seems to be an upwelling of deep and cold water, which rarely exceeds 45°F (6°C). Not surprisingly, there can be dense fog here when everywhere else is bathed in bright sunlight. Indeed, the fog can be dense enough to prevent your seeing the bow of your boat.

The constant movement of fishing vessels in this area, the most concentrated region of inshore fishing in the entire province, is another complication. Before I had radar, I never quite realized just how many fishing boats were out there, but it is rare to pass this place with radar on the 2-mile range, at any hour of the day or night, without finding at least two or three boats on the screen. Most of them have had close encounters with Liberian rust buckets or carelessly handled large draggers, so they are quite attentive and will often realize they are seeing a sailing vessel. In that case, they'll often keep clear of you.

A main turning point for commercial shipping lies a few miles offshore. The southern corner of Nova Scotia is on the great-circle route from the East Coast of the United States to Europe. About 10 miles offshore, and farther out, there is a constant procession of large ships.

It is difficult for a small boat to reach Cape

Sable from Yarmouth on one tide, as you would need to maintain at least 6 knots over the ground. Unless conditions favor this, it is better to stop somewhere on the way. Missing the tide here commits you to hours of bouncing around in the roughest waters of the East Coast.

Rounding Cape Sable via the Outside Route

This route is easier and safer than taking the inside passage.

Rounding Outside, from the West. Do not approach land closer than the whistle buoy "N2," which lies about 4.5 miles south-southwest of Cape Sable. From "N2," come on to course 108°M. When you are sure that the horn at Cape Sable is definitely behind you, bearing 340°M or less, a course of 075°M will take you safely to The Salvages and points east. If you round Cape Sable at the end of the ebb, make the latter course 085°M, rather than 075°M, to compensate for the inward set.

At a distance of 3 miles from Cape Sable lighthouse you will clear all dangers and the worst of the rips. Further out, it is smoother.

Rounding Outside, from the East. To round the cape from east to west, reverse the above instructions. If your depthsounder shows less than 90 feet (27 m) as you approach the cape, you are too close, and should head farther offshore. There is a racon at the lighthouse which makes it easy to identify the cape, and measure your distance off, with radar. The lighthouse is tall and prominent, so in clear conditions it's also easy to establish distance off by vertical sextant angle. As the banks on which the lighthouse sits are low, it seems to stick up straight from the sea. In hazy conditions, Cape Sable lighthouse can easily be overlooked because your attention is drawn to visible land far to the north. The horn, which blows one long blast every 60 seconds, is loud and usually heard anywhere in the vicinity of the cape.

Loran readings in this area tend to put you south of where you actually are (by about a third of a mile on my set) and so should be interpreted with caution. If all else fails, the radio beacons on Seal Island (322 kHz, Morse H . . . .) and Bon Portage (Outer Island) (270 kHz, Morse IN . . –.) may help.

Unless you have radar, always use this outside route when it's foggy. Do not rely on loran or GPS alone to make the inside passage.

Rounding Cape Sable via the Inside Passage

This route is somewhat easier if you transit from east to west.

Rounding Inside, from the West. Unless you're coming from Stoddart Island or Clark's Harbour, using the inside passage when you're approaching from the west doesn't save a lot of time. The buoys are not easy to see from the west, and if the tide is with you, you might find yourself in a difficult position because of an unexpected set.

Consequently, the outside route around Cape Sable is much safer under most conditions.

Coming from Clark's Harbour, you are out of most of the tide until you get to Black Point, but I still wouldn't advise your taking the inside passage in any wind-over-tide situation where the wind is more than 15 knots. You will have green water all over your deck, and unless your crew has a lot of experience, you may have a mutiny on your hands. Once you are committed to this passage, you can't turn back.

Rounding Inside, from the East. The tide off the cape turns about 2 hours earlier than it does in Yarmouth, and sometimes there is an eddy close inshore that starts up to an hour before this. Thus, going west, you might find a favorable tide at Cape Sable 3 hours 30 minutes after high water at Yarmouth.

The best time to pass the cape going west is at low water slack, as you will then have 8 hours of

favorable tide. In the right conditions, using the inside passage can save you half a day, but I wouldn't use this passage unless the tide were favorable.

Coming from the east, you'll need to approach the cape to within about 0.4 miles. Black Rock needs to be avoided if you are coming from Barrington Bay, and thankfully it is always visible. After rounding the cape, come to 315°M to head directly for bell buoy "NA." Pass close to it, and then come to 325°M to leave "NA2," a red conical buoy, close on your starboard side. Do not under any circumstances stray north of the track between these two buoys. After passing "NA2," a course of 330°M takes you to Bon Portage (Outer Island) Lighthouse. Green Island is close to starboard. Beware that the tide doesn't set you

on it. There is a mess of rocks close to port, but the minimum depth is 4 feet (1.2 m), and you will probably have at least 1 foot (30 cm) more depth. You would be very unlucky to hit anything if your draft is less than 5 feet 6 inches (1.7 m), though you can certainly frighten your crew easily enough.

Once you've passed Green Island you're clear of immediate dangers and you should be able to hear the horn of Bon Portage (Outer Island) ahead of you. It gives one blast every 20 seconds. If you are heading farther west than Woods Harbour, bear to port, because the tide tends to set you on to Bon Portage (Outer Island) or Duck Island.

I can usually get to Argyle in 4 hours in my 30-footer if I have a favorable wind, and pick up the first of the flood at the cape. Transit times to the Tusket Islands would be similar, and it should be possible to reach Yarmouth on one tide.

The South Shore: *Cape Sable to Cape LaHave*

Great Island, Medway Harbor

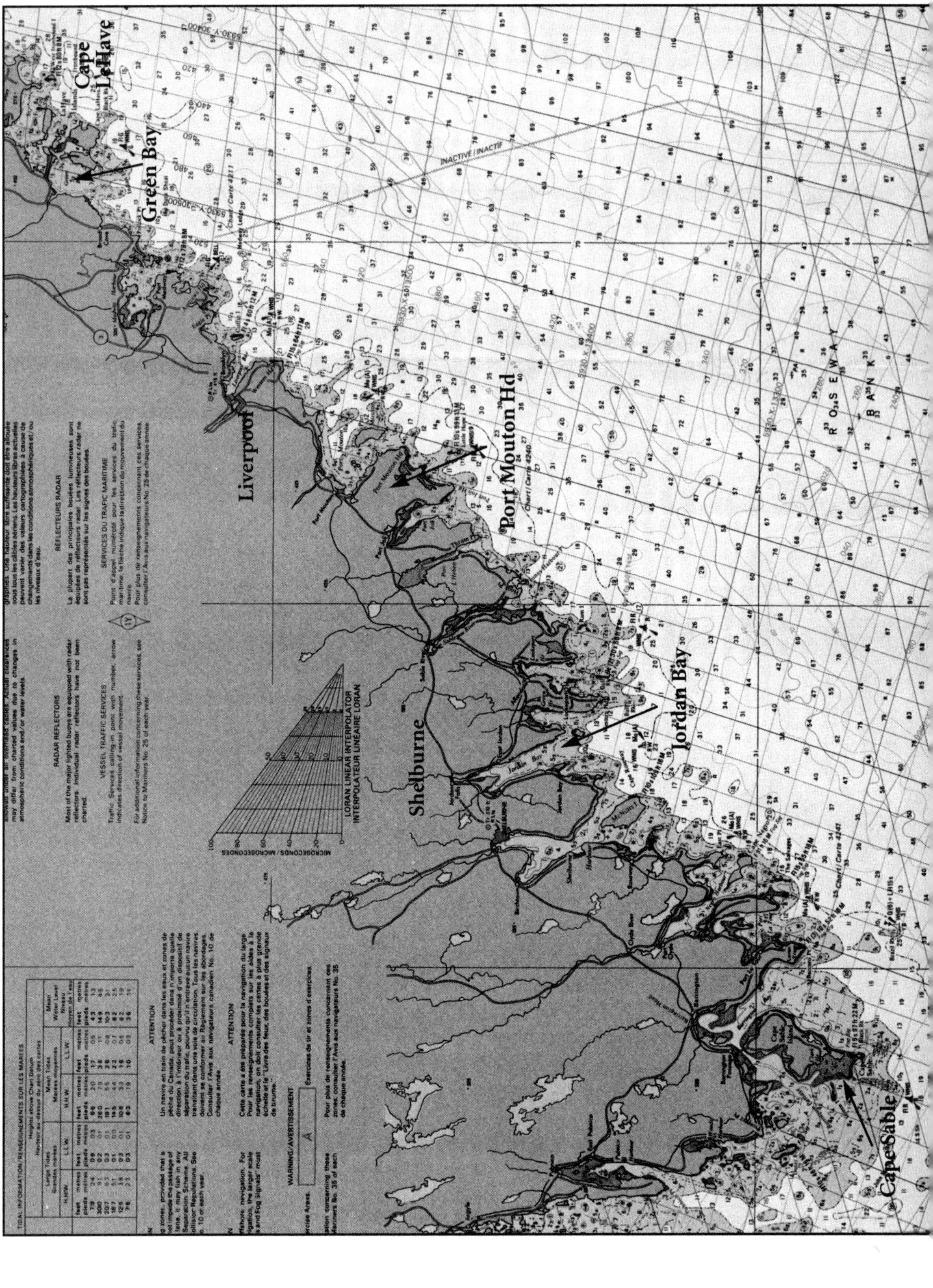

Based on CHS Chart 4012. Not to be used for navigation.

Cape LeHave

Green Bay

Liverpool

Port Mouton Hd

Shelburne

Jordan Bay

Cape Sable

LORAN LINEAR INTERPOLATOR
INTERPOLATEUR LINÉAIRE LORAN

MICROSECONDS / MICROSECONDES

WARNING / AVERTISSEMENT

For the purposes of this book, the South Shore of Nova Scotia extends from Cape Sable to Cape LaHave. This is not quite the same definition as that used by the Nova Scotia Department of Tourism, but as it is delineated by natural boundaries, I feel it is somewhat more logical.

About 3 or 4 miles east of Cape Sable, tidal streams become weaker, and, except in a few locations, are no longer a consideration anywhere in the remaining areas of this book. Between Baccaro and Lockeport, they average about 1 knot. East of Lockeport, they rarely exceed 0.5 knot. The sea becomes much smoother from about 4 miles east of Cape Sable, though there are other rough spots to which I will refer later.

From Cape Sable, a course of about 078°M takes you along the line of the outside buoys as far as Lockeport, then 065°M will take you to Cape LaHave.

The only communities of more than 1,000 people in this 70-odd miles of coastline are Shelburne and Liverpool. The numerous coves and inlets are either occupied by small fishing communities or scarcely inhabited at all. The area contains the best beaches on the Atlantic coast of the province, though many of them are too exposed to visit by boat.

Apart from shipyards in Shelburne and Liverpool, and a pulp mill in Liverpool, the only industry is that of the fishery. Though other areas of the province, notably the eastern shore, are even more sparsely populated, this area will seem almost deserted to those of you who have never gone east of Petit Manan. Though the area houses some rather economically depressed communities affected by the fisheries crisis, it remains quite prosperous on the whole. There is not the population base to support a large yachting community, but I have no reservation in nominating the yacht club in Shelburne as the friendliest in the province. The trip up Shelburne Harbour is, admittedly, a bit off the beaten track, but the diversion will be rewarding. For further details, see the section on Shelburne.

Harbors on the East Side of Cape Sable Island

Charts: **4241, 4230,** 4215

It seems more natural to include these harbors in this region, as going from the east side to the west side of Cape Sable Island is not a simple business. Many amateur sailors in Nova Scotia regard Cape Sable with trepidation, and never venture west of it.

The best chart is 4241. Now-obsolete 4215 has more detail, but shows very few of the buoys correctly. Chart 4230 does not really show enough detail to enter any harbor in this area, though it might suffice in clear weather.

South Side (Daniels or Donald Head on the charts)

★★

Chart: 4241

The largest fish-processing plant on Cape Sable Island is in this harbor, and it makes an excellent radar target. The harbor is surprisingly clean despite this, but it is naturally a very busy place. The best place for visiting yachts is on the west side of the wharf in the middle of the harbor, so that the plant is directly to your west.

You will almost certainly have to lie outside another boat. I have tied up here late at night alongside a fishing boat, having had a long beat to the west, or a long day rounding the cape, to find myself neatly tied up to the wharf in the morning, the crew of the inside boats having been kind enough to move out without waking me. It is easier for them to do this if you run long bow and stern lines to the wharf.

Incidentally, no local inhabitant uses the names on the chart.

Approaches. Coming from Cape Sable, you should round Black Rock, which shows 3 feet (1 m) at high water. From there, a course of 060°M brings you to bell buoy "JS55." You can pass inside of the first bell buoy, "JS53," but it is better to pass "JS55" on the correct side, that is, leave it on your port hand. From here, the course is 008°M to entrance buoy "JU50," after which 275°M will lead you to the end of the breakwater. You can pass "JU50" on either side, but go close to it before turning for the breakwater, as there is a rock, with just 3 feet (1 m) over it at low water, which is not shown on chart 4241.

I have entered this harbor in thick fog with no radar, but I don't recommend it for strangers. There is a fog signal, sounding every 30 seconds, 200 yards south of the breakwater. Don't confuse it with the identical fog signal at Cripple Creek, 2 miles north.

Flood tide here runs to the south, and the ebb to the north, fortunately at only 1.5 knots—but this can cause confusion if you are not aware of it.

Coming from the east, a course of 305°M from Bantam Rocks brings you to entrance buoy "JU50." On the east side of Barrington Bay, by the way, the flood runs northwest and the ebb southeast, just to keep navigators on their toes.

Anchorage, Dockage. The tide rises and falls much less here than it does on the west side of Cape Sable Island, the range being about 8 feet (2.4 m) at springs. If you prefer to anchor, it is possible to do so in the bay just north of the wharf, provided the wind is from the west. There is considerable swell in this anchorage if the wind has any easterly component. The wharf is well sheltered. Diesel and ice may be available.

Ashore. There is a clean sandy beach just north of the wharf, and it is possible to explore South Side Inlet in a dinghy. Uncharted power lines cross the inlet with a clearance of about 35 feet, (10.6 m) just by the fish plant. The power company won't tell me what the safe clearance is, or even admit that the lines are there. In view of this, it is inadvisable to enter the inlet in anything other than a skiff or a small dinghy.

Lobster-boat races take place in Barrington Passage, usually during the first week of August. The boats are stripped until they're no more than open shells, 35 to 40 feet (10.5 to 12 m) long, with enormous engines. Many of these boats are stored on the east side of South Side Inlet.

Stoney Island and Cripple Creek

These are small harbors, 1.5 and 3 miles north of South Side, respectively. They are more difficult to enter, and for this reason I have never used them.

North East Point and Barrington ★★★★

Charts: **4241,** 4215

There is a delightful little anchorage at North East Point, formed between the causeway and the dunes that have built up since it was built. It is particularly good if you have children aboard, as the water is reasonably warm and there is a beach composed of the finest white sand—which you may have to warn the kids not to bring back on board the boat!

Approaches. Approach via Barrington Bay, favoring the west side slightly, on a course of about 325°M, until you come to buoy "JS70," on the western edge of Wesses Ledge. Then come to 323°M and leave green spar "JS73" close on your port side. Incidentally, these spars are difficult to see until you are right on top of them. Then come to 270°M, and you will see the causeway ahead of you. Pass between the two pairs of spars correctly, as shown on the chart. Then, when you are about 30 yards from the causeway, turn south, pass the end of the sand dune on your port hand and anchor anywhere you can find space. Depths are between 12 and 20 feet (3.6 and 6 m), and there is at least 20 feet (6 m) all the way in. The last time I came in here, I was under full sail in a 25-knot southeasterly. It certainly brought the traffic on the causeway to a grinding halt.

Anchorage. This anchorage has become more popular among local boats over the years, though I haven't seen many yachts other than myself or our traveling companions. The sandy bottom makes good holding ground, and you're sheltered here from everything but a hurricane from the northeast. I have ridden out ordinary easterly gales here in comfort.

It is not the quietest anchorage, because of the constant traffic on the road, but I think its good points compensate for this.

Ashore. The sand dunes are a nesting ground for the piping plover, an endangered bird, and at certain times of the year (usually before July) there will be signs asking you to keep off the dunes, though walking on the beach is still allowed.

The commercial center, Barrington Passage, is just north of the causeway. That places it a half-mile from the anchorage, so the activity won't bother you much. There is a wharf off Sherose Island, and an extensive, though shallow, bay to the northeast. Approaches to everything but the small and crowded wharf are very narrow, and considering the ease of anchoring at North East Point, not recommended. If you have a decent dinghy, it could save you the half-mile hike to the stores. It can be tied up at the ruins of an old wharf just east of what is called Clement's Point on chart 4241.

Barrington Passage has large grocery stores, banks, drug stores, a post office, and fast-food outlets. You'll find doctors, lawyers, and five restaurants, though none of the latter feature what could be called gourmet meals. This makes sense, though, when you realize that the local preference leans more toward Captain Morgan's rum than fine wines. Nonetheless, if your needs are those of steak, fresh fish, or chicken, you will be well fed at a reasonable price. Despite the local tastes, the small liquor store in Barrington Place, just to the right of the causeway,

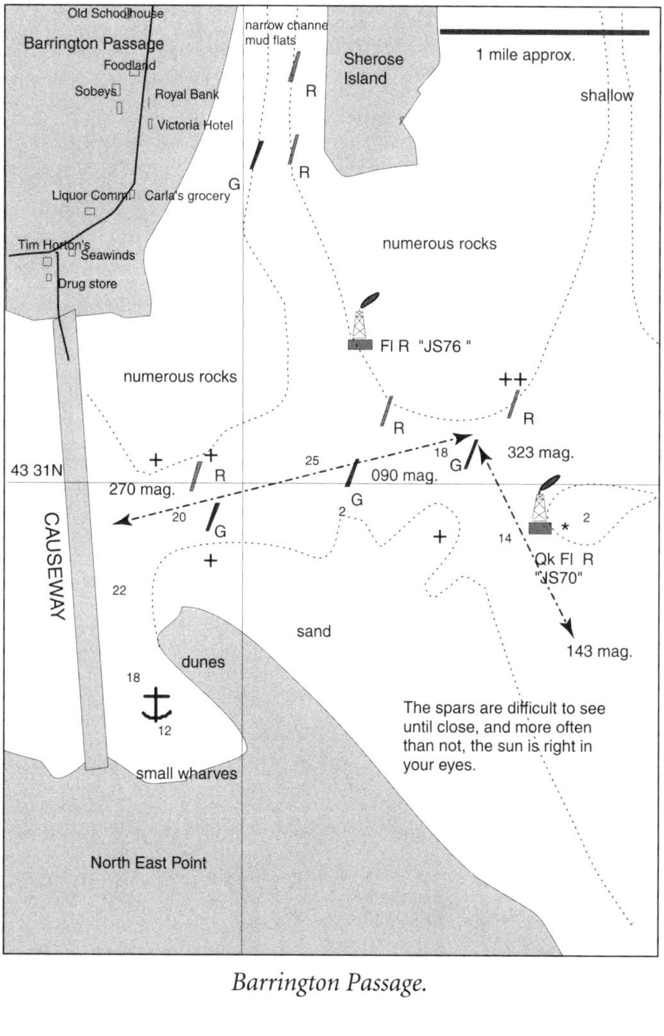

Barrington Passage.

83

has the best selection of wine in western Nova Scotia. The Old Schoolhouse restaurant is about 1 mile from the causeway going northeast. It was built by members of a religious commune whose puritanical ways were considered too extreme, even by the standards of the locals, who at one time set a record for the highest rate of teenage pregnancy in all Canada. After about 10 years, the commune moved out, and the place was bought by one of the more colorful fishing captains from Woods Harbor. It is now a bar and hotel, with a restaurant and live music—of the good-ol'-boy variety—from Thursday through Saturday. If you seek local color, this is the place to visit.

Port La Tour ★★★ 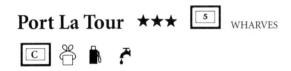 WHARVES

Charts: **4241**, 4215

Port La Tour lies north of Baccaro Point on the eastern side of the peninsula, and is a lot easier to enter if you're approaching from the east. The west entrance by way of Cuckold Rock is narrow, and I wouldn't try it unless visibility were a couple of miles or more.

If you are heading east, and looking for an anchorage for the night, it is only a mile or two more to go to Cape Negro from fairway buoy "JA." Cape Negro is much easier than Port La Tour to enter.

In 1994, the Coast Guard changed almost all the buoys in Port La Tour, a fact I discovered only after entering. To my consternation, there wasn't a single buoy positioned correctly according to my chart. Fortunately, it was clear and I could see the rocks.

Approaches. From fairway whistle buoy "JA," steer 340°M, which brings you to bell buoy "JN."

About 100 yards farther along on the same heading is a flashing green light on a small skeleton tower which you should leave close to port, passing midway between it and the red spar. Then come to 334°M and leave the red quick-flashing buoy "JA56" on your starboard hand. This will bring you to the bay between the two wharves. There is at least 8 feet (2.4 m) of water all the way in.

You could also go the long way around, passing just south of Blind Dick, and north of Mohawk Ledge, but I didn't see any buoys marking those hazards last time I was there.

The latest chart indicates a buoyed channel leading to the basin south of Cape Negro village, which would appear to have about 4 feet (1.2 m) at low-water springs. It looks quite intimidating on the chart and I have never tried it, though I understand it to be pretty and well sheltered.

Port La Tour looks a little intimidating too, because of the small scale of the latest chart. It is straightforward enough in good visibility, and reasonable at night, but I wouldn't try it in fog without radar.

Anchorage, Dockage. You can anchor in firm sand between the wharves with about 8 feet at low-water springs, or tie up at either of the wharves. They are quite busy, though, and the boats tend to get going at about 0400. Both wharves have been upgraded in the last few years, and are now substantial structures giving protection from any normal storm. There is plenty of water if your draft is 6 feet (1.8 m) or less.

Ashore. Diesel, ice, and fresh fish may be available at the northern wharf. There is also a small store with very limited supplies. The bottom of this bay is fine, white sand, and the water is beautifully clear, though usually only 54°F (12°C). There are some small sand beaches.

Port La Tour was one of the earliest sites of European occupation, having been settled by Claude De LaTour in 1610 or thereabouts. Claude was quite a character, wheeling and dealing between the French and the English in the interminable

COASTAL HAZARDS

The coast between Barrington and Cape Roseway is encumbered with a great number of outlying rocks, and should be closed with caution. Going east from Barrington, the first headland is Baccaro Point. This has a very conspicuous radar dome on it, which in clear weather is recognizable from at least 12 miles. I presume this was named by Breton and Portuguese fishermen, probably before the time of Columbus, Baccaro being an English corruption of the Portuguese word for cod.

Anywhere between Baccaro Point and Brazil Rock, 5 miles to the south, is still a good place to jig for fish, though you are more likely to get pollack or haddock than the endangered cod. There is a great concentration of small vessels, usually 30 to 40 feet (9 to 12 m) long, doing just this in summer. As they are usually anchored while fishing, with engine and radar turned off, they can be a hazard in thick fog.

Bantam Rocks, marked by red whistle buoy "JS56," is a drying rock about 1.5 miles south-southwest of Baccaro Point. Local fishermen usually keep inshore of it, but the tide runs quite hard off the point, so I don't recommend this practice. Apart from this particular spot, there is not a lot of tidal stream to worry about.

wars of the seventeenth century. He was French, but Protestant and not politically correct. Claude's wife, Marie, died a nasty death after a particularly vicious siege (in a place near Saint John, New Brunswick) laid by a French nobleman, Seignior d'Aulnay. There is a monument to La Tour about a mile to the south of the lower wharf.

The Salvages

Chart: 4241

To the east of Port La Tour lie The Salvages, as nasty a mess of rocks as you are likely to see anywhere. They are steep-to on the southern end, but don't take that as an invitation to close with them. The surf they generate can easily be heard at the anchorage at Cape Negro Island, 3 miles away— and the spray flies this distance also.

Negro Harbour can be entered from the west, the side on which The Salvages lurk, through the West Entrance marked on the chart, but it is full of unmarked rocks, and the look of them from the outside will deter all but the most foolhardy. I don't recall a lot of the local fishermen using it

either, for that matter. There is an unmanned lighthouse on the biggest rock, which must be like a submarine in the winter. It has a loud fog signal, three blasts every minute, and can easily be heard for miles.

Cape Negro Island ★★★★

   NO FACILITIES

Charts: 4241, 4216

There are a few cottages and some interesting ruins on wasp-waisted Cape Negro Island. Like many offshore islands in the province, it was permanently inhabited 50 years ago, but not now. There is an old graveyard on the northern island. A few years ago I looked through the old, ruined, two-story house and found newspapers dated 1958, so permanent habitation was relatively recent. The island is much used by duck hunters in the winter. In summer most of its residents are sheep.

There are a number of trails over the island,

85

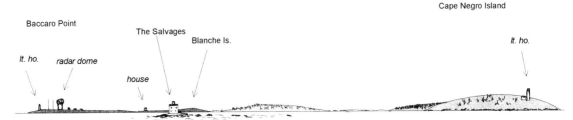

The Salvages from two miles to the southeast.

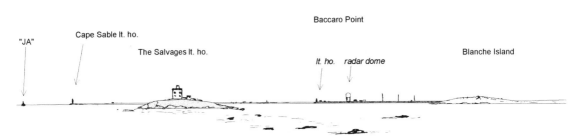

The Salvages from one mile to the east (as when going west from Cape Negro).

and the sheep keep the vegetation down, making for easy walking. There is a pond between the twin shingle banks joining the northern and southern parts of the island and I have been intrigued to see that this pond has a permanent population of frogs. As sea water is supposed to be a barrier to frogs, I often wonder where they came from.

In 1992, the *Gentry Eagle,* a 70-foot (21-m) powerboat trying to break the transatlantic record, grounded on the rocks just south of the anchorage. Her crew apparently mistook the radar image of the island for a rainstorm. At the speed they were doing at the time, 70 knots, they were fortunate not to be killed. As I had been anchored here a day before this incident, I was much relieved that I hadn't been in the way.

Approaches. You can round the southern end of the island at a reasonable distance off, and approach from the east, taking care to avoid the spit that sticks out between the island and bell buoy "SN51."

Alternatively, you can steer 313°M from the fairway whistle buoy, "SN." This will bring you to "SN51," which lies just east of Budget Rock. It is actually difficult to hit Budget Rock if it is more than an hour after low water and your boat draws less than 5 feet (1.5 m). I have, however, seen the kelp on a few occasions. Go 100 yards past Budget Rock, turn to 260°M or so, and go in as close to the beach in East Cove as you can.

It is possible to go west of Budget Rock, leaving the red spar close to starboard. This spar is not easy to see and is a poor radar target, so perhaps this approach should be reserved for clear weather.

The horn on the lighthouse has a distinctive sound, reminiscent of a wailing tomcat. In the days before radar was available for small boats, I entered this harbor by finding the buoys as above, going a short way past the bell, and coming to 260°M. When the depth got to 10 feet (3 m), I dropped anchor. I had been here some four or five times before I ever saw the island.

Occasionally, you'll find gill nets set close to the eastern side of the island. These things are a

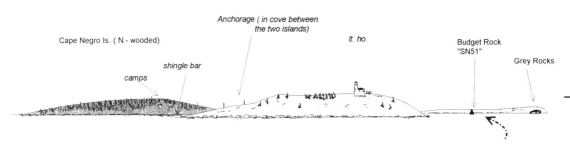

Cape Negro Is. (S- mostly bare)

Anchorage (in cove between
the two islands)

Cape Negro Is. (N - wooded)

lt. ho.

Budget Rock
"SN51"

Grey Rocks

shingle bar

camps

Cape Negro Island from one mile to the south.

curse, especially if your boat has a fin-and-skeg underwater profile. They are just under the surface, never well marked, and I've no idea how you're supposed to miss them in the dark.

Anchorage. The anchorage in East Cove is sheltered from every direction except north-through-east. If it is one of those rare weeks where there has been an easterly wind for days, some surge runs into the anchorage, though it won't bother anyone who has ever anchored in the Caribbean. I usually anchor about level with the ruined house in the northwest corner of the cove. Watch out for some drying rocks in this corner. Anchoring here will keep you clear of the electric cable supplying the lighthouse. I have dropped the hook here some 30 times, and had to move only once. This anchorage gets a bit of a bum rap in other guides but I have found it pleasant and relatively free of bugs. Furthermore, there is an unlimited supply of firewood on the beach.

The holding ground is good, in firm sand, and no one is likely to run you over if you don't have a riding light set at night.

Ashore. The island is, in fact, a double island connected by an enormous shingle bar. This bar was broken through during an extra-tropical cyclone in March 1993, and the islands are now separated at high water. This may affect the quality of the anchorage if the break continues to widen. The storm surge also removed a lot of the driftwood, but I've no doubt it will soon be back.

Ingomar ★★★ 4   B

NO FACILITIES

Charts: 4241, 4215

If the anchorage at Cape Negro is untenable, Ingomar is a close-by alternative. It's very well sheltered from the easterly winds that will have forced you out of the island. A course of 015°M from Cape Negro Island anchorage takes you right in to the harbor. Watch for Grog Rock on your starboard hand. Flashing red buoy "SN54" can be passed close on either hand. To starboard ahead, you'll see the peninsula called Apple Island, and once you've passed it, favor the east side of the buoyed channel.

Anchorage. There are numerous fishing boats on moorings here, but there is plenty of anchoring space between them. As they all depart at 0400 on weekday mornings, riding lights are essential. There is a small store close to the wharf: Just walk up the road and turn right. The holding ground is good, in mud, and the anchorage is more sheltered, even from the south, than the chart suggests.

Clyde River
(Negro Harbour)

★★★ [4] [C]

NO FACILITIES

Charts: **4241**, 4215

The adventurous might enjoy a diversion up the Clyde River, called Negro Harbour on the chart. I am not sure of the origin of this place name, though I believe it dates back to Champlain's voyages.

Once you've cleared the northern end of Cape Negro Island, there are few hazards until you come to Davis Island, which is called Big Island on the new charts. Going north, pass to the east of Big Island, midway between it and Round Island to starboard. These islands are quite high and easy to see.

Continue toward red spar "SN70," leaving a small islet on your port hand, then come to about 330°M. A drying rock, marked by a green spar, lies on the west bank. There may be other spars farther up, but the channel is reasonably clear and offers a depth of a little over 5 feet (1.5 m) at low-water springs.

You may anchor in any convenient spot, and you'll probably find one of the local boats moored here. In the upper reaches, there is a current of about 2 knots, though you'll not find it elsewhere in the harbor.

The Clyde River is famous for its salmon fishing, which, in recent years, has been threatened by acid rain. But the river now seems to be recovering somewhat.

The abandoned railway bridge at Port Clyde is the limit of navigation for any boat with a mast, though a canoe can traverse another 40 miles to the central part of the province and an elevation of some 400 feet (120 m).

Ashore. Just past the railway bridge is a challenging golf course, in the process of being en-

larged to 18 holes. If you have the energy, a walk of a mile or so along the roads on either side of the river brings you to the village of Clyde River, where there is a service station and a well-stocked country store.

Cape Negro to Cape Roseway

East of Cape Negro, the coast turns to the north. There are a few off-lying dangers—Grey Rocks, Gull Rock, and Grey Island, in that order, going north—but they are all at least 20 feet (6 m) high, and easily seen or heard. If you stay at least 1.5 miles off the headlands, you'll clear them all.

McNutts Island straddles the entrance to Shelburne Harbour, creating two passages called the Eastern Way and the Western Way.

The Western Way is marked with a couple of spar buoys, but it is shallow, with only 3 feet (1 m) at low-water springs. It is also more exposed to the prevailing southerly swells. Consequently, it has never appealed to me very much. The Eastern Way is much more straightforward.

Shelburne Area

Charts: **4241, 4209,** 4230, 4012

For this area, chart 4241 is the most-used coastal chart. Chart 4209 is new, and includes Lockeport Harbour and Shelburne Harbour. It's a useful chart, but it might be hard to find. I have always entered Shelburne Harbour with 4241 or the older charts. Incidentally, charts 4214 and 4213 are now outdated, but they still have much better detail than 4241. The only problem with them is that the numbering of buoys will not be correct, and some buoys may be missing or incorrectly shown.

Charts 4230 and 4012 are small-scale charts for offshore passages, and not really suitable for entering harbors. If you are desperate, and have

McNutts Island Cape Roseway lt. ho. NE Bluff Government Point Jordan Bay

"SAC"

"S51"

**Entrance to Shelburne harbour
(Eastern Way)**

Entrance to Shelburne Harbour from one mile south-southeast of Cape Roseway.

no other charts on board, you could probably get into Shelburne with one of them.

Shelburne Harbour ★★★★★

Charts: **4241, 4209**

Shelburne Harbour is an official port of entry into Canada, but it's also home to the Shelburne Harbour Yacht Club, by my reckoning the friendliest yacht club in the province, if not anywhere. The club's vice-commodore, Harry O'Connor, tries to greet every visiting boat personally, either at the club or the town wharf, and he sees that all their needs are attended to. He can often be contacted on VHF Channel 16 or 68. Not surprisingly, Shelburne is visited by increasing numbers of cruising yachts every year, and the number now is in the order of 150 between the end of June and the middle of September.

Shelburne Harbour Y.C. is a working-class club, and there are no paid employees. There are therefore no club officials on the premises until about 1600, but the door at the back is left unlocked, so there is access to the washrooms and hot showers. The treasurer would be grateful if you patronized the bar during your visit. There is racing every Tuesday night and alternate Sundays. Visiting boats are welcome to participate. Club members own at least 30 boats, which indicates a very high degree of participation in the sport of yachting, considering that the town's population is less than 2,000.

Approaches. Shelburne is by far the easiest harbor to enter in this area of Nova Scotia. Almost all vessels of any size use the Eastern Way. Entrance at night is straightforward, and even in fog it's reasonably safe, as there are few submerged hazards. You can get in here at any state of the tide and in any wind conditions. There are a lot of fishing boats around, as well as the occasional large vessel, such as a cruise ship. Shelburne could be entered in fog using only GPS or loran, as long as you are aware of the limitations of these instruments. If there is thick fog outside, it is usually clear inside Sandy Point after 1000. Shelburne is probably the easiest port of entry for those of you without a lot of experience navigating in fog. It is well worth the extra time spent going farther north into the harbor.

89

From the west, steer approximately 030°M from Jig Rock bell buoy "S51," and when you have Cape Roseway light abeam to port, come to 019°M and head for fairway buoy "SAA." Just west of buoy "SAA," a compass needle on the chart indicates the pilot station. On your starboard bow, on Government Point, you'll see prominent buildings that until recently were the shore terminal of the SOSUS system for detecting Russian submarines.

When you have "SAA" abeam to starboard, come to 330°M which will take you to Sandy Point bell buoy "S54." I always go north of "SAB," but if you draw more than 8 feet or it is blowing a southeasterly gale, veer a little to port and pass this buoy on your starboard side, the correct orientation. If you have an old chart, it will show a fog signal on Sandy Point, which is no longer there.

If you're approaching Shelburne Harbour from the east, steer 325°M from outer whistle buoy "S" to reach "SAA." There is a rock, Bell Rock on Old Cow Reef, awash at high water, about a half-mile to starboard on this course. It is marked by flashing red bifurcation buoy "SAC." Once you've arrived at buoy "SAA," follow the instructions above to buoy "S54" at Sandy Point.

Sandy Point to the Government Wharf. After rounding Sandy Point, come to 027°M. There are two leading marks, white daymarks with red stripes, in a vertical line, behind you on Surf Point to keep you on this heading. At night, the marks show fixed green lights. Check your heading to ensure it is the marks you are following and not some shore light. This course will take you safely right to the end of the government wharf, 4 miles up the harbor.

A large aquaculture holding tank is located 1.6 miles north from Sandy Point light, less than 100 yards east of the course marked by the leading marks. The latest charts indicate its approximate location. The tank is nearly 1,000 feet (300 m) long, and its owners are sometimes not as conscientious as they might be about lighting it. On most occasions when I've passed it, it has had radar reflectors, and sometimes it's had flashing yellow lights. But on occasion there's been no indication at all of its presence. If you get fouled up in this thing, you might need a tow and a diver. There is another tank on the west side of the harbor, farther north, but this is a lot farther from the line of the leading lights and not such a hazard.

On the starboard side going north, just past the fish tank, and below a small wharf and fish plant, is the Shelburne Harbour Yacht Club. There is a small floating dock here, and a number of the members' boats are moored outside of it.

There is not a strong tidal stream here, and the rise and fall at springs is only 7 feet (2.1 m).

Between McNutts Island and Sandy Point, the wind funnels through Western Way, often increasing to 25 knots when it's blowing 10 knots everywhere else. This can be quite exciting if you have a spinnaker up. Another peculiarity of the wind is that on fine days, with the wind in any direction with south in it, a stiff breeze will start blowing straight up the harbor by about midday, build to a peak at about 1500, and die away to nothing by evening. The afternoon wind can be in the order of 25 knots even if it's flat calm first thing in the morning.

Birchtown Bay. This is the western arm of the Y that forms Shelburne Harbour, and it contains a lot of rocks. In the main harbor, however, there are virtually no significant hazards until you get north of the government wharf.

Shelburne Town

Chart: 4209

Three miles north of Sandy Point, on the starboard side, there are some large fueling dolphins, owned by the Department of National Defence. Close to the north of them are the premises of Shelburne Marine, where large vessels are usually under repair, so it is quite conspicuous. You may pass either side of the dolphins, assuming you draw less than 12 feet, (3.6 m) but be sure to give the rails of the marine railway a decent berth.

Anchorage, Dockage. While there is usually space to tie up at the government wharf, the town dock is a far better berth. It's about a half-mile farther up at Bruce's Wharf. There is space for two berths alongside on each side of the wharf, but I don't recommend the south side except in the calmest conditions, because of the daily southerly blast to which this berth is exposed. Approach the berth at right angles to the shoreline, as there are submerged ruins sticking out from the shore at all sorts of odd places. For the same reason, do not follow the shore between the government wharf and the town dock too closely. If

the town dock is occupied, there are a number of substantial moorings just off the dock. No one has ever asked me to pay for using these facilities, but I suppose it could happen if you stayed more than a few days. In August 1994, the water temperature at the town dock was 79°F (26°C), warm enough for even an old graybeard loon like me to go swimming.

For the Boat. Shelburne Marine has a travel lift, one of the few in the province, with a capacity of about 30 tons, enough to handle most visiting yachts. They store most of the yacht club boats, so you can be sure they're experienced in this sort of work. Virtually any repairs can be done here. *Gentry Eagle* was repaired here after she piled up on Cape Negro, and Shelburne is a major repair center for the offshore fishing fleet.

Ashore. Shelburne is a port of entry at present, but because of government cutbacks, may not be after 1996, when clearance will have to be made by phone—(902) 875-2324.

A few years ago, the Town Fathers cleaned up the waterfront, and it is now one of the most attractive in the province. As all the power cables have been buried, and as many of the buildings still have their original early nineteenth century facades, the waterfront has starred in several historical films. In 1994, *The Scarlet Letter,* a Disney film starring Demi Moore, was shot here, the waterfront having been made to resemble Boston in the early eighteenth century.

Shelburne itself has an interesting history, having been settled shortly after the American War of Independence by United Empire Loyalists from Philadelphia. For a short time afterward it was one of the biggest towns in North America. Unfortunately, Shelburne County hadn't the natural resources to sustain a township of

Shelburne Town

provincial park

shopping mall 1 mile

Water Street

park | Dock St.

5 R

2 ++

G

tourist inf.

liquor Comm.

Coopers Inn

CUSTOMS

bank

7

Bruces Wharf

R

10

12

Town Dock
+ watch for this rock

grocery

shallow

3 G

shallow

R

18

tie up on north side of town dock

R

10

MOORINGS

22

GOVERNMENT WHARF

Tie inside, i.e. east side, if you want to use government dock.

Shelburne Marine slipway

fueling dolphins Red Lts.

1 mile approx.

some 10,000, and the population rapidly dwindled to its present level of about 2,000. The streets retain the spacious grid pattern of 1783, and it is a pleasant walk from the waterfront around to Water Street, one block up from the water.

There are all the usual stores within easy walking distance of the town dock. There is a shopping mall with a larger grocery store about 1 mile to the north. The Liquor Commission store is a fair hike down the Sandy Point Road toward the hospital. I've occasionally been lent a shopping cart by Grovestine's grocery store to trundle my supplies to the dock.

There are a number of banks in town and there are at least five restaurants within easy walking distance of the wharf. The fanciest is The Cooper's Inn, right on the waterfront. I've had some excellent meals there in the past, but you'll have to judge for yourself because it recently underwent a change of ownership. The original owners had the misfortune to sink on a passage from Bermuda to the Caribbean in winter, always a tricky business. They were lucky enough to survive, though their boat did not. The Cooper's Inn is small, and reservations are certainly advised. I have also had good eating at the Loyalist Inn, with somewhat less strain on my overdraft. The other restaurants offer more standard small-town fare, but are all adequate, and by Nova Scotian standards, quite economical.

McNutts Island ★★★

    NO FACILITIES

Charts: **4209,** 4241

There is a quiet anchorage on the west side of Mc-Nutts Island. After approaching from Eastern Way, round the long spit that extends from the northwest corner of the island, and then head east toward the dock. Anchor in any convenient spot. There is at least 7 feet (2.1 m) all the way in. If you draw 5 feet (1.5 m) or less, you'll find better shelter by going a little farther south to what is called

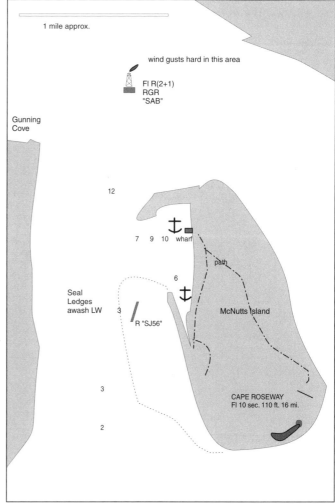

McNutts Island

Hagars Cove on the new chart. There is about 5 feet (1.5 m) here at low-water springs and it is sheltered from all directions.

The main (northern) anchorage is a little open, but is better than it looks on the chart. There is a path from the wharf to the lighthouse, which makes a pleasant walk of two hours, there and back. The wharf comprises open pilings, and is less than ideal for overnight moorage. Some years, a charter boat uses this wharf for day-trips on a fairly regular basis, but there was no such activity last time I was here.

Lower Sandy Point ★★ | 4 |

| A | NO FACILITIES

Charts: **4209**, 4241

Lower Sandy Point provides convenient anchorage if you arrive here late and don't want to spend another hour-and-a-half going north to Shelburne town. Just turn to starboard after you reach buoy "SAB," and tie up to any convenient fishing boat. There is about 8 feet (2.4 m) at low-water springs. There are no facilities either here or at McNutts Island.

Gunning Cove ★★ | 4 | | C |

NO FACILITIES

Charts: **4209**, 4241

The approaches to Gunning Cove, 1.5 miles west of Lower Sandy Point, are rather shallow, with less than 3 feet (1 m) at low-water springs. Consequently, the last time I visited this area with the intention of anchoring in Gunning Cove, I ended up at Sandy Point instead. Depending on the draft of your boat, you might think it a wise move, too.

Jordan Bay and Green Harbour

Chart 4241

Five miles northeast of McNutts Island, little Blue Island stands sentinel to two fingers of water leading north, Jordan Bay to the west, and Green Harbour to the east.

Jordan Bay, entered between Blue Island and Jordan Bay Gull Rock, offers good anchorage if the wind is offshore, but is untenable if the wind has any south in it. Gales from the south drive right into Jordan Bay and create heavy seas.

Lower Jordan Bay, a small harbor 2.5 miles west of Blue Island, is shallow, with only about 4 feet (1.2 m) at low-water springs, and I have never visited it. The entrance channel is buoyed along a course of 323°M.

Green Harbour, entered between Blue Island and Western Head, also is wide open to the south, and for this reason I have never anchored in there, either.

West Green Harbour, 1.4 miles north of Pattersons Point, has a public wharf providing shelter for small craft, and the channel is buoyed. But, once again, it is shallow, having only 3 feet (1 m) alongside at low-water springs.

Lockeport ★★★★ | 5 | | B |

Charts: **4240**, 4209

Lockeport looks a little intimidating from the chart, but is well marked and a lot easier to enter than you might think. It is not far off the beaten track, and perhaps deserves to be used more often. Protection, from a substantial breakwater capable of accommodating a storm surge of 10 feet (3 m), is complete in all winds, and this would not be a bad place to ride out a hurricane.

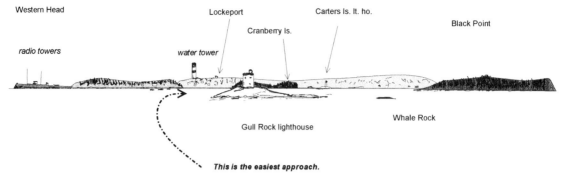

Western Head

radio towers

Lockeport

water tower

Cranberry Is.

Carters Is. lt. ho.

Black Point

Gull Rock lighthouse

Whale Rock

This is the easiest approach.

Entrance to Lockeport Harbour from one mile south of Gull Rock.

Even at the height of activity in the fishing industry, Lockeport Harbour was very clean, and it is now spotless. There are beautiful white sand beaches just feet from the wharf, though the water is cold. My children, being tougher than I am, have swum in it, however.

Approaches.   For some reason, the water in the approach is rather rough, possibly because of the irregular and rather shallow bottom. The flood sets east-to-west across the entrance, and the ebb the other way. The maximum rate is slightly less than 1 knot so it isn't likely to bother you much.

My loran indicates a position in this area 0.6 mile south of where I actually am. This could be hazardous to your health, so don't rely overly on those black boxes in this area.

From the west, approach Gull Rock lighthouse on any convenient heading. It is a house-like structure on a big rock, with the light (occulting every 10 seconds) on the roof. Old charts give a visibility range of only 8 miles for this light, but to me it has always seemed brighter, and the new chart gives a more realistic range of 14 miles.

If you're coming from Shelburne, you don't need to go all the way outside Bull Rock. The water half-a-mile south of Western Head is deep, and there are no obstructions. Unless you draw more than 15 feet (4.5 m), you don't need to take much notice of the spars south of Gull Rock either.

From just west of Gull Rock, a course of 025°M takes you right up the harbor. Don't pass on the wrong side of green spar "KK57" because

it marks the end of Chain Ledge. Leave it to port. The bell buoy "KK61" can be left to starboard, as long as you don't come too close to Round Rock, which always shows. Follow the spars when you come level with the south end of Cranberry Island and alter course there to 018°M.

When you get to bell buoy "KK69," which can be passed close on either side, turn west on to a course of 284°M. That will take you right to the harbor entrance. Carters Island, a small grassy island with a lighthouse on it, will be ahead of you on the approach to "KK69."

The east side of lower Lockeport Harbour—that is, the bay outside the artificial harbor—is full of drying rocks, but Cranberry Island is steep to except at its northern end, so keep to the west side of the harbor, preferably following the spars.

From the east, you can approach Lockeport Harbour through the Ram Island Passage, or from farther offshore. Ram Island Passage is shorter by several miles, which is no bad thing after a day spent beating to windward.

On the approach to Ram Island Passage, keep clear of Black Rock, which lies about one-third of a mile east of Hemeons Head, then come on to a course of about 285°M to take you midway between Ram Island and Hemeons Head. There is at least 12 feet (3.6 m) of water, and I've been through here against a 25-knot westerly without a lot of distress. Radar makes it easier to keep in the middle, though.

When you are clearly through the passage (when you can see breakers on Potter Ledge, south of Ram Island), head directly for Western Head on a course of 262°M. When you can see Carters Island clear of Black Point and bearing 342°M or more, you are clear of Black Point Rock. The rock is now marked by red buoy "KD62," which you should leave to starboard. Now you can head toward flashing green bell buoy "KK61," and follow the spar buoys to the harbor entrance as described above.

Spars "KK58" and "KE60" mark shoals with at least 12 feet (3.6 m) over them, so unless you have a megayacht you don't have to worry about them.

If you're approaching offshore from the east, you'll most easily find whistle buoy "K38" about 4 miles out to sea. Alternatively, you can try to find red buoy "KE52" 2 miles closer in. But this small buoy is a bit difficult to see in a slop or in poor visibility.

From "K38," steer 346°M all the way in to "KK61." You will pass red bell buoy "KE56," green spar "KE57," west cardinal "KE," and red spar "KE60." The only thing you can hit is Whale Rock, drying 5 feet (1.5 m), a half-mile to port, midway between "KE56" and "KE57."

From "KE52," if you can find it, steer 316°M to "KE." Don't go north of "KE52," because there is a reef a mile-and-a-quarter long extending from Ram Island, on which the chart shows a wreck—though I can't recall ever having seen one there.

The sea breaks around almost all the rocks in the approaches to Lockeport, perhaps from the continuous swell, so you're not likely to hit anything in decent visibility. I was peacefully tied up in Lockeport one day when I was hailed by the owner of a 40-foot (12-m) French catamaran, a man called Oliver, who had sailed it from the Caribbean.

"Is this Lockeport?" he asked.

On being told it was indeed, he explained that his Michelin road map didn't show any rocks, so when he was approaching the coast he asked a fisherman for directions. He thought the entrance easy, as you could see all the breaking rocks. Mind you, his craft drew only 3 feet (1 m), so you might need to be a little more circumspect with your boat. I've had no problem entering here at night, however, and have done it a number of times in thick fog.

The Coast Guard changed all the buoys in 1993, so be sure your chart is up-to-date.

Anchorage, Dockage. Having reached Carters Island, you'll encounter no problems entering the harbor itself. There are numerous wharves. A new marina was built in 1996, just south of the Clearwater plant, which is the best place to tie up. If your boat is more than 40 feet long, or the marina is full, use the south side of the public wharf. There are shallow areas in the harbor—see the sketch chart for details.

You may be tempted to anchor in here because the harbor is nearly half-a-mile square, but I'd advise against it as the holding ground is poor, and the very size of the harbor allows a considerable chop to build up. Although Lockeport has been seriously affected by the decline in the East Coast fisheries, large vessels still occasionally go to the Clearwater fish plant on the western side of the harbor.

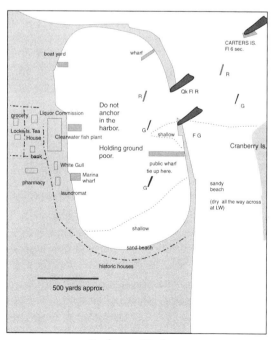

Lockeport Harbour.

Ashore. There is a bank, a liquor store, a drug store, a laundromat, a grocery, and a hardware store handy to the marina. With the marina, and the much-improved grocery store just one block away, Lockeport is now an excellent stop to provision. In 1996, you weren't charged to stay at the marina if you had a meal at the White Gull, a restaurant at the marina. Two blocks away there's a very acceptable restaurant called The Locke Island Tea House.

For some reason, possibly to do with the amount of steel in the public dock, you may notice that your compass shows 40 degrees of deviation when you tie up here. If you have a steel boat, and stay more than a day or two, you might want to check the residual deviation.

Lockeport is one of the few places in this part of Nova Scotia where you will find able-bodied adults hanging round on street corners. While I have never been panhandled here, I have found this a little disconcerting, even though I am more or less a native. It might be enlightening if I explain the situation.

Since about 1990, the numbers of so-called groundfish (cod especially, but also haddock, redfish, and so on) in this area have dwindled catastrophically. The inevitable result was that the Canadian government closed almost this entire fishery, resulting in massive unemployment in Newfoundland, the Eastern Shore of Nova Scotia, and a few spots like Lockeport. Most of western Nova Scotia has been relatively little affected by this, but Lockeport, 30-odd miles by road from the next community of any size, was badly hit. The major employer here was a groundfish processing plant employing 400 people. But Lockeport refuses to die. Last time I was there, it showed signs of rebirth—a few new businesses, and a little rekindling of the fishery for non-traditional species.

The laundromat and the liquor store are the closest to the wharf anywhere along this coast.

I'm sure any purchases made by visiting boats will be welcomed.

The upper reaches of Lockeport Harbour are, unfortunately, wide open to the south, and rather encumbered with unmarked rocks.

Sable River ★★

NO FACILITIES

Charts: **4240**, 4213

If you still have an old copy of chart 4213, it shows this section of coast in much better detail than does chart 4240. East of Lockeport the coast becomes much more sparsely inhabited, and for the next 25 miles there is scarcely a house visible from offshore. There are few outlying dangers, except Bantam Rock in the middle of the entrance to Sable River, and the sea always seems fairly calm here.

Approaches. The mouth of the Sable River has a shallow bar with a minimum depth of 3 feet (1 m), leading to a winding channel that is completely unmarked and not suitable for any deep-draft vessel.

Little Harbour lies on the west side of the entrance. It might be useable on a calm night, but it's open to the east and has only 5 feet (1.5 m) at low water.

Jones Harbour, on the east side, is similarly shallow and unmarked. There is a conspicuous building on the south point of Harding Island which makes it easier to locate Jones Harbour.

Little Port l'Hebert ★★★

 NO FACILITIES

Charts: **4240**, 4213

Determined gunkholers might want to try Little Port l'Hebert, which is entered about 1 mile east of Harding Island. Beware of the unmarked rock 400 yards to the southwest of Green Island. It is much easier to enter this harbor with chart 4213 than the newer 4240.

There is between 6 and 12 feet (2 and 4 m) in this anchorage, and it's reasonably well protected, except from easterly gales. A long spit extends from the southern side of the entrance. Neither this place nor the other two mentioned above should be visited in any but the clearest conditions. There are no facilities.

Port l'Hebert ★★★

 4   **B**   NO FACILITIES

Charts: **4240,** 4212

Port l'Hebert (pronounced "lebear") is fairly easy to enter, but is better shown on old chart 4212 than on new chart 4240. There is a lot of swell in the entrance and I wouldn't try this place in a southerly gale. It might be a little tricky at night, too, unless it's clear and calm.

Approaches. From fairway buoy "UX," a course of 008°M brings you right up the middle of the entrance to a small lighthouse on a shingle beach. On your starboard side is a long white shingle beach, and to port is a big hill called

Richardsons Head on the old charts and Tillys Head on the new ones. Favor the east side going in, keeping the green spar and flashing green buoy "UX55" to port. When you have passed "UX55," veer to port and keep in the middle.

There is a tidal stream of 1.5 knots in the entrance, but it sets straight in or out. High water

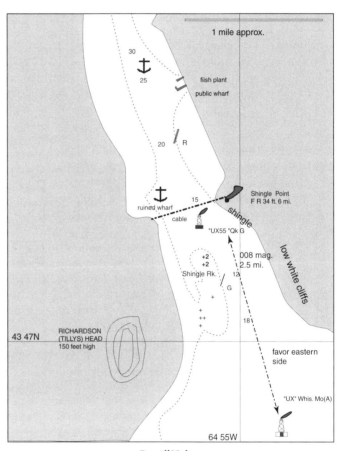

Port l'Hebert.

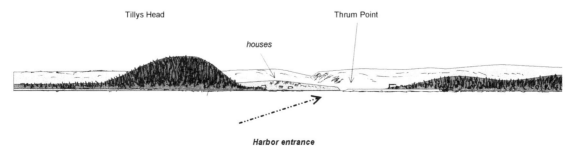

Port l'Hebert from two miles to the southwest.

here comes at the same time as it does in Liverpool. Above the fish plant, the harbor widens out and becomes shallow and winding, with poor shelter. The upper reaches are much more suited to ducks than boats. Shelter around the stretch of river by the fish plant is quite reasonable.

Anchorage. There is a reasonable anchorage just north of a ruined wharf on the west side of the river, where one of the few local boats has a mooring; or you may anchor just north of the fish plant. You could also tie up to the wharf here, but there is not a lot of room. Whether the fish plant is operating or not seems to depend on the availability of government grants. They seem to be scarce, because the plant is not in operation much. Consequently, there's little noise or pollution here, but riding lights are advisable. The settlement of East Side Port l'Hebert is remote even by road, so there are no facilities there.

The Coast Between Port l'Hebert and Port Mouton

Port Joli, the next harbor east of Port l'Hebert, is completely open to the south, and essentially offers no shelter.

Two miles east-southeast of Port Joli Head, Little Hope Island tops an undersea hill. I've never known whether this particularly bleak island was named after a fellow called Hope, or if it has the more obvious meaning, namely that there's little hope for you if you hit the thing. It is a concrete tower on a pile of rocks. There are fringing reefs extending almost a half-mile to the south, and slightly less in other directions. You can hear the surf a long way off. It's all right to pass inside it in any reasonable weather, but give it a wide berth. The lighthouse makes an excellent radar target, but has no sound signal. There is a whistle buoy a mile to the south, though. This is hard to hear if you are coming from the west, and not a lot of use if you are coming from the east.

Port Mouton ★★★★★

Charts: **4240,** 4212

You wouldn't know from its name that Port Mouton is one of the most beautiful ports in the province. Champlain, in more mundane mood, named it for a sheep that fell overboard. The locals, incidentally, call it "Port Muhtoon."

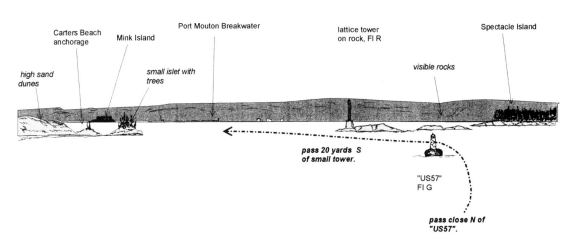

Approach from the south-southeast to Carters Beach and southwest Port Mouton.

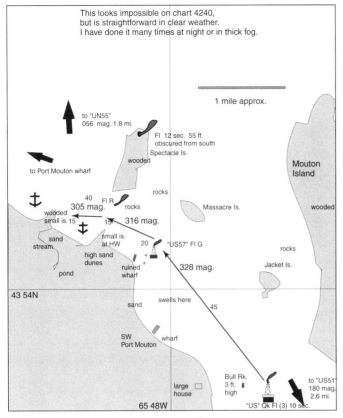

This looks impossible on chart 4240, but is straightforward in clear weather. I have done it many times at night or in thick fog.

1 mile approx.

to "UN55" 056 mag. 1.8 mi.

Fl 12 sec. 55 ft. obscured from south

Spectacle Is.

wooded

to Port Mouton wharf

Mouton Island

wooded

rocks

40 Fl R rocks

305 mag.

wooded small is.15

316 mag.

Massacre Is.

sand stream

small is. at HW

20

"US57" Fl G

high sand dunes

ruined wharf

+ +

328 mag.

rocks

Jacket Is.

pond

43 54N

sand

swells here

45

SW Port Mouton

wharf

large house

Bull Rk. 3 ft. high

to "US51" 180 mag. 2.6 mi.

65 48W

"US" Qk Fl (3) 10 sec.

Port Mouton anchorage.

Approaches. Chart 4240 is misleading in this area in some respects. For example, it looks impossible from the chart for a boat to pass to the south of Spectacle Island, but it is in fact very straightforward—and a valuable shortcut if you're coming from the west.

When I approach from the west, I always use the Western Channel. From whistle buoy "U36," south of Little Hope Island, steer 032°M to bell buoy "US51" off Port Mouton Head. From there, a course of 000°M brings you to the east cardinal buoy "US" off Bull Rock. Pass close to the east of "US," then come to 328°M and head toward flashing green buoy "US57."

Bull Rock always shows, and my radar usually picks it up. There are no real hazards in the entry until you reach Bull Rock, and I have never had any problem from the sea state in the entrance. My loran is not accurate here, however, and indicates a position at least 600 yards south of where

I actually am. This would tend to put you solidly on Port Mouton Head, which has a rather nasty set of outlying rocks.

Even if there is thick fog at sea, by mid-morning the fog usually lifts inland of Bull Rock, and the rest of the approach is clear. If the wind is southwesterly, the land seems to refract it, so that after you've rounded Bull Point, the breeze turns to the west-northwest, warms up nearly 20°F (12°C), and increases in strength. There are many times I have come in here, running before a gentle 10-knot southwesterly, only to have my boat turned on its ear by a 35-knot blast from the northwest after rounding this corner. This can cause more excitement than you might like if you have a spinnaker up. Many southeast-facing harbors do this if the land is hot, but rarely to the extent that this one does. There is always a swell off the beach at South West Port Mouton, just north of Bull Point, so if you want the best anchorage you have to go farther in.

Pass close east of "US57," come to 316°M, and pass about 20 yards south of the small tower with the flashing red light on it. There is at least 16 feet (4.8 m) on this track at low-water springs. All the local boats use it constantly.

If you're approaching from the east, a course of 254°M from Western Head takes you about a half-mile off White Point. There is a conspicuous large building just east of this point, at the |resort called White Point Lodge. From this position off White Point, steer 280°M to bell buoy "UN55." From there, steer 236°M for the anchorage, keeping the small lighthouse on Spectacle Island to port. The only problem in the dark is the aquaculture cage just west of Spectacle Island.

There is no tide to speak of here. The only hazards are some rocks 100 yards or so off White Point, and Brazil Rocks, east of Port Mouton Island. The sea breaks on all these hazards and the surf can easily be heard.

99

Although some of the old books recommend you go east around Port Mouton Island in bad weather, when coming from the west, I suspect the authors haven't actually tried this. Running before a southwesterly gale, rounding Devastation Shoal and Brazil Rocks, and then beating back into Port Mouton after having jibed, with the rocks of White Point just ahead of you, is a lot more work than running up the western channel into progressively smoother water.

This harbor is well marked with lighted buoys, so entry at night presents no special problems, though entry in fog without radar may not be so straightforward.

Anchorage. Carters Beach, or Wobamkek Beach on the old charts, is one of the prettiest in the province, comparable to Roque Island, Maine.

Once you've left the small tower with the flashing red light about 20 yards on your starboard side, anchor anywhere off the beach on your port hand, or off the next one up. Small Carters Island separates these two beaches, and on the south side of this island a small stream runs into the sea. There is fine white sand, and the beach extends about 2 miles to the southeast, back as far as Bull Point.

Anchorage is in fine sand, in depths of 15 to 25 feet (4.5 to 7.5 m). It's wise to keep out of the stream of traffic traveling between the tower and Mink Island. There used to be 20 fishing boats going past every morning at 0500, but the fishing cutbacks have reduced this number considerably. The holding ground is generally good, but the fine sand is sometimes a little unreliable, so make sure your anchor is well dug in before you go off to the beach.

The anchorage is open to the northeast, but this is a rare wind in summer, and I can only recall having had to move twice in the 30 or so times I have anchored here. If you have to move, Port Mouton Harbour is only 1 mile away. This

has become a popular anchorage by Nova Scotia standards. Twenty years ago you could anchor here for a week and not see another boat, but in summer there's now at least one boat here every night. Because of the nocturnal fishing boat traffic, a riding light is essential here.

Ashore. Although this is one of the most beautiful beaches in Nova Scotia, it's rare to see more than a dozen people on it. South of the small tower are sand dunes 50 feet (15 m) high, with spectacular views from their tops. My children used to call this the sand mountain, and got very upset if we sailed past it without stopping for a day or two. You can paddle through the little stream at low tide, or take a dinghy across at high tide. The water is fresh and warm, in marked contrast to that of the sea, which never exceeds 50°F (10°C) and is usually colder. Near the head of this little stream there is a pond deep enough for swimming. It is overlooked from the south by a big rock that bears a remarkable resemblance to a grinning frog. On a sunny day, the white sand and the turquoise water look almost like the Caribbean—though this illusion won't last long if you put your toes in the water.

Port Mouton Wharf

Chart: Inset 4240

If the wind starts to blow from the northeast while you're at Carters Beach, Port Mouton Harbour offers shelter just 1 mile to the north.

Approaches. From the anchorage at Carters Beach, pass to the east of Mink Island, whence a course of 320°M brings you to entrance buoy "UN59." The channel to follow is the one to port as you go in. Follow the spars and buoys exactly, as there are shoals and rockpiles all over this harbor. There are two public wharves, and you can usually tie up alongside somewhere. There is a lifeboat station here (the building with the tall radio mast), and if in doubt, ask for advice. The other channels are a little shallow for the average yacht. The dock in Port Mouton is very well protected and you could ride out any gale here. The rise and fall of tide is about 8 feet (2.4 m) at springs, and high tide occurs at the same time as it does in Halifax.

Ashore. There is a convenience store at the head of the wharf—just follow the road and turn right. You can row your dinghy to it if you prefer. You'll find another one further along the same way, if you go as far as the Halifax road and turn right again. There is a small restaurant here also.

Five miles toward Halifax (if you can get transport) is Summerville Beach Provincial Park. It has a good restaurant, The Quarterdeck, with a spectacular view. White Point Lodge is about 2 miles farther on.

Port Mouton Island

Chart: 4240

Fifteen years ago there was a substantial house on Port Mouton Island, but I haven't seen it lately, and it may have burned down. Like many similar offshore islands, this was once inhabited year-round, and supported a small farm.

The island offers no sheltered anchorage, but on a calm day the beach at the northwest end can be cautiously approached for an interesting ex-

ploration ashore. This would be easier if you had an old copy of chart 4212.

Hunts Landing ★★

NO FACILITIES

Chart: 4240

This is a very small, crowded harbor 3 miles east of Port Mouton and 1 mile west of White Point. It can be approached by steering 020°M toward the end of the wharf. Any other approach risks hitting unmarked rocks. A few local fishermen tie their boats between the two breakwaters. Because there is always a swell here, they occasionally have ropes strung across the entrance. Because of the lack of room, I doubt that you'd be welcomed here with open arms.

Liverpool Bay

Charts: **4379,** 4240

Liverpool Bay can be approached safely from any convenient direction. There are fringing rocks all around Western Head, but they do not extend more than 100 yards offshore. The Sow and Pigs, a half-mile south of Moose Point, extend eastward about 500 yards.

Western Head is a bad place for gill nets, which

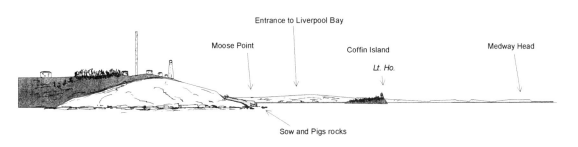

Approaches to Liverpool from the south.

101

are impossible to see at night, and difficult to avoid by day. Particularly if you have a boat with a propeller on a strut, it would be as well to keep at least 1 mile offshore. Be aware that any chart of Liverpool Bay, including large-scale chart 4379, is based on a survey done 25 years ago or more.

Moose Harbour ★★

NO FACILITIES

Charts: 4211, 4240, 4379

Moose Harbour is a real hole-in-the-wall that pops up as you turn the corner from a westerly direction into Liverpool Bay. It lies at Moose Point, and there is currently a flashing green buoy just outside. The Coast Guard has changed the configuration of this buoy three times in the last 15 years, so it may not be green when you see it. If you draw 5 feet (1.5 m) or less, this can be a useful spot if you are fed up with beating to windward.

Approaches. Round buoy "UB1" on the correct side, (currently leaving it to port), and aim for the end of the breakwater, which should also be on your port hand. There is a pile of rocks at the base of the breakwater that sticks out about 10 feet (3 m). If you aim for the middle of the entrance you should be all right. There is a fog signal, but it's on the west side of the harbor, about 30 yards from the entrance. If you aim for this from buoy "UB1," you'll hit something. There is about 5 feet (1.5 m) in the entrance, and the same depth in the harbor, at low-water springs. There should be room to tie up alongside one of the fishing boats.

I once managed to get 100 gallons (378 liters) of fuel here when I couldn't get it in Liverpool. But you would have to be made of sterner stuff than I am to attempt this harbor at night.

Liverpool ★★ 4 A

🍽 🛒 📷 🔧

Charts: **4379,** 4211, 4240

Liverpool is a decent-size town with all the usual stores within easy walking distance of the wharf. There are taverns and restaurants, mostly of the "good ol' boy" variety—as befits a place that gave the world Hank Snow Jr.

The latest publication from the Nova Scotia Department of Tourism mentions a marina at Liverpool, but I have not yet found it. There is even a telephone number—(902) 354-5741—which, I think, relates to the small slipway just above the fixed bridge.

30 yards approx.

"UB1" Fl G

6

Fl G

rocks
2

5

rubble
at base
of breakwater

fog signal is here

5

fish plant

wharf

5

4

Moose Harbour

Approaches. From offshore fairway whistle buoy "UM," set a course of 328°M to bring you to inner fairway bell "UMA," halfway between Moose Point and Coffin Island. From there, a course of 318°M fetches bell buoy "UM53" at the entrance to the harbor proper.

A tidal stream setting northeast can cause you to pile up on the rocks on Forbes Point, which is not far from this track. I did this once myself. For this reason, it is safer to favor the port side going in. If there is thick fog outside, it often clears halfway up the bay. You will also be able to smell the pulp mill at Brooklyn that, despite having the most up-to-date technology in North America, still manages to advertise its presence several miles downwind.

As it does in Port Mouton, the wind often swirls around the land, so that there can be a steady south-westerly outside, and a gusty west-northwesterly inside. Occasionally the heat from the land hits you with a great blast. This is not entirely unwelcome if the fog outside has been of the drippy, freezing-cold variety.

On the way in, there is a public wharf at Brooklyn, just east of the mill. There is a new marina at Brooklyn, which might be a better spot than Liverpool, though it is two miles from the town. I haven't tried it myself.

At "UM53," turn to 270°M and follow the buoyed channel in. The lighthouse at Fort Point is no longer in operation. Once you are past it, however, all the spars are red and should be left to starboard. I mostly seem to arrive here in mid-afternoon or later, when the sun is right in my eyes. When that happens, you can't see the color of the spars. Just remember, they're red. You will go aground if you get out of the buoyed channel.

The channel offers at least 12 feet (3.6 m) at low-water springs. You'd think a healthy swell would run in from the east, but I've spent some time here waiting for breaks in easterly gales and never thought the swell too bad.

On the south side of the river are the premises of Steel and Engine Products, an Irving subsidiary. Large vessels are usually undergoing repair on the marine railway. There are occasionally similar-size structures moored in the river, all of which should be passed with caution.

The Mersey River drains the largest lake in the province, Lake Rossignol. The tidal stream at the bridge is in a permanent state of ebb, and if it has been raining a lot, it runs strongly. It is difficult to approach the dock under sail for this reason.

Dockage. Tying up at the wharf is a difficult business. Mersey Sea Products, which has a plant adjacent to the government wharf, has for the last 15 years or so frequently had a large and almost derelict stern trawler tied up to the handiest spot, occupying half the available space. The inside of the wharf is always occupied by trawlers coming and going, so if you can't find a place to tie up to,

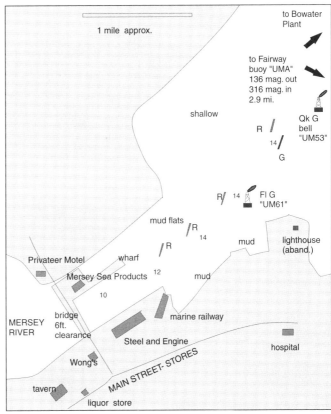

Town of Liverpool.

make fast to the derelict trawler if it is there.

Ashore. It is almost impossible to get fuel here. The large oil storage depot at the head of the wharf won't sell it to you; the service station on the west side of the bridge doesn't have diesel; and the nearest service station that does have diesel is a mile to the east. There is a conspicuous sign on the fish plant that no small amounts of ice are available.

In contrast, I have found the stores at Steel and Engine Products quite helpful for engine parts, filters, and the like. There is traffic on the bridge all night, and the town's rowdier elements seem to get their jollies from making tires squeal at 0300. In all fairness, though, I have to say that I have never been hassled at the wharf by drunks or other forms of lowlife.

One of the better Chinese restaurants, Wong's, is located southwest of the bridge. The Privateer Motel, just the other side of the road from the government dock, is a little more sedate.

Just over the bridge from the wharf is a small park with tourist information. The upper reaches of the Mersey River are picturesque. If it hasn't been raining too hard, an outboard-powered dinghy can ascend the river for several miles.

It seems a pity that the town's disadvantages outweigh its convenient location, its compact town center, the ease of access to stores, and so on. Perhaps one day the town fathers will wake up to the economic benefits to be gained from making the place a bit more attractive to visiting yachts. Maybe some grants from the government trough (in the name of tourism) will be the catalyst.

Coffin Island ★★★

NO FACILITIES

Charts: **4379, 4211**

Most boats bound east after leaving Liverpool will go outside Coffin Island. The course from the outer buoy to Cape LaHave is about 068°M. But it is possible for boats drawing less than 5 feet (1.5 m), to cut inside Coffin Island. The best water is about a quarter-mile off the mainland. I wouldn't recommend this inner passage, however, if there were much of an onshore breeze.

For those adventurous souls whose boats draw less than 5 feet (1.5 m), there is a delightful anchorage at the north end of Coffin Island. Let me stress, though, that the harbor should only be en-

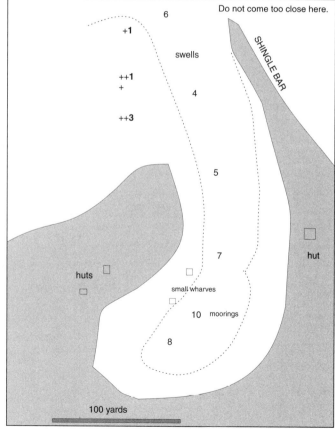

Coffin Island.

tered on a calm day. I would never attempt it in fog or at night. The configuration of the bar may change in severe storms, so the following instructions should be used with caution.

Approaches. Identify the shingle bar that protrudes from the northeast corner of the island, and give it a good berth if you are coming from the east. Enter the harbor on a heading of about 200°M, favoring the western side, but avoiding the drying rocks farther west. There is always a little swell in the entrance. The last time I was here, it was dead low water. Contrary to what chart 4379 indicates, I found at least 4 feet (1.2 m) all the way in. My boat draws 4 feet 8 inches (1.45 m), and she didn't scrape bottom. Inside, a pool deepens to a minimum depth of 8 feet (2.4 m) and although a couple of moorings were revealed, I tied up to one of the small wharves.

Ashore. You will almost certainly share this place only with the abundant bird life. There is a half-mile path to the lighthouse.

Eagle Head and West Berlin

These pretty little harbors, lying on the mainland between Wolfs Point and Blueberry Point, are be-

set by numerous unmarked reefs that have deterred me from visiting by boat. They are both open to the south, but offer shelter behind the small government wharves.

Medway Harbour

Medway Harbour is extensive, but most of it is less than 12 feet (3.6 m) deep. It is also one of those places where the Coast Guard has whims about the buoyage, and it can be very disconcerting to find—as I did one recent summer—that none of the spars is on your chart. The upper reaches of all the coves in Medway Harbour are full of unmarked rocks, not all of which are on the chart.

Approaches. Medway Harbour is simple enough to enter in clear weather, because Medway Head has a distinct and unusual profile. In restricted visibility, though, it needs considerable thought.

From outer buoy "UA51," which has a bell, not a whistle as you might imagine, steer 012°M. On your port hand, the shore between East Berlin and Medway Head is a writhing mass of unmarked rocks. There is a small harbor here called Long Cove, but getting in and out would certainly defeat me. To avoid these hazards, keep Medway

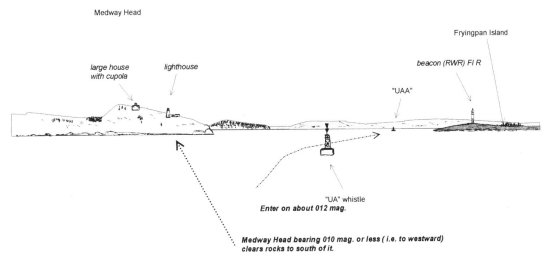

Entrance to Medway Harbour.

Head bearing less than 010°M on your approach.

To starboard, there is first the inner south cardinal whistle buoy "UA," then a flashing red light on a small lattice tower on Fryingpan Island. Then, dead ahead, you'll find bifurcation buoy "UAA."

Once you're past Fryingpan Island, favor the western side. I was once beating out of here in thick fog in a boat with no radar. The breeze was fairly stiff, and I was relying on the depth-sounder to keep me out of trouble. But the rocks on the west side of Toby Island go from 40 feet to 0 in about two boatlengths, and I hit something. Fortunately, after tacking the boat immediately, I got off. I would therefore advise you to keep to the west side once you are inside Medway Head.

Port Medway ★★★

Port Medway is probably the best anchorage in the harbor. There is also a substantial wharf here, and usually room to tie up.

Approaches. From buoy "UAA," turn to 300°M and go straight to the end of the wharf. If you draw less than 7 feet (2.1 m), Middle Ledge, half-a-mile northwest of "UAA," is the only thing you can hit. Pass south of flashing red buoy "UA64" marking Fosters Islands.

If you prefer to anchor, carry on a bit farther and drop your hook a little way west of the old ruined wharf. This is a bit open if it is blowing hard from between west and northwest, when anchoring just east of the village is preferable. The adventurous might try going a bit farther up the Medway River.

Ashore. Port Medway is a pretty little community, alas reduced to a shadow of its former self by the decline in the fishery. There are two convenience stores, and you might be able to get fuel and ice at the fish plant.

Voglers Cove

Voglers Cove has two wharves separated by Calf Point. The wharf northwest of the point is easier to get to, but the wharf to the east offers better shelter. There is not a lot of room at either place if the fishing fleet—or what remains of it—is in. If that's the case, Port Medway is a better bet.

Approaches. You'll need to pay sharp attention while approaching Voglers Cove because the navigation is intricate. I wouldn't recommend that you try to enter here in poor visibility. The east wharf has an uncharted drying rock about 15 feet (4.5 m) from its outside end, which could present

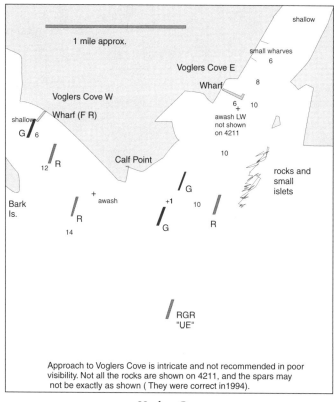

Voglers Cove.

a major problem if you approach the end of the wharf from any direction other than parallel to it.

Anchorage. It may be possible to anchor in the cove a little distance to the north.

Ashore. There is a small convenience store just east of the east wharf whose owner is very obliging. He's looking to retire, though, and may not be in business when you get there.

The best-maintained parts of both these wharves are the large and expensive signs proclaiming in both official languages that the wharves are operated by the Small Craft Harbours Division of the Federal Department of Fisheries. You'd think it might be more appropriate to use the wood to repair the wharves, which were not in the greatest shape in 1994.

Port Medway to Cape LaHave

Apple Cove, Cherry Cove, and Broad Cove are small harbors east of Port Medway. All are shallow, with less than 6 feet (1.8 m) at low-water springs, and for that reason I have never visited them by boat. If you can reach them by land, though, you'll find them to be attractive little communities.

For Green Bay and Crooked Channel, see Region 3.

Cape LaHave to Peggys Cove

Riverport at the mouth of LaHave River

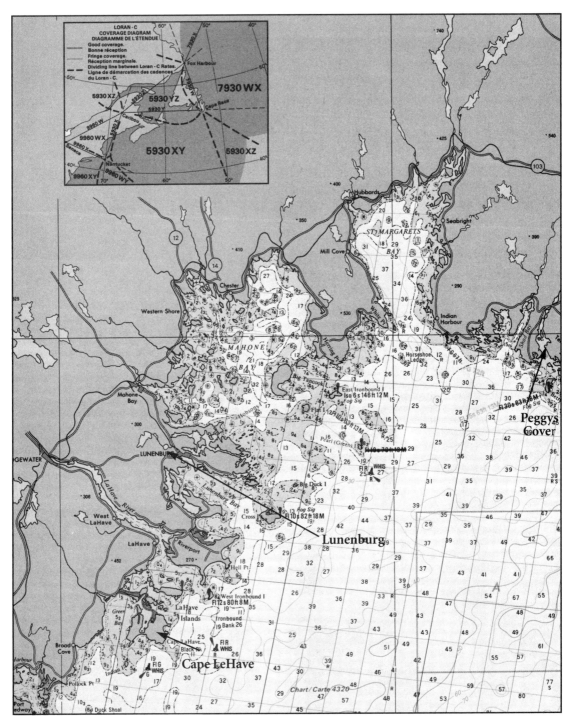

Based on CHS Chart 4012. Not to be used for navigation.

This region encompasses the LaHave Islands and the LaHave River, Lunenburg Bay, Mahone Bay, and Saint Margarets Bay. Lunenburg County, the major part of this region, was settled originally by Protestants from Germany in the 1780s, and many family and place names are of German origin, though in Nova Scotia these are often called "Dutch." Lunenburg itself takes its name from the German town of Lüneburg, on the River Elbe. Many small farms and heritage buildings make this a visually attractive area, and it is the most popular yachting area in the province.

Although Lunenburg is the home of the largest fish-processing plant in North America, and is the center of the offshore fishery, the fishing industry does not dominate the whole area in the way it does further west. There are traditional fishing communities on the LaHave Islands, at Nova Scotia's largest remaining island community (Big Tancook Island), and at a few other small places. Lunenburg's fisheries museum and picturesque waterfront make it a harbor that no cruise to Nova Scotia should omit. Forestry and Michelin Tires constitute the major industries in the hinterland of the western part of the region, though from the coast these activities are not apparent. The eastern portion of this area is increasingly populated by commuters working in Halifax.

While easy access to the metropolitan area has caused major waterfront development, by Nova Scotian standards at least, there are still many uninhabited islands and anchorages, including some of my favorites. The process of waterfront development, whereby wealthy non-natives buy up desirable property and inflate its value beyond the reach of most locals, is not unique to this area but it has been going on here longer than anywhere else in the province. As in most other areas where this occurs, relationships between natives and non-natives are sometimes strained. You will still find unrestricted access to any beach in this area, however, at least if you arrive by boat. No self-respecting Nova Scotian would take kindly to any "come-from-away" telling him or her: "You can't picnic on my beach." Any portion of the beach below the high-water mark in the province is Crown land, or public property—a right jealously guarded by the natives, and protected by provincial and federal legislation. High-profile outsiders occasionally contest this long-standing right of access, but the locals' displeasure usually wins out in such confrontations. Most of the more secluded private palaces are on points of land and rocky crags that are, in any case, not very accessible by dinghy, thus reducing potential confrontations.

While the right of access across private property from a beach to a public road is not quite as clear-cut legally, and has rarely been tested in court, I can't imagine any rural Nova Scotian objecting to your landing a dinghy and quietly walking to a road. If you see a native, it would be well to pass the time of day, and ask permission, just so you are not mistaken for a drug smuggler. As a minor waterfront landowner myself, all I ask is that you don't leave a mess.

This is the one area of the province where it is easy to find provisions and boat-repair facilities. Bridgewater is the commercial center of the western part of this region, with respectable-size towns at Lunenburg and Mahone Bay. Repair facilities can be found in the LaHave River, Lunenburg, Chester, and Saint Margarets Bay.

Passage East of Cape LaHave

If you are bound east of Mahone Bay, your course now passes a little farther offshore, as Mahone and St. Margarets Bays form a large bight some 50 miles in extent.

From whistle buoy "T34," 3.5 miles east-south-east of Cape LaHave, courses to the following destinations are:

LaHave River: 358°M, 4 miles.
Entrance to Lunenburg Harbour: 038°M, 9 miles.
Entrance to Mahone Bay: 048°M, 14 miles.
Prospect Bay: 070°M, 28 miles.
Entrance to Halifax Harbour and points east: 088°M, 38 miles.

111

Tidal currents are not strong here. They affect your course only at entrances to the largest bays. The outside courses are quite a long way offshore and often out of sight of land. They're also in the shipping lanes used by large vessels en route from Halifax to the U.S., so you should keep a good lookout.

The LaHave Islands ★★★★★

   NO FACILITIES

Charts: 4384, 4394

Chart 4384 covers the area from Cape LaHave to Lunenburg. It does not show the spar buoys in the LaHave Islands, but you can certainly get to Bridgewater with it. Chart 4394 shows the northern part of the LaHave Islands and the entrance to the river, which is a handy thing to have if you are traversing the islands. Charts 4395 and 4391 are large-scale plans of the river that I have never had. Chart 4320 is for coasting from Cape LaHave to Ship Harbour, and not really suitable for entering harbors, though you could get by with it in a pinch.

The LaHave Islands, a scenic group, were connected to the mainland in 1973 by a road and a bridge. There was, at that time, a plan to make the islands a national park. Naturally, as is usual in these matters, the two or three hundred permanent inhabitants were not consulted, and later raised vigorous objections to having their land confiscated for the benefit of tourists from central Canada. They didn't really want a bridge either, certainly not one like the bridge that's there now. Although the bridge was eventually built, the plans for the park were shelved.

The first European inhabitants of these islands were German-speaking, part of the influx of the late eighteenth century that settled Lunenburg county. Most of the inhabitants have Germanic-sounding names even now, though German as a spoken language died out here early this century.

A fixed bridge with a clearance of 22 feet (6.7 m) now connects Bush and Bell Islands, effectively cutting off the easiest passage through the islands for boats with masts. It is still possible to pass through the islands via other routes, though, if your boat draws less than 5 feet (1.5 m).

There are dozens of potential anchorages in the LaHave Islands, and I certainly can't claim to have visited them all. The buoyage consists of spars and the occasional stake, and the markings can be quite eccentric. If I am unsure of the channel, I stop and sound out the best route in the dinghy, and I suggest you do the same.

In the Bell Channel, the (relatively) deep water is between mud banks covered with eelgrass, and the edges of the channel are difficult to find. If you can see the top of the eelgrass, and it is bent over, you will definitely run aground. Because the eelgrass grows in great profusion everywhere around the islands, it is perhaps one of the few places in which a Danforth-type anchor may be more reliable because the sharp points of its flukes penetrate better.

The LaHave Islands are the worst place in the province for gill nets, and you should be on the lookout for them in the approaches. Fishing boats are on the go at all hours of the day and night, so riding lights are essential. There are no stores on the islands, and no fuel or water except possibly at the wharf by the bridge at Bush Island. Fresh fish can be bought at the plant at the wharf. On a quiet day, you can anchor just about anywhere in the islands, but with a stiff fog breeze, one has to be more circumspect. My charts show some of the places I have found satisfactory, but there are no doubt more places to be found by the adventurous, especially if you have a shoal-draft boat.

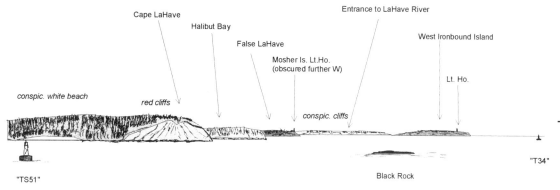

Cape LaHave

Halibut Bay

False LaHave

Entrance to LaHave River

West Ironbound Island

Mosher Is. Lt.Ho.
(obscured further W)

Lt. Ho.

conspic. white beach

red cliffs

conspic. cliffs

"TS51"

Black Rock

"T34"

The LaHave Islands from the south.

Approaching the LaHave Islands from the West

Cape LaHave is a bold headland that cannot be mistaken. In most lights it looks reddish, but when you get up close, it seems to turn gray. This part of the coast is not well lit, and there is a permanently dry ledge (Black Rock) 1 mile to the southeast. This ledge is not lit, and at night or in thick fog can be extremely dangerous. I usually follow a course between the ledge and the cape when going east, and while this route is quite clear and unobstructed, you must be sure you know where the rock is. You'd think the last thing you'd see here would be a large vessel, but I came within 30 feet (9 m) of colliding with a tug towing a large barge here one foggy night, so I cannot stress enough the importance of keeping a good lookout. Naturally, technology such as radar makes this a great deal easier. Big swells are frequent here, and though they are usually benign they can be alarming to the inexperienced. They have never prevented me from entering the anchorages.

Apart from Black Rock, the swells, the concentration of gill nets, and the resident population of whales, there are no other hazards in this approach.

Crooked Channel

I would enter Crooked Channel from the west only in the clearest of conditions. There is a large drying ledge to port on the way in, which usually shows. There is plenty of water for the average yacht at low water, but if the banks are covered, you can very easily go aground. On this approach, if you can clearly see both sides of the bridge at Bush Island and you steer about 068°M, you won't hit anything until you are actually in the islands. If you want to go farther than the bridge, the easiest way around is through Wolfe Gut, which carries about 5 feet (1.5 m) at low-water springs, and is marked. The markings may not be the same from year to year, though, and may even be missing, so if you get confused, do what I do: Anchor and sound out the deepest water from the dinghy. The channel south of Tumblin Island, which leads to Cape Bay, certainly looks interesting, but I have never done it. The best state of the tide for traversing these shallow channels is just after low water, when you can see all the banks.

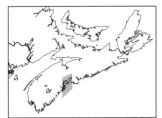

Petite Riviere

Chart: 4384

On the mainland to the west of the islands, across the head of Green Bay, is Petite Riviere. The entrance to the river is not charted, and isn't really accessible to deep-draft boats, but is notable as the site of Covey Island Boatworks, the best boatbuilders in the province. The owner, John Steele, started this operation on Covey Island (see page 115), but limited access there forced him to move to the mainland. The firm specializes in epoxy-saturated wooden boats. Whenever I visit this yard I have mixed feelings about my own frozen-snot vessel. However much I try, and however much less maintenance she requires than does a wooden boat, I cannot consider fiberglass in any way aesthetically pleasing.

At present, the yard is involved in planning a replacement for the *Bluenose,* a symbol of the province, which was built in the traditional cheap-and-dirty fashion of the province's workboats. Now, after 30 years, she's falling apart.

Fancy composite spars of spruce and carbon fiber are also being made at the boatworks and exported to the Sultan of Bahrain as replacement spars for a fleet of racing dhows. A visit to John Steele's yard is always fascinating, and well worth the difficulty of the journey.

Halibut Bay ★★★

B   NO FACILITIES

Chart: 4384

This anchorage on the east side of Cape LaHave Island appears to be wide open to incoming ocean swells, so I have never anchored there. But I am told the swell may not be a problem, particularly in the southwest corner. There are drying rocks to avoid in the northwest part of the cove.

Bell Channel

Chart: **4394**

This is the next entrance channel to the islands, going east. It leaves Cape LaHave Island to port and bends northward toward Bell Island. But the northwestern end of Bell Channel is shallow, and it is difficult to see where you are. For these reasons, I never use Bell Channel. I always use False LaHave, a much friendlier passage a mile north.

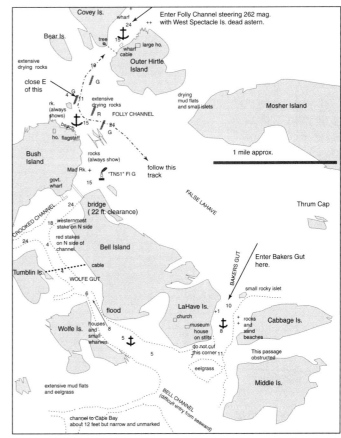

Anchorages in the LaHave Islands.

False LaHave, Bakers Gut, and Wolfe Gut ★★★★

 NO FACILITIES

This is a very pretty area, with houses on some of the islands. There are a number of small sandy beaches on Cabbage Island that make good picnicking sites.

Approaches. From bell buoy "T51" (not to be confused with whistle buoy "TS51" to the southwest) steer 330°M. This leads to the entrance of the Folly Channel (see below). It is not possible to go between Outer Island and Middle Island, but there is a passage between Cabbage Island and LaHave Island (Bakers Gut). Pass to the west of the small island in the entrance, and then favor the starboard side going south.

Pass the house on stilts on the southwestern corner of the passage and turn to starboard without cutting the corner. You need to be careful here as the channel is quite narrow. You have now rejoined the Bell Channel.

Come to 305°M to pass between Bell Island and Wolfe Island. It is shallow here, with just over 4 feet (1.2 m) at low-water springs, but it is quite flat, and if you have enough water when you are due south of the little church you won't hit anything. In the middle, between Bell and Wolfe Islands, there is about 5 feet (1.5 m).

Continue northwesterly, through Wolfe Gut, which was, in 1996, staked with small trees on the south side of the channel to which red balloons had been tied. Note that the westernmost tree/stake is on the north side (see illustration on page 114). The current is not strong here, but the tide floods northwest, although a strong northerly wind can reverse it. By now, weed may be scraping your keel, but the ground is flat and the mud soft. When you have double figures on the depth sounder again you have rejoined Crooked Channel.

Anchorage. I often anchor in Bakers Gut, just south of the visible house with the little slip.

Though you would think this anchorage absolutely protected, one night at 2300 I was anchored here in a raft of three boats when a sudden squall blew right out of the northeast. That was the only (and then only marginally) open direction, and the winds exceeded 80 knots, creating more excitement than anyone would wish for. Other boats in the islands were similarly afflicted and one sank. This would be unlikely to happen to you, but it's certainly worth checking that your anchor has penetrated the eelgrass.

It is also possible to anchor just north of Wolfe Island, though you'll be in quite a busy passage. There are numerous other anchorages, depending on wind direction, for the adventurous, but pay attention to the tide and the depth, which makes for difficulties if you draw more than 5 feet (1.5 m).

Mosher Island ★★★

NO FACILITIES

Charts: **4394, 4384**

Mosher (pronounced Moazher) Island guards the deep-draft entrance to the LaHave River, and has on its eastern extremity a small lighthouse with a fixed white light. On a nice day, if you are sure the wind is going to remain in the west, it is possible to anchor in the little cove just west of the lighthouse. There is a mooring here, usually with a small boat on it, used by the people who live on the island. I must confess this is not a place where I would sleep soundly at night.

Folly Channel (Covey Island)

★★★★   NO FACILITIES

Charts: **4394, 4384**

With the spit on West Spectacle Island dead astern, enter Folly Channel steering 262°M, just a shade to starboard of the middle of the channel. Though there are unmarked rocks either side of

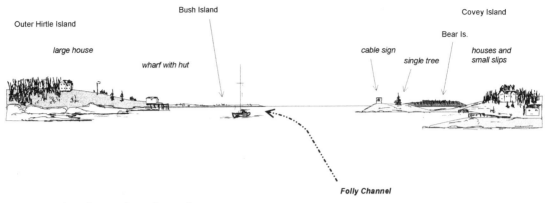

Covey Island anchorage from the northeast.

the entrance, I have never found this entrance very difficult. On the starboard side of the channel are the buildings of the original Covey Island Boatworks. The owner still lives there and commutes by boat.

Going south, leave the first green spar to port. If you then swing east toward the False LaHave Channel, leave the second green spar close on your starboard hand, then leave the next red one to port. Be aware that the orientation of the buoyage changes between the two green spars.

Anchorage. There is a reasonable anchorage in mid-channel between Covey and Outer Hirtle Islands, though the fact that it's the main thoroughfare makes a riding light absolutely essential. There are some patches of kelp on the bottom, but I've never dragged here. I have anchored off the small beach just south of the red spar buoy on the north side of Bush Island, and it was very pleasant. There are many small, dry reefs with rock pools just to the east—very good fun for small children.

Bush Island, a half-mile to the southeast, is connected to the mainland by a causeway, and to Bell Island by the infamous bridge.

If you carry straight on to the south, along the west coast of Bush Island, and if you can avoid the multitude of small islands, you will come to the north side of Crescent Beach, a provincial park much favored by tourists of the terrestrial type. There is slightly deeper water—between 6 feet and 12 feet (1.8 m and 3.6 m)—about a half-mile north of the beach.

Snug Harbour ★★

NO FACILITIES

Chart: 4394

Snug Harbour, mentioned in some older cruising guides, lies on the mainland just west of Bushen Island. The channel immediately adjacent to the mainland here is deep, but there are many unmarked rocks, and chart 4384 is of too small a scale to be a lot of help.

I have found Snug Harbour a disappointment, as it is almost too small to anchor in, and is surrounded only by woods and rock. There are no beaches or trails to walk. I suspect that the Snug Harbour mentioned in previous books is, in fact, Sperry Cove, just to the west, which is a much better bet. If you try it, be sure you are going in the correct entrance, which is the one farthest west, past the small group of 24-foot-high islands on your port hand. If you haven't got chart 4394, you need to be very careful about this. The rest of this enclosed bay has numerous unmarked rocks, especially the area to the northwest of Covey Island, and because of the small scale of chart 4384, it's difficult to find your way around.

The LaHave River

Charts: **4384, 4394**

Big swells occasionally set into the entrance to the LaHave River. These are usually benign, and not breaking, but I have seen them 12 feet (3.6 m) high when the outside swell was less than 3 feet (1 m), and this can be alarming if you are not aware of it. For this reason, it might be better to shelter in the LaHave Islands rather than try the river entrance in severe southerly gales, though I have entered the LaHave River myself in pretty dirty conditions without breaking anything.

Approaches. From the south, pass between Mosher Island and bell buoy "T52," southwest of West Ironbound Island. It is unwise to pass between "T52" and Ironbound itself because Ironbound Breaker, a nasty set of teeth awash at low-water springs extends almost a half-mile from the island.

From outside whistle buoy "T34," east-southeast of Cape LaHave, a course of 358°M will bring you to the fairway bell buoy "TA." From a spot midway between Cape LaHave and Black Rock, a course of 034°M will bring you to roughly the same spot. Though there is not a lot of tidal stream here, there may be enough on this latter heading to set you into False LaHave. If Mosher Island light becomes obscured, you have been set too far inshore on the approach from the south, and you need to make easting.

From the east, it is perfectly all right to pass north of West Ironbound Island under any normal conditions, there being 30 feet (10 m) of water in the middle. Shag Rock, to the northeast of Ironbound, always shows, and can usually be heard. Mosher Island light bearing 283°M puts you on the direct line between Mosher Island and bell buoy "TC52" off Hell Reef, and provides a safe range (transit) for this passage.

From the fairway buoy "TA," steer 316°M to bell buoy "T54." It is not necessary to follow the big ship channel west to Dublin Shore unless your draft is more than 12 feet (3.6 m), or it is blowing hard from the south. It is, in fact, undesirable to follow the channel, as it recurves to pass east of Bull Rock, which dries about 6 feet (1.8 m). From "T54," steer 008°M to a spot midway between Krout Point and Fort Point. The only hazards are Oxner Rock to starboard, marked by a small red spar which is difficult to see, and Bull Rock to starboard, marked by bell buoy "T63." Neither of these is really close to the track and should not be a problem. This is straightforward in the dark, and feasible in fog. Most of the time the fog will clear at least enough to see the sides of the river by the time you get to Fort Point.

The wind speeds up in this entrance, usually when it's blowing from the south. This is naturally more of a problem leaving the river than entering it. A number of times I have sailed peacefully downriver toward the sea and rounded the corner to be met by an icy blast that had me scurrying back into the river to reef. After such an experience, the crew naturally shows great enthusiasm for the forthcoming 20-mile beat to the next harbor. More than once I have gone only as far as the LaHave Islands, and waited for a better day.

Ships of 20,000 tons use this river on a regular basis, and since there are lots of narrow spots, you need to keep clear. In addition, below Riverport offshore draggers come and go all the time.

Lower Reaches of the LaHave River ★★★★

Chart: **4384**

There are few hazards in this stretch of the river, the only problem being that the wind usually blows straight up or straight down, and with my luck, always seems to be adverse. It is difficult to get lost in the LaHave River, and there are few submerged hazards, so I have always felt chart 4384 adequate.

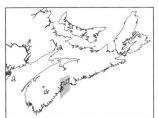

Ashore. On the port hand, about a half-mile past Fort Point, is the LaHave Bakery and Outfitters. There is a small floating dock here that can accommodate about four boats, and there are a few moorings. Diesel fuel and showers are available, as is overnight alongside berthing for a very modest price—$10 in 1994.

Excellent fresh-baked goods are available at the bakery, and there is also a small coffee shop. Water in this area is a bit of a problem, as the whole area depends on well water, and in dry summers the levels are often at a critical level.

The lower floor of the building next to the dock is occupied by a boatbuilder whose specialty is small dinghies. I have seen a lot of boats, and those built in this shop are some of the finest. In the summer of 1994, he had just completed a Herreshoff tender that was a work of art. It was for sale at just over $2,000, which, to be sure, is more than the cost of your usual plastic bathtub, but I certainly thought it was underpriced. It's more important here to like making boats than it is to make money, I guess. It's a real pleasure to visit this shop.

A little farther upstream, a chain ferry crosses the river. Give it a wide berth. If you haven't yet met one of these beasts, they are, in essence, a barge connected to both sides of the river by a long chain on each side. Power-driven pulleys in the barge haul it across. The chains, which have links 12 inches (30 cm) in diameter, lead from the bow and the stern of the barge, one from each corner. The ones on the pulling side are under some tension and extend just below the water surface in front of the ferry for three or four boatlengths. It is as well not to get caught up in all this machinery, and as the ferry cannot do anything but go ahead, astern, or stop dead in its tracks, it has the right of way. The ferrymaster will usually wait for you to pass if he is about to leave the dock.

Two miles farther up the river, also on the port hand, is the LaHave Yacht Club, just past Miller

Head on the chart. There are 20 or so boats here, so you can't miss it. Showers, a bar, food, fuel, and (the state of the groundwater permitting) water, are available. The club is friendly and berthing may well be available alongside—no bad thing, because shelter in the LaHave River is not as good as you might think. Though Nova Scotia is usually considered a less-than-affluent province, if you look at some of the houses on the port side as you go upriver you may rethink this somewhat simplistic view.

Upper LaHave River ★★★

  NO FACILITIES

Charts: **4384**, 4395, 4391

There are few hazards in this stretch of the river, but the best water north of the yacht club, and as far as Little Island just south of Upper LaHave, is on the starboard side. North of Little Island, and as far as Weagle Island, the port side is favored.

On the starboard side going upriver is Snyder's Shipyard, where the replica of the *Bounty* used in the classic film was built. They are one of the few yards in the province still building wooden vessels. For some reason, wooden fishing boats are still quite popular in Lunenburg County, and 65-foot (20-m) longliners continue to be built.

From just downstream of Little Island, it is necessary to pay attention to the spars. One in particular, "T84," just upstream of Weagle Cove on chart 4384, always seems to be on the wrong side of the river, being close to the port side going upstream. It is not, and you must pass to the west of it. This is quite a sharp bend in the channel, and if you meet one of the fully-laden timber vessels that load at the Bridgewater wharf every two weeks during summer, you'll have your hands full. In fact, ascending the LaHave under sail alone is a challenge my crew prefers to forgo—but I have seen it done.

Bridgewater ★★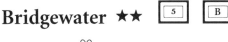

Charts: **4384, 4391**

The river channel is marked as far as the government wharf—a substantial structure nearly 700 feet (213 m) long—that lies a mile below the town. There is usually space here for visiting yachts, but it's a fair hike to the town. If you draw less than 6 feet (1.8 m), you can take the river all the way to the highway bridge in the town center. The channel is on the port side going upstream, and you will surely go aground if you stray from it. There is at least 5 feet (1.5 m) of water at low-water springs, and the tidal range is 5 to 7 feet (1.5 to 2.1 m). There is a small floating dock on the port side at the head of the river.

Ashore. While Bridgewater cannot be called scenic or quiet, it is a handy place for shopping. There is a large mall, with a liquor store, a few yards over the bridge. There is another mall on the west side of town, about a half-mile up from the bridge. In fact, Bridgewater has the best shopping of any town on the coast of Nova Scotia outside of Halifax, and virtually any supplies or services are available.

Main Street runs along the west side of the river. Just a little way to the east there is another mall, and the regional hospital. If you can't find what you need at any of these places, go south when you get off your boat, then turn right and walk up the hill for about a half-mile to the first set of traffic lights, where you'll see another shopping center. Unfortunately, Bridgewater lacks gourmet restaurants, but there are plenty of places where you can get a decent steak.

Lunenburg Bay

Charts: **4328, 4384,** 4394, 4320

Passage between LaHave River and Lunenburg

As noted in the LaHave River section, if you are coming from the LaHave River, especially if the wind is in the southwest, it is much easier to pass between West Ironbound Island and the mainland. Steer 103°M, with Mosher Island lighthouse dead astern of you bearing 283°M. This brings you to bell buoy "TC52" off Pollock Shoal. The names of Hell Reef and Point Enrage on your port hand should be sufficient warning not to stray too far inshore of this buoy. A little way past "TC52,"

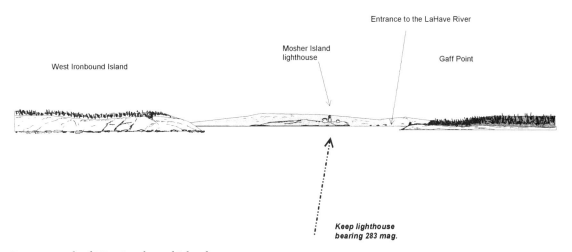

West Ironbound Island

Mosher Island lighthouse

Entrance to the LaHave River

Gaff Point

Keep lighthouse bearing 283 mag.

Passage north of West Ironbound Island.

come to about 032°M, which will take you clear of Rose Point.

Hartling Bay and Kings Bay are pleasant to visit by land, but their southerly exposure and the constant surf, even when the wind is in the northwest, have deterred me from exploring by sea.

There is, however, an anchorage on the western shore of West Ironbound Island that could be interesting if the wind is east, although I have never had the right conditions to try it. The owner of the house on the island keeps a mooring in this little bay, and you can anchor either north or south of the small islet that divides the western side of the island, depending on which looks more sheltered—but don't try this without chart 4394.

Approaches to Lunenburg

Charts: **4384, 4328**

From the southeast, Lunenburg Harbour is very easy to reach. Pass anywhere between Cross Island and Rose Point, and aim straight for Battery Point lighthouse on the end of the harbor breakwater. The course from whistle buoy "E50," south of Cross Island is 330°M for 7.2 miles. Pass south of Sculpin Shoal, marked by bell buoy "E52," and north of Long Shoal, marked by two green spar buoys, and flashing green buoy "E57."

Approaching from the north, for example from Mahone Bay, I usually pass inshore of Little Duck Island. You have to be careful of Hell Rackets and Gimlet Ledge on the approach. Then from whistle buoy "EA51" you should steer 192°M to

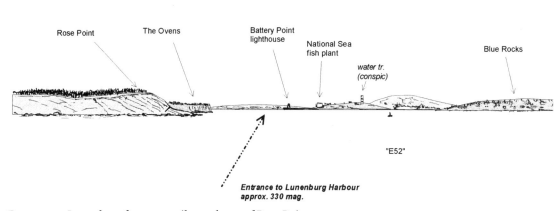

Entrance to Lunenburg from one mile southeast of Rose Point.

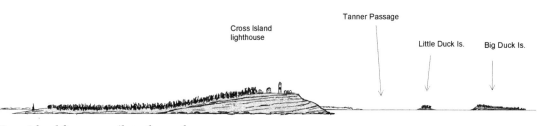

Cross Island from one mile to the south.

bell buoy "EDA." Incidentally, the whistle on "EA51" is a rather miserable, constipated thing, possibly because the lack of wave action doesn't give it enough pressure to hoot properly. When you reach "EDA," come to about 296°M and head for the harbor. As long as you stay more than a quarter-mile offshore, you won't hit anything.

Rose Point always appears to me to be shaped exactly like a dolphin's beak. The rocks are dark gray, almost black shale, and the layers have some yellow mineral, probably iron, that in certain types of light shines just like gold. This rock formation is present all the way to St. Margarets Bay. Many of the beaches have black sand formed from this rock. There is nothing quite like this found anywhere else on the coast of Nova Scotia, and if you are up at sunrise to catch this effect, you will certainly have some outstanding photographs.

Dangers in Lunenburg Bay. One of the remnants of our navy is sunk off Sculpin Shoal to provide a diving park. The superstructure used to lie only 12 feet (3.6 m) below the surface, as the old frigate refused to cooperate when she was sunk, remaining upright rather than turning on her side as planned. But the latest news I have is that the old girl has now decided to rest on her side after all, so there is now more water than this. The wreck is marked by a flashing yellow buoy that lies (I think) to the west of it. Frankly, I would give this area a wide berth.

The main dangers in the entrance to Lunenburg Harbour are the large draggers that go in and out constantly. There was a major accident a few years ago when two draggers collided a few hundred yards off the breakwater, in clear weather and daylight. There was considerable loss of life, and the handling of the larger vessel, one of National Sea's large stern trawlers, was criticized at the subsequent public enquiry. I haven't seen much evidence of improvement, having been nearly run down myself by one of these cowboys in 1992. Legal constraints prevent me from saying what I really think. You would be well advised to keep clear of all draggers, whether you have the right of way or not.

Lunenburg can be entered at any state of wind or tide. There is no problem at night, and (making appropriate allowance for the fishing boat traffic) it's even feasible in fog.

Rose Bay ★★★

NO FACILITIES

Charts: 4328, 4384

Rose Bay is open to the east, but I have anchored here a few times when I've tired of constant beating. There is a drying rock 100 yards north of Rose Point, but no other dangers in the south part of the bay. The north entrance to the bay is not so favored, and The Ovens should not be approached too closely as there is a drying reef extending nearly a half-mile south of Ovens Point. Although Rose Bay is an open roadstead, for some reason there is never much swell, and I have slept quite well here. The best anchorage is in the southwest corner of the bay.

If you have chart 4328, you might be tempted to try the little pool in the buoyed channel leading to the government wharf, near "EQ57." Every time I have been here, though, it has been foggy or late at night, so I haven't been able to try this myself. All the communities on the Rose Point peninsula are picturesque, and determined gunkholers might find this an appealing challenge.

Lower South Cove

Chart: 4328

This is another challenging anchorage that I have never had the time to explore, but it is well marked and accessible to boats drawing 7 feet (2.1 m) or less. You must have chart 4328 to try this, but the entrance presents no great problem.

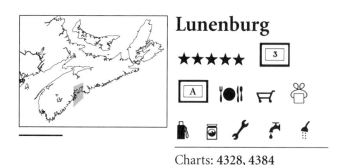

Lunenburg

★★★★★

Charts: 4328, 4384

Lunenburg's waterfront is unique. It is picturesque enough to grace one series of the Canadian $50 bill (it looks like Mystic Seaport), but it remains a working town. Indeed, the tourist business developed here only over the last 10 years or so. One of the old-established businesses, Lunenburg Foundry and Engineering, will still sell you parts for an engine first made in 1906. I had one once, the same beast described in Farley Mowat's book, *The Boat Who Wouldn't Float*. Other enterprises include blockmakers and blacksmiths. Incidentally, if you like historic buildings, this is the place for you. Lunenburg is filled with them, and most of those in the downtown core are original, dating from the eighteenth century.

Approaches. Entering Lunenburg Harbour is straightforward; just turn to starboard past Battery Point lighthouse, and aim for the flashing red buoy "E66" off the marine railway operated by Scotia Trawler. There is very little to worry about anywhere in this harbor if you draw less than 7 feet (2.1 m). The buoyed channel bears to port, to pass the Fisheries Museum of the Atlantic.

There may be large, laid-up steel trawlers in the first part of the anchorage. Having decimated our fishery, most of these boats have now been sold to third-world countries (where they will no doubt do the same thing) and so have gradually disappeared from this anchorage. There weren't any in 1996, though they may reappear at any time. They are usually lit, but watch out for them if you're entering in thick fog.

Anchorage, Dockage. Due south of the museum there are about a dozen mooring buoys with very

substantial gear maintained by the Dory Shop (634-9169). You may also be able to tie up to one of the museum's wharves, but space is limited. Large sail-training vessels and the like use these wharves on a regular basis in the summer. They are also covered with tar and exposed to any gawking landlubber from a bus tour, or worse, drunken scallopers on a Friday night. There is however a small floating dock for dinghies which is very handy. There may also be space at the small government wharf right at the head of the harbor, though this is in constant use by inshore fishing boats.

The moorings, on the other hand, are a blessing because the harbor mud is a foul, sulphurous slime that only a high-pressure hose will move from your anchor chain.

The harbor is a little open to the south, and a slop can build up in southwesterly gales, though not usually enough to bother anyone at anchor. Rowing a dinghy to the museum dock in these conditions, however, requires a little more care. Anyone rowing a dinghy at night should have a flashlight, as there is constant coming and going from the Lunenburg Foundry dock at the head of the harbor. Riding lights are not required if you are at a mooring, and not really needed if you are anchored in the general mooring area.

Ashore. Scotia Trawler, in the northeast corner of the harbor, just west of the marine railway, has a fuel and water dock with just over 6 feet (1.8 m) at low-water springs.

There are actually a few yacht services in Lunenburg. North Sails has a loft on Pelham Street, which is one street back from the waterfront, and Scotia Trawler has a chandlery, The Yacht Shop, one block up from their fuel dock, next to the boatyard. Major repairs can be done at this yard and at Lunenburg Foundry.

One block up from the Fisheries museum is the customs. At the time of writing, Lunenburg is a port of entry.

To reach the provincial campground, go toward the big water tower overlooking the east end of town. Showers with unlimited hot water can be had there for $1.

The Liquor Commission outlet is about a mile out of town, on the road to Bridgewater, and my advice would be to go to the post office and catch a taxi. They're cheap in Lunenburg and the cab drivers are very helpful. They'll drive you around to shop for hard-to-find items such as block ice.

One block east of the post office and customs, and another street up from the water, is a supermarket. There are numerous other stores of all types, including craft stores and art galleries.

The Fisheries Museum dominates the middle of the waterfront and is well worth a visit. Scattered around it are numerous restaurants, but the sheer number of tourists sometimes saturates the facilities. The Rumrunner Inn has an adequate restaurant, and rooms if you are fed up with the cold and fog and want a drier berth. I've enjoyed excellent dining at the Compass Rose, just up from the museum. Magnolia's Grill, a hole in the wall on Pelham Street, is hard to find, and I still haven't experienced its pleasures myself, although I've had favorable reports.

One of the few drawbacks to Lunenburg is the lifestyle of some of the people involved in its major industry, particularly the offshore trawlers and scallopers. They are at sea for two weeks and are paid in cash at the end of each trip. The greenest recruit may earn several thousand dollars a trip. Combine that with a powerful thirst for firewater and it explains why the waterfront taverns can get pretty rowdy late on a Friday night, though things seem to have become more sedate recently. When I come to Lunenburg I prefer to stay on one of the moorings.

The Lunenburg Peninsulas

There is a series of fascinating creeks northeast of Lunenburg, and on the east side of Cross Island. The same rock formation that is seen on Rose Point extends to Mahone Bay and its outer islands. The rock is deeply fissured with cracks running east and west, forming a series of narrow inlets that create some of the prettiest anchorages in the province.

Blue Rocks

Chart: 4328

I have never visited this harbor by boat, though the entrance should be straightforward enough in clear weather. Beware of the 6-foot (1.8-m) drying rock off the end of the breakwater. It's just north of red spar "EC66."

Blue Rocks is a crowded fishing community much loved by photographers and filmmakers, and room is very limited. There are, in this immediate area, other little cracks between the rocks in which you will see boats moored. If you have a calm day, chart 4328, an adventurous bent, and nerves of steel, you could well find some fascinating gunkhole of your own.

East Point Gut ★★★★

 NO FACILITIES

Chart: 4328

It's much easier to enter East Point Gut from the east. If your boat draws more than 4 feet (1.2 m) and it is low water, you will have to be careful at the entrance. A bearing of 278°M on the little lighthouse on East Point Island provides a safe approach line. When you near the first spar, "EC51," veer a bit to the north to avoid the long spit that comes out from the lighthouse. Keep south of "EC52," which marks a pointy rock, and when you have passed the next spit that extends from the southeast end of Little East Point Island, favor the north side of the gut all the way through and out the other side. The deepest water lies north of west cardinal buoy "EC" at the west entrance.

Anchorage. You can anchor anywhere in the gut, though swinging room is limited. I once saw a 100-foot (30-m) barque anchored in here, though, so I know it can be done.

123

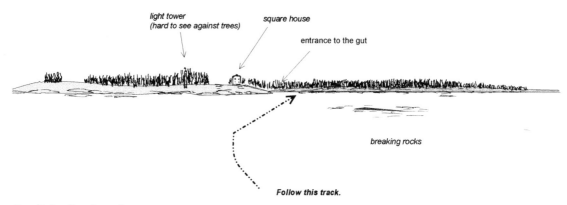

light tower
(hard to see against trees)

square house

entrance to the gut

breaking rocks

Follow this track.

East Point Gut from the east.

Cross Island ★★★★★ 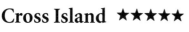 5

 C NO FACILITIES

Chart: **4328**

I sailed past this anchorage several times before I realized it was there. One day, as I was passing, I saw a 40-foot (12-m) schooner emerge from this crack in the rock under full sail. As he was much bigger than I was, I figured I would fit in there too, so I tried it. I have never seen any sailing directions for this anchorage in any previous guide to the province. It could be that those who know about it want to keep it for themselves, and I might get lynched for providing directions. Nonetheless, as it is my favorite anchorage (I've spent several of my birthdays here) I feel I should spread the word.

The mere mention of Cross Island anchorage causes agitation among my crew, though I have only run aground once in the dozen times I have come here. I must admit, though, that the entrance is difficult for strangers, and extreme care is required. I would never, ever, try to reach this spot at night, or with anything of an easterly wind. I don't advise it in fog, either, with or without radar. The best time to creep in here is at low water, with a rising tide, provided you don't draw

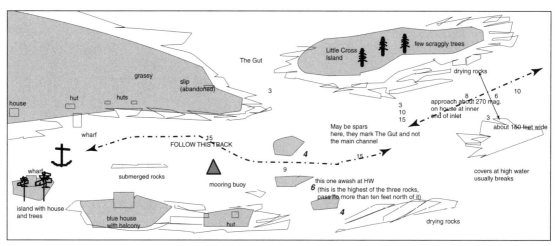

Cross Island.

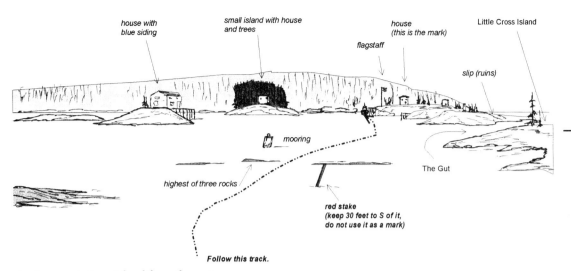

Labels on illustration:
house with blue siding
small island with house and trees
house (this is the mark)
Little Cross Island
flagstaff
slip (ruins)
mooring
highest of three rocks
The Gut
red stake (keep 30 feet to S of it, do not use it as a mark)
Follow this track.

Anchorage at Cross Island from the east.

more than 6 feet (1.8 m). In addition to my chart, you must carry chart 4328, even though it doesn't show the anchorage in any detail.

Approaches. Approach from the east, keeping at least a quarter-mile east of a line drawn from the easternmost point of Cross Island to Little Duck Island. Find Little Cross Island, a small grassy island about 20 feet (6 m) high with a few straggly trees on it. The passage leading to the anchorage lies to the south of it. When you can see down the channel, look west and identify the small house at the extreme western end of the channel. It's the one shown on my sketch chart, on the north side of the channel. There are other houses on the south side of the channel.

From your offshore line between Cross Island and Little Duck Island, approach on a heading of exactly 270°M straight toward this house. To port is Black Rock, a big smooth rock that covers at high water. It will be visible at most states of the tide, and there is usually a lazy sort of swell over it when it's covered. Pass about halfway between this rock and Little Cross Island.

A big flat ledge extends north from the rock and comes nearly halfway across the channel. The width of the whole channel at this point is about 100 feet (30 m), and it's about 6 feet (1.8 m) deep at dead low water in the deepest part. It would

pay at this point to send a crewmember aloft or to the bow to watch for rocks. The water is very clear, and they certainly can be seen if the sun is not in your eyes.

When you draw level with the seaward end of Little Cross Island, veer just a little to port, as a similar ledge sticks out from the southern side, though not nearly as far as the one from Black Rock. When the middle tree on Little Cross Island is abeam, change course to 260°M and steer straight for the blue house with the substantial wharf and patio. (I hope Wayne, the owner, will not change the color and confuse you.) There will now be a red spar ahead of you. It does not mark this channel, and you should pass about 20 feet (6 m) south of it. Ahead of you now are three big flat rocks with little space between them. Pass between the middle one, the highest, and the one to its north, staying within 10 feet (3 m) of the middle rock. If the tide is high, the middle rock will be awash, and the other two will be invisible.

Up ahead, you'll notice a big orange buoy looking rather out of place. This is a mooring buoy, and if by now you are in need of a drink, tie up to it. If you want to go farther in, keep to the north side as there is a rock ridge in the middle of the channel. I usually tie up to the little wharf by a hut with "Chateau au Law" written on it, on the north side of the channel. If you want to

125

anchor, do so fore-and-aft so you don't swing around a lot. Bear in mind when entering this place that it's so narrow that you can't turn around without backing up (at least in my boat you can't). This can cause a problem if there is a stiff crosswind. If your boat is more than 40 feet (12 m) long you may have to warp her around to face outward.

Ashore. This spot is perfectly sheltered from anything except a hurricane from the east. The owner of the camp at the extreme end of the in-let has marked a path that leads to the west side of the island. There is a picnic table with spectacular views of Lunenburg Bay. If you take your dinghy and row through the various cracks in the rock in a southerly direction you come to an abandoned wharf and a series of small beaches. If the tide is high in the afternoon, the black rocks will heat up the water so that paddling, at least, is reasonably pleasant. The wharf is at the start of what used to be a well-maintained dirt road to the lighthouse on the southern end of the island. This is a very pleasant walk, up and down little hills and valleys, of about a mile. On a clear day there are spectacular views of East Ironbound Island and Saint Margarets Bay. The lighthouse is now automated, so there is no lighthouse keeper. Consequently, the road is no longer repaired after winter storms, and has deteriorated, though it's still passable on foot.

There is all sorts of animal and bird life on Cross Island, because natural predators are few. One recent summer, my son saw a large unidentified animal which I think was a juvenile moose. Moose and deer are strong swimmers, and have no trouble crossing to the mainland. But the long swim is too much for the coyotes that prey on them.

A fair-size community lived around the anchorage in the first part of this

century. There was a school, a fish processing plant, and a graveyard, but all is overgrown now, and it would require a major archaeological dig to find them. There are no facilities on Cross Island other than the natural beauty of the place. It can get quite crowded at weekends I am told, though I have never found it so. My traveling companions and I have been the only sailboats here on the numerous occasions I have stayed.

This is my favorite anchorage in the whole province, and I like to think you haven't really cruised the coast of Nova Scotia until you've been here.

Tanners Pass ★★★★★ 5

B NO FACILITIES

Chart: 4328

Tanners Pass is at the northeastern end of the Lunenburg peninsula, and it's a lot easier to enter than is the Cross Island anchorage. From whistle buoy "EA51," shape a course of 310°M to take you right in. Leave the two spar buoys to port, and when you come to the second one,

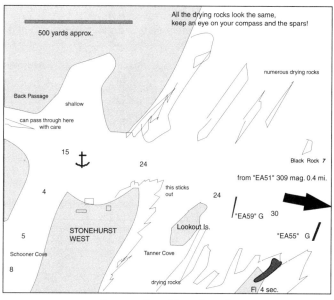

Tanners Pass (Stonehurst).

Gunning Point Island
lighthouse

houses
(Stonehurst West)

Anchorage

"EA59"

"EA57"

"EA51"

numerous dry ledges

**Steer approx. 309 mag.
from "EA51" to enter the pass.**

**The two green spars are difficult to see until you
are right on top of them.**

Tanners Pass from the east.

"EA59," come to 300°M and stay in the middle of the channel. I usually anchor in the little cove by Stonehurst West, but the adventurous might want to turn south and explore a little farther, down to Schooner Cove. It's also possible to go a little way up Back Passage, which leads to Lunenburg Back Harbour.

There is a little pool about a half-mile west in Back Passage that carries about 8 feet (2.4 m) at low water. The channel is scarcely wider than your average boat and it can be intimidating, as there is no room to turn round. If your boat behaves as badly as mine does with sternway on, this can cause a severe problem. The best advice I can give if you want to try this is to sound the depths from the dinghy first. It is certainly an interesting passage in a small boat.

There are no facilities in Tanners Pass, but on the little hill to the north of the cove there are large quantities of blueberry bushes and raspberry canes. Anchoring may require some patience, as there is a profusion of eelgrass on the bottom that interferes with penetration by CQR and Bruce-type anchors. This is one of the places where a Danforth-type anchor may be better.

Mahone Bay

Charts: **4381**, 4320

Mahone Bay is one of the two major sailing centers in Nova Scotia, the other being Halifax. There are two decent-size towns, Chester and Mahone Bay, two yacht clubs, four marinas, and about 400 boats based here. I have never failed to find room to anchor, though, except during Chester Race Week. More about that later.

The tourist guide mentions 365 islands. I don't think there are that many, unless you count half-tide rocks, but there certainly are a great number of anchorages. Almost every anchorage in Mahone Bay has plenty of water for boats drawing up to 6 feet (1.8 m), and most can accommodate 9 feet (2.7 m) with a bit of care.

One problem in this area is that, because of the high hills between here and the transmitter at Ketch Harbour, southeast of Halifax, VHF communication with the shore station is difficult and may even be impossible in places. There is an inshore lifeboat, which can be summoned by calling Mahone Bay Inshore Rescue on Channel 16. Luckily, there's no problem with this service, or with cellular phone coverage.

Approaches from the South. When coming from Lunenburg, I always pass inside Little Duck Island. From bell buoy "EDA" in Lunenburg Bay, steer 012°M to whistle buoy "EA51." Don't expect to hear it, though, until you are right on top of it. From the buoy, steer at least 020°M to keep away from Hell Rackets and Gimlet Ledge. The ledge always shows, being 5 feet (1.5 m) above high water, but it is not a good radar target. If the weather is clear, you will see Big Tancook Island

127

fine on your starboard bow, and Star Island, a tiny, grassy lump 800 yards west of Tancook, dead ahead. When all the small islands that comprise Hell Rackets are aft of your beam, you can ease off to the west if you're making for Mahone Bay town or Princes Inlet, but don't cut this corner too close or you will hit something. It's not safe to pass inside Chockle Cap bell buoy, "M55."

I have made this passage many times in thick fog and at night, with and without radar, but it requires some care. There is not a lot of tidal stream to worry about, and you can probably get away with using GPS or loran. I have never seen the buoys out of position here in the summer, and they can probably be used to check the accuracy of your loran. The Rackets can certainly be impressive in easterly gales, and this is one time when it might be better to go well outside of Little Duck Island.

Approaches from the Southeast. The easiest approach from offshore is to pass either side of Big Duck Island, depending on your line of approach. It is quite steep-to, and a clearance of a quarter-mile is sufficient. Leave red buoys "M52" and "M54" to starboard, then also leave Big Tancook Island to starboard. The channel is wide and clear here, and if you plan to stay in the middle you can safely pass through even if you're relying only on loran or GPS.

A course of 344°M will take you from "M52" to green flashing buoy "MC55" off East Shoal. With a bit of luck, the fog will clear as soon as you pass Big Tancook. Beware of Middle Ledge, east of "M52," and Bull Rock, northeast of "M54." I've known boats to hit each of these hazards, and in one instance a yacht sank.

In clear weather, you can safely pass either side of Pearl Island, then between East Ironbound and Flat Islands, and between the Big and Little Tancooks. A course of 348°M takes you from whistle buoy "D32," south of Pearl Island, to the middle of the pass between the Tancooks, 8.2 miles away.

Approaches from the East. If you're coming from Halifax, for example, pass north of East Ironbound Island. It is just possible to make this passage on one tack against the prevailing southwesterly wind. There are a couple of little caveats, however. Firstly, don't come too close to the north side of East Ironbound; there is a rock (Grampus Shoal) 250 yards off the northern point that is awash at low water and usually doesn't break.

Secondly, the tops of the Aspotogan Peninsula and East Ironbound are the same shape. If you can see only one, it is the Aspotogan Peninsula, so don't be tempted to ease sheets to pass north of it, or you'll end up in St. Margarets Bay. Incidentally, there is a tidal stream of about 1 knot at the mouth of St. Margarets Bay. This is advantageous if it is ebbing, as it pushes you to windward, assuming the usual close haul for this passage. But on the flood you can be set 3 miles downwind, to end up on Seal Ledge.

The wind always seems to pipe up in the vicinity of East Ironbound. On many occasions I've passed by here, grumpily contemplating the bother of hauling down another reef, when only a mile or two farther on, by Little Tancook Island, the wind has died away completely.

Having passed East Ironbound, it is usually easier to pass north of Little Tancook, rather than to pinch up into the pass between the Tancook Islands. The distance lost to leeward is more easily made up in the calm waters of Mahone Bay than it is outside the islands.

Even when there is the thickest of fogs outside, once you're inside the outer islands, Mahone Bay is usually clear, at least by midmorning. For this reason, and because the few hazards are well marked, the bay is very popular with sailors.

Lunenburg Back Harbour

Chart: **4381**

Back Harbour is a long way from a main road and is therefore quite peaceful. While not many houses are found here, there are some farms, which are rare on the Atlantic coast of Nova Scotia. There are no facilities other than the boatyard and the sailmaker, unless you go all the way in to the government wharf and walk the half-mile to Lunenburg. There is, however, sheltered anchorage in just about any spot you care to stop.

Approaches from the East. The route to Lunenburg Back Harbour is intricate, and I don't think I'd try it in thick fog. I'd also think twice about doing it at night.

First find Chockle Cap bell buoy, "M55," and steer approximately 275°M. There is an island, 35 feet (10.6 m) high, just ahead of you on the port bow. This has the typical dark-orange striped rocks found on the Lunenburg Peninsula, and it's topped by a few scrubby trees. Farther to port is the mess of rocks that makes up The Rackets.

The entrance you're seeking is between Lucy Island and Sacrifice Island, neither of which are easy to pick out against the mainland if the sun is in your eyes. There is a long rocky bar, almost totally submerged, running from the unnamed island near Chockle Cap buoy, "M55," to Sacrifice Island, so you need to stay north of that line. The water on that side, the starboard side going in, is clearer in any case, and if you draw less than 6 feet (1.8 m), you have only to avoid Nose Shoal, a half-mile north of Sacrifice Island. There is a large house, shaped like a lighthouse, on Bluff Head, three-quarters of a mile northwest of the entrance, which helps you find the gap.

Approaches from the West. Northeast of Bluff Head, find the green spar buoys "ME57" and "ME55," and leave them to starboard, as the channel buoyage is oriented as if you were proceeding to sea.

After passing "ME55," turn to 210°M to head just east of Lucy Island, and enter the anchorage. Near buoy "ME55" there is a very long spit that extends westward from Hobsons Island. It is not at all apparent from the chart, but it extends at least two-thirds of the way from the island to the spar buoy, so stay quite close to the spar.

Heckmans Anchorage, where you now find yourself, is a little open for most people's taste, so it is better to go farther in. After passing Lucy Island, remain in mid-channel until you're abeam of Goreham Point, where you need to favor the starboard side. On the latest edition of chart 4381, green spar buoy "MM61" marks the rocks right in the middle of this little bay—but the buoy wasn't in place last time I was there.

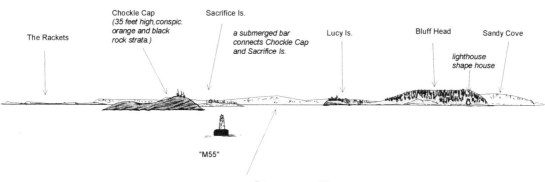

Heckmans Anchorage and the entrance to Lunenburg Back Harbour from the east.

Anchorage. It's possible to anchor anywhere in here, provided you make allowance for rocks. The channel to Lunenburg Back Harbour passes through two sets of narrows, which are generally free of obstructions. There seems to be a lot of water, but it's an illusion: There are a number of mudbanks that show only at low water. Heckmans Back Harbour, to the southeast, is full of these banks, but it's navigable by dinghy all the way to Tanners Pass.

To the west it's possible (if you keep off the mud) to go as far as Lunenburg Back Harbour government wharf. One of my friends kept his 75-foot (23-m) converted motor fishing vessel (MFV) here one winter. Her draft was nearly 10 feet (3 m), so there is certainly enough water if you can keep to the channels. The best time to make this passage is just after low water, when you can see the extensive mud flats. You'll notice they're not quite as they're shown on the chart.

Ashore. Close northwest of Heckmans Anchorage, in a small cove north of Little Island, is a boatyard run by the Stevens family. David Stevens, the patriarch, died in 1992. He was famous as the designer of *Atlantica,* built in Montreal in 1967 to celebrate the centenary of Canada's founding. She is still around, as is the pale-blue *Kathi-Anne 2,* the last boat he built.

Farther up the hill, at the tip of Second Peninsula, is the original home of R. B. Stevens, sailmakers. It was taken over by North Sails sometime in the early '80s and moved to Lunenburg. The old shop has been reopened as Peninsula Sails. I have to say that the sails I had made here nearly 20 years ago set every bit as well as the newfangled things with computer-assisted design. Going here by land in the middle of winter to get sails repaired used to be quite an adventure. The road from Lunenburg is unpaved, and runs along the side of a deep inlet with no trace of any wimpy safety feature such as a guardrail. It wiggles and twists, and is quite an experience when

130

covered with ice. Every time I visited this place I was amazed to find they actually had electricity there, and—even more amazing—computers.

Rafuse Island ★★★

NO FACILITIES

Chart: **4381**

Rafuse Island is a popular anchorage with fine, sandy beaches, and, like nearby Mason Island, is well worth a visit in reasonably settled weather. It lies about 2 miles north of Hell Rackets and 1.5 miles west of Big Tancook Island.

Approaches. From the south, steer about 028°M from Mahone Bay whistle buoy "M," then 310°M from East Shoal Ledge buoy "MC55." Don't confuse this buoy with "M55," 2 miles south. This route brings you around Rafuse Island from the east, which is easier. I have done this many times in thick fog and there are not many hazards. Rafuse Ledge is a hazard if you're approaching from the northwest, though, but at least it's always visible in daylight. Enter the gap between Rafuse Island and Little Rafuse Island from the northeast, favoring the Big Rafuse Island side.

Anchorage. This is a popular daytime anchorage, protected by the bar between the two Rafuse islands. The bar is submerged at high water, but don't imagine it gets deep enough for you to sail through the gap.

The anchorage is just north of the bar. In the southeast corner there is a nice sandy beach, with low, grassy dunes behind it. Just off the beach, however, is a mighty hole, where the depths go from 6 to 50 feet (1.8 to 15 m) in a couple of boatlengths. This makes anchoring in the fine sand somewhat difficult. There's better holding ground to the northwest, toward Little Rafuse Island. The anchorage is quite sheltered, except from the northeast, and I have stayed here many nights, though the locals tend not to. I have dragged anchor quite a few times also, so I wouldn't say it's a place where you can sleep soundly.

Mason Island ★★★

NO FACILITIES

Chart: **4381**

Another popular anchorage is the crescent-shaped bay at the northeast end of Mason Island. It's close west of Rafuse Island, and has a delightful sandy beach nearly a half-mile long. It is open to the east, but makes a reasonably calm anchorage in stable summer weather. Give the extreme northeast end of the island a decent berth as a spit sticks out there.

When you're passing between Rafuse and Mason Islands, favor the Mason Island side as there is an unmarked rock a fair way out in the channel opposite the Rafuse Island bar. There are also outlying rocks to the southeast, southwest, and west of Mason Island, but they're all fairly well marked by buoys. The approach from the north is unobstructed.

There is a house on the island, owned by someone with a passion for skeet shooting. There are certain times when this island sounds like a war zone, and it might be wise to exercise caution if you are walking ashore.

Princes Inlet ★★★

Chart: **4381**

Princes Inlet lies north of Second Peninsula, about 2 miles north of Lunenburg. The coastline along Second Peninsula is almost unobstructed, and there is a fine beach at Sandy Cove where unusual speckled pebbles are to be found. They're about the size of footballs, and look like giant sea gull eggs. I have some around my fireplace at home. The only hazard here is the shallow water

off the western end of the cove that is marked by green spar buoy "ME59." Stevens' Boatyard, mentioned previously, is near Sandy Cove.

Princes Inlet continues west to the Lunenburg Yacht Club, between Hermans Island and Little Hermans Island. Beware of the spit that sticks out southwest from Backmans Island. It's long and unmarked. Also, stay south of red spar buoys "ME64" and "ME66."

It's possible to enter or leave Princes Inlet through the channel running north, but keep to the Hermans Island side and don't cut inside buoy "MJ51." Inshore of it is a drying rock.

You can anchor in the spaces between moorings, farther west in Princes Inlet along the Hermans Island side. On a calm day you can also make a picnic stop off the spit on the southwest corner of Backmans Island.

The yacht club has a dinghy dock, and there is water, fuel, showers, and a bar. The last time I was here, on a summer weekend, almost every boat was off its mooring and going somewhere by 0900 on Saturday. It struck me that this is a club of enthusiasts.

Mahone Bay Town ★★★★

Chart: **4381**

Mahone Bay is one of the most scenic towns in Nova Scotia, but has yet to be overrun by tourists. The head of the bay is dominated by the spires of the three churches that appear on postcards of the province. In summer, the sun sets right behind these spires, making for spectacular photographs. There are numerous restaurants, and a decent tavern with reasonable prices. In the same building as the tavern is an excellent bookstore, P. G. Joost, with a selection much more varied than those of the usual chains. Zwicker's Inn, one of the finest restaurants in the province, used to be at the head of the government wharf, but a couple of years ago it changed ownership and went bust. The original

owner, however, has another establishment, the Innlet Cafe, at the head of the bay just past the churches, which is well worth a visit. He has an excellent wine list and the best homemade ice cream and bread I have tasted anywhere in the world—enough to make a visit here quite memorable.

Incidentally, this is one of the problems with this type of guide. In the 20 years I've been cruising Nova Scotia, almost every restaurant in the major tourist areas has changed hands at least once, and when this happens there is no guarantee that the great meal you had last year will be repeated. I guess this is part of the adventure of eating out. Perhaps one day the income tax department will accept my argument that eating in every waterfront restaurant once a year is a legitimate business expense, and I'll be able to keep these things up to date.

Approaches from the South and East. Steer 296°M from Mahone Bay whistle buoy "M." This buoy is well marked and lit. The only hazards on your way in are Southwest Ledge and Gull Ledge, both to starboard, and Coveys Ledge to port. Both Southwest Ledge and Coveys Ledge are marked by lighted buoys.

As you approach Mahone Harbour, pass south of Westhaver Island, a little grassy lump with a small lighthouse on it. About one-third of a mile to the northwest, you can pass either side of flashing green buoy "M67," as long as you keep close to it, then you should swing north to clear Eisenhauers Point. (Eisenhauer is a common name in Lunenburg county, but has half-a-dozen different spellings, including that of the former U.S. president.)

A spit extends in an easterly direction from the northeast side of Eisenhauers Point, and it sticks out farther than is apparent from the chart. I have run aground there, but you can avoid that mistake by maintaining an offing of at least 100 yards. Several local boats are kept in Maders Cove, close west of Eisenhauers Point, and it is

possible to anchor there in depths of about 7 feet (2.1 m). It faces a busy main road, however, and is overlooked by houses, so it's not often used by visiting boats.

Approaches from the North. If you're heading southwest from Indian Point, favor the mainland (starboard) side. There are unmarked rocks off Andrews Island, and a drying spit extending from its northeast corner is not shown on the chart. All the passages between the islands are simple enough if you can cruise down the middle. It's when you're beating that you have to watch out. Enter Mahone Harbour north of Strum Island. Off Hyson Point, on your starboard side opposite Strum Island, is a substantial dock. This is owned by CIL, a large chemical company, and is used to load explosives. If there is a large ship here, you might want to give it a very wide berth.

In Mahone Harbour, pass either side of Strum Shoal, which is marked by spars, then go south of the little flashing red beacon just before you get to the town.

Anchorage, Dockage. Off Mahone Bay town, you can anchor anywhere west of the flashing red light. Lately, moorings have been laid for the wooden boat festival, and it might be possible to use one. The government wharf lies farther west on the south side of the harbor, and provides space alongside for about four boats. There is about 10 feet (3 m) at low water. Above the government wharf, the harbor dries out.

Ashore. Mahone Bay town is the best place on the bay to provision, much better than Chester. There is a large, well-stocked supermarket downtown, within a quarter-mile of the government wharf. For an hour or so either side of high water, you can row your dinghy to a spot close by. Don't delay, however, for if the tide goes out you'll find yourself wading through foul black mud to get ashore, or to drag your dinghy back to the water. Next to the supermarket is a farmers' market with a wide selection of fresh fruit and vegetables. There is even a department store called Bill's. One year, my boat's bedding was so damp from fog that we gave up the unequal fight of trying to dry it, and bought new sheets at Bill's. The liquor store is about a half-mile down the road to Blockhouse—that's my maximum range for carrying a case of beer. Also along this road is the headquarters of Suttles and Seawinds, a now quite well-known line of ladies' designer clothing.

There is a laundromat adjacent to the government wharf, certainly the handiest one in this area. There is, unfortunately, no dockside fuel. There may be water at a small marina just south of the government wharf, but this venture has not been operating long enough for anyone to know whether it will be there from one year to the next.

The Mahone Bay Wooden Boat Festival. This show has expanded recently to become one of the province's major attractions. Usually held the last week of July, it attracts 60 or so boats from all over North America. Last time I attended, there were boats from Bermuda, South Africa, and New Zealand as well. There are beer gardens, traditional music, boatbuilding competitions, small-boat racing, and the like. Quite often, the Nova Scotia Schooner Association coordinates its race week with this event. This group of enthusiasts keeps alive the tradition of wooden ships and iron men (and iron women, too, in this liberated age). Many of the boats are more than 50 years old, and 20 of them racing in a good breeze is a sight to behold. It's even more thrilling to be aboard one. I'll always remember sailing on *Sebim,* flying at 18 knots down Shelburne Harbour, heeled over about 60 degrees from vertical, with a 35-knot wind on the beam.

The organizers of the wooden boat festival set out to make it attractive to family groups, and seem to have succeeded handsomely.

Indian Point and Vicinity

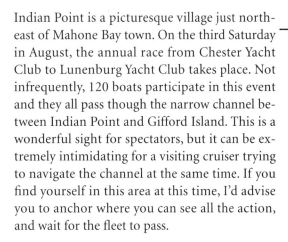

★★★★★   5   B   🍽

Chart: 4381

Indian Point is a picturesque village just northeast of Mahone Bay town. On the third Saturday in August, the annual race from Chester Yacht Club to Lunenburg Yacht Club takes place. Not infrequently, 120 boats participate in this event and they all pass though the narrow channel between Indian Point and Gifford Island. This is a wonderful sight for spectators, but it can be extremely intimidating for a visiting cruiser trying to navigate the channel at the same time. If you find yourself in this area at this time, I'd advise you to anchor where you can see all the action, and wait for the fleet to pass.

Approaches from the South. Coming from Mahone Bay town presents no major problems, though it is best to favor the mainland side. A long spit, not well shown on the chart, juts out from the northeast corner of Andrews Island. There are charted, but unmarked, rocks midway between this point and Gifford Island.

Approaches from the East. West of Big Tancook Island, on Kaulback Island, are two leading lights to guide you safely between Young Ledge and Bella Shoal. They are in line at 267°T, or 287°M, and the green flashing buoy "MN51," off the north side of Big Tancook, should be dead astern of you. The leading marks are fixed white lights, and they're difficult to pick out from the shore lights. The last time I came in here, neither light was lit, and I mistakenly thought a pair of street lights were the marks. In truth, there aren't many street lights either, but there is one pair that can cause confusion. My loran wasn't working at the time, and I was lucky to avoid Young Ledge. Nevertheless, it is perfectly feasible to enter here at night—just check your heading to be certain that you are following the right set of lights. You must keep

to the buoyed channel until you are past Bella Island, as there are drying rocks not far off the track.

Approaches from the North. From Chester, find Sheep Ledge bell buoy, "MC59," and steer 236°M. Don't stray to starboard or go the wrong side of the spars, as there is a vast expanse of unmarked rocks, mostly just below chart datum level. Round Island Nubble, a small lump with trees on it, has a bar extending a long way into the channel. Round Island has no hazards on its northwest side. When you reach the westernmost extremity of Round Island, change course to 268°M.

The channel narrows here, so leave green spar "MS55" close to port, and watch out dead ahead for Beacon Shoal light, a concrete block with an interrupted quick-flashing green light on it. If you get here in mid-afternoon, the sun is right in your eyes and it is difficult to see any of the spars, let alone their colors. While the nominally preferred channel is to starboard of Beacon Shoal light, there is 12 feet (3.6 m) of water if you keep to port of it and stay in mid-channel. There are some imposing mansions along this track; every year, a new one seems to spring up.

After rounding Beacon Shoal light, a turn to port leads you to Indian Point. Ahead, to starboard, is Martins River, a narrow buoyed channel. Just south of this lies a challenge for the adventurous: Narrows Basin, dominated by a new mansion bigger than many resort hotels. There is 5 feet (1.5 m) of water inside at low-water springs. Keep Crow Island, and the little unmarked island off Leg Point, to port going in. Numerous local boats are moored here, but there is usually room to anchor.

There is clear passage between most of the islands around Indian Point, except between Gifford Island and Ernst Island, which are connected by a sandy bar. There are a few shallow spots, and there is an uncharted spit extending from the northwest corner of Gifford Island that catches a few boats every year. You might want to mark it

on your chart as a reminder to give the spot a wide berth.

The wind often screeches through the passage past Indian Point, even when it is pleasant sailing elsewhere in the bay. More than once, I've been caught here with the rail under water. Another hazard is the cultivated mussel beds, this being one of the first areas in the province to get into this field. The mussels are grown on vertical lines, each of which is held up by a buoy, and there are usually a couple of hundred lines in a string. As there are no horizontal lines in the water, you're unlikely to run foul of them, but it's best to keep clear. Their locations may vary slightly from year to year.

Anchorage. Many of the islands are inhabited year-round. Most of the residents keep their boats at the government wharf at Indian Point so there is usually not much room for visitors. Anchorage is possible almost anywhere, however, and most of the bays have sandy beaches. Among the spots I've enjoyed are:

- The beach on the west side of Round Island. It has fine sand, and there's grass adjacent to the beach, making it a good place for a picnic, though the anchorage is a little too open for an overnight stay. There are spectacular views to the northwest.
- The bay on the northwest side of Young Island. It has no beach, but is usually beautifully secluded.
- Either side of the bar connecting Ernst and Gifford Islands. The north bay has mussel lines, but there is usually room to anchor inside them.
- The channel between Rous and Gifford Islands.
- In the bight formed by Goat Island, although this is somewhat open to the south.
- Either side of the government wharf at Indian Point. This is a little open to the southwest, but I and others have often anchored here overnight.

There is a small boatyard on Gifford Island, but no other facilities. Because there is a lot of small-boat traffic in this area at night, an anchor light is essential.

Oak Island ★★★

Chart: 4381

Oak Island may not look very prepossessing, but it is part of Nova Scotian folklore. During the late eighteenth century, two young men rowed ashore here and found an old block and a frayed rope hanging from a tree. There was a depression in the ground under the tree, and some superficial digging revealed what appeared to be an old mine shaft.

A longstanding rumor held that Captain Kidd had buried a vast treasure on an island in Mahone Bay, so reinforcements were brought in the next day, and the site was excavated to about 30 feet (9 m), revealing an 8-foot (2.4-m) square vertical shaft, lined with wood, with floors across about every 10 feet or so. Even in the 1780s the structure looked at least 100 years old, and it was apparent to the excavators that considerable care and effort had gone into its construction.

This was the discovery of the fabled "money pit," and the beginning of a controversy that would last centuries.

When the diggers returned on the second day, they found the pit full of water. It could not be pumped out, as there seemed to be a connection to the sea. The shaft caved in soon after this exploration, and to this day the pit remains flooded. During the following 200 years there have been diggings galore, drilling, legal disputes, conspiracies, several deaths, and all sorts of mayhem, as well as reports of gold coins having been found. Drilling has shown the shaft to be at least 120 feet (37 m) deep, but the pit has kept its secrets, and still no one knows who built it, or why, or even when—though a date in the mid-1600s seems as good as any. There is a museum a short walk south of the marina that details the mystery.

It seems to me that exploratory efforts so far have been fairly low-tech affairs, and I have to wonder if modern techniques such as ground-penetrating radar would finally solve this puzzle, which some theories have linked to UFOs, little green men, and ancient Egyptians. Amid the maze of speculation, one fact stands out: The amount of money expended on the digging outweighs, by several orders of magnitude, the possible value of any buried treasure. So Captain Kidd, whether in heaven or the warmer place, is probably having a damned good laugh.

Approaches to Oak Island. From Mahone Bay or from Indian Point, the route is straightforward: Pass either side of Sheep Ledge, and then either side of Apple Island. Don't confuse Apple Island with Round Island Nubble, a mile to the south, which looks quite similar. There is a rock southeast of Apple Island, so don't get too close to this part of it, or to the long bar extending from its northwestern side—which is not well shown on the chart. Then pass between Oak Island and Frog Island. There is reputedly a submerged rock in mid-channel here, and it is shown on the chart. I'm not sure whether it's really there or not, but caution may make you favor the Oak Island side.

There are a number of ledges in the upper bay, most of which are marked. If you're going from Oak Island to Chester, pass south of Warrens Ledge (which may be Warnes Shoal on older charts). If you're bound for Chester Back Harbour, go north of South Gooseberry Shoal; and if your destination is Chester Front Harbour, pass south of the shoal.

Anchorage, Dockage. Oak Island Marina, a substantial facility, was built with a government grant in about 1974. For many years, it was the only commercial marina in the province with docking alongside. Things seemed to slide downhill in the 1980s, with the loss of the marine slipway and boatyard. The hotel attached to the property went into receivership, and a few years ago was taken over by the Best Western hotel

chain. While one wonders if marina management is their strong point, the situation has stabilized. Fuel and water are available, and there may be guest moorage. In July and August it is certainly advisable to call ahead. The toll-free number is (800) 565-5075, but make absolutely sure that the person who answers the phone understands you want a berth in the marina, not a hotel room.

Conveniently, visitors berthed at the marina may use all the hotel facilities for the modest price of the slip—about $15 a night for a boat of 30 feet (9 m). There is a tolerably good restaurant, a good bar, and an indoor swimming pool kept warm enough to thaw out even my creaky bones. If you have seen nothing but cold, drippy fog for a week, this can be a very welcome respite. About a quarter-mile inland is the main road, with a grocery store, a fast food outlet, laundromat, and a tavern.

Gold River

Chart: **4381**

Two miles north of Oak Island lies the Cross Marina at Gold River. This operation was started by the Cross family, who for many years operated Gabriel Aero-Marine Instrument, Ltd. in Halifax, dealing largely in charts and electronics. But the 1980s were not kind to the company, and while I think the chart agency is still in operation, at the time of writing the marina is in receivership. It had a large number of boats using it as a base, however, and I'm pretty certain someone will buy it and keep it in operation. Until that happens, however, I can't give you a phone number to call.

136

Approaches. If you're approaching from the south, it's easier to stay outside Big and Little Islands, and then follow the buoyed channel in. At the time of writing, the marina was marked with a light buoy, but the Coast Guard has a habit of removing such navigation aids as soon as a commercial operation fails.

Chester Basin ★★ 4 B

Chart: **4381**

Chester Basin lies in the extreme northwest corner of Mahone Bay, and while this anchorage can't be considered scenic—it's surrounded by houses—it is certainly a convenient place for pro-

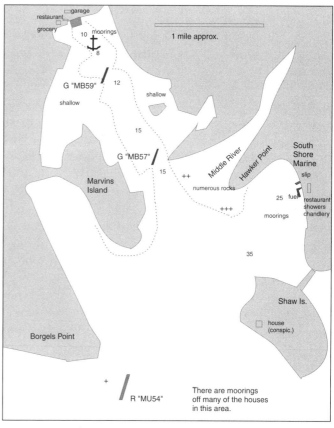

Chester Basin and South Shore Marine.

visioning. It's much easier to get groceries here than it is in Chester, as you can wheel your cart right onto the boat, instead of having to walk nearly a mile.

Approaches. Chester Basin is entered between Marvins Island and Hawker Point, north of Shaw Island. Favor the Marvins Island side, as there are drying rocks off Hawker Point. The area is unlit and visitors may find navigation difficult at night.

Leave green spar buoys "MB57" and "MB59" to port, and be aware that they're difficult to find unless you know exactly where to look. At the head of the basin, just beyond "MB59," is a small government wharf with about 8 feet (2.4 m) of water at low-water springs.

Anchorage. The holding ground is good if you anchor just to the south of the few local boats. The anchorage is sheltered, except for a narrow gap to the south. An ordinary summer gale won't bother you here, though, even from that direction.

Ashore. At the head of the wharf is a large grocery, a pharmacy, and a small restaurant, famous for fish chowder, which includes among its regular clientele some of Canada's rich and famous, such as Pierre Trudeau. But don't let that deter you; there's nothing pretentious about it.

The garage is a rendezvous of the local teenagers, and I prefer to anchor out here at night, even though the mud is foul and sulphurous.

South Shore Marine
(Stevens Cove) ★★★★ | 3 | | A |

Chart: 4381

This is one of the few marinas in the province, and although it does not feature rows of docks and slips, it offers good moorings and virtually all the services expected of such an operation. There is, in addition, an excellent boatyard, with

one of the few travel lifts in the province. The manager, Steve Moody, is a noted local sailor who for many years owned a 50-year-old classic boat. (I think the labor and expense of maintenance must have finally got to him, as he now has one of fiberglass.)

Approaches. The route to South Shore Marine is straightforward, and involves little more than turning east around the northern end of Shaw Island. The major hazard is all the moored boats. Not much of a sea gets in here, so the moorings are quite safe in anything short of a hurricane.

Ashore. There is no overnight docking unless things are very quiet, but there is almost always a vacant mooring, with an overnight charge of about $10. Fuel, water, and showers are available. There is a chandlery, and you can get block ice here, too—a rarity in the province. There's also an excellent restaurant and bar. The marina telephone is (902) 275-3711; Fax: (902) 275-2416. Marina staff also monitor VHF Channels 16 and 68.

The fuel dock is at the head of the cove. It is exposed to westerly winds, and coming alongside in a stiff crosswind with a vessel as unhandy as mine will test the skills (and humor) of the crew.

I especially like the restaurant, and often eat there when traveling to and from Halifax by land. I have never had a bad meal there. A stop there is a wonderful treat for any crew that has been beating through fog for a week. The view from the restaurant on a summer night is spectacular, and I think matched only by The Old Argyler in my home community. Reservations are advisable for the restaurant in summer. The telephone number is (902) 275-4700.

Chester ★★★★

4 BACK HARBOUR

2 FRONT HARBOUR

A 🍽 🛏 🔧 🚰 🚿

Chart: 4381

Chester has two harbors separated by a peninsula running north and south. Front Harbour, on the eastern side of the peninsula, is completely open to the south, and is best avoided unless you are visiting the yacht club or the restaurant. Back Harbour, to the west of the peninsula, is the preferred anchorage in Chester.

I must confess to having ambivalent feelings about Chester. It has become a hangout for Canada's rich and famous, as will quickly be apparent when you look at some of the houses. This has either enriched the community or ruined it, depending on your point of view. It's the uneasy relationship between this group and the lesser mortals of the community that accounts for my ambivalence.

Approaches. From the south, the approaches to Chester are straightforward. A course due north (000°M) from East Shoal buoy "MC55" will bring you to the west side of Quaker Island, a large grassy island with a small, red-flashing light tower.

From the east, from Halifax for example, pass north of Coachman Ledge, then shape a course of 315°M from whistle buoy "MA55." There are few obstructions in the approach, and it is not difficult at night. Thick fog presents more of a problem, though I have done this many times without hitting anything—so far.

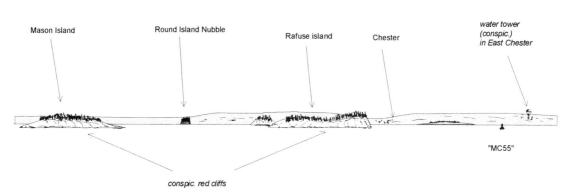

Approaches to Chester from the south—five miles out.

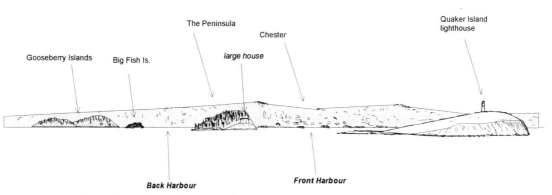

Approaches to Chester from the south—two miles out.

If you are a stranger to Mahone Bay, watch your compass, and keep a proper plot. There are numerous islands that look similar, and you can easily get confused.

To the north of Quaker Island, at the end of the protruding peninsula, is a wooded hill with some very impressive houses on it. One mansion faces offshore from the southern tip of this peninsula, which divides Front Harbour, on the east, from the approach to Back Harbour, on the west.

There is a long narrow spit, or shoal, north of Big Fish Island, just to the west of the imposing house on the end of the peninsula. There is also a spit joining the two Gooseberry Islands, and yet another spit north of Big Gooseberry Island. I have hit this one and come close to some of the others.

Anchorage, Dockage. Front Harbour is the site of the yacht club and, a little farther north, the Rope Loft restaurant.

Between them is the government dock. Don't tie up here, as you might at other government docks in the province; this is the terminus of the Tancook Island ferry. The ferry makes a run about every three hours during summer, and while it is quite maneuverable, it is best to keep out of its way.

There is temporary docking alongside at the Rope Loft, and there may be at the yacht club, if you want water. But the Chester Yacht Club is not the sort of place where you can tie up your boat and leave it while you visit the sights of the town. I suspect the members would not be amused.

If you're heading for Back Harbour, you can pass Little Fish Island on either side, but there is a bit more water to the east. The best anchorages are in the south, just off the government wharf, or in Mill Cove to the north. There are a number of local boats moored in Back Harbour, but there is usually room to anchor there, unless it's Chester Race Week. The holding ground is a little unreliable, and you should keep an eye on your boat if it blows hard from the northwest.

Ashore. Ben Heisler's boatyard is at the south end of Mill Cove. This is a local institution as Ben built most of the Chester "C"-Class boats, one of

the few remaining fleets built to the old International Rule that included the old Meter classes. Ben, in his 80s, had a designated seat in the local tavern, which I, for one, would not have the gall to usurp. (Don't worry that you may commit this sin by accident: It has his name carved on it.) Ben died in 1996, but I still wouldn't usurp his chair. It might bring bad karma.

Going up either of the roads from Back Harbour (ahead or to the right) leads you to the center of the village and a real tavern, The Fo'c's'le, which lies alongside Rosie O'Gradey's, a fast food establishment. The tavern has a hatch into the eating establishment so that patrons can order food directly without interrupting their beer consumption. It's a good place to get a steak that doesn't cost an arm and a leg.

Farther down Front Harbour is the Rope Loft restaurant, telephone (902) 275-3430. It has a small dock outside for patrons who arrive by boat. I've enjoyed some excellent meals here, though I must warn you that it has recently changed hands. Nearby is an interesting gift shop, the Warp and Woof. Right next to the Back Harbour wharf is another restaurant, The Captain's House. This has had several owners, with effects on its quality. I haven't tried it lately, though I'm told the present owners have improved it greatly.

The liquor store is a bit farther along this same road—it's a long way to walk with a case of beer. There is a bank, a pharmacy, a good hardware store, and a few other stores. Business moves at a different pace in villages like this, and if there are three people in the bank you'll have a long wait for service. But there may be an automatic teller machine to make this less than an hour's stop. There is no laundromat—at least I've never been able to find one—and there are no taxis. The supermarket is at least a mile from Back Harbour, on the road toward East Chester and the golf course. It is so out of the way that provisioning here is only for the desperate. There is a new mall to the northwest of the village, on the way to Chester Basin.

Chester Summer Theatre has some excellent productions, handy to the village center. Chester

also has a famous brass band that gives occasional performances on the green by Back Harbour.

Chester Race Week. The largest regatta in Atlantic Canada, Chester Race Week, is held during the third week in August. Usually, about 100 boats participate. I have mixed feelings about this event—though I have competed in it, and even won a trophy once when everyone else got lost in the fog. Some insoluble problems beset race week. Volunteers do their best with organization, and sacrifice a great deal of their spare time, but the protest meetings that follow the racing are more acrimonious than some countries' military uprisings. The truth is that there is really not sufficient room for all the boats. Furthermore, the racing crews, some of whom exhibit extraordinary thirsts, are not overwhelmingly welcomed by the natives. If you dislike a rowdy party atmosphere, you might want to avoid race week, especially if you have on board children under the legal drinking age of 19 years.

Chester Area— Other Anchorages ★★

B NO FACILITIES

Chart: **4381**

Among the anchorages in the Chester area are, from west to east, Borgels Point, Sandy Cove, and Marriotts Cove. All are exposed to southerly winds, overlooked by houses, and obstructed by moorings of local boats. There is nothing to recommend them.

Meisners Island

Chart: **4381** (Chester Harbour inset)

You can anchor off the western extremity of this island in calm weather. The views of Chester are good, and it's quite scenic. The owner is a very famous central Canadian "come from away" who doesn't like locals walking on his island. They are reported not to like him, either, but they do like his island, and use it for duck hunting. The one time I stayed here, the mosquitoes were so bad that after killing several hundred of the little fiends we upped anchor and fled at midnight.

Graves Island

Chart: **4381**

Graves Island, a provincial park with picnic facilities, lies a mile north of Lobster Point. The northwest corner, in Scotch Cove, offers the most sheltered anchorage, being open only to the northeast. As you approach, give a wide berth to Cye Ledge on the northeast corner of the island.

Occasionally you will see boats anchored off other nearby islands, and in calm weather you can get away with this during daylight, but I'd be reluctant to recommend any of these spots for an overnight stop.

Deep Cove ★★★★★
NO FACILITIES

Chart: **4381**

Deep Cove is a spectacularly beautiful cleft in the hills extending almost a mile into the 500-foothigh (150-m) Deep Cove Mountain on the eastern shore of Mahone Bay. It is wonderfully protected and I once sheltered there from a hurricane.

Approaches. From Lynch Shoal bell buoy "MA57," off Chester, steer 086°M for 4.3 miles.

From Blandford bell buoy, "MK52," steer 030°M for 3 miles. These courses will take you to a conspicuous gray cliff just north of Deep Cove. The entrance to Deep Cove is difficult to see until you are north of it. Keep close to the port side going in—the land drops away steeply, and if you stay only a boatlength off the cliff you won't hit anything. There are ledges obstructing the southern side, marked by small red spars that can be difficult to see. There is a small wharf, used by local fishermen, on the south side just past the ledges. Chart 4381 shows a red flashing buoy there, but it was removed following the demise of the marina.

Anchorage.   At its head, the inlet expands into a small basin where there is a small fish weir. There is plenty of room to anchor at least a dozen boats, however. A small grassy area on the south side of the basin is ideal for picnics.

A marina midway down the inlet, on the north side, was in receivership at the time of writing. But it's a facility on which at least a couple of million dollars has been spent, so I'm sure the receivers will try to sell it as a going concern. With or without the marina, this is one of the most scenic anchorages in Nova Scotia, and well worth a visit. The road is nearby, but it can't be described as busy, and doesn't detract from the ambiance.

Blandford Area

Chart: **4381**

Of the three harbors in the Blandford area—Upper Blandford, Blandford, and New Harbour—two are dominated by fish plants. Upper Blandford is the exception. None offers any facilities for visiting yachts, and, with more attractive harbors nearby, I've never been tempted by any of them. New Harbour offers the best shelter, and Blandford has the most difficult approach. You will almost certainly have to moor alongside a fishing boat, most of which leave at 0400. If you need immediate shelter from the weather, all will provide adequate protection in anything short of a hurricane.

Big Tancook Island ★★★★

Chart: **4381**

Big Tancook Island is Nova Scotia's largest remaining island community, having a winter population of about 180. There is an elementary school on the island, but high-school students must take the ferry to Chester. Fishing is the only industry, though the local delicacy, sauerkraut, was originally made here, and the island is still famous for its traditional boat, the Tancook whaler, a double-ended gaff schooner typically 35 to 40 feet (10.5 to 12 m) in length. Several were built as yachts. One of the earlier ones was described in *The Saga of Cimba,* by Richard Maury, in the 1930s. If my memory serves me right, he sailed from Nova Scotia to Fiji, where the boat came to a sticky end on a reef. Another was built for the noted rumrunner William ("The Real") McCoy. I am not sure when the last one was built, though I have tied up alongside one completed as late as 1979. A recent book, *The Tancook Schooners—*

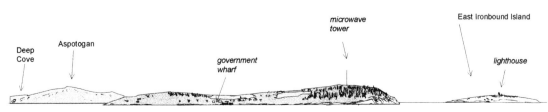

Tancook Island from the southwest.

An Island and Its Boats, by W. M. O'Leary (McGill-Queen's University Press) gives much detail about this tradition.

Many Lunenburg County family names in the boat-building business originated on Tancook Island, among them (with original German names in parentheses):

Stevens (Steebing, or Steubing); Cross (Krass, or Krauss); Baker (Becker); and Heisler (Haussler). Two other names, Mason and Langille, come from French Huguenots who settled in Lunenburg County at the same time as the Germans.

Approaches. The entrance to Northwest Cove is easy in clear weather, even at night, provided you keep clear of Star Island Ledges, off the northwest coast of the island. If you're coming from the north, head for the light on the end of the government wharf in Northwest Cove. If you're approaching from the southwest, don't get closer than a half-mile to Tancook Island. If Little Duck Island, 4 miles south, bears less than 190°M—or if Star Island, a half-mile west of Northwest Cove, bears more than 040°M—you are safe. Don't cut too far inshore of flashing green buoy "MN51."

Anchorage, Dockage. The wharf in Northwest Cove is crowded and you will have to tie up alongside a fishing boat. Again, this is a place where the fishermen are early risers. The ferry arrives five or six times a day and its space must not be usurped. It is possible to anchor close west of the government wharf, though if the wind swings to due west you will be exposed. Shelter at the wharf itself isn't great in strong westerlies either, though it's usually adequate in summer.

As an alternative, you can visit Southeast Cove, where the best anchorage is west of the ruined wharf. It's shallow, though, and completely exposed to the southeast. Swells will roll into the cove if the wind has a southerly component.

Ashore. Though the anchorages are indifferent and facilities limited, Big Tancook Island makes an interesting stopover as long as you keep an eye on the weather. The road going south from the government wharf leads across the top of the island and affords spectacular views of the whole of Mahone Bay. A small restaurant and a general store are within easy walking distance of the wharf.

One word of caution: Beware of the cars. Tancookers don't have to license or insure their vehicles for use on the island. A multitude of vehicles, many of which would normally be buried in wreckers' yards on the mainland, come here to die. But before finally expiring, they raise great clouds of red dust during the dry periods. There must be a source of fuel for all these vehicles and you'd expect it would be available to visiting yachts as well, but I never have discovered it. I suspect it's brought over on the ferry in large drums and is not for resale.

Little Tancook Island ★★

  NO FACILITIES

Chart: **4381**

Little Tancook is home to about six families, and the wharf is somewhat more exposed to westerlies than Big Tancook's is. My chart shows a marina here, but it doesn't exist. There may be a little more room at the wharf than there is at Big Tancook's, but the island doesn't have the historic attraction of its bigger neighbor.

East Ironbound Island ★★★

  NO FACILITIES

Chart: **4381**

The views from the lighthouse on East Ironbound Island are spectacular. The wharf provides only marginal protection in strong westerly winds, but it's substantial enough to handle large amounts of building material for a very substantial summer house for one of the barons of the fishing industry. The ferry no longer calls, and you may find room at the wharf for an overnight stay if the weather is behaving. The island is the background for a famous painting of a dory fisherman by Jack L. Gray, the renowned American artist.

The wind always seems to pipe up between East Ironbound Island and the mainland Aspotogan Peninsula, at least when it is in the southwest. Sometimes, when you pass the island, you'll run into a wall of dense fog and a great blast of wind at the same time. Be prepared for this little idiosyncrasy of the local wind gods.

St. Margarets Bay

Chart: **4386**

St. Margarets Bay has been neglected by yachtsmen, including me. I usually bypass it when I'm sailing between Halifax and Chester.

The northern and eastern parts of the bay, being only 15 miles from Halifax, have succumbed to a sort of suburban blight. Of course, this view reflects my own rural prejudices, and I'm sure the inhabitants think it's the very finest kind of place. Nevertheless, bedroom communities are not the usual destinations of cruising yachtsmen. In the southeast corner of the bay, for example, Peggys Cove is overrun with tourists by the hundred thousand. To add to the difficulties for yachtsmen, the larger food stores are situated in strip malls—very handy for motorists, but miles from the water.

Despite everything, there are anchorages that are attractive and sheltered from bad weather. There are yacht clubs at Hubbards, and at the Head of the Bay, and there's a marina in Tantallon. As I did with Mahone Bay, I'll describe the anchorages going clockwise from the southwest.

Approaches to St. Margarets Bay. Chart 4386 is the preferred chart of this area. Chart 4320 shows too little detail for entering any harbor in this area except in an emergency. I'm sorry to say, though, that 4386 is not a very good chart. Even

recent editions are based on a 50-year-old survey, and I'm certain not all the rocks are charted. As for the smaller anchorages, chart 4386 is only marginally useful, and when it comes to the inshore waters of the bay, I'd advise you not to trust the chart implicitly. Luckily, there are very few hazards in the open water of the bay. Like Mahone Bay, St. Margarets Bay is often clear of fog, especially the upper end, when it is of the dungeon variety outside.

The white granite rocks around St. Margarets Bay are dramatically different from those farther west, and form conspicuous headlands. Shut-In Island, for example, is unmistakable when the sun shines on it.

From the west, the entrance to St. Margarets Bay is obstructed by Seal Ledges and Horseshoe Ledge. In clear weather, you might be tempted to go inside one or the other, but I don't recommend doing that at night, and it could be dangerous in fog. Be particularly careful about the extensive drying rocks and ledges south of Gravel Island. The local fishermen go between Gravel and Saddle Islands, but I definitely don't recommend this. A course directly on the line between Seal Ledge bell buoy "MA54" and Aspotogan fairway bell buoy "DF," steering 060°M inbound, or 240°M outbound, will keep you safe if you can see buoys.

A vessel approaching from the east will encounter no dangers provided she keeps a reasonable distance off Dover, Peggys Cove, and other headlands. From Pennant Bay whistle buoy "A30," a course of 312°M for 12 miles brings you to Peggys Cove bell buoy "DA." From there, a course of 348°M leads you up the middle of the bay.

St. Margarets Bay is affected by tidal streams in the entrance, flowing northwest on the flood, and south-to-southeast on the ebb, at about 1 knot. These streams are not charted, but they're greatly affected by winds, barometric pressure, and rainfall. You need to keep track of your drift when visibility is less than clear.

Aspotogan

★★★★  ☐3 ☐C

NO FACILITIES

Chart: **4386**

Aspotogan is a neat little spot, as pretty as Peggys Cove, but undiscovered by tourists. The approach is a little tricky and I would not attempt it at night or in fog. From fairway buoy "DF," steer 332°M, midway between Gravel and Black Islands. Close to the headland, turn north. Stay on the port side going in, about 100 to 200 yards off. Black Rock dries 6 feet (1.8 m) so it almost always shows right in the middle of the cove. There are other rocks to the east of it, marked with a small red spar buoy. The cove will open up to port when you think you can't go any farther. The small government wharf is likely to be occupied, but there's room for one or two boats to anchor in the middle. A swell enters during southeasterly gales, but in an ordinary summer southerly the harbor is all right. There are no facilities, but with the 530-foot-high (160-m) mountain just ahead of you, it is certainly a pretty spot.

On the way in, there is reportedly an anchorage north of Saddle Island, but it's exposed to southerly winds and I haven't tried it.

Bayswater ★★★ ☐1 ☐C

NO FACILITIES

Chart: 4386

Close south of Aspotogan, Bayswater is best approached from the north. It has a beautiful sandy beach, but is open to winds from the south and east, and I would use it only in the calmest of conditions. There is usually a swell here.

Owls Head

Chart: **4386**

Southwest Cove: ★★★ ☐4 ☐C

NO FACILITIES

Northwest Cove: ★★ ☐3 ☐B

NO FACILITIES

Owls Head offers two anchorages, a reasonably well-protected and pretty one in Southwest Cove, and a more open, busier one in Northwest Cove.

Approaches. If you are coming from Aspotogan or Mahone Bay, you can run inshore of Southwest Island, but keep clear of the shallow patch in the middle by staying just outside a line from White Point to Owls Head.

Charley Rock, a half-mile east of Southwest Island, has 11 feet (3.3 m) over it, so you are unlikely to hit it. The greater danger is that of running into its unlit buoy at night.

To enter Southwest Cove, pass about 150 yards north of the north end of Owls Head Island, turn toward the mainland on a course of approximately 290°M, and get within 20 yards of the shore. You can then turn south, avoiding a rock, awash at low water, in the middle of the channel near the northern tip of Owls Head Island. The rock sometimes has a tiny buoy on it. I'd think twice about doing this at night, especially without radar.

Anchorage. The few local boats moored at the head of the cove leave plenty of room to anchor. The holding ground is good coarse sand, and you're sheltered here from anything but a real screecher from the northwest.

On the mainland side near the head of the cove is a small waterfall. The bottom rises beyond the waterfall until the water is less than 10 feet (3 m) deep. Just opposite, on the island, stands an impressive stone home in the form of a castle, which by now might be completed. A fixed bridge connects the island to the mainland, with a small sandy beach north of it on the island side. If you go east over the bridge, away from the mainland, you'll end up in a little bay with a view all the way across to Peggys Cove. The latest (1995) chart shows a power line with a clearance of 18 feet (5.4 m) across the southern part of the bay, just south of the little waterfall. It definitely wasn't there last time I visited, and I think the chart refers to the lines just north of the bridge, which have a clearance of only 2 feet (600 mm). I have to advise caution, however, as overhead power lines are difficult to see against trees, and running into one could ruin your day.

Northwest Cove. This harbor is easier to enter than Southwest Cove. It is buoyed all the way in, with light buoys north of Horse Island. It's less scenic, more crowded, and more open to the east. It's possible to anchor just west of the small government wharf. An alternative anchorage in Tilley Cove is partially obstructed by aquaculture cages.

Hubbards Cove ★★★

Chart: 4386

Hubbards is the commercial center of St. Margarets Bay, and has banks, stores, and a liquor store. There is a restaurant, the Dauphinee Inn, that is reputed to have moorings and slips for overnight dockage, and a laundromat. The inn's phone number is (902) 857-1790 or (800) 567-1790. I haven't stayed here, but it has been in business since 1927 so is quite likely to still be there if you want to patronize it.

Approaches. Hubbard's Cove is easily approached along almost unobstructed shorelines. The Royal Canadian Navy has a communications center at Mill Cove, little more than 2 miles south, and although they don't advertise how they're spending our tax money, electronic interference with lorans

and other instruments seems to be a common thing. So be a little skeptical of electronic readouts in this vicinity. The tiny government wharf at Fox Point was washed away in a winter storm in March 1995, and I doubt that it will be replaced in the near future. It was, in any case, very exposed to southerly winds.

Hubbards Cove is one of the easier places to enter in thick fog. From whistle buoy "DP," off Owls Head, steer 000°M for about 5 miles to bell buoy "DY52" and pass it on either side. Then come to 350°M to enter the cove.

To port, locate the fixed red light on Green Point, and to starboard, the small red spar marking Slaughenwhite Shoal, which dries 4 feet (1.2 m). The spar is at the inner end of the shoal for some reason, so don't pass southeast of it. There is an 18-foot (5.4-m) shoal in the middle of the entrance, but this shouldn't bother the average yacht. The anchorage is to starboard past Dauphinee Head. The shoreline is quite built up, as befits a suburb of Halifax, but the anchorage is well sheltered. A slight swell gets in if it is blowing a gale from the south or southeast but is not troublesome.

Anchorage. You can anchor anywhere, but just past the yacht club is as good a place as any.

From Hubbards, the bay trends more or less northeasterly to what the chart calls Head Harbour. Indenting this coastline is a series of beaches and coves, all exposed to the south, and all therefore of limited interest because there is almost always some sort of swell present. One of the beaches, Queensland, is a provincial park.

Head of the Bay
(Head Harbour) ★★★

Chart: 4386

A very sheltered series of coves nestles in the northeast corner of St. Margarets Bay. In the upper

reaches of Head of the Bay, or what the chart calls Head Harbour, I think you could probably ride out even the worst of storms. For my own tastes, the urbanization of this harbor, just 12 miles from Halifax by road, has reduced its attraction. Of course, if you come from west of Penobscot Bay it may not appear at all urban to you, and you may be wondering what the hell I'm talking about. It's all a matter of degree.

Approaches. Croucher Island guards the entrance to the harbor, flashing its white light. You may pass either side, and both sides are unobstructed, but the eastern side is wider. A course of 040°M from Ringdove Shoal bell buoy "DA58," off Franks George Island, will bring you past the eastern side of Croucher Island. When you are close to the shore, and when you can see red buoy "DA66" to starboard, north of Clam Island and just forward of abeam, come to 104°M to enter the harbor between Mason and Mackerel Points. From here on in, hazards are marked with buoys shown only on the latest charts. Be sure to pass them on the correct side, as most of them mark drying rocks.

If you're going to the marina on the south side of the entrance, just past Mackerel Point, an approach from the northeast—all the way around Mink Island—may be safer and easier.

Anchorage, Dockage. The Dockside Marina, close east of Mackerel Point, provides all services including, I believe, a 15-ton travel lift. Their phone number is (902) 826-7234.

There are numerous other coves farther in, not well shown on chart 4386, and best seen on my chart. The shores here are lined with cottages and houses, the traffic on the road is continuous, and the water is dotted with moorings for local boats, so I have never lingered. Nonetheless, if the weather outside is in one of its less humorous moods, and you need shelter, this is not an unreasonable place to find it.

French Village Harbour
(Glen Haven) ★★

| 4 | | B | NO FACILITIES |

Chart: 4386

The coastline south of Head Harbour is deeply indented, forming a dozen little coves of varying attractiveness. Again, if the population density were lower, this would be a very attractive cruising ground. The entrance to Glen Haven (French Village Harbour) lies 1 mile southeast of Croucher Island and has an unmarked rock with 9 feet (2.7 m) of water over it right in the middle. The harbor is open to the prevailing southwesterlies, but the more adventurous, in search of a really sheltered spot, might try going northeast to Frostfish Cove. There is another rock right in mid-channel, marked "PA" (position approximate) on my chart. This means that the Department of Fisheries and Oceans, which is responsible for the charts, is not sure where this rock really is, or if it is there at all. If you draw 6 feet (1.8 m) or less, favor the east side going in, and be careful. There is a sheltered anchorage just around the corner, with about 7 feet (2.1 m) at low-water springs.

Seabright (Hubley Cove) ★★

| C | NO FACILITIES |

Chart: 4386

Entering Seabright (called Hubley Cove on the chart) is a little tricky, but I have done it at night. Simply leave green can buoy "DT57" to port, and turn toward the north. There are depths of about 9 feet (2.7m) and it is more sheltered than the chart makes it appear, although it's somewhat exposed to strong westerlies. The founding director of the Maritime Museum of the Atlantic, Nils Jannisch, lives here.

Franks George Island ★★★

  NO FACILITIES

Chart: **4386**

There is a good anchorage at the eastern end of the bay that forms the northeastern side of Franks George Island. Part of this bay may be an aquaculture site, but there is room to anchor east of it. Most aquaculture sites coexist with other marine interests without much conflict, but not this one. The 1980s were full of reports of cut nets, sabotage, and incidents with shotguns at Franks George Island.

The bar at the east end of the island sticks out a long way to the north, so don't pass south of flashing red buoy "DV52" that marks its end. There is just one house on the island, and a sandy beach where the water is quite warm for Nova Scotia.

Glen Margaret ★★★

NO FACILITIES

Chart: **4386**

Immediately south of Franks George Island is a series of coves around Mosher Island. Daylight access is not difficult, but entry will be trickier at night. The most sheltered is that of Glen Margaret itself. Luke Island has a nice sandy beach each side of the 4-foot (1.2-m) drying rock in the middle.

Boutilier Cove is a little open to the northwest, but otherwise all right, if you are comfortable with the narrow entrance. Hacketts Cove, northeast of McCall Point, is another possibility, and there's more shelter if you use the cove to the south. I have not anchored overnight in any of these coves, but the entrances present no undue difficulty.

Going farther south, do not be tempted to go inside Shut-In Island; there is a rocky bar between it and Mackerel Point (the second Mackerel Point

in St. Margarets Bay, if you are confused) on which the rocks are unmarked and may not be correctly charted.

Indian Harbour ★★★

 NO FACILITIES

Chart: **4386**

I have always been dissuaded from visiting Indian Harbour by the need for intricate pilotage, and by the fact that every time I've been in the vicinity, the weather has been dirty. However, it is well marked and in calm weather you might be tempted to have a go at it. Don't mistake the fixed green light at the entrance with that at Peggys Cove, 2 miles southeast.

Peggys Cove

Chart: **4386**

Peggys Cove, home to a fishing fleet of about six small boats, is one of the most-photographed areas in Nova Scotia, or in Canada for that matter.

An old account by G. Peabody Gardner of Brookline, Massachusetts, tells how a 50-foot (15-m) schooner with a 7-foot (2.1-m) draft entered the cove in 1953. I'm not sure if anyone has tried it in a similar vessel since then, but I am certainly inhibited by the constant swell, the narrow entrance, and the hordes of tourists. If you did manage to get in, I'm not sure you would be welcomed with open arms. There certainly isn't room to anchor, and there probably wouldn't even be a place to tie up to.

147

Halifax Harbour and the Granite Coast

Ketch Harbor, near Halifax

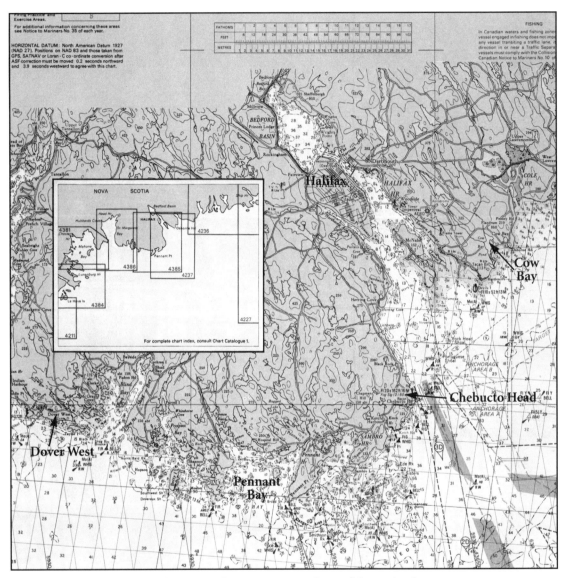

Based on CHS Chart 4320. Not to be used for navigation.

Halifax Harbour, one of the largest ports on the east coast of North America, is well marked, well charted, and easily navigated in clear weather. In thick fog, however, dense commercial traffic can make this area a nightmare if you don't have radar. In these conditions, I've been very grateful for the assistance of Halifax Traffic (see pages 160–161). I advise you to monitor them on VHF Channel 14 as you approach the harbor, and then on Channel 12 when you're inside the harbor limits.

Unfortunately, the attractive coves and anchorages west of Halifax have not been well charted by the Hydrographic Service. None of the charts of this area seems to be without problems. The scale of chart 4320 is too small to allow safe entry to any harbor in this region. Charts 4385 and 4386 also lack detail, and the surveys on which they are based were undertaken at least 30 years ago, and possibly as long as 50 years ago. To top it all, you need both 4385 and 4386 to enter one of the most picturesque and popular anchorages, Rogues Roost. But as these charts are all that are available for the area between the Aspotogan Peninsula and Pennant Point, you are stuck with them. There is a marked contrast between the urban shoreline of Halifax Harbour and the rocky coves to the west, many of which have so far escaped the urbanization characteristic of the upper reaches of St. Margarets Bay.

The Granite Coast

The Granite Coast, extending 15 miles from Peggys Point to Pennant Point, was named, as far as I am aware, by the late Dr. Dan Blain, of the Cruising Club of America and the Chester Yacht Club, in an article—or possibly a book—written in the 1950s. It is, unfortunately, long out of print, and I have never been able to find a copy. There have been a few changes since Dr. Blain's time (though, in this area, maybe fewer than you would think), and I trust there will be no objection to my following in his wake, as it were.

The coastline here is all sparkling white granite, and as the topsoil is only a few inches deep, those bits of it not pounded by the continuous surf are colonized by the hardiest type of spruce trees, interspersed with the odd bog and blueberry patch. In the 15 miles between Peggys and Pennant Points, there are at least a dozen good anchorages, and, despite the proximity of Halifax, you may well not see another boat, even at the height of the season.

While there are few outlying dangers, this coast is very steep-to, and depths can change from 120 feet (36 m) to 0 in a few boatlengths. Furthermore, the shore you're likely to end up on would almost certainly be surf-pounded rock. There always seems to be an onshore swell here, even during northerlies, and the Granite Coast attracts more than its fair share of fog.

Don't rely solely on loran or GPS to enter most of these harbors, because there might be a considerable error—the horizontal datum of the charts is North American Datum 1927, and corrections must be made to electronic devices using NAD 83, as notes on the charts point out. While I have entered most of these places in thick fog, or at night (sometimes both), the pilotage is quite intricate, and unless you have radar, or have been here before, you will find it a lot less tense if you explore the area in good visibility.

The rise and fall of the tide here is a maximum of about 7 feet (2.1 m). During the summer months, it's usually more like 5 feet (1.5 m), and there is very little tidal stream to worry about, except in and around the Sambro Ledges.

Dover ★★★★

NO FACILITIES

Chart: **4386**

Dover Harbour is well protected from the south by numerous islands and offers cruising boats a wide choice of scenic anchorages in snug coves.

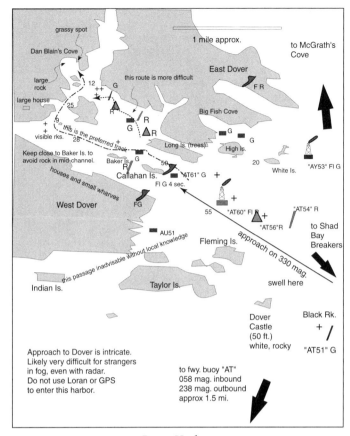

Dover Harbour.

Within the map image, the following labels appear:

grassy spot
Dan Blain's Cove
1 mile approx.
to McGrath's Cove
Dan Blain's Cove
large rock
12
this route is more difficult
East Dover
F R
large house
25
G
Big Fish Cove
9 this is the preferred track
visible rks.
28
G R
R
G A R
G
G
Keep close to Baker Is. to avoid rock in mid-channel.
houses and small wharves
Long Is. (trees)
High Is.
White Is.
20
"AY53" Fl G
Baker Is.
G
50
"AT61" G
Callahan Is.
Fl G 4 sec.
West Dover
FG
55
"AT60" Fl R
"AT56"R
"AT54" R
to Shad Bay Breakers
AU51
Fleming Is.
approach on 330 mag.
this passage inadvisable without local knowledge
Indian Is.
Taylor Is.
swell here
Dover Castle (50 ft.) white, rocky
Black Rk.
"AT51" G
Approach to Dover is intricate. Likely very difficult for strangers in fog, even with radar. Do not use Loran or GPS to enter this harbor.
to fwy. buoy "AT" 058 mag. inbound 238 mag. outbound approx 1.5 mi.

Approaches. From fairway whistle buoy "AT," steer 058°M—or from bell buoy "AT50," steer 020°M—until the small lattice tower (the red-white-red daymark) on Callahan Island bears 330°M. On this approach, Dover Castle, a conspicuous white rock 45 feet (14 m) high, will be to port. Southeast of it, and closer to your track, will be Black Rock, 2 feet (60 cm) high, marked with green spar buoy "AT51," which is not easy to see. If you can see the spar (or Black Rock itself), you can cut this corner a bit.

When the Callahan Island mark is bearing 330°M, turn on to that heading and follow the red buoys in, leaving them to starboard. The buoyed channel lies north of Callahan Island, but most of the local boats pass close to its south side, going to the fish plant on what is called Soi Point on the chart. Bear in mind that the outside buoys are exposed to the full force of the North Atlantic Ocean and may not be in exactly their charted positions.

There tends to be a lot of swell in the entrance, and this passage is quite narrow. Fleming Island is steep-to, and there are drying rocks north of spar buoys "AT54" and "AT56," so favoring the port side going in is a bit safer. When the sun is in your eyes, as it will be if you are entering after 1800, these spars are difficult to see. Once you are past Fleming Island, the water becomes much smoother, though the pilotage is still intricate.

Anchorage. Close to the harbor entrance, a really pretty sheltered spot, is the gut between Taylor and Moore Islands. There are spectacular views from the top of Taylor Island.

Farther in, the buoyed channel leads north of Privateer Island, but there is a mess of rocks at the north end, sometimes marked, but not always. For this reason, I prefer going around the west side of Privateer Island. As you go in, keep Baker Island close to port as there are unmarked rocks in mid-channel between the island and green can (may now be a spar) buoy "AT67." Leave the two little islands southwest of Privateer Island close on your starboard hand, then swing north between the last island and a small rocky ledge that always shows. You then enter a small channel with a number of coves on your port hand. The third one up, known locally as Dan Blain's Cove, is a delightful, sheltered anchorage. In the southern part of the cove is a large rock—one much used by my children for jumping off—and on the northern side there is a grassy area suitable for picnicking. A road lies somewhere off to the west, but it's not intrusive, and no houses overlook this cove. The last time I was here, the water was warm enough to swim in—for the children, at least.

One of the few drawbacks of Dover Harbour concerns the weak flushing action of the tidal stream. Every plastic bag thrown overboard by local fishermen ends up on shore. While fishermen in general are now more environmentally aware than they were a few years ago (some of them still regard environmentalists as eccentrics with more regard for seals than for people) it will take years for the plastic garbage to disappear from this particular harbor.

Incidentally, there is a passage south of Dover, between the mainland and Moore Island, leading west toward Indian Island and Polly Cove. This looks straightforward enough, though I wouldn't advise anyone without local knowledge to enter it from seaward, and I've never been there myself. I have seen boats sailing through there, however, so I guess the adventurous could try it at their own risk.

East Dover, however, is quite easy to enter—simply follow the buoys in. Keep on the south side after passing Leary Point as there are unmarked rocks extending from the northern shore. A government wharf situated halfway up the cove, on the north side, has about 8 feet (2.4 m) of water at low tide. A low swell finds its way in here in southerlies.

If you keep close to the southern side of the inlet, you can pass into a little basin at the head of the cove, which is much more sheltered. I'd advise you to check this out from the dinghy first, because it's very narrow. The anchorage is overlooked by houses, though, which reduces its attraction for people like me.

East Dover ★★★

NO FACILITIES

Chart: 4386

Close east of Dover Harbour, there is a multitude of coves forming the west side of Blind Bay. Most of them are well sheltered and surrounded by islands covered with spruce trees. In recent years, this area has been discovered by "rich people from away" who have built enormous houses overlooking some of these coves and bays. Whether this has improved the area or not depends on your point of view.

If you're heading north from Dover Harbour into Blind Bay, you may safely pass between High Island and White Island, where there are depths of more than 20 feet. The swell can be intimidating, however, and you should favor the eastern side.

The first cove going north from Dover Harbour is Big Fish Cove, which, from the outside, looks a little congested. I have never used it.

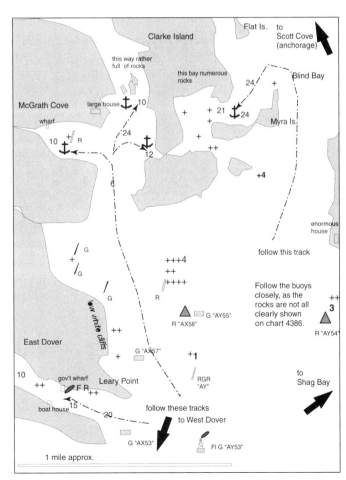

East Dover and McGrath Cove.

153

McGrath Cove

★★★★

NO FACILITIES

Chart: 4386

McGrath Cove is actually a series of coves, perfectly sheltered and roomier than East Dover. Be sure to follow the buoys, as there are a lot of rocks in the entrance. If it is foggy (the usual state, it seems, when I have been there) finding the buoys can be quite exciting, though the approaches are quite sheltered if it's not blowing a gale from the south or southeast.

The quietest anchorage is off the west side of Clarke Island, though there are other suitable places. Some of the space is occupied by the moorings of local boats, and some fishing takes place here, but it is not really a busy place, and there has always been plenty of room to anchor. Some of the large houses overlooking the various coves are quite spectacular. A minor drawback is the dearth of places suitable for a walk ashore.

There are a number of other potential anchorages farther up Blind Bay, some of which look very attractive, but I have no personal experience of them. There seems to be no undue difficulty in the pilotage, provided you remember the smudges on the chart are actually unmarked rocks.

Shag Bay ★★

Chart: 4386

Shag Bay is free of hazards in its main reach, but it's exposed to southwesterlies. Nevertheless, there are a few anchorages at the northern end of the bay, and the village of Shad Bay (whose name is spelled differently to confuse those from away) has a tavern and a restaurant within walking distance of the government wharf. As this area is just 10 miles from Halifax, the nearby highway is pretty busy.

Approaches. The approach to Shag Bay is somewhat encumbered with rocks, like most of the harbors in this region. From the west, that is from fairway buoy "AT," steer 058°M straight for Outer Gull Island, which is 44 feet (13 m) high. Keep clear of Shag Bay Breakers, which are marked by green spar buoy "AS53" on their eastern side. Be careful here, because the buoys can be confusing. If you leave red buoy "AT50" on your starboard side while heading northeast, as you should, don't be tempted to aim for spar "AS53" and to try to leave it to port. If you don't leave it far to starboard you will run into Shag Bay Breakers.

When you come to Outer Gull Island, leave it to port and pass up the bay close to the eastern shore. There are other passages up the bay, but they're more difficult.

If your approach brings you from the east, stay about a quarter-mile off the Prospect shore, and when you round Shag Head, just follow the eastern side of Shag Bay as described above.

Anchorage. Northwest Cove, branching off the bay to port, is open to winds from the southeast, but otherwise looks satisfactory.

Shag Bay is reasonably well sheltered, but be careful to follow the buoys. You cannot circumnavigate Cochran Island because of overhead power cables with a clearance of 28 feet (8.5 m) on its northeast shore. There is a similar cable from the mainland to a small island a half-mile to the south.

Anchoring is possible west of Cochran Island, and the anchorage is more sheltered, although the main road is a distraction.

Ashore. Shad Bay has a tavern and a restaurant that I visited one night after arriving in the dark. When I set sail next morning, there was thick fog, so I still don't know what it looks like in daylight. The nearby highway is quite busy, as it is less than 10 miles from downtown Halifax.

Prospect ★★★ 4 A

NO FACILITIES

Chart: **4386**

With its conspicuous church steeple standing on a small hill, Prospect is a picturesque community from seaward. It has a government wharf, but it's somewhat less urbanized than other communities in this area and, for me at least, somewhat more attractive as a result.

Approaches. If you come from the west, a course of 105°M from offshore buoy "AT" takes you near red bell buoy "AM62" at the entrance. On this approach, you'll notice a series of small islands to starboard, extending northwest from Betty Island. The northernmost island, Norris Bald Rock, is quite close to your track. It's 24 feet (7.3 m) high, has a good radar profile, and you can usually hear surf breaking on it.

The approaches from the east are more difficult—follow the directions given below for Rogues Roost.

When you reach bell buoy "AM62," change course to 316°M, and enter close to the northern side of Saul Island, which shows a fixed white light. There is a small government wharf, with depths of about 8 feet (2.4 m) at low water, and

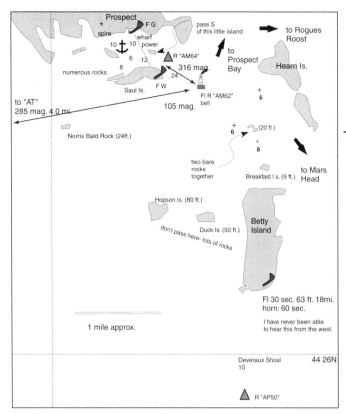

Approaches to Prospect.

you may anchor just west of it, in about 10 feet (3 m). Power cables on the sea floor run from the wharf to Saul Island, so don't anchor in the eastern part of the harbor. Getting into Prospect doesn't leave much room for error, and while it's easy enough on a fine day, I'd have reservations about doing it at night.

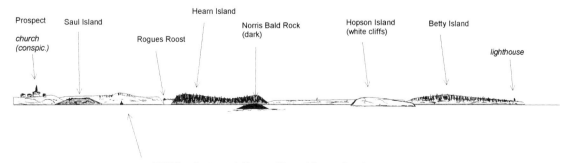

Approaches to Prospect from the southwest.

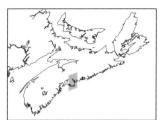

Prospect Bay ★★

Charts: 4386, 4385

Anchorages. Prospect Bay is dominated by Pig Island and the bigger Purcell Island to its north. While the west side of the bay north of Purcell Island is built up with houses, there are several coves and anchorages offering good shelter for small craft.

Approaches. Instead of turning to port at bell buoy "AM62," come on to a heading of 038°M and watch for green buoys "AN55" and "AN57" ahead. Leave them to port. Kelly Ledge, marked by "AN57," can actually be passed either side, though the recommended passage is to the east. If you choose to pass west of it, keep well over toward the Prospect side. Farther up, keep close to the eastern side of Purcell Island as there is an unmarked rock in mid-channel at the northern end of Whitehorse Cove.

The first cove north of Prospect, just south of Kelly Point, is obstructed by numerous rocks, and best avoided.

Murphy Cove, on the west side of Prospect Bay a little less than a mile north of Kelly Point, has depths of about 25 feet (7.5 m) but is obstructed by rocks at the entrance. There is a passage through these rocks, with roughly 6 feet (1.8 m) of water at low tide, but I've never been through it. If you want to try it, sound it out in the dinghy—the passage is more or less in the middle. I've seen boats in there, so I know it can be done.

Pig Island provides sheltered anchorage from all directions, though access is a little shallow. Favor the Pig Island side, as there is an unmarked rock on the mainland side of the entrance, just where you turn east into the cove. Rounding Purcell Island from the north reveals another sheltered anchorage that's a bit easier to get to.

Prospect Bay is navigable as far as White's Lake, at the head, but there's a 4-foot (1.2-m) shallow patch just before you reach the lake. I

have had the indignity of running aground on it. Although White's Lake is quite a sheltered anchorage, it always seems as if thousands of commuters are using the major road junction at the head of the bay.

Ashore. There is a shopping mall on the road north of Purcell Island that has a decent-size grocery store. Getting there involves anchoring somewhere nearby, rowing ashore, and clambering over some big rocks. As the local inhabitants are almost all landlubbers, this activity may reward you with the kind of glares usually reserved for the latest arrivals from Colombia.

Rogues Roost ★★★★★

Chart: 4385

Rogues Roost is one of the most famous anchorages in the province, and you really can't say you have cruised Nova Scotia unless you've been there. Despite its popularity, I have always found plenty of room, and I think the maximum number of boats I have seen there at once is about eight.

Approaches from the West. One of the problems when you're approaching Rogues Roost this way is that you have to change charts from 4386 to 4385 just as you are about to find the entrance, which can be damned irritating. It is also difficult to pick out the entrance until you are right on top of it. The first time I took my wife there, she thought I was aiming at a solid wall of rock. She wondered if I'd gone crazy.

From Prospect bell buoy "AM62," steer about 072°M to pass just north of Hearn Island. The island has a few offlying rocks, but as long as you stay out 50 yards or so, you'll be safe. When the sound east of Hearn Island opens up, steer 100°M. There's a green spar to starboard, "AN53," that marks a rock uncovering 1 foot (30 cm) at low water, according to chart 4385. The rock def-

here for the first time at night or in thick fog, though I have managed it a number of times.

Approaches from the East. Find Grampus Rock bell buoy "AM52," then steer 350°M toward the northern end of Betty Island, leaving the line of three red spars to starboard. From the last spar, "AM58," it gets a bit tricky, but the safest way is to come immediately to 334°M, leave the two small islets close to port, and then swing just a little more to port to miss the drying rock off the southwest corner of Hearn Island. When Prospect bell buoy "AM62" is abeam, follow the instructions above for an approach from the west.

This sounds a little complicated and, indeed, I have found it more than a little tense at night or in fog. I hit one of the spars once—they were big cones then—and everyone thought we were going to sink. It looks possible to round the south end of Burnt Island, and I've done this a couple of times, but I'm sure the chart doesn't show all the rocks, and its small scale makes this passage difficult.

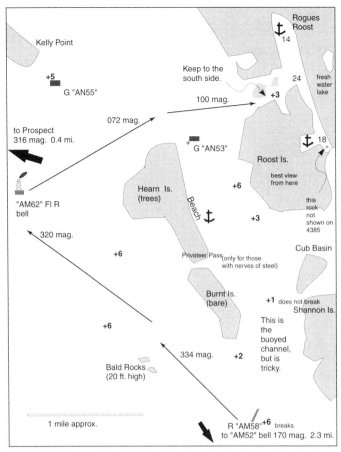

Rogues Roost.

initely is not there. There might be a submerged one, though I have never seen it.

If you keep going, the entrance—between Roost Island and the small island to the north—will open up in front of you. A large flat rock, drying about 4 feet (1.2 m), obstructs the middle of the channel close inside the entrance. Pass south of the rock, keeping only a few feet off Roost Island.

A small cove will open up to starboard, but it's not the main anchorage. Go on a bit farther, keeping to the south side. At the end of the inlet you can turn either to port or to starboard. The most popular spot is to starboard—a little basin carved into Roost Island at the end of the cleft in the rock. There's plenty of water here, at least 12 feet (3.6 m) all the way in. One of my friends regularly visits this place with a 50-foot (15-m) schooner. It would be a little daunting to enter

Anchorage. The holding ground is thick mud in depths of 20 feet (6 m) or so, with all-round shelter. I have ridden out the odd hurricane warning here, and the wind did bluster around a bit, but extra security can be had by putting a line around a tree.

While there are many small, enclosed anchorages in Nova Scotia, what makes this one unique, I think, is the view. On the west side of the south cove there is a little shingle beach where you can land the dinghy, and a path, tramped by generations of sailors, that leads to the bare rocks on top. It's not a difficult climb, even for old graybeard loons like myself, and the view from the top is stunning. On a clear day, you can enjoy a 180-degree panorama, from the little church in

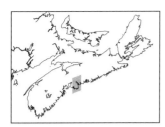

Terence Bay in the east, over the inlets of Cub Basin and Back Bay, south to Betty Island, west over the islands south of Prospect, and northwest to the village of Prospect itself. Watching the sunset from here is something to be remembered. It is difficult to believe you are only 10 miles from Halifax. There is a small plaque on the north side of the cove in memory of John Snow, late of the Armdale Yacht Club, who had the misfortune to slide off the causeway to the club in the middle of a winter storm, and expire, while still in his vehicle, almost under his own boat. John Snow was a frequent visitor to this cove, and the plaque states that this was his favorite anchorage. Many local yachtsmen refer to it as Snow's Cove.

Once when I was anchored at Rogues Roost, a couple of dolphins swam down the inlet, around the little cove with its anchored boats, and back out again, jumping out of the water occasionally. Less welcome, perhaps, are some of the locals, who do the same thing in high-powered skiffs, trailing enormous wakes. However, this usually only occurs at weekends, and may not happen at all.

If the south cove is too crowded for your taste, the cove to the north is just as sheltered, and some people prefer it. I have to say, though, that most of the times I've visited here, the only boats present have been our own and our friends'.

Opposite the northeast corner of Roost Island, on the mainland, is a path leading to a freshwater lake that warms up enough in summer for swimming. The only trouble is that the enormous population of sea gulls has the same idea, and, as they have besmirched the rocks somewhat, you may not end up as clean as you intended.

It is not possible to pass into Cub Basin from here, except in a small dinghy.

Hearn Island ★★★★

NO FACILITIES

Chart: **4385**

If you tire of Rogues Roost, and particularly if you have dogs or small children in need of a run on a beach, Hearn Island is the place for you. From the entrance to Rogues Roost, go southwest to the midpoint of Hearn Island, leaving green spar "AN53" to starboard. You'll find a white beach, plenty of grassy spots for picnicking, and pleasant walking on most of the southern part of the island. It is reasonably sheltered, but I've usually gone back into the Roost at night. Some of the residents of Prospect Bay camp on the island during the summer, but there is plenty of room for all.

Cub Basin ★★★

NO FACILITIES

Chart: **4385**

If you feel your way carefully out of the south end of the sound east of Hearn Island, you can enter Cub Basin, which is somewhat larger and marginally less sheltered than Rogues Roost. The bottom is rocky and less reliable as an anchorage. For that and other reasons, I have never used it.

Rogues Roost to Mars Head, including Ryan Gut

To anyone studying the chart, Back Bay and the area south of Shannon Island appear to be a mass of unmarked rocks. It looks even worse in real life.

To leave Prospect Bay via the east side of Betty Island, follow the line of red spars (leave them to port, as you are leaving harbor), on a course of about 170°M. This, after 2.5 miles from the end of Burnt Island, leads you safely to Grampus bell buoy "AM52." If you are coming along the shore from Chester or St. Margarets Bay, you should stay just outside a line drawn between "AM52," Betty Island, and Dover fairway buoy "AT," on a course of about 132°M. There is a foghorn on Betty Island giving one blast a minute, but I have never heard it when I've been coming from the west.

There is a shortcut to Pennant Bay through Ryan Gut (north of Ryan Island), but it's narrow and difficult. Captain T. F. T. Morland, a retired naval captain who wrote extensively about the coast of Nova Scotia 40 years ago, states that it's inadvisable to try this passage unless you have on board someone who has been through it before. I am not usually deterred by this sort of advice, and maybe one day I will pass here when there's not a big swell running, a 30-knot southwesterly blowing, and thick fog obscuring everything. Although I've been here some 30 or 40 times, it hasn't happened yet.

It has been my policy in this guide not to describe a passage unless I've done it myself. But as this could be a useful shortcut, and as you might come upon it on a flat-calm day with good visibility, I will make an exception.

The passage is entered from the west, close north of red spar buoy "AM54." Pass north of Dollar Rock, which usually breaks and is not difficult to see, and then hug the north side of Ryan Island. This channel is buoyed, but the buoys are not shown on the chart. They are also arranged as if you were leaving port, which means you must leave the red spars to port. When you reach the eastern end, the channel turns more to the south-southeast. The last spar "AH53," relates to another channel, and although it's green you must leave it to port also. If you haven't hit a rock by now, nothing will get you. Whenever I have approached this channel from the east, the whole area has seemed full of rocks, and appeared even more intimidating than it does from the west.

As you head south, the last point of land on Mosher Island is Mars Head. The sea always seems to be rough when I round it. A reef extends three-quarters of a mile south, almost all the way to bell buoy "AM52." Give this area a wide berth. The captain of the *Atlantic,* a White Star Line steamer, did not follow this advice. He ran aground there on April 1st, 1873, at 0300. Five hundred passengers drowned or died of hypothermia. Many of them are in the graveyard at Terence Bay. This was one of the worst shipping disasters prior to the loss of the *Titanic.* Although there were hundreds of women and children aboard, few survived, and the subsequent Court of Inquiry made pointed remarks that subsequently led to the policy of allowing "women and children first" into the lifeboats.

Terence Basin ★★

NO FACILITIES

Chart: **4385**

There are a few aspects of Terence Bay, in the northwest corner of Pennant Bay, that are not at all apparent from the chart. It has a longstanding reputation for being what is euphemistically called "a rough place." In my experience, the natives have been less than friendly and tend to disturb you with wakes from powerboats. Most of them don't seem to realize that passing an anchored boat while dragging a big wake tends to make the affected crew hostile. It also induces apoplexy in any captain who spills his gin in his lap. This situation may be improving, however, as the community gradually becomes yuppified with commuters from Halifax. I know this anchorage is quite popular with Halifax sailors, so perhaps they are more inured to this sort of behavior—or perhaps I've just had a few bad experiences.

Approaches. Terence Bay is totally landlocked and provides good shelter from anything but a hurricane—but the approach is difficult for strangers, especially at night.

When approaching from the west, steer 058°M from bell buoy "AM52" off Mars Head. Pass either side of Terence Rock and gradually come round to about 330°M. Give Tennant Point, which has a fixed red light on it, a berth of at least a half-mile as there are outlying shoals.

If you're coming from the east, steer 338°M from bell buoy "AA50" off Pennant Point and leave red lightbuoy "AD56" fairly close on your starboard side.

A government wharf comes into view just before you enter the basin, on the port side. This is close southwest of the "T" in "Terence Bay" marked on chart 4385. There's no great difficulty getting to the wharf, but it serves a busy fish-processing plant, and there's not usually much spare room.

Anchorage. The entrance to Terence Basin is narrow, so stay in the middle. Small wharves project from the western side of the gut, and toward the top end of the gut there is a shoal patch with 4 feet (1.2 m) at low water, so watch the tide if you draw more than that. The bottom is covered with long eelgrass that sometimes returns depth-sounder echoes, making you think you are aground when you are not. After about three-quarters of a mile, the passage opens out into a little bay divided in two by a rocky outcropping on the eastern side.

The bay in the southeast corner, Grover Cove on the chart, provides the most secure anchorage. The last time I came here it was about midnight. After picking my way through Pennant Bay, and creeping up the gut, I rounded the corner here and ran into an unlit aquaculture tank. A torrent of abuse came from one of the houses overlooking the channel. Had there been a cannon on board, I would cheerfully have returned fire. Eventually I found an unobstructed space higher up. Don't try to get to the head of the basin, as there is an overhead power cable with a clearance of only 18 feet (5.4 m). There are moorings for local boats at the top of the basin. I wouldn't suggest picking one up, the locals might take umbrage at this and sink you.

The rest of Pennant Bay is so infested with unmarked rocks exposed to the prevailing southwesterlies that I haven't explored it further.

Halifax Harbour Outer Approaches

Charts: **4385, 4237**

Halifax is the deepest major harbor on the eastern seaboard of North America, and handles well over 1,000 commercial ships a year. Their movements constitute the biggest hazard for small boats in this area. Halifax is also the largest naval base in Canada, and there is considerable fishing-boat traffic. Dodging ships isn't much of a problem for visiting cruisers in clear weather, but it can give you white knuckles in fog.

On the west side of the approaches to Halifax are the Sambro Ledges. They cause an awful slop, so I usually go inside when I'm coming from the west. There are fewer hazards in the eastern approaches, but you should be aware that it is an area much used for naval exercises.

Halifax Traffic uses VHF Channel 14 for vessels

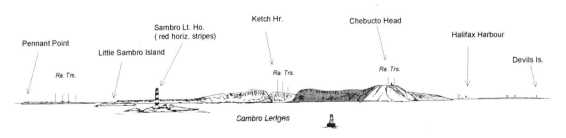

Entrance to Halifax Harbour from the south—five miles out.

outside the harbor, and Channel 12 for vessels inside Sandwich Point. Vessels less than 65.6 feet (20 m) in length do not have to report to Halifax Traffic, but may if they wish. Vessels longer than 65.6 feet (20 m) must report on crossing a line extending from Pennant Point to the west, or Shut-In Island to the east. I have found Halifax Traffic very helpful in informing me of shipping movements, and on one particularly trying day, with visibility so bad I couldn't see the decks of the harbor bridges when I was directly beneath them, they guided me to a berth. They cannot, however, for reasons of legal liability, tell you whether it is safe to cross the path of other vessels. They will only tell you that such-and-such a vessel is in your vicinity, doing this speed on that course. They have a blind spot on their radar display inside Sambro Light and west of Chebucto Head. They track all vessels continuously and can identify an individual vessel by its VHF transmissions. If you call for assistance, they may ask you to hold down your mike button for a few seconds to identify you. If you're out here, perhaps with no radar, and the fog shutting in, and darkness falling, with engine noises all around you, call them. Don't plug on stubbornly and hit some large and unyielding object. Many of the controllers are yachtsmen themselves and understand the difficulties of entering port in poor visibility.

Charts. The preferred charts are numbers 4385 and 4237. They are much the same scale, but 4237 is a newer metric chart and gives slightly more coverage to the east of 4385. Be sure not to confuse the meter soundings of chart 4237 with the fathom soundings of 4385—and watch out for heights in meters instead of feet.

Charts 4201, 4202, and 4203 are large-scale charts of Halifax Harbour. Chart 4201 is the only one that shows the Bedford Basin, and if this is your destination, you should probably have it on board. Incidentally, all these charts are unhandy things, 3 feet by 4 feet (1 m by 1.2 m) in size, and designed for big ships' chart tables. It's impossible to look at them unfolded in the cockpit of a small boat. You can probably get away with chart 4237

or 4385 if you are going no farther than downtown Halifax, or to the Northwest Arm.

It would be unwise to use small-scale charts 4012 and 4013 to enter Halifax Harbour, although you might get away with using 4320 in an emergency, as long as you realize that few buoys are shown on it.

Chart 4318 is an obsolete chart of the Sambro Ledges, a larger scale than 4237, and shows the ledges somewhat better. Don't throw 4318 away if you want to go into Sambro Harbour.

Approaches. Coming from the west, I prefer to go inside Sambro Ledges rather than the much longer way around the outside. Of course, if you're approaching from offshore, this is not such a consideration. It is always rough near the ledges, but ducking inside Pennant Point gets you out of the worst of the swell. I used the inside passage about a dozen times with my better half on board, at night and in thick fog. Then, one fine day, she was able to see all the breaking rocks and promptly banned this practice until I had a decent radar set—which, I admit, does tend to make things less intimidating.

From bell buoy "AM52," off Mars Head, steer 110°M for 3.3 miles to bell buoy "AA50," off Pennant Point. The easiest way from here, especially if you have radar, is to pass 0.3 miles off the peninsula, steering about 072°M toward bell buoy "HS6," about 3 miles distant. Eldad Rock, ahead, may be difficult to find if it is not breaking, but Bull Rock, about 0.3 miles to starboard, always breaks, and is usually visible, only covering at the top of high spring tides. You can usually hear it, too.

Island Rock, the next hazard to port, always shows. Torpey Ledge, to starboard, is awash at low-water springs, and usually breaks. Fairweather Rock, ahead to starboard, is 10 feet (3 m) high, a good radar target, and always heard. North of Fairweather Rock is bell buoy "HS6."

From the buoy, head north to round Inner Sambro Island, leaving it to starboard as you pass between it and Cape Sambro. There is 12 feet (3.6 m) of water here in the middle, so it shouldn't

161

be a problem for any boat of reasonable draft. When you've passed Lobster Claw, marked by green lightbuoy "HE13," resume a course of 072°M and head for bell buoy "HD5," just south of Chebucto Head.

It is tempting to creep up the western side of the approaches to Halifax Harbour if visibility is poor, heading roughly north. I have, in fact, done this many times, but if you choose to do it, remember that you're going against the flow of vessels in the traffic separation scheme, and you really need to watch yourself. At the base of Chebucto Head is a big pile of rocks, and I've had the nasty experience of spotting one of them through the murk a boatlength ahead, even though there was still 100 feet (30 m) of water under the keel.

There is virtually nothing to hit in the inner approaches, though—apart from ships—as long as you stay clear of Thrumcap Shoal, south of McNabs Island.

Sambro Ledges Passage. The buoyed passage through Sambro Ledges follows a magnetic bearing of about 068°, but is only marginally wider than the inside passage, and tends to be rougher, as the tide is stronger here, running at about 1 knot. The flood runs southwest, and the ebb northeast, most of the time.

Outside Route. If you prefer to go the long way around, a course of 124°M from buoy "AM52," south of Mars Head, brings you to bell buoy "HE2," off Smithson Rock, after 5.6 miles. From there, it's 104°M for 2.1 miles to whistle buoy "HS." Note that there is a drying rock one mile to the north of this track. From "HS," steer 078°M for 2.3 miles to bell buoy "HD3," thence 038°M for 3.4 miles to buoy "H1." The Sisters, a nasty pair of drying rocks, is just to port after you pass "HD3." Closer in, you can usually hear bell buoy "HD5" off to port when you get within a mile of

Chebucto Head. Sambro lighthouse, the oldest in Canada, a high tower with red and white horizontal stripes, dominates the scene if you can see anything at all. It's a high tower and has a loud fog signal (two blasts every minute) that you can hear anywhere in the vicinity, and a radio beacon broadcasting on 296 kHz—Q (– – · –). Chebucto Head fog signal blows twice every minute, but you sometimes lose it close in to the west. This outside route always seems to have an awful slop, but is probably safer if you have no radar and are relying on GPS or loran. The other routes are more demanding unless you are sure of the errors of your instruments—in this area my loran gives a position 0.25 miles to the south and east of where I actually am, which could certainly cause difficulty. There is frequently fog off Sambro, with 50 feet (15 m) of visibility, while Halifax Harbour bathes in bright sunlight.

Halifax Harbour Inner Approaches

Charts: 4385, 4237

When you're coming from the east, approach whistle buoy "HP," about a mile south of Devils Island, from any reasonable direction, and then steer 282°M. After 1.9 miles, you come to bell buoy "HN6," south of Thrumcap Shoal. It is unwise to cut very far inside it. Having passed it, come to 344°M to enter the harbor. Don't cut between buoy "H14" and the nearby lighthouse (flashing yellow every 30 seconds) on Maugher Beach. You may, however, cut inside bell buoy "H12." Off Maugher Beach is the narrowest part of the big ship channel and you need to be careful here. When approaching from the east, the entire area from Shut-In Island to Devils Island is a naval exercise area, where big ships, charging about in all directions, occasionally shoot things. I have not heard of any yachts being sunk, so the range control officer must be keeping a good lookout.

Eastern Passage. If you have been beating all day, and can't stand another tack, you can try the Eastern Passage, provided you are confident of your position, provided there isn't a stiff southwesterly blowing, and provided you draw less than 6 feet (2 m).

From buoy "HP," south of Devils Island, steer 342°M to bell buoy "HP2," then 000°M to buoy "HP3." Don't cut inside "HP2" or "HP3." The passage between the mainland and Lawlor Island is narrow but has 10 feet (3 m) of water at low-water springs, and is out of the slop. It isn't scenic, being dominated by a large oil refinery, but it's sheltered and out of the big ship traffic. If you are really adventurous, you can go inside Devils Island. There is a shoal patch of about 5 feet (1.5 m), but it is marked by quick-flashing green buoy "HY1." If you are brave enough to try this, don't go north of bell buoy "HP2."

Night Approaches. There is generally no problem entering Halifax at night in clear weather, though you can get confused by the multitude of lights. I've occasionally had near-misses by mistaking the identity of the buoys, so now I try to pass close enough to read their numbers.

Approaches from Offshore. From offshore, the approaches to Halifax Harbour must be the easiest of any harbor in the province. Simply aim 000°M at Chebucto Head. Halifax can be entered in any conditions of tide or wind. The rocks and cliffs west of Halifax Harbour are almost white, and those to the east are dark gray, which may enlighten you if you arrive from far offshore and are uncertain of your position.

Local Weather Patterns. If you are leaving Halifax to go west, be aware of the following common wind pattern. The day starts calm, and by 0900 a light southeasterly is blowing, which shortly becomes southerly. By noon, the wind is established in the southwest and can increase up to 25 or 30 knots. By 1700, the wind is dying out, and veering to the northwest.

Thus, you can have a headwind all the way from the Northwest Arm to Chester, a frustrating experience, to say the least. There is no way to ease the pain without using your engine once in a while.

Sambro ★★★

NO FACILITIES

Charts: **4237, 4385,** 4318

Ten years ago, Sambro was an extremely busy fishing port, mostly dedicated to longliners and swordfish boats, but it's now much quieter. If you're going up or down the coast, and don't want to be distracted by the fleshpots of Halifax, this is the best harbor in the area.

Approaches. Navigation in Sambro Harbour is a little complex, especially in fog, though it is often clear in the harbor when there is thick fog at Pennant Point.

From bell buoy "HS6," just southwest of Inner Sambro Island, steer 026°M. Leave Inner Sambro Island close to starboard, and Isle of Man, a 15-foot-high (3.6-m) bare rock, just to port. You can usually see the rock through the murk, and there is little tidal stream to push you off course. After 1.4 miles, you come to flashing red buoy "HS12," where you should alter course to 354°M to enter the harbor. Follow the buoys in to the wharf.

Anchorage, Dockage. The best place to tie up is inside the T-jetty, on its northeast face—anywhere else is rather exposed. This spot is just ahead of the lifeboat berth. Here, you are safe from anything but a hurricane from the southeast.

If you prefer to anchor, it's possible to go a little deeper into this cove, to venture into the cove to the west, or to go around to the northeast side of Powers Island. There is only 3 feet (1 m) at low-water springs in the Powers Island gut. Anywhere you anchor in Sambro Harbour, riding lights are essential.

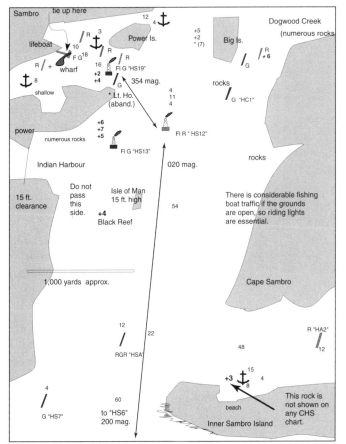

Sambro Harbour.

Map labels:
Sambro · tie up here · 12 · Dogwood Creek (numerous rocks) · lifeboat · R 3 · Power Is. · +5 +2 *(7) · Big Is. · R +6 · lifeboat · 10 · R · R · R +6 · F G 18 · wharf · 16 +2 +4 · Fl G "HS19" · G 354 mag. · rocks · R 8 · shallow · · Lt. Ho. (aband.) · 4 11 4 · G "HC1" · power · +6 +7 +5 · numerous rocks · Fl G "HS13" · Fl R "HS12" · rocks · Indian Harbour · 020 mag. · 15 ft. clearance · Do not pass this side · Isle of Man 15 ft. high · +4 Black Reef · 54 · There is considerable fishing boat traffic if the grounds are open, so riding lights are essential. · 1,000 yards approx. · Cape Sambro · 12 · 22 · RGR "HSA" · 48 · R "HA2" 12 · +3 15 4 8 · 4 · G "HS7" · 60 · to "HS6" 200 mag. · beach · This rock is not shown on any CHS chart. · Inner Sambro Island

Inner Sambro Island

★★★★

NO FACILITIES

Charts: 4237, 4318

There is a delightful anchorage in the little bay at the western side of Inner Sambro Island's northern edge. It is open to the east, but I have chanced it and stayed there overnight a number of times. Beware of a drying rock that's not shown on any of the official charts. I've been thankful for this haven, limited as its shelter is, on many occasions, particularly after beating all day. There is a white sand beach by the anchorage, and you can walk all over the island, which is fringed by white granite slabs pounded by the ever-present surf. Away from the water, wild strawberries proliferate. From the island, there's a splendid view to the south of Sambro Light and its surrounding rocks.

In the summer, some of the residents of Sambro may be camping on the island. It makes a good stopover if you have small children or dogs that need their daily run ashore.

The keener-sighted among you may want to try looking west one mile to what the chart calls Coote Cove. This is known locally as Crystal Crescent Beach. It's actually three beaches, the southernmost of which is reserved for nudists. Given that the water temperature here rarely exceeds 50°F (10°C), and that there is often an icy fog breeze blowing off the water, this behavior seems to me to smack of masochism.

You cannot get into Indian Harbour if you have a mast, as there is only 15 feet (4.5 m) of clearance under the utility wires. The rest of Sambro Harbour has many unmarked rocks, and I don't recommend it.

Ashore. There was a convenience store about a half-mile left of the wharf, but it hasn't always been in operation when I've been there. The lifeboat station has accepted my garbage on occasion (there being nowhere else to dump it), but they might not be able to cope with garbage from a dozen visiting boats a week.

Ketch Harbour ★★

NO FACILITIES

Chart: **4237**

Ketch Harbour is another spot that could be considered for an overnight stop while passagemaking, but it's less sheltered than Sambro. Entry is straightforward. From whistle buoy "HE 19," steer 350°M for 0.6 of a mile. Inside the harbor, there is some shoal water marked by red spar buoys. If you have any doubt about the entrance, there is a ruined gun emplacement on the headland to starboard going in.

The harbor is wide open to the south, and often gathers sufficient swell to make it difficult to sleep at night if you are anchored. Right at the top of the harbor there is more shelter on the north side of the government wharf. Although the swell makes this place an indifferent anchorage on any but a calm night, the natives are quite civilized, and there is unlikely to be anything in the way of vandalism (see Herring Cove below). There are no services of any kind available here.

Duncan Cove

If you look at Duncan Cove on the chart, you might be tempted to try it as an anchorage, but I've never tried it myself. In fact, I've never seen a boat in there, or seen any reference to vessels using it.

I suspect the cove falls prey to a continuous swell, but this may not be the only reason why cruisers tend to avoid it. During the 1960s, Duncan Cove was the site of much partying—and for all I know, it might still be.

Herring Cove

Herring Cove is the first harbor north of Chebucto Head. The approach is well lit and the harbor is completely protected from the weather, but it's another place I have never visited. I've been put off by its unsavory reputation for vandalizing visiting boats—a habit that stretches back 30 years.

It is inescapable that Spryfield, one of the roughest suburbs in Halifax, is within spitting distance up the road. While I may be maligning the place with hearsay, I cannot recommend it.

Halifax Metropolitan Area

Halifax, the capital of Nova Scotia, is the largest conurbation in Atlantic Canada. All the facilities of a leading North American city are there—and so, of course, are all the failings. Two major attractions of Halifax are its compact city center and its waterfront, which is one of the most attractive on the eastern seaboard.

There are some drawbacks to visiting Halifax by boat, however. Dockage is available at most of the yacht clubs, and at the downtown Maritime Museum of the Atlantic, but the yacht clubs are far from the city center, and the berths at the museum may be occupied. There is, furthermore, a requirement that boats be able to shift from the museum berths at 15 minutes' notice—in theory, at least. These berths also are subject to much commotion from passing wakes. A few more berths are available at Queens Wharf, but access to shore may be difficult.

The city council does not go out of its way to welcome visiting cruising boats. While Saint John, New Brunswick, has a marina 40 yards from the downtown core, no such facility exists in Halifax.

Not surprisingly, the council commands little respect from the peasantry—partly because of its inept handling of the city's sewage problem. The untreated sewage generated by 300,000 people is deposited directly into the harbor, despite the expensive machinations of a sewage commission for 10 years, and despite the imposition of a pollution abatement tax.

To be fair, not all the operations of the coun-

cil are reminiscent of the Keystone Cops, but to most Nova Scotians they are more a source of comic relief than objects of admiration—except, of course, that it would be funnier if we weren't paying.

I have to say that because of this, and because of the increasing crime rate in the downtown region, I have found Halifax less of an attraction than I once did. These days, I usually keep going right past the entrance. Of course, I may be turning into an old curmudgeon, tired of the spice of life. I have to admit that when it's at its best, Halifax is still one of the most attractive small cities in North America, and it's certainly worth visiting at least once. If you are going farther east, and you're low on stores, you'll have to stop here to reprovision anyway, as such facilities are few and far between on the Eastern Shore.

The Northwest Arm ★★★ [5]

Charts: 4385, 4237, 4202

About a mile north of Maugher (pronounced Major) Beach, the Northwest Arm opens up on your port bow. Directly ahead of you, on Point Pleasant, is a large cross, a monument to the men of the merchant navy who perished in World War II. Fine on the starboard bow, on the east side of the downtown Halifax peninsula, are the large cranes of the container terminal.

A shoal extends southeast from Point Pleasant, and you can easily run aground there (I've nearly done so myself) if you cut any of the corners—so make sure you identify the buoys correctly. There are no submerged hazards in the arm itself. On the east side—to starboard heading into the arm—are the expensive palaces of the Halifax upper class, and numerous private docks where you will not be welcome.

Royal Nova Scotia Yacht Squadron. About a mile from the entrance, on the west side, is the Royal Nova Scotia Yacht Squadron—(902) 477-5653—the oldest yacht club in Canada, if not on the continent. It is much favored by the Halifax establishment, but is regarded by others of us as being somewhat stuffy. Of course, if you turn up here after the Marblehead Race in a grand-prix 50-footer, I'm sure you'll receive a fine welcome. If however, you beat all the way from the Caribbean, and arrive in a scruffy 30-footer with rust streaks down the sides and weed on the waterline, the barman may sniff and suggest you need a jacket and tie before he can serve you a beer.

A friend of mine once bought a boat from one of the members here (the member was a fine fellow, not at all like the apocryphal steward), a transaction that afforded him some kind of temporary membership until he moved the boat to the outports of the province. When he repaired to the bar after the deal was done, to recover from the pain of signing the check, the barman told him: "I don't think we can actually handle cash here, sir. You have to have a bar account."

Perhaps I am just being a little envious. Theoretically at least, there is free dockage for the first night for visiting yachts, after which a small daily fee is charged if a berth is available. If the club manager likes the cut of your jib, you will find at your disposal a full-service boatyard, fuel, water, showers, a laundromat, a bar, and a restaurant.

A mile northwest of the Squadron, also on the west side, is a conspicuous tower, called The Dingle by the locals, and Fleming Tower by the city fathers. It is located in a park variously called Dingle Park or Fleming Park. There is a little cove just past it in which it is possible to anchor. I have done so on occasion, as it is one of the few spots out of the traffic. There is a no-anchoring zone all the way up the middle of the arm. While it is possible to anchor outside of it, I suggest you don't, because quite apart from the congestion of the moorings and the wakes of tourist boats, all sorts of racing takes place here, and it's difficult to find a space that's not going to obstruct someone's start line.

Armdale Yacht Club. At the top of Northwest Arm, still on the west side, is the Armdale Yacht Club—(902) 477-4617. In a previous life it was a naval prison, and, as befits its heritage, it welcomes those of us from the lower orders with wide-open arms. (Incidentally, all the metropolitan clubs except the Squadron have cash-flow problems, so their treasurers would be delighted for your patronage of the bars and facilities.) I have stayed at the Armdale Yacht Club many times, and found it very satisfactory. I tied up behind Mike Ritchie's *Jester,* of singlehanded transatlantic race fame, in 1987 or thereabouts. She was having a few minor repairs done before her last, ill-fated voyage, so Mike must have found Armdale a satisfactory place, too. There is a full-service boatyard, fuel, water, showers, a bar, and a restaurant. The boatyard has numerous classic wooden boats in various stages of restoration. Many are worked on by their owners, and it is interesting for a Luddite like myself, who has never really adjusted to fiberglass boats, just to walk around the yard.

You don't have to worry about crime or vandalism at any anchorage in the Northwest Arm. It's far removed from the seedier parts of town—but it's also far removed from the stores. If you don't want to take a taxi, there's a little park due north of the club where you may safely leave your dinghy. A half-mile away you'll find the West End Mall on the left—you can't miss the big Sears sign. If you're not filled with dread by the thought of rowing your dinghy slightly less than a mile, and of walking about the same distance for the round trip, you'll find all the shops you're ever likely to want. It's a long walk back with a case of beer, though, I have to admit. If you want to go downtown, you'll need to take a bus or a cab, unless you are a fitness freak.

You might find it a challenge to sail down the arm, with the wind wiggling around every hill and building, but be aware that on Wednesdays and Saturdays there are yacht races. If you run into a dozen boats under spinnaker, all expecting you to yield the right of way, you might want to think about starting your engine.

Downtown Halifax ★★★★

Charts: 4385, 4237, 4202

If, instead of taking the Northwest Arm, you continue north to the city of Halifax, you will pass inside Georges Island, a grassy lump with a few ruins on it, and some radar installations. Landing is not allowed, and the entire area is a prohibited anchorage. A few hundred yards past the container terminal and the headquarters of the tugboat company, you'll come to the Maritime Museum.

The ships exhibited there, the CSS *Acadia* and HMCS *Sackville,* are conspicuous, but if you have any doubts, they're moored just before the distinctive Xerox Building, and Sheraton Hotel, which shows a copper roof. Between the two ships is a dock you may use if there is room. There is also another pontoon just south of the *Sackville.* Dockage is free, but you must sign an agreement relieving the museum of any liability for any mishap. Call the museum at (902) 424-7490—but make quite sure you talk to someone who knows about the dockage. The museum staff are very helpful, but as there are frequent visits by training ships and the like, visitors' moorage is not always available.

When docking at the Maritime Museum, you will be asked to sign a form saying you are able to move at one hour's notice, and change berths at 15 minutes' notice. You can usually stay a night or two if there is space (the dockmaster usually knows when big boats are due), but the above requirement presupposes at least one crew member stays on the boat, though this is usually not enforced. You definitely shouldn't expect to leave the boat unattended for more than a few hours.

The dock is exposed to the wakes of passing vessels, and is pretty open to the southeast. Every morning at about 0700, a hideous, slab-sided workboat from the naval dockyard drives past, making more wash than a destroyer at 35 knots, and if you are not prepared, it will rock you out of bed and take your rubrails off.

167

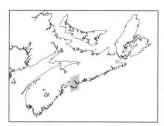

Queens Wharf is immediately north of the Maritime Museum. It consists of two new docks, each 100 feet long, but unfortunately there are only two ladders in this length. Dockage may be less than convenient for boats under 40 feet. There's only one float at the inshore end of the wharves, and it's oriented crossways, making it damned difficult to get at in my sort of boat without running warps everywhere. The telephone number for the wharf attendant is 902-422-6591. There's power on the docks, but no fuel, water, or showers.

North of Queen's Wharf, off Historic Properties, is a wharf for patrons of the restaurants and stores, where there might be space—though you should expect your boat to behave like a bucking bronco in the slop from passing powerboats. The intervening spaces are usually occupied by tour boats, or the *Bluenose 2* (see below). You may also be able to creep into the dock on the north side of the Sheraton.

If you can't find any space, but are desperate to sample the fleshpots of downtown Halifax, try the Cunard Wharf, south of the Maritime Museum of the Atlantic. You can identify it by the oil tanks. You'll usually find a fishing boat tied up at Cunard Wharf, and as they'll be in town for a little rest and recuperation, they won't mind your tying alongside for the night, especially if they're from Shelburne or Yarmouth counties. Don't ask at the office: They'll tell you to go somewhere else.

Anchoring is prohibited anywhere between McNabs Island and the A. Murray MacKay Bridge (the northern one), unless you are a large ship in one of the designated anchorages.

Ashore. There are any number of bars and restaurants within walking distance of the museum, an institution well worth a visit. The museum has two permanent floating exhibits, the survey ship CSS *Acadia,* and the World War II corvette HMCS *Sackville.* I always feel humble when I visit the *Sackville.* Little ships like these, with their crowded accommodation and foul

motion in rough weather, were largely responsible for winning the Battle of the Atlantic.

The major shopping areas are at Spring Garden Road, three blocks up and a little to the south; Scotia Square, two blocks up and to the north; and Historic Properties, a tasteful development on the waterfront just north of the museum. Barrington Street, one block up the hill from the waterfront, used to be the prime retail area, but some bad decisions by the council resulted in a severe case of urban blight.

I have found pretty good eating at O'Carrolls, which has live Celtic music Thursday to Saturday, and at The Five Fishermen. The prices may give you a fit, though. Georgio's, in the Prince George Hotel, also has a good chef, and the prices are less stratospheric. Reservations are advisable at any of the better downtown Halifax restaurants. There are many other attractions for visitors including the Halifax Citadel, an eighteenth-century fort, and the Nova Scotia Museum—not to be confused with the maritime museum.

There is live theater at the Neptune, and a symphony orchestra (under some financial difficulty at present) that operates at the Rebecca Cohn Auditorium of Dalhousie University. Major festivals take place at the Forum, attached to the World Trade and Convention Centre, which sports a big *Bluenose* windvane. The Nova Scotia Tattoo takes place the first week of July. If you are here at this time, you must see it. (I think this is the only "must see" in this whole book, and it's certainly the only event of this type I'd be prepared to drive to Halifax for.)

Halifax started life as a military garrison, and the Tattoo, modeled after the original one in Edinburgh, is a celebration of that tradition. The Navy and the Scottish regiments that founded the military establishment here are well represented, so you had better like bagpipes and military bands.

If you want a few laughs, you might, on the way to the Citadel, want to stop at the seat of the Nova Scotia government, or at that of the Halifax City Council—though this latter body has now been absorbed into a regional government.

In the summer, the symbol of Nova Scotia, the

Bluenose 2, is moored at Historic Properties. She is a replica of the famed *Bluenose* racing schooner. Unfortunately, both these fine vessels have experienced trouble in old age. The original *Bluenose,* after being cut down to a coal scow, died on a Jamaican reef in 1946. The replica, built in Lunenburg in 1961 by a brewing company, was constructed to the quick-and-dirty standards of Nova Scotia workboats from non-durable timbers and iron fastenings. She now has terminal rot. The endless patronage scandals regarding her management and crew have further sullied her reputation. She had been condemned as being unfit to carry passengers, but was reconditioned for the G7 conference in June 1995, receiving palliative treatment so that she could carry these august politicians without springing a plank. Long-term plans call for a replacement, but patronage is making this complicated, and there are now two rival *Bluenose* projects on the horizon.

Halifax is a safe city by North American standards, but it's not nearly as safe now as it was 10 years ago. There are, for example, five or six times more homicides in the Halifax-Dartmouth area than there are in similarly-sized Portland, Maine. Crack cocaine is here with a vengeance, and the capital region seems to be the country's breeding ground for juvenile prostitution. All these activities take place around the waterfront, and are only too obvious if you look around. North of the Sheraton is one such area, and you'd be well advised to keep clear of it late at night, especially if you're alone. There's a similar area around the Cunard Wharf, by the old Nova Scotian Hotel, near the railway station. Another suspect zone is the upper part of the ferry terminal, which, after dark, becomes a hang-out for drug dealers, despite being only 40 yards from the Law Courts. There are a number of rather dark holes going back to the docks at the Maritime Museum, though before midnight the area should be safe enough. Almost anywhere is safe in daylight, though lax laws applying to teenagers tend to encourage a few muggings and purse snatchings. Curmudgeons like me would suggest importing a Minister of Justice from Singapore, but this is not politically acceptable to our social democratic elite, so I guess these problems are here to stay.

The nearest food store of any size is Sobey's on Queen Street, a half-mile west. The nearest liquor store is also here, though there is a specialty wine store in Historic Properties, quite handy to the museum berths.

Halifax Airport (YHZ) is 25 miles out of town on the road to Truro—a $30 cab ride. The shuttle buses that leave every hour or so from the major hotels charge slightly less. All the usual car-hire companies are represented here, but I have to say Halifax has the worst signposting of any Canadian city I have visited, so be sure to get a map.

The Narrows

The area between the Angus L. Macdonald Bridge and the A. Murray MacKay Bridge is known as The Narrows. The clearance of the bridges is 185 feet above high water, which will only be the concern of the captain of *Endeavour* and other J-class boats. On the west side, it is largely occupied by the Naval Dockyard and the ship repair facility of Halifax-Dartmouth Industries. The eastern side is dominated by a large power station.

An old Indian curse is said to have doomed to failure most previous attempts to bridge the harbor. The present bridges, aged 40 and 25 years, look solid enough, but the curse may have settled on the treasury, which now owes more money on them than it did the day they were built.

This is also the site of the infamous Halifax explosion of December, 1917. Two munitions ships, the *Imo* and the *Mont Blanc,* collided in The Narrows and caught fire. The *Mont Blanc,* carrying 10,000 tons of picric acid—a temperamental and dangerous chemical used in detonators—exploded. The whole north end of Halifax was flattened, and about 2,000 people died. The anchor of the *Mont Blanc* flew two miles through the air and landed near the present site of the Armdale Yacht Club.

The possibility of a collision bringing down one of the bridges still causes apprehension

among traffic controllers, although the rock piles at the bases of the bridge towers are designed to prevent such a catastrophe. Commercial vessels have the right of way in The Narrows, as they do within the entire harbor area, and with the constant movement of container ships and naval traffic, you need to keep a careful lookout. This is not a safe place in thick fog, especially if you lack radar.

After passing north beneath the Mackay Bridge, you'll see to port the Fairview container terminal—which you would do well to steer clear of, unless you happen to be delivering 40,000 tons of car parts.

Bedford Basin ★★ 5

DARTMOUTH YC

Charts: 4201, 4230

Landlocked Bedford Basin, mostly deep and unobstructed, contains commercial shipping wharves, a naval installation, the Bedford Institute of Oceanography, and two yacht clubs.

Approaches. It's advisable to consult chart 4201 if you're going anywhere in the Bedford Basin, though you may be able to get by with chart 4320 in clear weather. None of the other charts show it at all. There are few obstructions in the basin, apart from naval activity and anchored ships. The Western Ledges and the Chicken Rocks, which are hazards, may be easily avoided by staying more or less in the middle of the basin.

The town of Bedford lies at the northwest extremity of the harbor, and flashing green buoy "H45," together with flashing red buoys "H46" and "H48" make Bedford a straightforward approach, even at night.

Bedford Yacht Club. The club is on the western side of the Bedford Bay, at the head of the basin. There is docking alongside, but depths are only about 5 feet (1.5 m) at low-water springs. Outside the mooring area, the water is also shallow, and there is not a lot of room to anchor among the moorings. Some of the fanatical club racers dry-sail their boats, and if you moor alongside you may get in the way of their crane. There are showers, a bar, and water, but no fuel.

The Bedford downtown area, with its numerous stores, is handy to the club, but I don't know if that makes up for the long sail through the basin, particularly as moorage is at a premium. It may be worth calling the club—(902) 835-3729—to see if a mooring is available. Bedford is a sedate place and you are unlikely to be bothered by the drug or body trades.

Heading southward from Bedford town, Long Cove is reported to be an adequate anchorage, though I have never used it myself. It is open to the west. Farther along the shore is the naval ammunition depot, with its attendant jetty, another place to avoid if loud noises make you nervous.

Dartmouth Yacht Club. Wrights Cove, centered on the eastern shore of Bedford Basin, is the site of the Dartmouth Yacht Club. Its marina is protected by Navy Island and a breakwater, making it one of the most sheltered places in the harbor. The two berths nearest the club bar are reserved for visiting boats, an impressive policy that should be more widely emulated. All facilities are here, including a full-service boatyard. The club's telephone number is (902) 468-6050.

If you feel in need of a dry bed, a Howard Johnson hotel is adjacent to the club. The stores are distant, but every time I've been here it's been easy to get a cab. This is a most unpretentious club, and I have been made very welcome here.

This is the club of John Hughes, the only Canadian ever to complete the BOC Round-the-World Race. As his was an unsponsored entry, complicated by a dismasting that required him to round Cape Horn under jury rig, you may be assured that club members won't mind if you turn up with the detritus of an ocean passage hanging on your hull. Like Bedford, Wrights Cove is a spot where you don't have to worry about running into the lower forms of life.

Farther south in Bedford Basin, just north of the MacKay Bridge, is the Bedford Institute of Oceanography, another place well worth a visit, though you must call in advance. The east side of The Narrows is dominated by the power station and various other industrial plants.

Downtown Dartmouth

Chart: 4385

South of the Macdonald Bridge (the southern-most one) is downtown Dartmouth. Just north of the ferry terminal's parking lot there is a small marina. It is reported to be operated by the Alderney Sailing and Boating Association—(902) 423-7159. If the association is still in operation, it's certainly a convenient berth from which to visit downtown Dartmouth.

Dartmouth is a city of suburbs, and the major shopping centers are far-flung. I have never visited here by boat for this reason. The city has a few rowdy bars, but the lower orders of life are much less visible than they are in Halifax.

Shearwater Yacht Club. Going south from Dartmouth, you come to the Coast Guard base (indicated by the moored icebreakers), a dock where cars are imported, and then a large oil refinery. Just off the eastern mainland shore are the designated big ship anchorages, a source of some anxiety if the fog shuts in and you have no radar.

Opposite the north end of McNabs Island, still on the eastern mainland shore, the Shearwater Yacht Club is operated by the armed forces. I have never stayed there, but I'm told there may be space for visiting yachts. Call them first, if you can, at (902) 469-8590. The club has showers, a bar, and water, but no fuel. It is a little exposed to winds from the northwest.

McNabs Island ★★★

Chart: 4385

Though Halifax Harbour provides few quiet anchorages, there are a couple of spots worthy of consideration on McNabs Island. One is Wreck Cove (Back Cove), between McNabs and Lawlors Islands, and the other is Maugher Beach, in McNabs Cove. The shallows of Wreck Cove (on chart 4237) or Back Cove (on chart 4385) are full of rotting hulks, so anchor in 15 feet (4.5 m) or more at low-water springs. While the backdrop of the refinery cannot be considered scenic, the anchorage is well sheltered.

At Maugher Beach, anchor just north of the spit going to the lighthouse. This is open to the northwest but is otherwise satisfactory, although a wake may disturb you when a ship goes past. You don't see much overnight anchoring here, and I've never done it myself, but I can see no reason why these anchorages—especially Wreck Cove—shouldn't be a welcome alternative to the noise and bustle of downtown Halifax.

McNabs Island, though largely owned by the Department of National Defence, has some sort of park status, and provides interesting walking. A tearoom operates on the island during the tourist season, but as it is only accessible by boat, crowds are not usually a problem.

The Eastern Shore: *Halifax to Cape Canso*

Eastern Shore of Nova Scotia

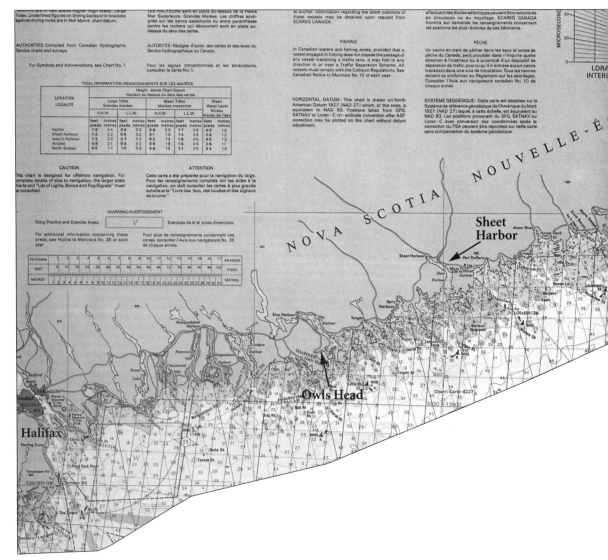

Based on CHS Chart 4013. Not to be used for navigation.

From Halifax to Canso is about 130 miles, but after the first few miles, when the suburbs of Dartmouth disappear below the horizon, you enter a completely different world. The main road, such as it is, lies well inland, and there is scarcely a sign of human habitation from offshore. This is certainly the least densely populated area in the province, and it may well be the most sparsely populated coastline on the entire eastern seaboard south of the St. Lawrence River. There is a mere handful of yachts to be found in this entire area, and, following the catastrophic failure of the inshore ground fishery, there are damned few fishing boats as well.

Some of the harbors that catered to 30 boats when I first visited them 20 years ago now have none. You can go for a week without seeing another boat, and it is rare to share an anchorage. The outstanding natural beauty of this area, and the solitude, make it a favorite cruising ground of mine, though it may not be to everyone's taste. It's a pity that so many yachts pass it by in the rush to get to Cape Breton.

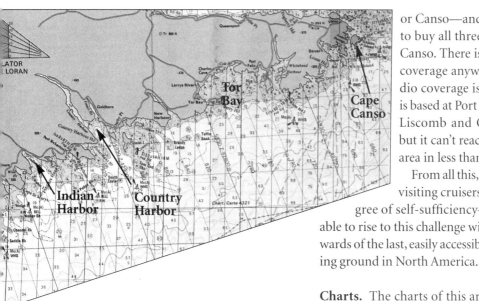

or Canso—and you won't be able to buy all three at once, except at Canso. There is no cellular phone coverage anywhere, and VHF radio coverage is patchy. A lifeboat is based at Port Bickerton, between Liscomb and Country Harbour, but it can't reach many spots in its area in less than four hours.

From all this, you will gather that visiting cruisers require a large degree of self-sufficiency—but those of you able to rise to this challenge will enjoy the rich rewards of the last, easily accessible, unspoiled cruising ground in North America.

Charts. The charts of this area still in print are numbers 4236, 4235, 4234, and 4233. They are rather miserable things, of too small a scale for yacht navigation. You would scarcely know that many of the harbors existed, let alone want to enter them.

Obsolete charts that show the inshore waters better than the new ones include numbers 4352, 4353, 4289, 4364, 4355, 4356, 4285, 4283, 4282, and 4280. No matter how moth-eaten your obsolete charts may be, I'd certainly advise keeping them. If you can't lay hands on any of the old charts, the sketch charts in this book may make your progress a little easier, though they should never be relied upon as your primary navigation references, of course.

This really is an ironbound coast, and careful attention to pilotage is required in the inshore passages. Neither loran nor GPS provides sufficient accuracy to navigate some of the passages. Some of the depths shown on official charts are not accurate enough, either. Nonetheless, the inside passages are calm, and I always use them when beating.

The 60 or so miles between Jeddore and Liscomb are particularly hazardous, with very exposed offshore reefs, and in this stretch I advise you either to keep to the inshore passages and pay very careful attention to your pilotage, or—if the weather and visibility are poor—to stay well offshore. A number of large, visible wrecks on the reefs will remind you of the penalty for being uncertain of your position. Remember that rescue facilities are limited and the population is small. Running aground on one of the offshore reefs could result in the loss of your vessel, or worse.

Hundreds of snug harbors line this region, and it would take more than one lifetime to sample them all. Nevertheless, I think this book describes a pretty good selection.

The Eastern Shore offers little in the way of facilities for small yachts. If you need groceries, fuel, or water, you must go to Sheet Harbour, Liscomb,

Passage Eastward from Halifax

If you plan to head east from Halifax, leave Thrumcap Shoal, south of McNabs Island, to port, and take your departure from whistle buoy "HP," a mile, or so south of Devils Island. A course of 096°M will bring you off Three Fathom Harbour after 9 miles, and Jeddore Head after 19 miles.

If you're coming from west of Halifax Harbour, a course of 076°M from whistle buoy "HS,"

2 miles south of Sambro Island light, takes you to Jeddore Head after 26 miles.

There is little tidal current to speak of here, except in the river entrances. The cliffs west of Halifax are almost pure white granite, while those east of it are dark-gray slate.

Between Devils Island and Graham Head lies a major naval exercise area, where all sorts of large vessels, helicopters, and submarines speed hither and thither, sometimes shooting at things. A large number of cautionary, orange-flashing buoys marks the area. Some of the buoys are on the chart, but some are not. They change from time to time, and even the latest chart may not be correct. You can be certain that any vessel drawing less than a destroyer could drive right up to one without running aground. I believe that military vessels have the right of unencumbered passage through this area, though I have never seen this officially proclaimed. I have never been stopped or asked to alter course, and I have never heard of any collisions or near-misses.

The coast between Osborne Head and Graham Head consists of sandy beaches at Lawrencetown, Cole Harbour, and Terminal Beach. There are small inlets at these places, but they dry at low water, and are further obstructed by the remains of the old railway line. The surf can be heard from 2 miles offshore, and a special breed of hardy surfers tells me that in winter the waves are the biggest on the East Coast. This would seem a good place to keep clear of. Shut-In Island, at the eastern end of this forbidding section of coast, marks the western side of Three Fathom Harbour, which should not be confused with the much smaller inlet at Terminal Beach. This inlet, west of

Graham Head, and named Lower Three Fathom Harbour on some charts, has only 1 foot (30 cm) of water at low tide, and is not suitable for any deep-draft boat.

Three Fathom Harbour ★★★

NO FACILITIES

Chart: **4236**

The little creek called Three Fathom Harbour is very rarely visited by yachts, and I would enter it only in good conditions and daylight, even though it's lit at night. Steer 000°M from fairway bell buoy "HX." When you pass Rat Rock with its flashing white light on small tower, veer a little

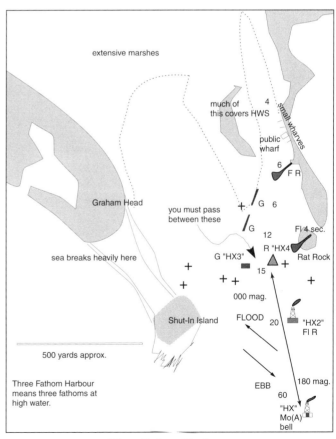

Three Fathom Harbour.

to starboard and follow the spars. There may be space at the outer end of the small public wharf. The wharf is quite well sheltered, though southerly gales will send a swell into the harbor. There is a depth of 6 feet (1.8 m) at low-water springs, with perhaps a little more at the end of the wharf. North of the public wharf the water rapidly becomes shallow. There are numerous fishing-boat docks, because the harbor was bought by the Department of Fisheries and Oceans to preempt residential development.

The marshes and sandbars have a certain austere attraction. The fishing boats are mostly older and less technologically advanced, perhaps more like those you'd expect to find in a maritime fishing harbor. Tidal streams average about 1 knot.

Three Fathom Harbour is an intriguing little spot, very different from the developed communities to the west—but you'd have to be a better navigator than I am to enter it in fog, or when a strong southwesterly is blowing.

Chezzetcook Inlet, Petpeswick, and Musquodoboit Harbour

To the east of Three Fathom Harbour are three inlets whose entrances present a degree of difficulty rivaled only by the spelling of their names. I have never had the good fortune to pass them when the weather was calm enough for me to try to enter. Petpeswick (pronounced Pesick), looks the easiest from seaward, and there is a small yacht club at its head, devoted mostly to small boats. From the land, these inlets remind me of creeks in the Essex and Suffolk estuaries in England, and they would present an interesting challenge to adventurous, shoal-draft

cruisers. Musquodoboit (pronounced Muskadabit) has a particularly intricate entrance, and it will have to be a calm and clear day before I try it.

Jeddore Harbour ★★★★

 NO FACILITIES

Charts: 4236, 4347

Jeddore is the first harbor east of Halifax that can be entered in most weather conditions. I have entered it at night and in fog so thick I could hardly

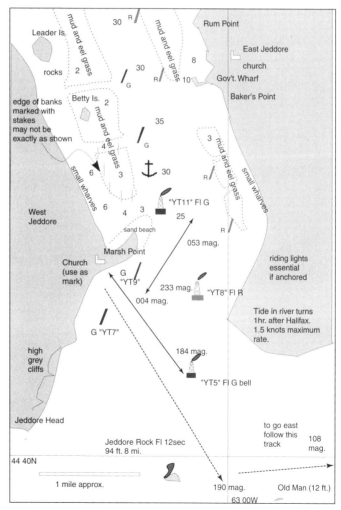

Jeddore (lower part).

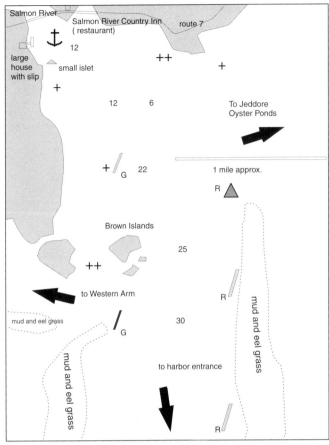

Jeddore Harbour (eastern arm).

see the dinghy I was towing, though it would be a lot safer with radar. Because it is a large enclosed harbor with a constricted entrance, the tide runs out at nearly 2 knots, and wind-against-tide conditions in a stiff southerly can be rough. If you stay in deep water, however, you should be all right.

Approaches from the West. Pass between Jeddore Head, a high slate cliff, and Jeddore Rock on a heading of approximately northeast. Jeddore Rock has a lighthouse on it flashing every 12 seconds. The lighthouse is held up by external steel scaffolding, and I suspect this is a sign of the ferocity of winter storms in this area.

After rounding bell buoy "YT5," steer a course of 004°M straight for the little white church. If it's not blowing hard from the south, I ignore Thorn Shoal, as it has 10 feet (3 m) over it at low-water springs. When you get close to the beach, come to 053°M to round Marsh Point. Favor the west side as rocks extend quite a way out from the starboard side going in.

Departure to the East. Departing from Jeddore, bound east, involves intricate pilotage, and you need to be careful in the fog or at night. The way I go (though there are others) is to steer 190°M

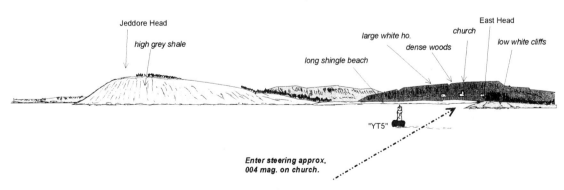

Entrance to Jeddore Harbour from the south—two miles out.

from the church for about 2.7 miles until Jeddore Rock is on the starboard beam. Old Man, a bare rock 14 feet (4.3 m) high (a good radar target) will be a close ahead. When Jeddore Rock is abeam, come to 108°M. Keeping Jeddore Rock astern, you pass close inside Egg Island, another windswept rock with a light tower reinforced with steel rods, and south of Bald Rock. This takes you right over Macdonald Rock (The Squince on the new charts), but there is 12 feet (4 m) over it, and I've never found it a problem. From here you can pass into Owls Head, or points farther east. I have done this a number of times in the vilest of conditions; but if you don't like the look of it, leave Jeddore Rock to port and maintain a course of about 200°M until you hear Arnold Rock bell buoy, "YT3," astern of you, then come to 150°M to go all the way outside Brig Rock, marked by flashing red bell buoy "YT2." In the usual southwester, this involves a beat out to sea of about 5 miles—sufficient to encourage me to use the inshore passage. Incidentally, don't steer directly from Jeddore Rock to bell buoy "YT3," or you will hit Arnold Rock. For some reason, the chart assumes you will pass between Jeddore Rock and the Old Man, but that's not safe in poor visibility.

Anchorage. Jeddore is a large, enclosed body of water, but the deep channel is constricted, in the lower reaches, by two parallel mud flats covered at high water. There are stakes marking the deeper channels (see my chart), but their positioning is sometimes confusing to strangers. Anchoring is possible almost anywhere, but many anchorages may be exposed at high water. Just past flashing green buoy "YT11," at Marsh Point, is a reasonable place to anchor. If you need more shelter you can go into the channels along the shore, but their entrances are shallow at low water. If you get this far into the harbor without mishap, you will usually find the fog lifting during the day, even if it is a thick pea-souper outside.

I usually tie up at a small government wharf at Bakers Point, East Jeddore. There's usually a longliner berthed there, and I tie alongside. I've only seen it move once in the last six years, but it may be gone by the time you get there. If you use this wharf, beware of the drying banks that extend to the north and south. To avoid them, approach the wharf from mid-channel on a course of roughly 110°M.

Between the two parallel mud flats—which, apart from a few breaks, extend all the way down the harbor—the main channel is narrow at low water. Deeper channels lie between the mainland and these banks, something I haven't seen anywhere else, and a number of small fishermen's wharves border these channels. If you wish to navigate them, check them from the dinghy first, as the local boats don't usually draw much more than 3 feet (1 m). There was a lot of fishing activity here 20 years ago, but it is now sadly reduced. Even so, it's still advisable to use riding lights at night.

The tidal current runs at about 1.5 knots, and if you are anchored at Marsh Point, you might get swirled around a bit when tide and wind are opposed; but I've never bothered with two anchors here as the holding ground is good. If you have sailed in England (or the Carolinas), you'll remember that all the rivers have tidal streams like this (or stronger), so that anchored boats usually lie aligned with the current rather than the wind. It's nothing to worry about, but a big anchor with chain does reduce any anxiety you may have about grounding on the banks.

Jeddore Harbour extends almost 4 miles from Marsh Point, and I have found it a pleasant sail up the harbor to the top. The eastern arm is less encumbered with hazards than the western arm, and is buoyed most of the way, but watch for the rock just north of Brown Islands, which usually has a green spar on it. I have found the best anchorage to be just south of the west end of the Salmon River Bridge. Because of the large size of Jeddore Harbour, anchorages are somewhat exposed, but this one is all right as long as the wind is not blowing hard from the southeast.

Ashore. If you want to eat out, there is a restaurant in a country inn just by the eastern end of the bridge. A few years ago I anchored here, just

below the big house with the slip. The owner of the house was fitting out a beautiful, 40-foot (12.2 m) teak, bronze-fastened ketch, originally built by Fife to Lloyd's 100-A1 specifications. He had acquired the boat for a ridiculously low price from the RCMP after a drug bust.

Apart from this fairly remote inn, there are no facilities in Jeddore Harbour. Some yachtsmen don't like this place, but I've always found it attractive because it's unspoiled and there is abundant wildlife. It reminds me of the more remote parts of Poole Harbour, in England. It's difficult to believe, sometimes, that it's only 25 miles from Halifax.

Passage East of Jeddore. Jeddore could be considered the western end of the famous inside passage, but I have reserved that term for the section between Sheet Harbour and Liscomb. If you intend to bypass this beautiful section of coast, simply head out to sea until you're about 5 miles south of Jeddore Head, and turn on to a course of about 110°M to fetch whistle buoy "Y28." From there, a course of 088°M will keep you clear of dangers all the way to Whitehead. The *Sailing Directions* warn large ships to stay in depths of more than 40 fathoms (73 m), and if you're making the offshore passage, this is not bad advice for smaller vessels, either. It's especially valid for those with no radar, at night or in fog. The *Sailing Directions* warn of drying rocks only a cable-length (200 yards, or 183 meters) from the 40-fathom contour line.

Little Harbour ★★★

NO FACILITIES

Charts: **4236, 4352**

Little Harbour lies at the eastern end of Clam Bay, a place I have avoided, as it offers no shelter, and is full of rocks and continuously breaking surf. Nearby Owls Head Harbour is considerably eas-

ier to get into. Determined gunkholers can approach Little Harbour from Egg Island, keeping to the east of Flint Ledge—and giving it a wide berth—then leaving bell buoy "YS6" to starboard, and buoy "YS9," at the top of the entrance, to port. This looks quite narrow from outside, and I wouldn't try it in any but ideal conditions. You will also be more comfortable if you have an old copy of chart 4352, which shows all the approaches to Ship Harbour, northeast of Little Harbour, better than does the new chart.

Owls Head Bay ★★★

NO FACILITIES

Chart: **4236**

Although Owls Head Bay is somewhat exposed to the southeast, and therefore enlivened by swells when the wind is blowing from that direction, and for a day or two afterward, I have been grateful for its shelter, especially at the end of a long day or a longer night. Entry is not difficult under most conditions, and I've done it in fog using radar a number of times—I think I've only actually seen the bay once. There is not a lot of current to set you off track.

Approaches. A southeastern approach is the easiest. Keep Owls Head light bearing less than 354°M, but more than 322°M. Flashing red bell buoy "YP2" is in the middle of this approach lane, and a heading of 334°M from the buoy takes you to Owls Head light. Incidentally, buoy "YP2" is exposed to the ocean weather, so don't rely on its being exactly on station. Keep clear of the ledge to starboard, extending to the southwest of Friar Island, which is awash at high water. Black Ledge, the danger to port, is 6 feet (2 m) above high water, and usually easy to see.

Anchorage. On passing Owls Head light, don't go into the first cove, which is full of rocks. Anchor in the next cove, marked "Southwest Cove" on most of the charts. Turn to the southwest, and

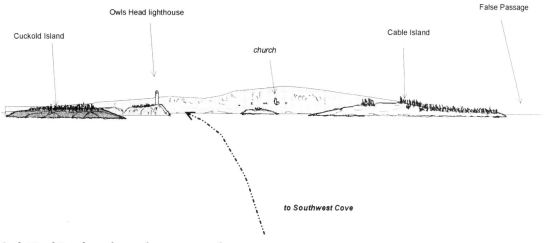

Cuckold Island

Owls Head lighthouse

church

Cable Island

False Passage

to Southwest Cove

Owls Head Bay from the southeast—one mile out.

anchor in about 10 feet (3 m). The anchorage is reasonably sheltered from anything but east-northeasterlies. Owls Head is not usually considered a great refuge in easterly winds, but I once rode out a severe easterly gale anchored just off the northwest end of Cable Island (called Green Tickle on the new chart, opposite Southwest Cove), in reasonable comfort.

False Passage from Owls Head Bay. It's possible to pass east into Ship Harbour through False Passage if you draw 5 feet (1.5 m) or less, if it is half-tide or more, and if it is calm. Pass east of Shag Rock, 30 feet high, then west of Little Shag Rock, the western tip of which always shows. The last time I wanted to use this route, the wind had been blowing from the east for a week, and the look of the passage made me chicken out. Theoretically, you can also pass inside Friar Island, but the bottom here is very irregular and subject to heavy swell.

Ship Harbour ★★★★

NO FACILITIES

Chart: 4236

Ship Harbour is an area of outstanding natural beauty, having been formed as a deep valley be-

tween some of the highest hills on the Eastern Shore. It takes its name from Ship Rock, 1.1 miles northwest of Tuckers Head—a distinctive landmark described by the *Sailing Directions* as "a remarkable clay slate cliff 75 feet (23 m) high, which, when seen from a distance seaward, resembles a ship under sail."

Access to Ship Harbour is a little difficult if visibility is poor, however, and I wouldn't try to get in there at night or in fog without radar.

Approaches. Head toward the lighthouse on Wolfe Point on a course of 342°M if coming from the west, or 316°M if you're approaching from the east. This will keep you off Bear Rock, which lies in the middle of the approach. Submerged rocks extend at least 400 yards southwest of the dry part—6 feet (1.8 m) high—of Bear Rock. Don't approach Wolfe Point lighthouse directly from either of the outer buoys, "YM1" to the west, and "YM" to the east, or you will hit something hard.

Anchorage. If you don't want to go all the way up the harbor, there is a satisfactory anchorage in Day Cove northwest of Passage Island (a bit farther in than indicated by the anchor on chart 4236), or in between the two arms of the northeast side of Passage Island, though the latter anchorage is a little cramped. Both these anchorages are open to the east.

181

As you go farther north, pay careful attention to the spar buoys as there are a surprising number of rocks in the middle of the harbor. As the hills disperse the fog somewhat, most of the time you can see where you're going. The best anchorages are in Marks Cove, just past Eisan Point, or in the Ship Harbour River at the head of the harbor, just past the small farmhouse on the west side of the river. Watch out for a 6-foot-high (1.8-m) rock here.

The eastern side of the head of Ship Harbour is occupied by the Nova Scotia Aquaculture Research Station, and a number of tanks obstruct the fairway. Ansteads Cove, north of Mussel Island, on the east side, looks quite reasonable as an anchorage, as long as the wind is not blowing from between west and north—but beware of the rock northwest of Mussel Island. The main road goes past there, but it is not busy.

There is a government wharf in Lower Ship Harbour, south of Caroline Island (Laybolts Island on the new chart) and about 0.5 mile northwest of Bead Point, where some local fishing boats moor. An anchorage is indicated on the charts, and it is all right in the usual southwester, but it's a little exposed for my tastes.

Inside Passage to Shoal Bay. Position yourself midway between Tuckers Head on Charles Island (Borgles Island on the new chart), and Bald Island, and then steer about 032°M. At the northwest end of Charles Island it is slightly easier to pass no more than one boatlength outside Round Island, which is 20 feet (6 m) high. There is 14 feet (4.2 m) of water here in the deepest part. There are other routes through here, most notably by way of Ship Rock, but they are more obstructed.

Shoal Bay ★★

NO FACILITIES

Chart: **4236**

Shoal Bay is generally free of hazards but I have found it rather exposed, compared with the many alternative anchorages nearby.

Approaches. From seaward, enter midway between Tangier Island and Charles Island and come on to a heading of about 340°M. Two passages branch off into Tangier Harbour, though they are not at all apparent on chart 4236.

To pass inside Baltee Island, steer 048°M from Borgles Bluff on Charles Island. This course keeps you clear of Eve (Shag) Ledge and Gravel Island. Then follow the spar buoys, which are red to star-

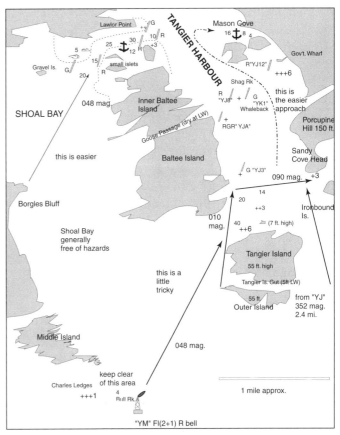

Shoal Bay and Tangier Harbour.

board all the way through, going east. This passage has a sort of dogleg in it (best shown on my chart), so don't go straight from spar to spar.

To pass between Tangier Island and Baltee Island, steer 048°M from bell buoy "YM." When the northwest corner of Tangier Island bears 190°M, come to 010°M. Outer Island will disappear behind Tangier Island at about this point. When the little cove on Baltee Island is abeam, and Sandy Cove Head bears 090°M, change course straight toward Sandy Cove Head. Keep Ironbound Island slightly open on the head. If they appear to touch, you are too far north. When the green spar "YJ3" is on your port beam, you can turn to the north if you are destined for Tangier Harbour, or continue straight on if you're going inside Ironbound Island to Sallys Cove (see page 84).

Incidentally, after you've cleared the northwest corner of Tangier Island, don't be tempted to head directly toward buoy "YJ3." It doesn't mark this channel, and you'll run aground. This passage is somewhat easier if you approach from the east of Tangier Island. Navigating in this area is much easier with chart 4353, but as it hasn't been published for 20 years, you most likely will have to make do with chart 4236, and the information on my sketch charts. Neither of these passages from Shoal Bay to Tangier Harbour looks possible on chart 4236, but the inside one is straightforward in clear weather. The passage north of Tangier Island is a little tricky, but I've done it in fog, aided by radar. I wouldn't try either in fog without radar, however, nor at night.

Anchorage. The charts indicate anchorage in the western part of the bay, which is Carter Cove on the old charts, but there appears to be an uncomfortably long fetch to the east—and many better anchoring spots close by.

Tangier Harbour ★★★

A NO FACILITIES

Chart: 4236

I once rode out a three-day easterly gale in Tangier Harbour, and never had to move. But there are no facilities there, despite the fact that Willy Krauch's world-famous smokehouse is in Tangier. The fact is that if you're in a boat, the smokehouse is more easily reached from Popes Harbour.

Approaches. If you are approaching from seaward, steer 352°M from the fairway whistle buoy "YJ." That course will take you straight to Sandy Cove Point, and the higher Porcupine Hill should be right in line behind it. This will keep you off 4-foot-high (1.3-m) Popes Rock, which always shows, and the much nastier Drunken Dick, which lies submerged in wait, halfway between Popes Rock and Ironbound Island—see the sketch chart of Sallys Cove, following.

Tangier Harbour is quite obstructed, and difficult to navigate in fog. Although the buoys suggest the west side of the harbor is the preferred channel, I much prefer the east side, leaving Whaleback and Shag Rock (not named on chart 4236) to port.

Anchorage. Masons Cove is a reasonable anchorage, but it's preferable to anchor farther in than the spot designated by the anchor on the chart—the "2" on 4236 marks a better place to anchor. That's where I sheltered from the easterly.

Tangier Island Gut has a minimum of 5 feet (1.5 m) of water, the deepest generally being on the north side. It might make an interesting anchorage, but I have yet to try it.

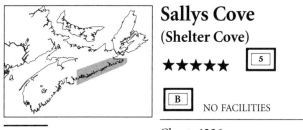

Sallys Cove
(Shelter Cove)

★★★★★ [5]

[B] NO FACILITIES

Chart: **4236**

Sallys Cove is one of Nova Scotia's prettiest and most sheltered anchorages. I've said it before about other harbors, I know, but this time I mean it: You really haven't cruised the province unless you have been there.

Approaches. From the west, if you're planning to go inside Ironbound Island, approach Sandy Cove Head on 090°M, and when you get to the head, swing a little to the south to avoid the 3-foot (1-m) drying rock on its south end. It is almost attached to the land, so an offing of 20 yards or so will suffice. Stay about halfway between Sandy Cove Head and Ironbound Island, and when the point at the south end of the little crescent beach on the east side of Sandy Cove Head bears 270°M, change course to 090°M. When you have passed the north point of Ironbound Island, where there is a rock awash at low water, change course to the south until the point at the south end of the crescent beach bears 284°M. The narrow channel between the mainland and the little island to the southeast of Sallys Cove will now be open. Now steer 104°M until you intersect a line between Popes Rock and green spar "YE5," marking Schooner Rock, to the north. Popes Rock, which is 4 feet (1.2 m) high, will be bearing 180°M due south.

When Popes Rock bears 180°M, steer 000°M to buoy "YE5" and leave it to port. From the spar, steer 320°M for 0.3 mile, then come to 260°M to enter the cove. This course keeps you clear of the two 4-foot (1.2-m) shoals on the direct course from Ironbound to "YE5." Hug the southern shore of the cove and anchor about halfway along.

You can take a shortcut: (1) if your boat draws 5 feet (1.3 m) or less; (2) if it is a calm day; and (3) if it is more than an hour after low water. Simply maintain a course of 090°M from Sandy Cove Head until you intersect a line joining Popes Rock and spar "YE5," as described above. Leave the spar to port and steer 320°M for about 0.3 mile, then turn on to a course of 260°M to enter the cove.

All this is quite intricate, and I have to confess to having been a little tense the first time I tried it. I hope my chart makes it a little less confusing. If you don't feel up to this challenge, you can steer 010°M from the Tangier fairway buoy "YJ." This takes you between

Sallys (Shelter) Cove.

Popes Rock and Drunken Dick. Popes Rock is 4 feet (1.3 m) high and this route is safe if you can see it. Rocks and shoals extend a half-mile to the south, and a little less to the east, of Popes Rock. The west side is less obstructed.

Alternatively, you can steer 036°M from "YJ" to Popes Harbour bell buoy "YE2." This course takes you over Popes Shoal, which has minimum depths of about 12 feet (4 m). If the weather is bad, however, you might be safer going all the way around Horse Rock, marked by green spar buoy "YE1."

From the east, this is all much easier. Just steer 320°M from buoy "YE2." Schooner Rock, over which there is about 5 feet (1.5 m) should be close to port after 1.2 miles. It is marked by green spar buoy "YE5." At exactly 1.5 miles, change course to 260°M, and you will come directly to the entrance of the cove. This is much the easiest approach at night or in fog.

If you go too far on course 320°M, you risk colliding with Black Rock, which is only 1 foot (30 cm) high—so watch your log.

When you enter Sallys Cove, favor the south side to avoid Sallys Rock—though you would be unlucky to hit it if you draw less than 5 feet (1.5 m). As different charts do not agree on the rock's position and depth, I made the effort to find it—and it certainly has at least 4 feet (1.3 m) over it.

Anchorage. Sallys Cove offers perfect shelter between low, spruce-covered hills. At the entrance is a delightful small sandy beach, an islet, and a little picnic spot in cleared land. The water off this beach is only about 4 feet (1.3 m) deep at high tide, so it warms up enough to encourage the hardy to swim. The locals are rumored to come here for picnics sometimes, but I have never seen them. You might find one or two other boats, as it's a popular spot for those who know about it.

If you go to the head of the cove, on the west side, and plow through the mud, you will come to another sandy beach. Going south, a small spit of land separates it from a twin beach to the east. These beaches are usually clean, white sand, but on a few occasions they've been somewhat degraded by massive amounts of rotting kelp. I suspect this happens only after major storms, and is not the usual state of affairs. The south extremity gives a clear view of Tangier Island and Ironbound Island. It also has some small tidal pools which, because of their south-facing aspect, get really warm. My children always much enjoyed this little spot.

Popes Harbour ★★★★

 NO FACILITIES

Chart: **4236**

Popes Harbour extends northwest from Sallys Cove. You can pass either side of Black Rock, but favor the western side of the harbor to avoid Barrier Reef. The little cove at the northwest corner of the bay has a 3-foot (1-m) rock right in the middle of the entrance. The adventurous can avoid it by keeping to starboard going in. This cove is nothing special, but it is the nearest access to Willy Krauch's smokehouse.

If you land the dinghy near the road, walk west for about a half-mile, and there, down a little road to the right, is the smokehouse. Willy died in 1994, but the firm of Willy Krauch and Sons still produces some of the world's finest smoked fish. They sell it to people all over the world, including the British royal family. You cannot find better smoked salmon—I order it by mail from home. The last time I was anchored in Sallys Cove, the crew commandeered the dinghy to avail themselves of some of Mr. Krauch's fish.

185

Gerard Passage

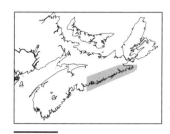

★★★★★   4

C   NO FACILITIES

Chart: 4236

Between Popes Harbour and Spry Bay, north of Gerard Island, runs the beautiful and sheltered strait known as Gerard Passage.

Approaches. From the west, round Harbour Island, avoiding the rock just off its northwest point. Then steer more or less east along the north side of the island, keeping clear of the spit that extends a long way from Long Island. When you reach the east end of Long Island, pass close to it, going north between the island and the 2-foot (60-cm) high rock that always shows. When you've cleared the rock, resume your easterly course and make directly for Dutchtown Point, northeast of which the passage joins Spry Bay. Just to make the pilotage interesting, a rock with 2 feet (60 cm) of water over it at LW encumbers the middle of the passage where it joins the bay. The rock is probably best avoided by

keeping close to Dutchtown Point, though the other side is clear also.

Anchoring is possible almost anywhere in here. If you use the little cove on the east side of Harbour Island, beware of the rock, submerged 3 feet (1 m) at low-water springs, in the northeast part. The little bay north of Long Island is easy to enter, but anchor close to the Long Island shore as the northern part of the bay is shallow. If you're going to Popes Harbour village, keep to the starboard side going in, as rocks extend most of the way from the west.

This is a delightful sail in clear weather, and I have done it in fog, but it could be a real challenge at night. It is very sheltered, however, so if you run aground you are not likely to get into serious trouble.

Spry Bay and The Bawleen

Chart: 4236

The bays at the top of Spry Bay, east of Gerard Island, are shallow and full of rocks. With such attractive alternative anchorages close at hand, I have never explored them. The most sheltered of these anchorages is just north of the old farmhouse on the northeast shore of Gerard Island.

The Bawleen, a large body of water to the south of Gerard Island, protected by Phoenix Island, unfortunately has only 3 feet (1 m) of water at low-water springs at each end, which has deterred me from exploring it also.

To exit Spry Bay, steer due south 180°M from the lighthouse on Tomlee Head. While there used to be two lights in line here, the light now has red and white sectors, with the white sector covering the safe departure bearing to keep you clear of Maloney Rock and Mad Moll, both of which show at high water. Fairway bell buoy "YA2" is 4.1 miles from the light-

Gerard Passage.

house, almost on the bearing mentioned above.

If you're headed for Sheet Harbour from buoy "YA2," steer 070°M for 4 miles to clear Taylors Head and fetch the entrance to the harbor. This course lies inshore of the unmarked drying rock known as Taylors Goose. If you are uneasy about this, steer 120°M from "YA2" for 4 miles to the Geddes Shoal fairway buoy "X26," then shape a course north to the entrance to Sheet Harbour.

Mushaboom Harbour and Malagash Cove ★★★

 NO FACILITIES

Charts: **4235**, 4289

Mushaboom has few permanent inhabitants, but is a popular site for cottages. There are reasonably protected anchorages for cruisers not planning to venture farther north to Sheet Harbour.

Approaches. Chart 4289, or the older chart 4361—which is a replica of British Admiralty chart 2807—show the rocks in this area in better detail than does modern chart 4235.

From "YA2," the Spry Bay bell buoy, a course of 050°M will take you a safe distance off Taylors Head and Pyches Island, both of which are steep-to. An offing of a quarter-mile is safe. Round Pyches Island at any reasonable distance, and come to about 354°M. There are two dry rocks off the southwestern end of Malagash Island: Bald Rock, 10 feet (3 m) high, and the larger but lower Gull Island, to the northeast. A bearing of 354°M on Gull Island clears all dangers, but the island might be difficult to see from a distance.

Ship Reef, off Salisbury Island, is a hazard in the approach, but if you can't spot Gull Island, you can use pre-electronic age technology to keep clear of Ship Reef. Simply make sure you can see the western end of Malagash Island while you're still south of Gibbs Island. If Malagash Island is not open behind Gibbs Island in the vicinity of Ship Reef, you're too far east and in danger of hitting the reef.

Incidentally, note that Gibbs Island is called West Gibbs Island on chart 4235, while Roach Island, to the east, is called East Gibbs Island.

As you close with Gull Island, The Gates will open up to starboard. There is not really anywhere to anchor in Mushaboom Harbour, so go through The Gates, heading about 098°M. The Gates carry about 8 feet (2.4 m) of water, and when you're coming from the west, this passage gets you into smooth water about a half-hour quicker than a passage around the outside.

Take the north passage of The Gates, and keep close to Malagash Island. A small, detached island almost a half-mile along Malagash Island's southern shore should be left to port, but as soon as you have cleared it, swing south, well into mid-channel, to avoid a rock, drying 5 feet (1.5 m), just to the east. Most of the time you will be able to see this rock.

You can pass north between Malagash and Monahan Islands, in depths of 24 feet (7.3 m), or continue your course toward Sheet Harbour.

A rock stands in the middle of Malagash Cove, at least 2 feet (60 cm) above high water. A drying rock lies off the north shore of Monahan Island.

It's also possible to navigate the MacPhee Passage, south of The Gates, between Carroll Island and Salisbury Island, but it's more difficult.

Incidentally, if you're leaving Malagash Cove for Sheet Harbour, pass north of Horse Island to avoid the mess of rocks to its south.

Anchorage. Malagash Cove offers satisfactory anchorage at its western end, being open only to the northeast. But it is surrounded by cottages, so I prefer anchoring in the little cove off the north side of Gibbs Island, east of The Gates, for this reason. Watch for the rock that dries 6 feet (2 m). Anchorage is also possible east of Jim Hubley Island, though I haven't tried it.

Hurd Cove, on the east side of the entrance to Sheet Harbour, is obstructed by the bridge, which has a clearance of about 4 feet (1.2 m). It is, in any case, a little too open to the west for my tastes. But if you wish to enter it, pass midway between Coombs Island and Gull Ledge, going south, and

swing east toward Sheep Island. Keep clear of the bars extending north and southeast of Gull Ledge. The best anchorage is almost up to the bridge, though it is constricted. This anchorage has some merit in a strong easterly blow, though I would prefer to be farther up the harbor if things got really dirty.

Sheet Harbour ★★★

Chart: 4235

Sheet Harbour is the only place on the Eastern Shore between Canso and Halifax where you can easily provision. It is also the easiest harbor to enter between Jeddore and Liscomb.

Approaches. From offshore or from the east, steer 014°M from Geddes Shoal whistle buoy, "X26," for 6 miles to Sheet Rock, which should be left to port. After "X26" you will come upon a green spar "XU1," off Yankee Jack shoal to port; then a starboard bifurcation spar, "XUC, which you needn't bother about unless you draw more than 20 feet (6 m); and then a flashing red buoy off MacDonalds Shoals to starboard. If you keep Sheet Rock bearing between 002°M and 044°M

you will clear all dangers. Rocks extend from the west side of Sheet Rock for about 200 yards.

If you're approaching Sheet Harbour from the west, pass through The Gates, between Malagash Island and Gibbs Island. Alternatively, approach from buoy "YA2" on a course of 068°M until Sheet Rock bears 044°M, when you can alter course straight for it. Once again, leaving Sheet Rock to port is much preferred.

When you've cleared Sheet Rock, change course to about 010°M and keep the Sheet Rock light dead astern of you to clear White Shoal, now marked by quick-flashing red buoy "XU10." After leaving "XU10" to starboard, come to about 030°M and stay in mid-channel. Dead ahead, off Watt Point, lies flashing red buoy "XU14," and apart from Salmon Island over to starboard 2 miles from "XU10," there's nothing to hit on the way.

About a mile north of Salmon Island the channel starts to trend westerly, running about 330°M, and you should be able to see ahead the fixed green lights of the new commercial dock. The port side of the channel is less obstructed in this section, and should be favored.

Hazards in Sheet Harbour's Upper Reaches. Sheet Harbour has lately undergone something of a renaissance as a commercial port, having languished since the pulp mill burned down in the early 1970s. There are 150 commercial shipping movements a year, most notably a tug towing a 300-foot (91-m) barge to a mill in New Jersey

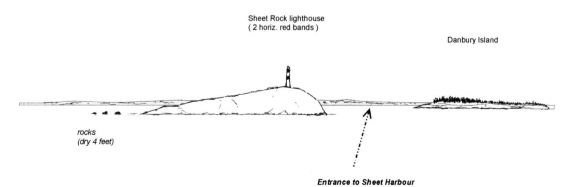

Sheet Rock lighthouse
(2 horiz. red bands)

Danbury Island

rocks
(dry 4 feet)

Entrance to Sheet Harbour

Entrance to Sheet Harbour from the south.

twice a week. You should watch out for this monster on your way in, especially in fog. While there is no port radio or traffic control, I'm sure a call on VHF Channel 16, asking for any commercial traffic in Sheet Harbour to identify itself, would not be unreasonable. There is no commercial traffic above the new dock. I have entered this harbor a number of times in thick fog, or at night, and occasionally both, without too much difficulty.

Anchorage, Dockage. Northwest of the new dock, Sheet Harbour divides into two arms. You can use either the eastern or the western arm. There is a government dock in the eastern arm, just before the bridge, which is well sheltered from anything but a hurricane—though friends of mine once rode out a hurricane there. The dock was repaired in the 1980s and is in good shape. A boat confiscated after a drug raid is submerged just off the wharf, with about 5 feet (1.5 m) over it. It's marked by a green buoy. There are plans to remove this wreck, but nothing has come of them yet. The problem with this wharf is that it is far from the town's stores. Boats able to cope with a bridge clearance of 27 feet (8.2 m) can ascend the East River for another 2 miles.

For reprovisioning, I would strongly recommend the western arm, unless there is a gale blowing, but watch out for the drying shoal off Church Point on the way in. You'll find a small slip and some moorings at the Fourwinds Motel, west of Halls Point. In previous years the Sheet Harbour Motel, a little farther south, maintained the same kind of facilities. I'm informed by a friend who lives in Sheet Harbour that there is good eating at the restaurant at the marina—telephone (902) 885-2502. There is reported to be fuel, too, but I'm not sure this information is accurate. There definitely is a reasonable supermarket where you will find fresh meat and the like. As the town is the commercial center of the Eastern Shore, it contains most of the usual stores and the government watering hole, although selection may be limited.

At the head of the harbor is an impressive set of rapids, just above the ruins of the pulp mill.

The really thirsty can walk over the bridge at the head of the harbor to a nearby tavern fashioned, believe it or not, inside an old oil-storage tank. It used to be called The Tank, in fact, but now has a more highfalutin' name. They have live music there occasionally. By the way, if you find all this walking too hard on creaky joints, Sheet Harbour does have taxis.

While it's not an unattractive community, Sheet Harbour can't really be considered a beauty spot—although it can possess a compelling allure for cruisers fleeing from a week of bad weather.

Passage East of Sheet Harbour

If you're on your way east from Sheet Harbour, and have had about enough of dodging rocks for a while, depart Sheet Rock on a course of 190°M, which, after 5.5 miles, brings you to Geddes Shoal whistle buoy, "X26." This course gives you a clearance of at least a half-mile from any rock, and is the safest route if you are relying on loran or GPS. From "X26," a course of 088°M takes you along the line of major outside buoys, most of which are whistles and can be heard in fog.

When I leave Sheet Harbour, however, I don't usually take this long tack out to sea. I go inshore of the two Shagroost Rocks, 3 miles southeast of Sheet Rock, which is safe enough under most normal conditions. If you'd like to try this route, steer 174°M from Sheet Rock to flashing red buoy "XU4," off MacDonalds Rock, then 104°M to Sheet Harbour Passage buoy "XP7." From the latter, steer 102°M to pass north of Pumpkin, Brother, and Beaver Islands. Although there's a nasty mess of rocks to the north of you on this course, the islands are steep-to on their northern sides, and this course is safe in most reasonable conditions.

If you want to go half outside, half inside, hold a course of 116°M from buoy "XU4" at MacDonalds Rock. That will take you inside Eastern Shagroost to whistle buoy "XK1," whence the course is 088°M to all points east, as above.

189

Sheet Harbour Passage ★★★

 4   B

NO FACILITIES

Charts: **4235**, 4361

While I have sailed past Sheet Harbour Passage many times, I've not stayed there overnight. However, as it provides excellent shelter not too far off the beaten track, I'm including it in this book.

Approaches. Enter Sheet Harbour Passage on a course of 004°M from buoy "XP7." This is the bearing of the leading marks, two fixed white lights. Like all such marks, they can be mistaken for shore lights—so check that your heading is correct, because this is not a good place to go aground. To prove the point, on the southern end of Sober Island, to port of the leading line, there used to be a substantial wreck—though it has degenerated into a pile of rust over the years. In passing, the best explanation I've heard for the name Sober Island was that a party of surveyors was unable to find a single house on the island capable of slaking their mighty thirsts.

As you progress north toward the leading marks, you will come to Factory Point, named Cameron Point on the old charts, on your port side. There, you should turn to the west and keep to the south side of the main channel, avoiding the drying banks to the north. You can anchor anywhere in the passage, or tie up at the public wharf if there's space. There may be fishing boat traffic at night, so riding lights are essential if you anchor.

There is a buoyed channel north of Softwood Island leading east in the direction of Beaver Harbour. I looked at it once, coming from the east, but was deterred by the enormous number of rocks. It is possible to pass between Round Island and the ledge north of it, thus cutting 5 miles off the journey to Beaver Harbour, but it is not very clear on chart 4235. What's more, the buoys that used to mark this passage have been removed, so

I can't recommend it. I once used the passage when it was rough, but the journey was very tense, and I've never tried it again. This whole area is full of rocks, has a very irregular bottom, is charted from an 1857 survey, and is very exposed to the prevailing southwesterlies. While you can cut inshore of Pumpkin Island with reasonable safety, I wouldn't venture in among the rocks to the north again unless the sea were flat calm and visibility 100 percent.

The Inside Passage

Smooth water, sheltered havens, and abundant wildlife—including whales—characterize the intriguing Inside Passage running 20 miles or so between Beaver Harbour and Liscomb. I always use this passage when I'm traveling west, at least in daylight. I wouldn't want to try it at night because there isn't a single light in it. The fog is usually less dense in here than it is offshore, though, and for this reason it may be easier to navigate the Inside Passage in fog than you'd imagine.

While opinions vary on the merits of the passage, it's one of my favorite places. The water is calm, and while the buoyage is a little eccentric, and the pilotage quite demanding, it's easy enough to find your way through the maze of rocks if you have a little patience. There are fewer buoys now than there were 20 years ago, but at least they're substantial steel spars that show up on radar. Before, the hazards were marked with a mixture of lobster-pot buoys, sticks, and God knows what, so you often had to stop and look around to find the mark. Thank goodness that's no longer necessary.

The names of rocks and islands vary from one chart series to the other, especially in this area. Local residents often know the same places by completely different names—but I've had to compromise. Even when I know full well that the locals don't call it that, I've used the name given on the latest chart, or in the *Sailing Directions*, so that visiting cruisers, who may be expected to be using those publications, will not be confused. Confusion happens all too easily aboard a small boat in times of stress, and there can be great danger in this. So in the interests of safety and simplicity I have tried as far as possible to use the exact names—misspellings, grammatical errors, and all—used by the Department of Fisheries and Oceans. Most of the buoys—those with numbers preceded by XM and XA—are placed as though you were entering harbor from west to east, that is, you leave the red ones to starboard, going east.

I've made every effort to ensure that the bearings and distances are correct, but this is an area where an unsuspected compass deviation error of two or three degrees could get you into trouble. Close attention to pilotage is essential, preferably using transits of islands, rocks, and other things that don't move around much. Many of the islands look alike, so I'd also advise you to keep a running dead-reckoning plot. One of the nice things about this area, though, is that there is little tidal stream, so at least you don't have to worry about that in your calculations.

Beaver Harbour
(Horsehead Cove) ★★★★

NO FACILITIES

Chart: **4235**

Horsehead Cove is a delightful, perfectly sheltered anchorage in Beaver Harbour, northwest of Beaver Point. It was named by Curtis Bok, of the Cruising Club of America, in 1953.

Approaches. Entering from the west or from offshore is straightforward— steer 336°M from buoy "XK3" off Beaver Island. If you have passed north of Pumpkin Island, keep going east off the north coast of Beaver Island, and don't turn northeast until Beaver Island lighthouse bears 170°M or more. That

will keep you off the rocks that extend quite a way east from the Horse Island Shoals.

The eastern side of Sutherland Island is steep-to, as is Beaver Point, which no longer has a light. The last time I was there, however, the point still displayed a white-red-white daymark.

After you've rounded Beaver Point, you'll see ahead two small green spar buoys marking rocks off Horsehead Cove.

Their position seems to vary, so if you can't find them, continue a northwesterly course almost to the point called Bluff Head on the chart, then turn south, following the shore, about 30 yards off. There are a couple of small wharves here, in pretty decrepit condition, unless they have been recently repaired. The entrance to the cove is quite narrow, and this deters some people, but it is deep in the middle. I have never found less than 10 feet (3 m) at low water.

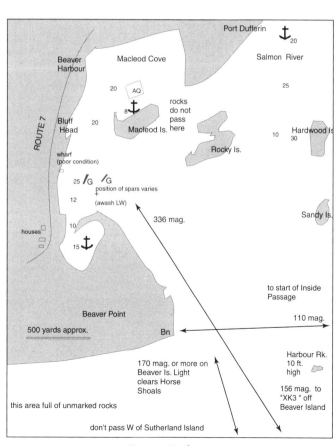

Beaver Harbour.

Anchorage. A few local skiffs moor in the cove, and on a couple of occasions I've found an aquaculture tank, but there is always room for a visiting yacht. The cove is protected to the north by a long shingle spit spattered with driftwood and wildflowers. It's a good place for walking or picnicking. A couple of houses overlook the cove, and the road from Sheet Harbour to Ecum Secum goes right by, but you couldn't by any stretch of the imagination call it a major road. Hardly anything moves on it after 2200. The holding ground is excellent, and you could ride out almost any sort of blow here.

There are other anchorages, such as the one north of Macleod Island (though you may have to share it with an aquaculture facility), and the one in the entrance to the Salmon River, northeast of Macleod Point. These places are certainly scenic, and in some ways more attractive than Horsehead Cove—Macleod Island, for example, has a little sandy beach—but they're more exposed to the weather. Indications of wharves on some charts are misleading: They're all turning into rubble.

You will notice some unusual environmental degradation in this region. It was very apparent on Sutherland Island the last time I was there, but no island is immune. There has been a population explosion of cormorants in the last few years. These noisy and unattractive beasts nest in the trees on offshore islands when they take over a new residence. Unfortunately, their copious droppings kill every plant they come into contact with—trees, grass, the whole works. Trees are the first things to go. They turn into dry sticks, as if there'd been a forest fire. Eventually the grass dies too, and the soil often washes away to reveal bare rock. It takes only 10 years to accomplish all this, and it may be 50 years before a tree will grow again. The smaller islands may be permanently reduced to bare rock. In the less sensitive parts of the province, the natives are given to shooting every cormorant they find nesting, but in this region the cormorants are left to flourish.

192

The Bay of Islands ★★★★★

  NO FACILITIES

Chart: **4235**

Despite the depredations of cormorants, on a fine day the passage through the Bay of Islands is one of the most scenic to be found anywhere. In good weather, anchorage can be had behind virtually any convenient island, though very few places are sheltered all-round, and you'll have to keep an eye on the weather.

These directions assume a transit of the Inside Passage from west to east. If you are traveling in the opposite direction, read this entire section before attempting the passage. The buoyage has been changed in recent years, and old charts will not show the buoyage correctly. I have been through here a dozen times, and there are always one or two spar buoys that are not on my chart. For this reason, I have tried to give transits and bearings on islands and landmarks that are more reliable.

There is not a single light in the passage, and very careful pilotage is required in fog. I would not recommend passage through here at night, or if the visibility is less than a mile, without radar. Loran and GPS cannot be relied on sufficiently to make this passage.

Approaches and Transit. From Beaver Point, steer 110°M to pass north of bare Harbour Rock—about 10 feet (3 m) high—and the wooded Harbour Islands. There may be a red spar just north of one of the outlying islets at the west end of the group, but often it has not been there. It is safest to keep the two green spars, "XM3" and "XM5," close to your port side. On a reasonably calm day with no swell, you can anchor off the north side of the Harbour Islands, the eastern end of the big one being better in this respect. Keep an eye on the depthsounder, though, as there are a few outlying rocks.

When Beaver Island light comes into line with the east end of North Harbour Island, change course to 038°M. You should at this time be in the vicinity of buoy "XM5." Leave it to port with Beaver Island light bearing 218°M dead astern of you.

When the highest part of 40-foot (12-m) High Island, to port, bears 264°M, come to 084°M. You should now be almost on top of red buoy "XM6," which should be left to starboard. There is a rock, with only 1 foot of water over it at LWS close east of this track, so veer a little to the west if you suspect the water is getting too thin. Apart from a drying rock 100 yards off the northeast point of High Island, the eastern side of the island is clear.

Continue on a course of 084°M, leaving buoy "XM7" to port and "XM10" to starboard. You need to be careful here, as there are drying rocks close either side of this channel. Buoy "XM10" marks a long reef extending west from Black Duck Island. The whole area south of this track is full of unmarked rocks, all the way to the Bird Islands, and should be avoided.

Round "XM10," leaving it to starboard, and change course to 102°M to pass midway between Baptiste and Black Duck Islands. Quoddy Hill, to the southwest, should bear 282°M behind you. On a good day, you can anchor just north of the reefs west of Black Duck Island.

To the north, on Turner Island, a conspicuous white house with two gables stands close west of a public wharf. If you'd like to tie up at the wharf, follow the buoyed channel in.

Branching northeastward off that channel is another, reasonably straightforward channel between Calf and Lobster Islands that enthusiastic gunkholers can take—with care—as far as Harrigan Cove. There are no marks, and the channel is winding, but there is deeper water on the Hog Island side.

Quoddy Harbour's unmarked rocks have always put me off, but it might well be a place of scenic and sheltered anchorages for the adventurous.

Necum Teuch, Felker Cove, and Mitchell Bay ★★★★★

 NO FACILITIES

Chart: 4235

Necum Teuch is a Mi'qmak Indian name, pronounced Necum Taw, and refers to a sandy place.

Approaches. After passing Black Duck Island, come to 082°M to pass midway between Torpey and Gold Islands. You need to keep in the middle as there are shoals extending from both islands, the Gold Island side being marginally better. Leave buoy "XM16" to starboard and "XM17" to port, then steer 078° directly for another island named High Island. This is the 52-foot-high (16-m) island southeast of Mitchell Point. This course will take you between Harbour Rock, 30 feet (10 m) high with a grassy top, and Dry Ledge, 2 feet (60 cm) high, shown as The Moll on the latest chart.

The 90-foot (27-m) high and conspicuous Ship Island will be on your port bow. Don't go north of a line between Torpey Island and Dry Ledge because it is full of ledges. The easiest way to get to Felker Cove, South of Moose Head, is to pass east of Ship Island, then to come to about 290°M, favoring the south side of the cove entrance to avoid the rock off Moose Head. This is a quiet and pleasant anchorage, but it's open to the southeast.

It's also possible to go between Torpey and Macdonald Islands, keeping close to the Torpey Island side at first (when traveling from west to east), then close to the east side of Macdonald Island. This is intricate and should only be tried on a calm day.

Moser River, running into the northwest corner of Necum Teuch Bay, looks as if it might offer good anchorage, but I have to say that it has a notorious reputation following a murder in the Halifax County Jail that enraged Nova Scotians, and brought the province's justice system into disrepute.

It all started when a gang of outlaws of the Hatfield and McCoy variety, heavily into drug dealing and welfare fraud, began terrorizing the inhabitants of Moser River. Most of the inhabitants were elderly, and the bullying went on for years. As the nearest policeman was at least three-quarters of an hour away, it wasn't difficult for the outlaws to thumb their noses at the law.

After his teenage daughter had been threatened by a gang member, one of the more determined members of the community decided he'd had enough. He forced the gangster's car off the road.

Instead of giving him a medal, the long arm of the law convicted the motorist of dangerous driving, and sent him to jail for two weeks. He hadn't been in the jail one hour, when one of the gang member's relatives, incarcerated for another offense, beat him to death. This resulted eventually in a first-degree murder conviction, an inquiry into the running of the jail, and substantial compensation for the motorist's wife from the province, which admitted liability. There is now a police officer stationed in Moser River. Some of the outlaws have been run out of town, and the place may now be a little more sedate, but I'd advise all except students of marginalized communities to give Moser River a wide berth.

Transit of Mitchell Bay

Chart: 4235

If you thought the pilotage challenging up to this point, think again. Mitchell Bay is where it gets really interesting. Continue on your course of 078°M across Necum Teuch Bay toward High Island until you come close to Hartlings Island (formerly called Lang Island),

then swing due south, passing about 30 yards off the west points of Lang/Hartlings and Calf Islands. This wide sweep is necessary to avoid Calf Island Shoal, which is no longer marked. Pass close along the south side of Calf Island (it is steep-to), until you are in the middle of Mitchell Bay.

Note that you cannot pass between Calf and Hartlings Islands—the passage is obstructed by rocks. You can pass between High and Hartlings Islands, but the remainder of the passage is a little more complicated if you do this.

From your position in the middle of Mitchell Bay, turn again to the south, but be sure to pass to the northeast of the small unnamed rock off Net Point. The rock is almost awash at high water, and it's difficult to see. At low water it looks quite unusual. If you're in any doubt about where it lurks,

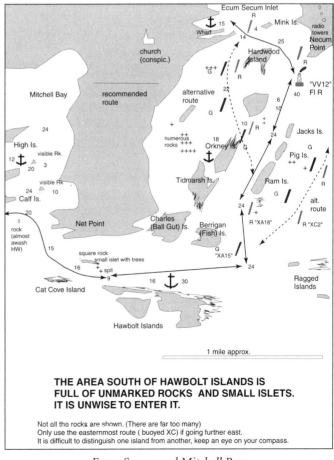

THE AREA SOUTH OF HAWBOLT ISLANDS IS FULL OF UNMARKED ROCKS AND SMALL ISLETS. IT IS UNWISE TO ENTER IT.

Not all the rocks are shown. (There are far too many)
Only use the easternmost route (buoyed XC) if going further east.
It is difficult to distinguish one island from another, keep an eye on your compass.

Ecum Secum and Mitchell Bay.

edge closer to Net Point. Pass north of Cat Cove Island, then south of the little unnamed island with the square rock on its northwestern point. When you pass this little island, alter course just a little to the south at its east end to avoid a submerged rock about 30 yards out. Pass close north of Hawbolts Islands, the long chain just ahead to starboard. Apart from a few obvious dry rocks, the islands are steep-to. This is the narrowest, shallowest, and most difficult part of the Inside Passage. It's also the one place where the southwesterly swell gets in, and it can get a little intimidating. My charts and illustrations will, I hope, make this a little clearer.

Once you get to the Hawbolts Islands you can breathe again. The minimum depth in this section is about 12 feet (3.6 m), and you can anchor behind any convenient island. The lee of Hawbolts Islands makes an excellent anchorage.

To continue from Hawbolts Islands, make for green spar buoy "XA15," off Berrigans (Fish) Island, on a course of about 105°M, and, when you reach the buoy, turn hard to port to 010°M. Leave buoy "XA18" to starboard, change course to about 072°M, and continue keeping Tidmarsh, Orkney, and Rocky Islands to port.

If you're making for Ecum Secum Harbour, you can, as an alternative, take the buoyed channel to the west of Rocky Island.

Again, you can anchor in perfect shelter between any islands. The little bay between Orkney Island and Tidmarsh Island, which must be approached from the north, is another excellent anchorage. The islands are covered with spruce trees and a few hardwoods, with big flat rocks forming the shoreline.

A course of 040°M from mid-channel between Rocky Island and Jacks Island will take you to red flashing buoy "VV12" marking the entrance to Ecum Secum Harbour.

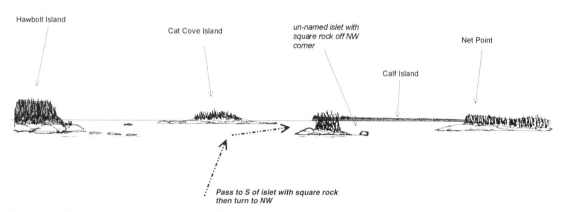

The Inside Passage, looking west near Net Point.

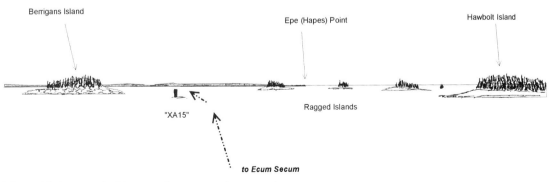

The Inside Passage, looking east from Net Point toward Ecum Secum.

195

I don't recommend the buoyed channel east of Rams Island unless you are going farther east, or are prepared to make a wide detour around Harbour Rock and Mad Moll.

Passage Outside Tuffin Island

Chart: 4235

If you feel the previous route is too much of a challenge, you can leave Harbour Rock to port and set a course of about 144°M for Tuffin Island. Leave flashing red bell buoy "XA4" to port, and then change course to 102°M to traverse the south side of Tuffin Island.

Incidentally, there is another quick-flashing red buoy ("XA6") 1 mile north of buoy "XA4," marking a channel through the rocks to Mitchell Bay. Don't confuse the two. Make sure you are heading for the more southerly buoy. When you come to green spar "VV7," which is difficult to see until you're right on top of it, you can turn to 014°M to go deeper into Ecum Secum Bay. Don't drift north of the line between "XA4" and "VV7," as you can hit Tuffin Shoal, 400 yards west of the spar buoy.

You might suspect the existence of a buoyed channel from the west side of Tuffin Island to Mitchell Bay and Ecum Secum—and there might indeed be one, because the "XA" series of buoys starts at one end and finishes at the other—but I'll be darned if I can find it. This whole area seems to be a mess of rocks and reefs best avoided by anyone with a draft of more than 2 feet (60 cm). It is also unwise to try to approach the area north of Tuffin Island from seaward. Either go through the Inside Passage or pass by.

White Islands ★★★

NO FACILITIES

Chart: 4235

About 1.5 miles south of Tuffin Island there is an interesting anchorage north of what the chart calls Round Island. It's more or less in the middle of the White Islands. Chart 4235 shows it in the inset labeled "Ecum Secum." It is best approached from the north, but there are few dangers for boats of modest draft. The islands are a bird sanctuary, and very scenic. As the anchorage is completely open to any wind with a northerly component, overnight stays should be contemplated only in the most settled conditions.

Approaches to Ecum Secum, from Seaward

You can pass inside or outside of the White Islands, the inside passage being somewhat easier if you are coming from the west. Give the west end of the islands a good berth, as a ledge sticks out a quarter-mile or more from Camp Island.

From Lockwood Rock whistle buoy "V24," steer 344°M for about 2 miles to the bell buoy "VV1," and from there change course to 014°M. Leave Tuffin Shoal spar, "VV7," to port, and Frenchmans Rock lightbuoy, "VV8," to starboard. A bearing of 210°M or more on the east end of Long Island clears Tuffin Shoal, and 230°M or less on the east end of Long Island clears The Hubbub, though the latter is usually easy to see.

Continue on a course of about 014°M until you find red spar buoy "VX6" marking Nags Head Rock. This rock frequently doesn't break, so you need to be careful. If you can't find the spar buoy, which isn't unusual, a bearing of 340°M on the radio towers just east of Ecum Secum Harbor keeps you clear of the dangers. You should be able to see Harbour Rock, 4 feet (1.2 m) high, on your port beam if you have any doubts. Be aware also of Ballast Shoal, halfway between Nags

Head Rock and Davidson Point. This course leaves the buoyed channel, the latter going to the west of Harbour Rock and Mad Moll. As there is an unmarked 2-foot shoal almost in the buoyed channel, it is much easier to pass to the east of Harbour Rock. From "VX6" a heading of 312°M takes you to Ecum Secum Inlet.

If you're approaching from Marie Joseph Harbour, it is easier to round Hapes Point (Epe Point on old charts), and stay about 100 yards to 200 yards off the cliffs and obvious outlying rocks to clear all dangers.

This passage could be a little tense at night, though I have done it a few times—but I wouldn't try it in the fog without radar.

Ecum Secum Wharf ★★

Chart: 4235

There is a small government wharf in Ecum Secum village, where it says Back Cove on the chart. There are a few boats here, and you may have to moor alongside one of them. A small convenience store is situated just west of the wharf.

Ecum Secum Harbour ★★★

  NO FACILITIES

Chart: 4235

Presumably just to confuse strangers, Ecum Secum Harbour is about a mile west of the village. Enter it by passing close to the east of Hardwood Island, then west of the red buoy off Mink Island. The channel here is narrow and if you can't see the spar, keep really close to Western Point, as there is a rock in the fairway here. If you draw less than 5 feet (1.5 m) you can pass close to the east side of Mink Island.

The anchorage is in the second cove to the

west, north of Middle Point, just past the small government wharf, in about 10 feet (3 m), over a mud bottom. The holding ground is excellent, and it's sheltered all-round. It's not as pretty here as it is in the islands, but you'll certainly get a good night's sleep.

The adventurous can go farther up the inlet, passing east of Hen Island to the little basin just above, but the channel is rather tortuous.

Passage East From Ecum Secum

From Ecum Secum through Marie Joseph Harbour, the Inside Passage is easy going, but if you want to take the outside route, it is safer to go west and south of Little White Island before you turn east. The passage between Little White Island and the group of islands forming the southern boundary of Marie Joseph Harbour is full of rocks. Most of them show, but they're unmarked and very exposed.

Marie Joseph Harbour

Chart: 4235

Marie Joseph Harbour is completely enclosed and outstandingly beautiful. Approaching from the west is easiest if you steer 108°M from Harbour Rock, which keeps you a safe distance away from Nags Head Rock. You can also avoid Nags Head, if you're approaching from Ecum Secum, by keeping about 100 yards off Hapes Point. There were once spars marking this track, but they haven't been there in the last few years.

If you're coming from the southwest, round Frenchmans Rock buoy, "VV8," and keep about 50 yards off the dry rocks at Blackbill Point.

To go farther into the harbor, leave Round Island to port. It is steep-to, and there are no dan-

gers on its southern and eastern sides. In the bay between Round Island and Turners Island is an enormous mussel-farming operation. (Incidentally, Turners Island was formerly called Hawbolts. There must have been too many of those darned Hawbolts around.) The first time I saw the mussel farm, I wondered if it was even possible for me to get past. There is, however, room between it and Round Island, with a minimum depth of 10 feet (3 m). It could be a major hazard, though, if you were brave (or foolhardy) enough to try this passage at night. The last time I was there it had radar reflectors, but no lights, and as it's at least a quarter-mile long on each side, it would be all too easy to get fouled up in it.

You can go west of Round Island to avoid the mussel farm, but Hapes (Epe) Rock lurks a quarter-mile to the northwest. You can avoid the rock by keeping close to Hapes Point, and waiting until Turners Point bears 110°M before you turn east.

Any of the little coves on Goose Island will make a fine anchorage, but look out for the fringing rocks, most of which are always visible. You'll find navigation much easier in this area if you have an old copy of chart 4356 around, because chart 4235 doesn't show much detail. Turners Island is best left to starboard, though it is clear all the way around. The northwest corner of Marie Joseph Harbour has several unmarked rocks and is best avoided. The same could be said of Salmoneaux Passage, between Goose Island and Barren Island.

Hawbolt Cove, north of Turners Island provides excellent shelter and is free of obstructions. It is west of Oxford Point, which is a conspicuous red bank. There is 10 feet (3 m) of water close north of the government wharf. If you draw more than 7 feet (2.1 m) you need to keep clear of the shoal in mid-channel just outside. There is still a small fishing fleet of a half-dozen boats based at Hawbolt Cove, and diesel fuel is available at the wharf. There is also a small store and a boatyard.

Smith Cove, east of Hawbolt Cove, is a little less sheltered and its northwest portions are obstructed. An interesting anchorage, when conditions are reasonable, may be found in the northeast corner of Smith Cove, in the shelter of the shingle beach north of Smith Point.

Departing Marie Joseph for Points East

Charts: 4235, 4234

From Marie Joseph Harbour, the shortest route to Liscomb lies between Thrumcap Shoal and Barren Island. A course of 088°M from the green buoy "VT7," north of Barren Island, will take you to bell buoy "VP5," off Liscomb Island. This is one of the few places on the Eastern Shore where there is a noticeable tidal stream. It floods to the west at just under 1 knot.

If you are headed farther east, rather than north to Liscomb, beware of the multitude of dangerous rocks that extend at least 2 miles east of Barren Island—though their impressive surf should warn you of their presence.

When you emerge from the lee of Barren Island, having come from Beaver Harbour without hitting anything, you will have joined the select group of navigators who have traversed the Inside Passage. You may by now be feeling the need for a decent meal and a stiff drink. Luckily, you are close to one of the few places on this shore where such luxuries may be found. I would certainly recommend that you visit Liscomb. I believe you'll find it well worth the effort of the passage up the river.

Liscomb Harbour

Chart: 4234

Liscomb Harbour, entered between Liscomb Point and Cranberry Point on Liscomb Island, is almost landlocked and almost free of obstructions. It is dominated by Hemloe Island in its center, which gives shelter to the settlements of Liscomb, northwest of the island, and Little Liscomb, to the north. Another small-craft anchorage, Spanish Ship Bay, lies west of a peninsula protruding into Liscomb Harbour from the village of Liscomb.

The western side of the harbor forms the mouth of the Liscomb River, where a small-craft channel leads to Liscomb Lodge, a provincial resort hotel and marina with fresh water, fuel, dining, and lodging.

Approaches. As previously described, a course of 088°M from Thrumcap Island at the entrance to Marie Joseph Harbour takes you to bell buoy "VP5," off Cranberry Point on Liscomb Island.

The approach from offshore is easy under any conditions of wind and tide, and could probably be attempted in fog without radar. Approach the lighthouse on Liscomb Island on any heading between 320°M and 012°M. From outside whistle buoy "VP," shape a course of 338°M and hold it for 5.2 miles. A bearing of 012°M or less on "VP5" will keep you a comfortable distance off the nasty mess of rocks east of Barren Island.

Outlying rocks off the southeast corner of Liscomb Island (Crook Shoals) extend nearly 1 mile east. If you're approaching from southeast, a bearing of 320°M or more on the Liscomb Island light will keep you clear of them.

Vessels with a draft of less than 6 feet (1.8 m), when approaching from the east in any conditions other than an easterly gale, will save time by going north of Liscomb Island. From Little Liscomb bell buoy "VM3," steer 308°M. If you can't see this buoy—not an uncommon occurrence if you get here in late afternoon and the sun is in your eyes—look for the conspicuous wreck on Barachois Point, bearing 026°M, 2 miles distant.

When you reach the northwest corner of Liscomb Island, a little caution is required. Go midway between the spit just before the old boathouse and Hog Island. This is not the spit joining Point of the Beach (Gravel Island) to Liscomb Island, but one just east of it. Gravel Island

(Point of the Beach) is a small island with a grassy top, and if you keep it bearing between 292°M and 294°M, you will be in the deepest part of the channel. When the ruins of the boathouse (which by now might be just a concrete slab) are abeam, swing a little to the north to leave Point of the Beach a couple of boatlengths on your port beam.

There is at least 7 feet (2.1 m) here—up to 9 feet (2.7 m) in fact, if you are right in the middle. There is a striking, large modern house on Hemloe Island, which seems quite out of character on this deserted coastline. When you pass it, you are in deep water again. I always use this route, coming or going, east of the Liscomb River, and it's not difficult in daylight.

Approaches to Liscomb from the West, or from Offshore. Unless it is quiet, it is best not to pass over Liscomb Shoal. There is always a swell on it, and it is nasty when the wind's blowing hard. You'll find the smoothest passage by keeping in the middle until you can see the Liscomb River open to port.

Little Liscomb Harbour

★★★★   3   C   🍽   🛒

Chart: 4234

The eastern entrance to Little Liscomb Harbour, which forms a protected, crescent-shaped harbor within Liscomb Harbor, is a lot wider than the western one. As you approach the eastern entrance, keep the green buoys to port, no matter how close to the mainland they look. If you tie up at the government dock at the village of Little Liscomb, beware of a rock, drying 3 feet (1 m) southeast of the wharf. It's not shown on chart 4234.

The western entrance to Little Liscomb Harbour is narrow enough to be intimidating, but at least it's deep. Go between green spar "VQ5" and the little island to its east. Leaving the buoy to port looks wrong, but you will hit something if you leave it to starboard. Don't try either

entrance at night if you've no local knowledge.

You can anchor almost anywhere in Little Liscomb Harbour, north of Hemloe Island, but it is a bit open for my tastes. The best anchorage is in the little bight between Hemloe and Hog Islands, a little farther west than the spot designated by the anchor on chart 4234.

Ashore. There's a small restaurant and a convenience store just west of the Little Liscomb government wharf. As this really is a long way from civilization, you can expect supplies to be limited. The restaurant is licensed, but I've never had the chance to try it.

Another public wharf northwest of Hemloe Island marks the settlement known simply as Liscomb.

Spanish Ship Bay ★★★★

 NO FACILITIES

Chart: **4234**

Spanish Ship Bay, in the western part of Liscomb Harbour, has a narrow entrance, and you should hug the east side going in. I've never stayed here overnight, but it's more protected than Little Liscomb is.

Like Little Liscomb, though, Spanish Ship Bay is a pretty place to anchor in, with spruce- and pine-covered hills surrounding the coves. Once again, entering at night would be difficult.

Liscomb River and Liscomb Lodge ★★★★★

Chart: **4234**

I have enjoyed some wonderful sailing on the Liscomb River, a clear and largely unobstructed waterway bordered by wooded hills and a few small farms. The farms on the south bank are now all abandoned, poignant reminders of a previous century, and the only signs of habitation on that side of the river are a couple of summer cottages. The main road runs along the north side of the river, but is unobtrusive.

Approaches. On entering the river, the first mark is a conspicuous, gray slate rock close to the southern shore, just south of the anchor shown on chart 4234. Don't try to go inshore of the rock. About 100 yards west of it lurks a small ledge—not at all well shown on the chart—that sticks out a little way from the shore. If you remain more than 50 yards offshore, however, you won't hit anything. Just west of the rock there are a couple of buoys, the port bifurcation buoy "VPA" (which you can ignore if you draw 6 feet—

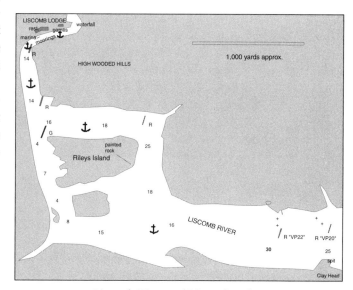

Liscomb River and Liscomb Lodge.

1.8 m—or less), and red buoy "VP16," which you must leave to starboard, going upstream. There is only 2 feet (60 cm) of water on the north side of it. The south side provides a clearer passage all the way up, except for a spit that extends a little way from Clay Head, just before buoy "VP22." Again, staying about 30 yards offshore will keep you clear. A half-mile past Clay Head, the river widens out into a small basin dominated by Rileys Island.

At the time of writing, the buoys in the river were constructed of painted polystyrene, and made poor radar targets, but they do have reflective tape to make them easy to see at night.

Anchorage, Dockage. Anchorage is possible anywhere in the basin, but the wind tends to blow straight up and down the river, and by far the most sheltered spot is up at the lodge. To get there, leave the basin by heading north along Riley Island's eastern shore. I believe it's also possible to go south of the island, but shallow patches plague this route. A sign painted on a big rock says Liscomb Lodge is another half-mile or so upriver. There are some buoys to guide you along this stretch of the river, but if you stay in the middle you won't go wrong, and you'll find depths of 12 feet (3.6 m) all the way up.

The river gets narrower, and the hills seem to get higher, until you end up in a channel so narrow that it seems you can reach out and touch the trees. Needless to say, it would be difficult to do this last section under sail, unless you have an easterly wind; but I've done it often enough under power on a pitch-black night. At the last bend, you will see the buildings of Liscomb Lodge on your port bow. There is a small dock, and two or three moorings. In the unlikely event that all are occupied, you can anchor just upstream (with care) or downstream of them. The water here is almost fresh and, with a little luck, will cause any barnacles on your hull to fall off. The stream is in a permanent state of ebb, the strength depending on the rainfall during the previous few days.

Nothing could trouble you here. The hills are 150 feet (45 m) high, and there are lots of bends between you and open water. I rode out a hurricane here in 1992, and though there was a mighty deluge, the wind bothered us not at all.

Ashore. Liscomb Lodge was opened in 1961 by George Wadds, a retired naval officer. It was bought by the government of Nova Scotia in 1976, and is now run as one of three provincial resort hotels. The others are Digby Pines and Keltic Lodge, at Ingonish, in Cape Breton. This is a splendid place in which to recuperate from a stretch of bad weather, and—being almost halfway between Halifax and St. Peters—it's also a good place to break a cruise into more digestible parts.

The lodge's facilities include an excellent restaurant, an indoor swimming pool installed in 1995, and a games room with a large-screen TV and a snooker table—more than sufficient to placate a fractious crew longing for the supposed pleasures of civilization. The marina has fuel, water, ice, a laundromat, showers and the like, and the marina manager, Chester Rudolf, is very obliging. He has, for example, lent me his truck to fetch supplies from Sherbrooke. The modest dockage charge ($10 a night in 1992) allows you complete run of all the hotel facilities—a real bargain. The marina office monitors VHF Channels 16 and 68 but, because of the hills, is difficult to raise until you are actually in the river. Liscomb Lodge's telephone number is (902) 779-2307, and the fax number is (902) 779-2700.

Close to the moorings is a set of rapids and a small waterfall. A hiking path laid out by hotel staff runs upstream from the road bridge. As the Liscomb River is one of Nova Scotia's more favored salmon streams, salmon are often seen jumping in these rapids, and indeed, all around your boat. Naturally, salmon features frequently on the restaurant's menu. Though this is one of the prettiest spots in the province, there are only two or three local yachts here, and you are not likely to feel crowded. Fiscal constraints caused by the province's financial crisis have so far not affected this operation, though it must be difficult to run it at a profit. There is no comparable facility on this entire stretch of coast, and from my experience,

those of you who make the diversion up the river will not be disappointed.

Incidentally, you might imagine nobody travels this river at night, but I've certainly done so, and I'd appreciate it greatly if you'd show riding lights if you're not on a mooring.

Liscomb to Canso

The nature of the coastline changes east of Liscomb, which marks the end of the Inside Passage. This area is part of Guysborough County, the most sparsely populated region in Nova Scotia, and this, in turn, is the least-populated part of the county.

The only industry in the area is a little inshore fishing, a couple of fish-processing plants, and part-time lumbering. The administrative center is Sherbrooke, a community of fewer than 1,000 people—which, incidentally, is difficult to approach by boat. There are a couple of dozen good anchorages in this stretch, most of which will be deserted. It's next to impossible to get much in the way of supplies or repairs, so you must carry sufficient provisions for the length of your stay. The hazardous offshore reefs that protect the Inside Passage are missing here, except off Country Harbour. If you stay 3 miles offshore, you'll be clear of all dangers.

This area has a lot of fog, and the sea is often rough. Loran reception is a little temperamental, and the 5930 Y and Z chains occasionally give better reception than the 5930 X and Y chains that work better farther west.

Charts for the Area Between Liscomb and Canso. Chart 4321, Liscomb to Canso, is a small-scale chart. You can probably get by with it for Liscomb, Country Harbour, New Harbour, and maybe Whitehaven. But don't try to enter Canso, Dover, Tor Bay, or the St. Marys River with it.

Charts 4234, 4233, and 4281 are the new inshore charts. They are better than the others in this series in most respects. Chart 4356 is out of print, but is the best for the Liscomb area. Chart 4282 is also out of print, but is slightly better for the eastern part of Tor Bay, and obsolete 4280 is very useful if you want to visit Dover Harbour, Louse Harbour, or Port Howe, which are not at all well shown on 4233.

Gegogan Harbour

Chart: **4234**

I have never visited this harbor, but I am told there is good anchorage in the basin above Rae Island. None of the new charts shows this harbor well. Keeping clear of Tobacco Reef and Shag Ledge is a problem, as they are unmarked. It is perhaps easier to enter between distinctive Tobacco Island and the wreck on Steering Reef (misspelled on the chart) a mile east of the island, or by passing between Redman Head and red buoy "VM6" marking the west side of Shag Ledge. There is not a single road going anywhere near the harbor, which will delight those who like solitude.

St. Marys River ★★★★

Chart: **4234**

Very few boats ascend the St. Marys River, and only the most adventurous take the winding, pretty channel the full 7 miles to the village of Sherbrooke. Those who do so are pleasantly surprised by the facilities ashore, which include a bank, a supermarket, a liquor store, and a couple of restaurants. There is also a small hospital. But even more surprising is the completely restored 1880s-vintage village, a reminder of the times when the hand of prosperity lay on Sherbrooke.

Approaches. There is a conspicuous wreck just west of the entrance to St. Marys River. It's an old "three-island" type of general cargo vessel of about 10,000 tons. I believe it went on the rocks here in a winter storm in the 1950s, and you can still see it for miles in clear conditions. The wreck has slowly deteriorated over the years, and the last time I was here, there was a large hole amidships.

From outer bell buoy "VK," steer 344°M for 4.3 miles to fetch the mouth of the river. The wreck will be a mile or so to port. Pass inner bell buoy "VK3" on either side.

The only light in the river—fixed green near spar "VK11"—is on a crib in the river entrance, which you must leave to port. In the lower part of the river, the deep channel is on the east side. The tide runs at about 2 knots here, and swirls unpredictably.

The leading lights are long gone, and it is best to keep the light on the crib bearing 346°M to avoid being set on to the shingle bank to the east. I would not consider entering this river except in daylight and reasonable wind conditions. In strong southerly winds the entrance is dangerous.

St. Marys River is one of the few places on the Eastern Shore where the tide is a major consideration affecting entry. It runs at 2 knots at springs—perhaps slightly more on the ebb, if there has been heavy rain. The range is about 6.5 feet (1.9 m) in the lower reaches, and slightly greater at Sherbrooke. High water occurs at roughly the same time as it does in Halifax.

Anchorage, Dockage. The government wharf at Sonora, on the eastern bank a mile upstream from buoy "VK8," is a miserable thing, and should be used only if there is no alternative. It is protected to the south by a breakwater, and the space between them is full of mud. The south face of the wharf has about 5 feet (1.5 m) of water at its end, and you may be able to moor there if your draft allows. There are no facilities.

The St. Marys River continues another 7 miles to Sherbrooke, a winding and pretty channel between wooded hills. It is quite well buoyed, but is best traversed in daylight on a rising tide. There is a lot of ice in this river in winter, and the narrow channel changes considerably. The spars are reported to be moved occasionally to mark the deepest channel, but there is no commercial traffic here, so they are sometimes out of position. Every time I've visited this river I have run aground at least once. Running aground on mud is not the worst hazard; there are rock piles left over from the cribwork of the log booms. This was an important lumbering area at one time and the rock piles are the size of small barns. They are everywhere along the banks of the river, and I think the winter ice may move some of them about. Because of the uncertainty of their position, even the latest chart may be inaccurate. In most reasonable conditions, you can anchor anywhere in the channel, and the tide is not as strong as it is at the entrance.

At the head of the river, the channel splits into two. The western arm is a hopelessly jumbled mess of rocks and abandoned log booms. But you can enter the eastern arm and anchor just downstream of the town. The holding ground is not good—I'm not sure whether it's smooth rock or old, rotten logs—so a fisherman-type anchor might work best.

Ashore. To get to the village, land your dinghy on the eastern bank, and walk northeast. As so few boats visit here, you can expect some strange looks. For the adventurous few who make it this far, the village comes as a pleasant surprise. Apart from the bank, supermarket, and liquor store, there are a couple of restaurants. I've enjoyed excellent meals at the Bright House. An interesting diversion is a visit to the Sherbrooke historic village restoration, a completely restored 1880s village. Sherbrooke in those days was a well-developed community supported by farming and timber. However, prosperity is damned scarce in Guysborough County 100 years later. Perhaps we will eventually learn and apply the doctrine of sustainable development.

Wine Harbour

Chart: **4234**

The next inlet east of the St. Marys River, Wine Harbour, was the scene of one of the biggest drug busts on the East Coast. It is shallow and obstructed by sandbanks, and not really suitable for deep-draft boats. Of course, if you have a big Zodiac dinghy and several thousand kilos, you may find it more to your liking—although you might be surprised at the intensity of the scrutiny you'd come under from the few inhabitants.

Indian Harbour and Holland Harbour

Chart: **4234**

The two small harbors in Indian Harbour have depths of less than 3 feet (1 m) at low-water springs, and are not really suitable for yachts. Holland Harbour is shallow and open to the southeast. With much better shelter nearby, I have not used either.

Port Bickerton ★★★

NO FACILITIES

Chart: **4234**

Port Bickerton is another harbor I have never anchored in, but I include it because it's the base for the only lifeboat on the Eastern Shore.

Approaches. Dangers in the approaches include Castor Rock and Pollux Rock. Each is about 5 feet (1.5 m) high, and visible in good weather—but they're a menace in fog.

If you're approaching from the west, a course of 070°M for 7.5 miles from "VK," the outer bell buoy off the St. Marys River, brings you to bell buoy "VCA," just off Port Bickerton.

If you're closing with the coast from offshore, find outer fairway bell buoy "VC." From there, steer 356°M for 4.1 miles to buoy "VCA."

The eastern approach is a little more complicated, as there are numerous shoals off Cape Mocodome. From whistle buoy "TT," 3.75 miles south of Country Island, steer 308°M for 2.3 miles, to bell buoy "TU2," just off South Easter, a nasty drying rock, thence 316°M for 4.75 miles to buoy "VCA."

If you're coming from Country Harbour, or Fishermans Harbour, head south to bell buoy "TY." Leave it to starboard and steer a course of 296°M for 3 miles to buoy "VCA." If it is a clear day, and the sea is not too rough, you can go between spar buoys "TY4" and "TY5," which mark the passage inside Rose Shoal.

The main harbor at Port Bickerton is called Mouton Harbour on the chart, and is well supplied with buoys and leading lights. There are three sets of leading lights to take you in at night from buoy "VCA."

Anchorage, Dockage. Large draggers use this port regularly, or at least they did before the fishery crisis. A large fish processing plant, owned by Mersey Sea Products of Liverpool, occupies most of the government wharf. Space may be available alongside the wharf, and I have heard of boats anchoring in the shelter of the breakwater, just south of red spar buoy "VC16," though there is not a lot of room. The best spot is on the north side of the public wharf. Go close to the tower with the quick-flashing red light to avoid the rock off the end of the wharf. The fish plant was not in operation much in 1994 because of the moratorium on East Coast groundfishing. This presumably affects the viability of the plant and its aids to navigation.

The lifeboat is stationed at the wharf in the northwestern corner of the harbor, where it says Port Bickerton on the chart. The approach is intricate. Don't be tempted to follow the leading marks right up the harbor, or you will hit something. With much easier harbors nearby, I don't go out of my way to use Port Bickerton.

Fishermans Harbour ★★★

  NO FACILITIES

Chart: 4234

While there are absolutely no facilities at Fishermans Harbour, it's not far off the beaten track, and it's easy to enter.

Vessels coming from Country Harbour should round Country Harbour Head at any comfortable distance. It is steep-to, and there are no outlying rocks.

If you're coming from any other direction, round Cape Mocodome, giving it a wide berth, then approach from southeast, halfway between the cape and Black Ledge, one part of which always shows. A bearing of 320°M on the fixed green light on the end of the spit forming Neverfail Cove keeps you clear of all dangers.

Anchorage. The best anchorage is not that indicated by the anchor on chart 4234, but the one tucked inside the spit. This deserted anchorage, miles from the nearest house, is a little open to northwesterly gales, but is otherwise satisfactory. There is a small public wharf in the south part of the cove, but it doesn't see a lot of activity.

Country Harbour ★★★

 NO FACILITIES

Chart: 4234

Country Harbour is a deep cleft extending some 8 miles inland between wooded hills, which rise to about 300 feet (91 m) on the western side. There is at least 65 feet (20 m) of water in the entrance, and 50 feet (15 m) as far as Mount Misery. I am surprised it has never been developed for deep-draft vessels, but perhaps this is to our benefit. The western side is completely uninhabited and miles from any road other than the cable-ferry terminal. Chart 4234 has a nice inset of Country Harbour. Though the chart shows nun and can buoys as markers, they are just as likely to be spar buoys that don't have to be hauled out in winter, and thus are cheaper to maintain.

Approaches. From the west, round Cape Mocodome inside or outside Rose Shoal, and turn north, carefully avoiding Black Ledge, which is marked on its western side by two spars. If you are going to Drum Head, southeast of the entrance to Country Harbour, a course of 050°M from outside bell buoy "VC" leads you close east of Rose Shoal bell buoy "TY," and takes you to the middle of the channel between Goose Island and Harbour Island.

For those of you approaching from offshore, a course of 346°M from outside whistle buoy "TT" will take you to Bear Trap Head, 8.5 miles away. The headland divides Country Harbour from Isaacs Harbour. Watch out for South Easter, on your port side (marked by bell buoy "TU2"), and Tom Cod Rock to starboard (marked by bell buoy "TT2"). The passage is wide, however, and shouldn't be too difficult.

Passage between Harbour Island and Goose Island is straightforward, but the channel between Goose Island and Country Island is shallow and irregular. It's best avoided. There is no longer a radio beacon on Country Island, so don't waste your time listening for it. It does, however, have a foghorn. The horn (one blast per minute) is usually easily heard on this approach.

When I come from the east, I always use The Sound, north of Harbour Island. A course of 294°M for 4.2 miles from buoy "TS6" off Coddles Harbour leads straight up the middle. Graham Shoal, marked with red buoy "TS10," is the only hazard.

Anchorage. Country Harbour is open to the southeast, and has a tidal stream of up to 1.5 knots at times, so there is often a swell in the lower reaches. The wind has a habit of blowing straight up or down the harbor, making the anchorages rather less sheltered than you might think.

The north cove of Mount Misery, 2.5 miles

northwest of Bear Trap Head, is widely used as an anchorage, but I have heard much of it is occupied by an aquaculture facility, and it won't give you much protection if the wind is blowing hard from the north. You can also use the south cove, but avoid the long spit off the southern peninsula.

At Stormont, 3 miles farther up the river on the eastern bank, there is a large wharf where you can tie up.

Incidentally, the anchorage shown off Stewart Cove, south of Stormont, may suit you if your vessel is 200 feet (60 m) long and displaces 4,000 tons, but it's far too open for my tastes.

The best shelter in Country Harbour, for those who have the time to get there, is probably around Widow Point, almost at the head of the harbor.

Isaacs Harbour ★★★

Chart: 4234

Isaacs Harbour, separated from Country Harbour by a peninsula 1.5 miles wide, offers better shelter closer to the coast. Entry is straightforward, just follow the buoys. You can go to the east of buoy "TT10," unless you draw more than 10 feet (3 m).

Anchorage. Webbs Cove, close to starboard after you've entered harbor, is a pleasant little anchorage. The spit between Hurricane Island and the mainland may cover at exceptionally high tides, but in most normal conditions the anchorage is well sheltered.

There are no submerged hazards in the harbor other than Sinclairs (Squinces) Ledge, on the western shore, south of the government wharf at the settlement of Isaacs Harbour. Good shelter is available at the wharf.

The best anchorage, other than Webbs Cove, is

not where the anchor on chart 4234 shows you, but at the head of the harbor.

Ashore. Eighty years ago, Country Harbour was booming. Though the earliest settlers had some horrendous experiences (hence Mount Misery and Widow Point), exporting lumber provided a good living, and gold was discovered in 1880. Goldboro, in fact, was a gold-rush community.

Unfortunately, gold mines do not last forever, and as sustainable forestry practices were unheard of (who could imagine a country like Canada running out of trees?), Goldboro and Isaacs Harbor became ghost towns. There is, however, still a small store in Isaacs Harbour—at least, there was in 1994.

Drum Head ★★★

NO FACILITIES

Charts: 4234, 4233

If you're looking for a convenient place to stop, and don't want to go all the way up Isaacs Harbour or Country Harbour, Drum Head is a good choice.

Just round the breakwater and tie up at any convenient wharf. Beware of the rocks southwest of the entrance, marked by red buoy "TS14."

When I first stopped here about 15 years ago, the harbor was home to about 30 fishing boats. When I visited again in 1993, I didn't see any at all—such has been the effect of the groundfishing crisis.

Harbour Island ★★★

NO FACILITIES

Charts: 4234, 4233

I have anchored quite a few times in the little cove on the north end of Harbour Island. Just go in as far as you feel safe. There is an old wreck there that has degenerated to the point where only the remains of parts like boilers are visible.

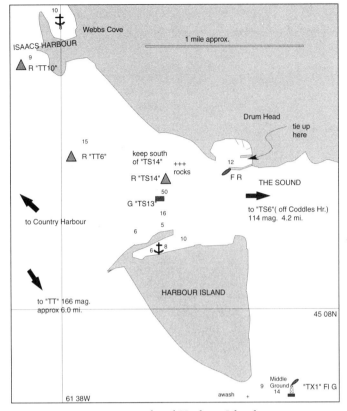

Drum Head and Harbour Island.

Text within map image (labels):
10, 8 (anchor) Webbs Cove, 1 mile approx., ISAACS HARBOUR, 9 R "TT10", Drum Head, tie up here, 15 R "TT6", keep south of "TS14", +++ rocks, 12, R "TS14", F R, THE SOUND, 50 G "TS13", to "TS6"(off Coddles Hr.) 114 mag. 4.2 mi., 16, to Country Harbour, 6, 5, 10, 6, 8 (anchor), to "TT" 166 mag. approx 6.0 mi., HARBOUR ISLAND, 45 08N, Middle Ground, awash, 9, 14, "TX1" Fl G, 61 38W

New Harbour ★★ `4`

`A` NO FACILITIES

Chart: **4233**

New Harbour lies 6 miles west of Berry Head and Tor Bay, and offers shelter from westerly gales. There is a very substantial government wharf behind a breakwater on the western shore halfway into New Harbour Cove.

The cove itself is not worthy of consideration as it is always affected by swells. Easterly winds will send a swell in to the wharf as well, though you should be all right in most normal summer conditions.

Tor Bay ★★★ `4`

`C` NO FACILITIES

Chart: **4233**

This anchorage is usually good enough in summer, but a few years ago an 80-foot (24-m) yacht anchored here one October night. A fierce northeaster blew up and she was driven ashore to become a total loss. When the easterly wind drives a swell in here, Drum Head is a better bet.

Seal Harbour and Coddles Harbour

Chart: **4233**

These small harbors are difficult to enter and for this reason I have never used them. There is possibly an anchorage north of Coddles Island, open only to the east—but with easier harbors nearby, only adventurous gunkholers with shoal-draft boats should try it.

Tor Bay contains the picturesque harbors of Larrys River, Charlos Cove, Cole Harbour, and Port Felix (called Molasses Harbour on the old charts). I have to say I have never visited Tor Bay by boat, having been deterred by the tricky and exposed entrances, and the proximity of Whitehead Harbour, where there is much safer shelter. For those adventurous cruisers who might like to visit Tor Bay nevertheless, I have included a brief description.

Approaches. Tor Bay is entered between Berry Head and the Tor Bay Ledges, which generate a great deal of noisy surf. The Berry Head side is safer, and if you stay 0.4 mile off Berry Head you will not hit anything. I definitely wouldn't try to enter in foggy weather, despite the fact that local fishermen went in and out of here in all sorts of weather, long before radar was invented. I

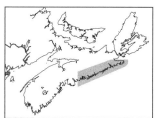

wouldn't try any of the passages between the Sugar Harbour Islands, inside Tor Bay, either.

Larrys River. The entrance to Larrys River, the most sheltered harbor in Tor Bay, is reasonably well shown on chart 4233.

The entrance to the river is between two parallel rubble breakwaters and is quite narrow. I'd presume there is a tidal stream, but I have been unable to get better information. The tidal range is 7 feet (2.1 m) at springs, 6 feet (1.8 m) at neaps. Tie up at the government wharf on the west side of the river. There is no room to anchor, and the river is shallow above the wharf.

Until a few years ago, Larrys River supported a French-speaking community, but I think the younger generation no longer speaks French. There are a couple of small stores with limited supplies. An interesting footbridge spans the harbor a few hundred yards above the wharf.

Charlos Cove. The little harbor of Charlos Cove looks inviting on the chart but has no anchorage or moorage deep enough for most yachts—only 4 feet (1.2 m) at low-water springs.

Cole Harbour. The northernmost refuge in Tor Bay, Cole Harbour, extends northeast for three-quarters of a mile, but is vulnerable to southwesterly winds and swells.

When approaching Cole Harbour, leave The Sisters to port. Leave to starboard the long spit that sticks out from the headland.

Port Felix (Molasses Harbour). If you're entering Port Felix from Tor Bay, you must dodge the rocks in the northeast part of the bay, and go north of Boudreaus Island (Mattee Island on the old charts), keeping close to the mainland side. There is about 9 feet (2.7 m) of water if you keep in the channel.

To enter Port Felix from the south, steer about 020°M from whistle buoy "TA4" toward the light-

house on Hog Island, leaving green buoys "TA7" and "TA9" to port, and "TA8" to starboard. Farther over to starboard are the Flying Point Shoals, marked by buoy "TA6," but you're not likely to hit anything there because they have a minimum depth of 9 feet (2.7 m). There always seems to be a heavy swell in this vicinity, however. When you are really close to Hog Island lighthouse, turn to starboard, and follow the buoys exactly. You can anchor in the cove on the east side of Hog Island, or off the northeast side of Boudreaus Island. There are also other anchorages farther up the harbor.

Whitehead Harbour ★★★★

 NO FACILITIES

Chart: 4233

Whitehead is an attractive harbor—if you can get inside without hitting anything. It's about 40 miles from St. Peters and from Liscomb, so it's a handy place to break up a long passage. I have long since ceased to find any pleasure in 80-mile slogs to windward. The road goes past the west side, but Whitehead Harbour is a long way from anywhere, and it certainly isn't busy. In Yankee Cove, for example, there is not a single light. Consequently, the night sky here is revealed in a glory never seen by urban dwellers. It's truly spectacular.

Whitehead is not a place where you would normally go for supplies, but I managed to obtain a V-belt for my engine here, at the small service station south of the wharf, after an unsuccessful hunt all over Cape Breton.

Approaches. Some earlier guides describe this harbor as "easy to enter." Well, I have in fact entered Whitehead in a stiff fog breeze without the aid of electronics, but I certainly didn't think it was easy.

On a clear day it's easy enough, though; and it's not even difficult at night if the weather is

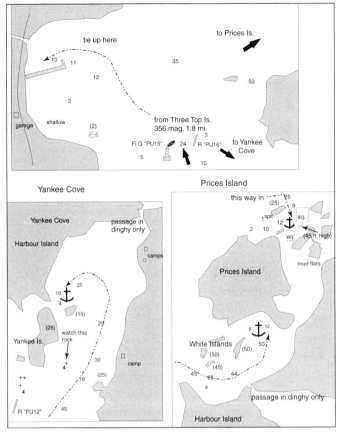

*Anchorages in Whitehead Harbour. Top: Marshall Cove
bottom left: Yankee Cove; bottom right: Prices Island*

with a small islet just south of Spry Point on a bearing of 068°M.

Most of the hazards on either side of this track are always above water, though there is a 9-foot (2.7-m) patch close south of Outer Gull Ledge that you should keep clear of if it is rough. When you get close to Three Top Island, swing a little to the south and leave Net Rock to port. When you're clear of Net Rock, change course to about 356°M to enter harbor. This heading, with the Three Top Island light directly astern of you, leads all the way to Marshall Cove in safe water. Though it's unlikely in good visibility, be sure not to confuse the light on Three Top Island with the much bigger light on White Head Island to the southeast. At night, make sure you can see both lights. If you can't, you are probably too far north of your track.

Approaches from the South. If you're heading for Whitehead Harbour from the south, steer 004°M from outside whistle buoy "PU." Leave bell buoy "PU1" close to port and change course to 018°M. Keep the next buoy, "PU5," fine on your port bow, passing between White Head Island and the Gammon Islands. Again, most of the rocks have more than 6 feet (1.8 m) over them, or show all the time. When you have passed Dogfish Point, on the extreme northern portion of White Head Island, come to 300°M, heading toward the light tower on Three Top Island. Turtle Rock will be close to starboard, marked by red spar "PU8." Don't get set north of this bearing. When you are close to the light, come to 356°M and proceed into harbor with the Three Top Island light directly astern.

Approaches from the East. I don't recommend an approach from the east at night or in fog, unless you have radar. The best route is to pass midway between the unnamed 25-foot (8-m) island

calm. But it can be a nightmare in thick fog with a stiff wind blowing—and unfortunately there seems to be a lot of fog in this region. I've been in and out of harbors around here many times, but there are some that I've only seen once or twice in daylight. My advice is not to attempt entering Whitehead Harbour while relying solely on loran or GPS.

Approaches from the West. Perhaps the easiest approach to Whitehead Harbour is from the west. Come toward the southern end of Three Top Island on any heading between 070°M and 036°M. You may be able to see the lattice tower of the light on the island, but it's obscured west of 055°M.

Net Rock, just southeast of the island, is in line

209

close east of White Head Island—which appears to be part of the island if you are too far to the west—and Paddy Ledge, on a course of about 326°M. Leave spar "PT3" close to port. When Three Top Island Light bears 300°M, steer for it, and then follow the instructions given above for entering harbor.

Anchorage. There are a number of anchorages in Whitehead Harbour.

Yankee Cove is quite popular, but favor the south side going in, as the 4-foot (1.2-m) rock shown on the chart is almost in the middle of the channel.

The best anchorage is just to the northwest of the little island. It is a pleasant row in the dinghy into The Basin, and on a calm day you can go as far as Prices Island.

Marshall Cove has a substantial wharf, and the best berth is on the north side of it. There is a little canal just north of the wharf, which affords passage for a dinghy to Port Felix at half-tide or more.

Prices Island, farther up the harbor, offers a choice of anchorages. The ones to the north of the island are obstructed by aquaculture facilities, but there still should be a little room.

The two upper arms of the harbor, stretching to the northeast and the northwest, go on for almost 3 miles above Prices Island. I have never had time to explore them, and the lower part of the Northwest Branch has a few rocks obstructing the entrance, but appears to afford excellent shelter.

Whitehead to Andrews Island

Many intriguing small coves and harbors dot the coastline between Whitehead and Canso, and most are overlooked by visiting sailors. I must admit I've always been in a rush to get to Cape Breton.

There are other reasons for avoiding this part of the coast, too. Frightful rocks fringe the shore, the southerly swell breaks continually, and there are very few aids to navigation. Thick fog is also common.

Chart 4280, though out of print, shows more detail of this area than the newer 4233, so if you still have one, don't throw it away. For those of you with the urge to go where "few others have gone before," I offer the following information, for use on a calm day. I have seen all these places from outside, but I must urge you to be very cautious when entering any of them.

Raspberry Cove West, Raspberry Cove East, Crane Cove, and Wine Cove

Chart: **4233**

These small coves east of Whitehead Island are reportedly snug anchorages.

Whale Cove and Raspberry Cove West on chart 4233 are rather open to the south. I suspect Raspberry Cove West is the place formerly called Fairweather Harbour. This can be entered by rounding the north side of the largest of the three islets northwest of Mink Island. Mink Island has trees on it and the island to round has the mark (4) inshore of it on 4233. Anchor right where this number is.

Raspberry Cove East is better shown on 4233, but requires some intricate pilotage.

Crane Cove, to the east of East Strawberry Cove looks difficult on 4233 and is open to the southeast.

Wine Cove is not shown at all on 4233, but is north of Whale Island. It must be entered from the east.

All these harbours are much better shown on the old charts 4282 and 4280, but it would have to be a calm day for me to try them. I couldn't recommend it if you have never been here and only have chart 4233 on board.

Port Howe ★★★

NO FACILITIES

Charts: 4233, 4280

If you're entering Port Howe from the south, keep over to the east to avoid Whale Rocks and Black Rock. The latter always shows and the former usually breaks. Inside Port Howe there are few submerged hazards. The usual anchorage is simply as far as you can go up the western arm, avoiding the two dry rocks that always show.

If you are entering Port Howe through Dover Passage, north of Dover Island, be mindful that the narrowest bit is only about 30 yards across. Avoid the shoal that protrudes north and east from the northeastern edge of Dover Island at the start of the passage. This route is sheltered from the prevailing southerly swell. There is a little cove at the west end of the passage that looks as if it would make an attractive anchorage. The rest of Port Howe, I suspect, is open to swells

if the wind is blowing hard from the south.

I haven't had the chance to use this anchorage, or the two following, but they look reasonably straightforward from seaward. Nevertheless, none of them should be tried except in good visibility and reasonable wind conditions.

Louse Harbour ★★★

 NO FACILITIES

Charts: 4233, 4280

The entrance to Louse Harbour is a little tricky as there is a rock, with 1 foot (30 cm) of water over it, extending from a submerged ledge on the starboard side going in. In the entrance to the most popular anchorage there are a number of rocks, with about 3 feet (1 m) over them at low water. If you are entering this harbor for the first time, I can only suggest you get in the dinghy and sound it out first.

If you like remote anchorages, either Louse Harbour or Port Howe should do, as they are at least 4 miles from the nearest road—and the road isn't much, either. One of the problems of these places is that you are likely to be the only large, warm-blooded animal for miles around, and you can be sure that every starving insect in the area will sniff you out in short order and have you for lunch.

Dover Harbour ★★★

  NO FACILITIES

Charts: 4233, 4280

My chart of Dover Harbour shows that it's rather shallow, having a minimum depth of only 3 feet (1 m) in the channel to the government wharf. The

Port Howe and Louse Harbour.

211

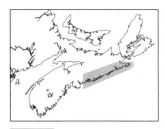

harbor is strewn with rocks not well shown on chart 4233, and the buoyage is confusing.

Little Dover Run, north of Little Dover Island, is reasonably easy to enter, though. The eastern entrance is probably better than the western: from outside bell buoy "PP1," steer 310°M and follow the spar buoys exactly. The Run affords snug anchorage at its western end. Earlier guides refer to the fishing fleet going through here at full speed early in the morning. I don't think this is likely to be a problem in the final decade of the twentieth century, given the state of the fishery. But in case there are still a few boats about, I'd keep out of the middle of the channel and put up a riding light. If you do go farther west in Dover Harbour (which I must say I haven't) bear in mind that the local boats rarely draw more than 3 feet (1 m).

Approaches to Canso

The end of the Canso peninsula points like a thumb toward the homeland of the Basques, the first Europeans to fish here. Offshore, the water is rough, second only in unpleasantness to Cape Sable, and there are a few aspects of its temperamental nature that are not apparent on the chart. The first is the tide, which has a range of nearly 8 feet (2.4 m) and a stream of up to 2 knots. No published predictions are available for the direction and rate of the tidal stream, but its speed, and the irregular bottom it runs over, make for rough conditions when the wind is opposed to the tide.

Immediately north of the Canso peninsula, the bottom plunges from average depths of about 120 feet (36 m) to 400 feet (122 m) or more in Chedabucto Bay. This underwater cliff extends 20 miles east. It doesn't take much imagination to figure out what happens when a strong northwesterly blows over it.

Canso is also subject to what the meteorologists call a "left-hand corner effect." This means that

when a northwesterly wind is blowing, the land of the Canso peninsula slows it down and increases the pressure gradient, accelerating the wind immediately offshore. The benign, 12-knot wind blowing when you leave St. Peters in the morning may accelerate to 35 knots by the time you're off Canso in the afternoon. There is also an upwelling of deep, cold water here that substantially increases the frequency of fog. I have only seen Cape Canso about a quarter of the times I have passed it.

To be prepared for all of this, keep constant track of your position, and pay careful attention to any drift from your DR track. Taking the inshore route via the Andrew Passage and Canso Harbour keeps you out of most of the rough water, and can save you hours if you're making for St. Peters, but because of the quirks of the tide, this route is very difficult—and it's not recommended in fog without radar.

Andrew Passage

Charts: **4281**, 4233

You need chart 4281 to make this passage safely. From the south, steer 352°M from bell buoy "PP1" off Little Dover Island toward spar buoy "PN6," south of Portage Cove. There are dangerous rocks off Madeline Point less than 200 yards on your port beam, and it would be wise to veer a bit to starboard here to be quite sure of avoiding them. Leave "PN6" a few boatlengths to starboard, then turn to the east, leaving the next spar, "PN7," to port. Buoy "PN7" marks a ledge that extends about 50 yards from the easternmost of the little islands just south of Pea Island, so give it a decent berth. Pass between the next pair of spars, "PN8" and "PN9," but don't head straight from there toward the next spar, "PN10," or you will go far too close to Britons Shoal for comfort. Swing a little to the east and then curve back gently to leave "PN10" to starboard. Alternatively, you can pass very close to "PN8" and take a straight line from there to "PN10." After you've rounded "PN10," just keep in the middle of the channel. Leave "PN15" to port and "PN16" to starboard to enter Glasgow Harbour.

If you're going on to Canso, change course at "PN16" to 070°M. Keep Charlotte Island dead astern bearing 250°M. This takes you midway between the two rocks in the entrance to Glasgow Harbour, which are not marked from this direction. When you have crossed the line between the two green buoys, "PM7" and "PM9," turn north again, heading 328°M for the end of the breakwater at Canso, which has a fixed green light.

If you need a rest, you can anchor in Portage Cove, which may be reached from the buoyed channel by rounding close north of Pea Island to avoid Haulover Ledge. Alternatively, you can anchor in Glasgow Harbour—but don't try to cut inshore of Charlotte Island. The northern arm of Glasgow Harbour is the more sheltered.

Canso is a rather bleak place, where every bit of vegetation has to struggle to stay attached to the underlying rock, and these coves are no exception. (The human inhabitants would probably describe their existence in much the same terms.) Portage Cove is exposed to the east, but the north cove of Glasgow Harbour is sheltered under most conditions.

Canso ★★★★

Charts: **4281, 4233**

Canso is the oldest continuously inhabited town in Nova Scotia, officially dating from 1604. There was undoubtedly a regular European fishery for at least 200 years before that—archaeological evidence reveals that Bretons and Basques fished in a number of places in eastern Canada in the 1300s, long before Columbus and Cabot arrived. Grassy Island is a national historic park, and there is an interpretation center next to the marina.

If you need to break up your trip to Cape Breton, or need to stop for a few supplies or a drink in the tavern, I'm sure you will be most welcome. A visit to Canso could be justified on the grounds of historical interest alone.

Approaches from the South. Canso is a large natural harbor with half-a-dozen approaches, all of which are well buoyed. Many are equipped with leading lights.

From the south, if you haven't come though Andrew Passage, approach via either channel south of Cranberry Island. There is still a radio beacon at Cranberry Island, broadcasting Morse code "G" (– – ·) on 308 kHz. It has a range of 150 miles. There are unmarked rocks extending 500 yards south of Cranberry Island lighthouse, so the western passage may be preferable to the eastern, although it's narrower. The western passage takes you close south of Black Rocks, whence a course of about 328°M takes you to the end of the breakwater. There are no lighted buoys marking this channel, and you might feel more comfortable using one of the other channels at night.

Approaches from the East. If you're coming in from the east, things are fairly simple. Just follow the fixed-yellow leading lights close north of Cranberry Island. They line up on a course of 289°M. Be sure to follow them exactly because the channel is quite narrow, and there are drying rocks close north of the track.

Approaches from the North. Getting into Canso from the north is a little more complicated. From whistle buoy "RW" follow the fixed-red leading lights on Hart Island on a course of about 191°M. Watch for Bald Reef to port. When you get to Hart Island, which has a conspicuous building on it, swing to port in the deep, unobstructed channel until you come to the second set of leading lights. This time they're fixed green, on a bearing of 188°M.

From the north, you may also use the False Passage entrance, but then you must pass under a high-voltage wire with a charted clearance of 67 feet (20 m)—and frankly, passing under these

things with less than 20 feet (6 m) of clearance always makes me nervous.

The harbor is nearly a half-mile long and a half-mile wide, big enough to make for some uneasy anchorages. Except in The Tittle (Tickle Channel), to the west, you don't have to worry about the buoys unless you draw more than 8 feet (2.4 m).

Anchorage, Dockage. There is a small, well-sheltered marina at the root of the Grave Island breakwater, south of Piscatiqui Island, and this is by far the best place in which to tie up. There is an anchorage in the little basin between Grassy Island and Piscatiqui Island but it has only 5 feet (1.5 m) in the entrance, so you have to anchor just north of the northwest corner of Grassy Island. The rest is too shallow. The Tittle (Tickle Channel) doesn't present any great problems if you don't draw more than 6 feet (1.8 m), but keep to the mainland side. There isn't much anchoring space, though.

Public wharves are situated west of the fish-processing plant, but the new marina provides much better berthing. There are interesting passages between the Derabies Islands to the north of Canso, which are used by the locals for picnics.

Ashore. Canso has an unfortunate reputation amongst cruising yachtsmen, from incidents that date back to the early 1970s. The town has seen some exceedingly hard times, some of them relating to its isolation. The nearest community of any size is an hour-and-a-half away by car, when driving conditions are good. But its major problems have stemmed from the fact that it's a company town whose workers have not found the company to be a particularly compassionate partner.

Yet my next-door neighbor, who has moored his dragger here for several months of each of the last five or six years, tells me that Canso people are very friendly, and bend over backward to help him out. I've gained the same impression from a couple of my colleagues, who have been physicians in the town.

Problems arose in the late 1980s when the groundfish quota was allocated. The company that owned the major fish-processing plant had about a dozen draggers operating out of Canso. But they decided to centralize operations, removed the boats, and closed the plant. As was the case in Lockeport, the company effectively owned the groundfish quota and it could not be fished by anyone else. The plant's 400 or so workers could find no other employment in this part of Guysborough County.

Fifteen years before, there had been a particularly bitter and prolonged strike against the company's predecessor, during which vandalism was directed at visiting yachts. That's what gave Canso its bad reputation. The irony is that the company exists only through the enforced generosity of long-suffering Canadian taxpayers, who have repeatedly bailed it out after poor business decisions.

Happily, the fish plant is now open again, albeit in a reduced capacity, processing under-utilized species such as hake and shrimp. And Canso is showing the first signs of recovery.

Chedabucto Bay to the Bras d'Or Lakes

St. Peters Canal into Bras d'Or Lakes, Cape Breton, Nova Scotia.

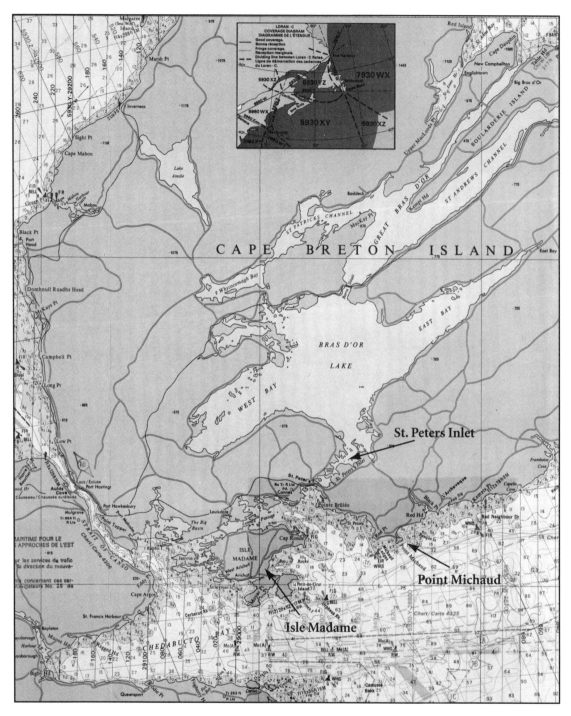

Based on CHS Chart 4013. Not to be used for navigation.

This, the final region of Nova Scotia covered by this cruising guide, describes two main areas of interest to visiting yachts—Chedabucto Bay, and the very popular Bras d'Or Lakes on Cape Breton Island.

In the Chedabucto Bay section I will alter the usual scheme of things by describing first the north shore of Guysborough County, then the passage to St. Peters and the canal, followed by Isle Madame, the Lennox Passage, and finally the rest of Chedabucto Bay.

Chedabucto Bay

Most people hurry across Chedabucto Bay on the way to St. Peters, never penetrating its inner regions. The bay tends to be a rough bit of water, much beset by high winds and thick fog. (See the section on Canso in Region 5.) The southern shores of the bay are inhospitable, offering real refuge only in Guysborough Harbour, to the southwest—a difficult place to enter.

The northwestern reaches of Chedabucto Bay support industrial areas next to the Canso Causeway (leading from St. Georges Bay to the lock at Balache Point) and the Strait of Canso (leading from the lock, southwest to Chedabucto Bay.)

The town of Port Hawkesbury, midway along the eastern shore of the strait, is the commercial center of the region, but it's unfortunately out of the way for most visiting yachts.

The north shore of Chedabucto Bay is dominated by Isle Madame—a fascinating and largely undiscovered cruising ground—and the entrance to St. Peters Canal.

Charts of Chedabucto Bay. Chart 4335 is a general chart of the entire area. It doesn't show the buoys in St. Peters Bay, which is a pity. If it did, you could do without all the others. Chart 4308 is a large-scale chart of Isle Madame. If you have 4308 you don't need 4275, which is a large-scale chart of St. Peters Bay. Chart 4279 is the chart of the southern parts of the Bras d'Or lake system; for some reason it has an enlargement of the Lennox Passage on it. Charts 4307 and 4306 are

large-scale charts of the Strait of Canso. I don't think they are essential, and I don't have them.

The chart references on chart 4335 are incorrect: 4279 is the southern part of the Bras d'Or lakes, not 4275; 4275 is St. Peters Bay, not 4279; 4308 is Ile Madame, not 4307. The boundries of 4308 re also incorrect on the chart catalogue.

Coves between Canso and Guysborough

Chart: 4335

Between Canso and Guysborough there is a spectacular coastline with hills 700 feet (210 m) high falling steeply to the sea. A number of coves could provide shelter from the prevailing southwesterlies. They are, from east to west, Fox Bay, Half Island Cove, Philips Harbour, and Queensport. One should be mindful, however, that this whole coast becomes a lee shore in any wind with a northerly component, and if such a wind were to blow with any strength, the situation could be very difficult, as there is no nearby shelter except Guysborough.

Guysborough Harbour

Chart: 4335

Guysborough Harbour is well sheltered from all winds, but entering it is another matter. This is probably the most difficult harbor entrance described in this book. The entrance channel is narrow, there is no good chart of the area, and the tidal streams are reported to run at up to 6 knots. Furthermore, the channel winds between shingle banks that are notoriously liable to change position during onshore storms—and there are several of those every winter. Yet the temptation to try to enter is great, because the nearest alternative port of refuge is more than 20 miles away.

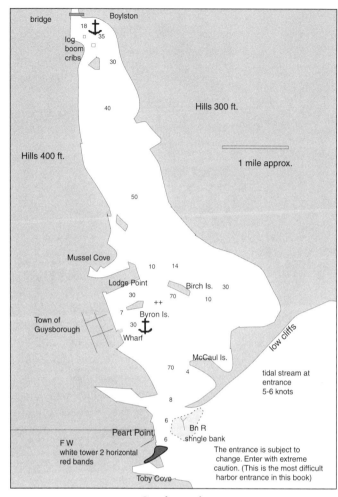

Guysborough.

are roughly the same time as Halifax.

It would certainly be ideal to enter Guysborough Harbour at or near slack water, but obviously no entry attempt should be made in strong onshore winds, or in any but ideal conditions of visibility and daylight.

Anchorage, Dockage. Once you're inside, Guysborough Harbour is deep and mostly unobstructed. It's also big, so you may have difficulty finding a sheltered anchorage if the wind is funneling down from the northwest. One reasonable anchorage is just off the town, below Byron Island, near the government wharf.

There is about 10 feet of water at the government wharf, but it was not in good shape when I was there in 1995. It is rather open to northwesterly winds.

Guysborough's fine old houses are a legacy of the area's prosperity in the nineteenth century, when it supported a booming lumber-exporting port. Unfortunately, prosperity is a rare commodity in Guysborough County these days, and many of the buildings look a little down at the heel.

You can move farther north up the river by going either side of Byron Island, but if you choose to go to the east of it be sure to miss the one rock you can run into in this harbor.

Mussel Cove, less than a mile north of the town, is the site of the Belmont Resort, which is reported to operate a small marina, as well as a golf course and a resort hotel with all the usual facilities. The chart states there are leading marks (red and white beacons) showing the best water. I have not stayed there, but further information can be obtained by phoning (902) 533-3904. There is cellular phone service in this area.

The harbor extends upstream to Boylston, a pretty little village that has the most sheltered anchorage in the harbor just below its road bridge. North of Priest Island, on the west side of the

At the time of writing, the deepwater channel ran close to the beach at Peart Point, that is on the port side going in, and most of the entrance was obstructed by a large shingle bank. There is a beacon on top of the bank, but it is far from the channel. There may be other spars marking deep water, but as there is no commercial shipping using Guysborough Harbour, their placement and maintenance is obviously not a priority. They were not there when I checked at the end of April 1995, but that was only a short time after the ice went out, and they might have been set later that season.

High water in Guysborough comes 20 minutes after it does in Port Tupper, the local reference port, and low water comes 35 minutes later. This means HW and LW at Guysborough

river, old cribs from the lumber trade still are a hazard, so it's best to favor the east side. While the river continues for nearly another 6 miles, and is unobstructed and deep, some Philistine in the Department of Transport designed the bridge at Boylston with a clearance of only 11 feet (3.3 m), effectively barring boats with masts from one of the prettiest rivers in the province. By the way, this part of Guysborough County enjoys some of the best summer weather in the province: hot days that are relatively free of fog.

From Guysborough, the shoreline trends northeast for 20 miles to the Strait of Canso, but there are no harbors suitable for yachts in this stretch. It is possible to tie up in Mulgrave, opposite Port Hawkesbury in the Strait of Canso, but the small-boat docks are pretty decrepit. The only decent place in which to tie up in the strait is Port Hawkesbury.

Cape Breton Island

No guide to Cape Breton Island would be complete without at least some mention of its socio-economic situation, which springs from a deep political rift separating Cape Bretoners and Mainlanders.

If you look at the fine homes on the shores of the lakes, you'll find it hard to believe the island's official unemployment rate of something like 20 percent. One has to give credit to the island's politicians, who howled loud and long about the island's poverty, bringing in billions of dollars in direct and indirect government grants. Grants to one steel mill alone account for nearly a quarter of the Nova Scotia government's total debt.

To boating visitors it will certainly not be apparent that this is one of the most economically depressed areas in Canada, except for a few isolated pockets. There may be fewer stores than you'd expect, though, and less variety in those surviving.

The St. Peters area could be regarded as a sort of suburb of the Strait of Canso area; many people commute to work in and around Port Hawkes-

bury (and would be mortified by this description). With the steady employment of the pulp mill and the port (the largest tonnage increase in Canada in 1995), Port Hawkesbury is the commercial center of this region and has been relatively stable economically. St. Peters makes a good place to stock up on stores for your return voyage. Its largely Acadian heritage also distinguishes it in many ways from the rest of the island, and I always think of it as a distinct region in itself.

One should also be mindful that some of the natives regard themselves primarily as Cape Bretoners, and you may be insulting them by addressing them as Nova Scotians. There is even resentment about the island's physical link to the rest of the province. One popular local comic, known as "General John Cabot Trail of the Cape Breton Liberation Army," always opens his shows with the rallying cry: "Down wi' the causeway, byes!" The local accent bears little relation to mainstream North American, the commonest speech sounding like a cross between the dialects of Newfoundland and Ireland.

No matter how they speak, the hospitality of Cape Bretoners is legendary. They have also undergone a recent cultural renaissance. A rural Cape Breton folk group, The Rankins, topped Canada's popular music charts for weeks in 1994, with a traditional folk tune—an amazing and welcome relief from rap and heavy metal groups. A large proportion of the inhabitants are musicians, writers, and artists and there are a number of live performances in summer. If time allows, you'd find it worthwhile to check local schedules—available at any tourist information center, library, or hotel—to see if any of these events would mesh with your itinerary.

Passage from Canso to St. Peters

If you're making directly for St. Peters Bay from the south, without visiting Canso Harbour, don't cut the corner east of Canso at Grime Rock. Keep to seaward, and leave whistle buoy "CV1" to port.

Only when you have passed the buoy should you steer about 022°M toward green flashing whistle buoy "NQ3," off Cap Ronde. As you come abreast of Green Island, you should see bell buoy "NQ1" marking Orpheus Rock. The buoy is almost on top of the rock, so leave it to port and don't cut inside it. The tidal stream is active here but there are no published predictions, so you must keep track of your drift.

If you're using loran, you may also find that the 5930 XY chain gets a little temperamental here, and you may have to change to 5930 YZ. My geriatric machine does not know how to do this for itself, but I understand some of the more modern beasts change over automatically.

From whistle buoy "NQ3," off Cap Ronde, steer about 000°M, leaving Cap Ronde to port, and continuing until the fixed red light on Jerome Point, close south of the canal entrance, bears 040°M. Don't succumb to the temptation to steer a direct line between buoy "NQ3" and bell buoy "NQ12," west of Point Brulee, or you will pass too close to the Samson Rocks for comfort—and at night you could hit one of the unlit spar buoys.

If you follow the bearing of 040°M all the way in, you won't be in the buoyed channel, but that's not important. You will have a minimum of 12 feet (3.6 m) of water under your keel. In fact, at night this course is preferable, because it helps you avoid collisions with the spar buoys. If you're passing by here in daylight, then of course you should feel free to follow the spars.

As you close with the land, keep the oil tanks to port, and the little lighthouse on Jerome Point to starboard, going about northeast. You will come right to the southern end of the St. Peters Canal.

The passage from Canso to St. Peters is usually fairly easy going north, but it can be a real dirty beat going back home if there is a stiff southwesterly wind blowing.

It is about 20 miles from Cape Canso to the canal, and as canal transits must be completed by 2030, it is all too easy to be late.

Passage from Canso Harbour to St. Peters Bay. If you are heading north from Canso Harbour, use the northern exit from the harbor, and steer 046°M. After about 14 miles you will be off Cap Ronde, having passed west of Green Island and the Petit Nez shoal, 4 miles north-northeast of the island.

If you arrive at St. Peters too late to pass through the canal, you can anchor in Grand Greve Harbour or (preferably) River Tillard. Before you try either of these, though, see if there is room for you at the dock just south of the canal on the western shore. I've always had luck there, and I much prefer it to entering unlit rivers at night. Sometimes I've found small cargo boats or tankers at the dock, but there has always been enough space for me as well. The dock affords reasonable shelter unless it is blowing a gale from the southwest.

St. Peters Canal ★★★★ ☐4

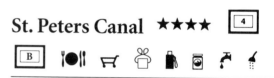

Charts: **4275, 4308, 4279**

The canal is open in July and August from 0830 to 2030. In May, June, and September, it's open from 0900 to 1700, but it may be closed on Sundays.

If you're approaching from the south, the lockmaster can see you and will usually have the lock gates open. You will be directed to tie up, usually on the west side, and sign in with your name, home port, and registration number. If you are not a Canadian vessel, you will be asked to produce a cruising permit. If you don't have one, I doubt you will be turned back, but there could be hours of form filling and interviews with the RCMP. So it's advisable that you get one on your way up the coast. I would suggest Yarmouth, Shelburne, or Lunenburg as the most suitable places with the least hassle.

In the event of your clearing customs and immigration by telephone, which may soon be the norm, the lockkeeper will ask you for your cruising permit number, which you should have

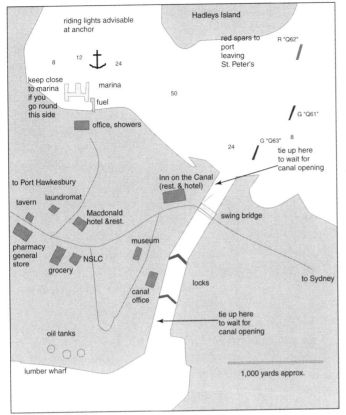

St. Peters Canal.

jigged all the way down the cut, keeping in time with the beat of the beast.

If you're approaching from the lakes, the lockmaster cannot see you, and you should tie up to the dock, again on the west side, just before the bridge. Use the telephone there to call the lockmaster. Make sure you don't tie up too close to the bridge—it needs room to swing.

The lock can accommodate vessels up to 260 feet (79 m) long, 45 feet (14 m) wide, and 16 feet (4.9 m) deep, so it would be a rare yacht that couldn't get through here. Of more interest to large yachts is the overhead power cable a little further into the lakes, which has 100 feet (30 m) safe clearance.

Entering locks for the first time can be a little intimidating, but this one is quite benign. It has a maximum rise or fall of 6 feet (1.8 m)—the lakes always seem to be higher than the sea in St. Peters Bay—and there is no significant turbulence. It is a lot easier than the Grootsluis in Amsterdam, or the Panama Canal, and usually you'll have it all to yourself, or at the most, share it with a fishing boat. But unless you are Nova Scotian author Silver Donald Cameron, who walks his engineless 28-footer through here, a decent source of auxiliary power is advisable.

Ashore. If you have been poking through the fog for a week, St. Peters is a welcome respite, particularly as the fog rarely penetrates much farther than the inside end of the canal. Twenty years ago, the St. Peters Lions Club established a small marina in Strachans Cove, close west of the canal's northern exit. It was originally a small A-frame building and a single fuel dock, but it now has space for about 20 boats and it stays pretty busy. The last time I was there, they had run out of space and I had to lie to my own anchor. All the usual services are available, and the overnight dockage fee is very modest—about $10 in 1992.

received over the phone. Be sure you get one at your port of entry.

There is no charge for using the canal, so, having satisfied the bureaucracy, you are free to exit the canal to the north. The lockmaster will have opened the swing bridge for you by the time you get there.

The passage into the lake, a narrow channel cut deep into the rock, is about a half-mile long. One of my abiding memories is going through here with my very first boat, which had a make-and-break engine made by Lunenburg Foundries. If you have read Farley Mowat's book *The Boat Who Wouldn't Float,* you will recognize this engine as the same surly Victorian piece of ironmongery he had. These engines have a very characteristic "pick-a-puck" sound, and the whole canal seemed to resonate with its noise as we passed through at two-and-a-half knots flat-out. Some small boys fishing in the canal were highly amused, and danced and

This is much the best place to stay in St. Peters, as the village is just a short walk away, up the hill. You can usually find charts of the lakes here, should you be missing one. The St. Peters Marina is fairly well sheltered, but might get a little lively in a severe storm with the wind in the north. Cape George Harbour would be a better bet then.

St. Peters is a bustling little place, and there are a number of grocery stores, restaurants, and the like. I have had excellent meals at the MacDonald's Hotel, just south of the marina, before you get to Main Street. The manager of the grocery store was kind enough to deliver my groceries to the boat. Although the commercial center of this region is Port Hawkesbury, about 20 miles away, a reasonable selection is available in the stores. I have always found it better to stock up the boat at St. Peters than at Baddeck. The home language of the locals is either English or French, and both languages are heard on the street. But everyone speaks English, so language is not likely to be a problem.

For further information on St. Peters Inlet, see the later section on the Bras d'Or Lakes.

Isle Madame

Chart: 4308

Isle Madame is a large island south of St. Peters, usually ignored by yachts rushing to the lakes. That's a pity in many ways because Isle Madame is a pretty place, with any number of little harbors, and you could cruise for a week here without seeing the same place twice.

Like many places on this coast, this one has suffered an extraordinary reverse of fortune in the late twentieth century. A hundred years ago it was one of the most prosperous parts of the province. Nevertheless, Isle Madame, has weathered the fishery crisis reasonably well, and certainly seems to maintain a facade of comfort, if not wealth. Most of the inhabitants of the island are French-speaking, or at least of Acadian origin, but English is spoken by everyone.

It's advisable to have chart 4308 for entering any harbor on Isle Madame.

Petit-de-Grat Inlet ★★★

Charts: 4308, 4335

Petit-de-Grat, the major harbor on Isle Madame, is a busy little place, being the site of a large fish-processing plant. But it does have a well-sheltered wharf you can tie up to, and a place to get groceries ashore.

Approaches. The way into Petit-de-Grat is well lit, at least as far as the fish plant, but it's a little tricky in marginal conditions, and I'd think hard about trying to enter while a southerly gale was blowing—though the locals do it all the time, of course.

From outside whistle buoy "CJ," steer 018°M, which will line you up with the two fixed-white leading lights. When Arrow Point is roughly abeam, come to 058°M and follow the second set of fixed-green leading lights until you reach the lighted buoys. Follow the buoys in, heading more or less north, to the end of the fish-plant wharf.

Dockage. The fish plant wharf is not a good place to tie up at. It's occupied with the comings and goings of large draggers. The preferred dock is a little farther up the harbor, so keep going north and favor the west side of the channel. This channel is quite narrow and probably not easy for strangers at night.

There is a substantial wharf on the west side of the inlet, just south of the road bridge, quite well sheltered on its northern side from anything short of a hurricane. There is only about 10 feet (3 m) of overhead clearance at the bridge, but the channel goes through to the Bay of Rocks. The

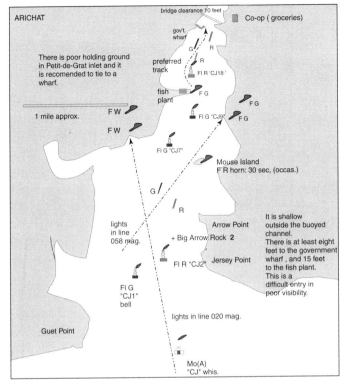

Petit-de-Grat Inlet.

large cooperative store east of the bridge will have groceries, and you may find it easier to row your dinghy to the nearby beach, rather than walk all the way around by road.

The northern entrance to Petit-de-Grat Inlet is rather shallow—there is certainly less than 3 feet (1 m) at low water, and there may be less. While it is used a lot by skiffs and small outboard runabouts, and while there is better shelter here than at the southern end of the inlet, I'd be reluctant to try it in a normal-size yacht.

Petite Anse

Charts: **4308**, 4335

Petit-de-Grat Island has another harbor on its east side, Petite Anse. I think I took refuge in it on a dirty, foggy night some years ago. I was rather worn out after two days at sea in thick fog

with no engine or electronics. Looking at it later in daylight, I couldn't see how I had managed to get in without hitting something. The entrance is narrow, and subject to a lot of swell. The wharf to which I tied up is now falling apart. Entering this harbor on any but the calmest of days, would, I think, be pushing your luck.

Arichat ★★★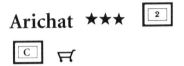

Charts: **4308**, 4335

Arichat, the next harbor west of Petit-de-Grat is a beautiful place on a fine day but is very open and exposed to the south. A small government wharf in the northern part of the harbor lies close to the center of the village and a large grocery store. If there's no room at the wharf, you can anchor at the head of the harbor, but you'll be vulnerable to westerlies.

The prettiest anchorage is off the northeastern beach of Jerseyman Island, open to the east this time. Although I've never done it, I think it would be possible to enter the little cove on the island; but you'd need to watch for rocks extending from both shores.

If you're heading west of Arichat Harbour, or making directly toward Port Hawkesbury from Canso, watch out for Cerberus Rock, 2.5 miles south of Arichat Head. An oil tanker, the *Arrow*, ran on to this rock in the early 1970s and caused massive pollution. As a result, the Lennox Passage was closed for years. It is an extremely dangerous spot, and the wreck of the *Arrow* is still there to remind you of the fact.

West Arichat and Janvrin Harbour

Charts: 4308, 4335

These small harbors occupy the remaining southeast coast of Isle Madame, Janvrin Island being attached to it by a series of little dunes and sandspits.

West Arichat Harbour, north of Crichton Island, has depths of 6 feet (1.8 m) or more all the way in, and looks reasonably easy to enter.

Leblanc Harbour, called Port Royal Harbour on chart 4335, has only 1 foot (30 cm) of water in its entrance at low water, blocking it off to any but the most adventurous gunkholers. There is a passage for small boats from Leblanc Harbour to Haddock Harbour, which leads out to the Lennox Passage.

Janvrin Harbour is entered by way of a gap between sandbars. They have a habit of shifting during major storms, so I would be very careful about entering this harbor—or either of the other two, for that matter. I haven't taken a boat into any of them.

Lennox Passage ★★★★

 NO FACILITIES

Charts: 4308, 4279

The Lennox Passage is a beautiful area, hardly ever visited by cruising boats, so although I have never traversed the whole passage by boat, this book would be incomplete without a description. I have, incidentally, visited all these places by land. The direction of buoyage in the passage is from east to west—that is, vessels traveling west should leave red buoys to starboard.

Approaches. When you're approaching from the east, keep clear of the shoals off The Goulet, a bay 2 miles west of Cap Ronde, the easternmost cape

on Isle Madame. Some parts of the shoals have only 3 feet (1 m) over them.

If you approach with Quetique Island—a conspicuous grassy island with a tall light tower—bearing between 308°M and 280°M, you will clear all dangers. As you near Ouetique Island, turn to port when the light on Grandique Point bears 284°M, and make toward the light on that heading until you pick up the buoys.

If you're coming from the west, you'll find the Lennox Passage unobstructed for boats of modest draft, except for Macdonald Shoal, almost in the middle of the extreme west end. The red spar marking the shoal is difficult to see, but if you keep over toward the northern side of the passage you'll avoid the shoal.

River Bourgeois

The easternmost harbor in the Lennox Passage is River Bourgeois, well known as the home of Farley Mowat, an iconoclastic writer of some repute.

Steer 000°M on the light on the east spit at the entrance to the inlet. The entrance channel is narrow, but has 6 feet (1.8 m) of water. The channel tends to twist and turn a little farther in.

D'Escousse Harbour

On the southern side of the Lennox Passage, sheltered by Bernard Island, is D'Escousse Harbour, home of the Lennox Passage Yacht Club.

Enter the harbor with Ouetique Island astern, bearing 010°M. A prominent red barn, sitting all by itself on a salt marsh, should be fine on your port bow. When you get close in, follow the buoys.

Anchorage, Dockage. D'Escousse Harbour is the last place you'd expect to find a yacht club. But indeed there is one, the Lennox Passage Yacht Club. A prominent sign welcomes visiting sailors, and there is mooring space alongside a small wharf. You may also anchor just off it.

This is the home of another writer, Silver Donald Cameron—Silver, because Nova Scotia is awash with lesser Donald Camerons. Among his numerous books is one called *Wind, Whales, and Whisky* (Macmillan Canada), which details a recent small-boat voyage around Cape Breton, which I recommend for a better understanding of the mores of the place.

Poulamon Bay

Poulamon Bay lies east and south of Grandique Point, and has three entrances formed by Crow Island and Eagle Island, which also divide the bay into two harbors. The eastern harbor is the deeper of the two, but it's a little too open to the north for my taste.

Couteau Inlet

On the north shore of the Lennox Passage, close north of Birch Island, the Couteau Inlet leads to Grande Anse. Entry looks straightforward—as long as you miss Goillon Reef at the entrance, and the few shoal spots inside. The bottom in most of these places is mud, so a grounding isn't usually a major disaster. Good shelter may be found in the small cove west of Knife Island, just inside the entrance. There is also reported to be good shelter off the north side of Indian Island, at the entrance to False Bay, northeast of Birch Island, but it's necessary to hug the west side of Indian Island on the way in.

Lennox Passage Bridge

Continuing to the west, the Lennox Passage begins to twist more, and the spars are difficult to see against the sun, but if your boat draws less than 5 feet (1.5 m), you aren't likely to hit anything as long as you stay in mid-channel.

The modern bascule bridge joining Isle Madame to Cape Breton Island opens on request during daylight hours in summer. The tide flows under the bridge swiftly, usually toward the west, and as the passage is open to westerlies here,

things can get quite lively. In theory, the tide floods to the east here, and ebbs to the west, but it's much affected by quirks of the wind and barometric pressure.

The bridge here was not always mechanized. Before the present one was built in 1976, its predecessor was operated by a rather temperamental horse. The stranding of the *Arrow* in 1970 caused such a massive oil spill that a temporary causeway was built at the site of the bridge to stop the oil from polluting the rest of the passage. When it was time to open the bridge again, the horse had been put out to pasture and the bridge itself had been pronounced structurally unsound. Though the province's bean counters were not thrilled at the idea of paying for a new lifting bridge, in an unusual case of farsightedness one was actually installed, preserving the passage for today's sailors.

Haddock Harbour ★★★★

  NO FACILITIES

Chart: **4308**

Haddock Harbour, at the northwest corner of Isle Madame, is a sheltered and deserted body of water entered between Campbell Island and Thorn Island. If you study chart 4308 you'll see spits sticking out from the some of the islands in the harbor, forming half-a-dozen sheltered anchorages. Small boats needing less than 10 feet (3 m) of overhead clearance can go through Mousseliers Passage to Leblanc Harbour and West Arichat. Though spar buoys are indicated on the chart, they may not be there when you actually need them.

Inhabitants Harbour

Charts: **4308**, 4335

On Cape Breton Island's southwest tip is another interesting and little-frequented basin with numerous anchorages. Inhabitants Harbour is easy

to enter with chart 4308, and even possible with chart 4335. Just keep over to the Evans Island side.

Though Inhabitants Harbour itself is a little large for a snug anchorage, anywhere behind Round Island, farther into the basin, or up the river just past Mussel Point, will suit.

Inhabitants Bay, at the mouth of the Inhabitants River, is a designated anchorage for large ships, but as the oil refinery is no longer in operation, and as most of the other mega-projects in the strait area have gone belly-up, it is hardly ever used for this purpose. I have never seen a large vessel passing through the adjacent Strait of Canso, so it is most unlikely that you will see the entire 14 anchorage spaces occupied—but it would be as well at night or in thick fog to be aware of this possibility.

Many of these anchorages around the Lennox Passage are every bit as attractive as the more popular ones in the Bras d'Or Lakes, and I am surprised that they are visited so infrequently.

The Strait of Canso, including Port Hawkesbury and the Canso Canal ★★

Charts: **4335, 4306,** 4335

The Strait of Canso is buoyed for tankers with drafts of 65 feet (20 m) or more, and so well supplied with navigation aids that the biggest problem is to sort them all out.

For yachts approaching from the south, the course from Canso North fairway buoy "PC" to Eddy Point is 334°M, about 14 miles. There are reciprocal ranges (transits) on Durell Island astern, and Port Malcolm ahead, on about 342°M and 162°M, but it may be better seamanship not to follow the exact line of these leading

marks, to lessen your chances of close encounters with large ships. Apart from the evil Cerberus Rock, there is almost nothing to hit until you are on the shore.

The controlling depth for this port is more than 90 feet (27 m). It's the deepest on the East Coast of North America, and there were once plans to make it a superport for large tankers and the like. The oil embargo of the early 1970s scuttled that idea, and while large vessels still go regularly to the pulp mill at Point Tupper, the oil refinery has been closed for years, as have many of the other government-funded mega-projects supposed to stimulate the area's growth.

As the Strait of Canso and environs is largely an industrial area, it is unlikely to be a primary destination for most yachts, but is the best practicable route if you are going to Prince Edward Island, the Magdalene Islands, the Northumberland Strait coast of Nova Scotia, or the Gulf of St. Lawrence. Once through the canal, you'll find warm water and no fog. At least, you'll find that in summer. In winter, it's quite something else.

Anchorage, Dockage. The only place to moor a small boat in the strait area is the government wharf at Port Hawkesbury, part of which is reserved for small boats. The wharf is just past the pulp mill, on the starboard side going north. It's a little exposed to strong southwesterlies, but as the wind tends to blow straight up or down the strait, under most conditions it should be all right.

There is a yacht club based in Port Hawkesbury, the Strait of Canso Yacht Club, and a few local boats are based here as well.

Port Hawkesbury is the commercial center of the area, and almost all services are available, except that fuel may not be available at the wharf. The stores are on the main road, the third road up from the water, about a half-mile from the wharf. It is the largest shopping area handy to a boat anywhere east of Halifax, and all major services are here, though like most regional centers in the province, the shopping area is designed for people with cars—it's a little unhandy if you are on foot.

Ashore.   Of the watering holes on the main drag, there is one that has a certain distinction: Billy Joe's Place. Billy Joe Maclean, at the time of writing, was the mayor of Port Hawkesbury. He was once a minister in the provincial government, but was convicted of fiddling his expenses and expelled from the House. His constituents, probably realizing that Billy Joe's misdemeanors were small beer compared to those of some of his political colleagues, promptly returned him to the House in a by-election.

He's a rather likeable fellow, though I don't know whether I'd want him to fill in my tax returns. Billy Joe has the gift of the gab and an outgoing personality. He was always rather good at putting the pompous and overblown media hacks from our National Broadcasting Service in their places. Billy Joe's Place features live music Friday and Saturday nights—and I've no doubt the owner could entertain you for hours with tales about the devious backwaters of Nova Scotian politics.

The Canso Causeway and Lock.   A little less than 3 miles north of Port Hawkesbury is the Canso Causeway and lock. The dock and the swing bridge occupy the east side. Call ahead on Channel 16 or Channel 11 with your estimated time of arrival, and everything will be ready for you. You can tie up temporarily on the south side of the lock, but the structure is designed for large ships, and much fendering is required. You will likely only have to wait if one of the two or three daily trains is passing. There is a small harbor of refuge on the north side of the locks, but it is on the western side of the strait, and the shelter is indifferent if it is really blowing.

When you pass though the locks, you are out in the open of St. Georges Bay, and there is no good harbor for 30 miles. Northwesterly gales make this a very dirty place, and the weather forecasts for this shore are not known for their reliability. When making this passage, you need to watch the weather, and be particularly careful if there is a forecast of a cold front approaching from the west. If there has been the usual south-westerly flow and fog, you will probably be all right.

The Canso Causeway, completed in 1955, was a massive engineering project for its time. Many of its effects were unforeseen in an era when environmental assessment studies were unknown. The difficult and rapid tidal streams of the area were much reduced, making navigation much easier and the flow of ice though the strait was permanently cut off. Before the causeway was built, the strait was jammed up with ice until the middle of May. This has had a profound effect on the climate as far south as Cape Sable, reducing the amount of winter ice to such an extent that most ports on the southeast coast are now effectively ice-free, and warming up the water by 5°F (2°C to 3°C), thus reducing the amount of fog. Most of these changes are considered highly favorable by Nova Scotians, and it is of some interest that, had today's review processes been in effect, this structure may never have been built.

A small museum shows the building process at the causeway, but it would be difficult to visit if you are in transit, as there is a distinct lack of suitable mooring places. You could, of course, visit it by taxi from Port Hawkesbury if you wanted to take a look at the lock before subjecting your boat to it.

The Bras d'Or Lakes

The Bras d'Or Lakes mark the limits of this book's coverage of the province. The Northumberland Strait coast, and the outside coast of Cape Breton Island, are farther than I have been able to travel on ordinary summer vacations. Traveling to the lakes represents a round trip in excess of 1,000 miles for me, and that has certainly been a challenge to complete in a month in some of the boats I have owned.

When you're planning a cruise to this area, I'd advise you to think carefully about the distances you can reasonably cover in a day, and the time that will be left over for exploring the lakes. If you're

coming from the Boston area, for example, it will probably take you one week to get to the lakes, and two weeks to get back. If you have a month's vacation, that gives you only one week in the lakes. It's a more demanding trip than you might imagine, unless you have a big boat or a powerful crew.

The two-week return trip represents a beat to windward, in the usual weather conditions, of 50 miles a day, every day for 14 days. For a man-and-wife team, it's tough going. It's certainly as much as my wife and I would like to undertake, and we would certainly prefer to go slower. And one storm can throw your whole schedule off. To meet this deadline you must be prepared for 16-hour days, or traveling overnight, and it is perhaps as well to be aware of this before you suddenly realize your home port is 400 miles to windward, you have five days to get there, and an intense depression is on the way from Cape Hatteras. My preferred strategy is to get where I'm going as quickly as possible, never wasting a fair wind, and then to take my time on the beat home. We find that beating in a traditional boat is not so bad if you know you can stop for dinner and a drink after a few hours.

The Bras d'Or Lakes look and feel much different from the outside coast of Nova Scotia. In summer, the water is about 18°F (10°C) warmer for a start. This means, at the modest price of no longer being able to cool your beer in the bilge, an almost total absence of fog. The tidal range is less than 1 foot (30 cm), and there are few underwater hazards. There are few lighted aids to navigation, which may explain why very little night sailing seems to get done on the lakes, though I can think of many places more difficult at night.

The only regular commercial shipping goes to Little Narrows, and then it's only about one boat a week. Fishing boats occasionally travel through, but the only commercial fishing in the lake is fish farming or oyster gathering, done from small boats. All this means your navigator can take a vacation, too. Eyeball pilotage is usually adequate,

which is certainly not the case in most other regions of the province. Distances are relatively short, and the water normally smooth, so a cruise in the lakes is usually pleasant sailing—pleasant enough, anyway, to persuade hundreds of sailors to put up with the ordeal of getting here every year.

A few hazards do exist, however. There are considerable tidal streams in the Barra Strait, and no satisfactory tidal predictions. When the west-going stream is opposed by a westerly wind, a remarkably nasty little sea arises in short order for a few miles west of the bridge. While it's unlikely to sink you, it can certainly make for an unpleasant few hours. Another weather tantrum to be aware of is the frequency of thunderstorms. I don't usually worry much about these things, but the last time I was crossing Bras d'Or Lake on the way back to St. Peters, I spent three hours watching lightning bolts strike a hundred yards or less from the boat. This experience made me a little more concerned about lightning protection, though I still don't know how to fix it.

The way many natural harbors were formed in the lakes will be of interest to visiting sailors. Natural harbors have three main forces acting on them: tidal streams, alluvial deposition, and the effects of major storms. In most of the lakes, there is little tidal stream, and there are no large sediment-carrying rivers, so storm waves and surges are the major natural force affecting harbors. What this means, in practical terms, is that a harbor formed by sand bars can have its entry changed overnight. Most of the survey work in the lakes is at least 20 years old, and it behooves you to enter any of these harbors with caution, especially where the entrance is exposed to winter storms. The west entrance of Pringle Harbor, in West Bay, is one such instance. The chart gives a depth of about 12 feet (3.8 m), but I suspect it is only half that.

Another matter of interest to visitors is that VHF coverage is notoriously unreliable in the lakes. While reception usually is good in the middle of big stretches of water, in most harbors it's problematic because of high hills. I must add, though, that I've always found it satisfactory in St. Peters and Baddeck. If you can get the signal, there is a local Bras d'Or Lakes weather forecast, updated twice a day. Cellular phone service is available in the Great Bras d'Or and St. Patricks Channel, which are near the Transcanada Highway, but very spotty anywhere else.

Fuel and piped water are available at St. Peters, Dundee, and Baddeck. All anchorages should be assumed to have no facilities, unless otherwise designated.

There is only one pumpout station, at Baddeck Marine, though humans tend to be greatly outnumbered by other beasts excreting into the water. Garbage disposal is best resolved by leaving it at the places where you buy fuel, as there are very few other disposal sites. The essentially closed nature of the system—it takes 10 years at least to change all the water in the lakes—makes garbage disposal even more of a problem than it is on the coast.

The pretty anchorages in the southern lake (Bras d'Or Lake), attract most visitors, with Washabuck and Baddeck being the most popular destinations in the northern lake (Great Bras d'Or). There are probably at least a hundred anchorages in all, and I will never live long enough to visit them all. It is difficult to get lost in the Bras d'Or Lakes, however, and I hope this guide will at least provide an introduction to the more popular places, with the expectation that you could safely find your own way to those more off the beaten track.

St. Peters Inlet

Charts: 4275, 4279

When you approach Bras d'Or Lake from St. Peters, leave the red spar buoys to port, and the green ones to starboard, just as you would while exiting any other harbor. But beware—the three lighthouses in the inlet are perverse. Leave the flashing reds to starboard, and the flashing whites to port.

The first hazard is the power cable at Beaver Narrows. This 500-kv line has a clearance of 100 feet (30 m). The deep channel lies on the south side of Beaver Island, and you should follow the spars and keep to starboard here. If you want to go into the cove north of Beaver Island, off Samsonville, you can only enter it at the western end. The eastern end has only about 2 feet (60 cm) of water. This is a sheltered anchorage, but it's next to the road, and with Cape George Harbour just 40 minutes away, I have never used it.

French Cove and Damions Cove also provide reasonably sheltered anchorages. The inlet joins the lake after exiting past Gregory Island, where there is a little lighthouse on the sandspit. Sailing out of the inlet into the lake always seems very pleasant. The wind is usually at your back, the water is smooth, and the fog seems to disappear as soon as you get a half-mile into the lake.

Fougeres Cove, just north of Gregory Island,

cannot be entered as there is less than 1 foot (30 cm) of water at its mouth. St. Peters Inlet is home to at least a couple of dozen bald eagles, and you'll usually see one or more when you make this passage.

Cape George Harbour ★★★★

  NO FACILITIES

Charts: 4275, 4279

This popular anchorage three-quarters of a mile south of the lighthouse at Cape George is easy to enter. Just keep in the middle between the south side and the sandspit. I have sailed in and out of here—admittedly after engine failure, and not by choice—so there are few problems with the entry. Most people anchor just behind the spit, up as far as they feel comfortable. As the beach is steep-to, it is possible to put your bow on the beach, and just run the anchor ashore. For those who prefer anchorages between tree-lined banks, you can go farther up the harbor. You should be a little careful of the spit that sticks out from the first branch, not shown on chart 4275. The water temperature here in August is likely to be 68°F (20°C), warm enough for hardy swimmers. There is a pleasant walk round the beach to the cape. The road goes past the head of the harbor, but you certainly can't see it, and you can scarcely hear it. There are no facilities of any sort here, but it is a pleasant spot with a beach ideal for walking and picnicking, but not of such fine consistency that it gets all over your boat. This is a small harbor, and could become crowded, but I have never seen more than four boats in it. This is a very protected anchorage and it is difficult to imagine anything short of a hurricane bothering you in here.

Chapel Island, Soldiers Cove, and Macnabs Cove ★★★

  NO FACILITIES

Charts: 4275, 4279

East of Cape George Harbour, on and near the shores of Cape Breton Island, are the harbors of Chapel Island, Soldiers Cove, and Macnabs Cove. They are not popular among visiting cruisers because of their tricky entrances and imperfect shelter.

Chapel Island is easily recognized by its small church and the cabins at its southern end. It has two anchorages, both on the eastern side. To enter the southernmost anchorage, approach the western side of Chapel Island with sufficient northing to clear the long spit protruding from Indian Point. Head south, 100 yards off the island, and pass between the spit and the island. When you see the gap into the basin opening up, turn to the east and stay in mid-channel. You can anchor in any of the coves in the center of the islands, but watch for the shallow spots if you draw more than 5 feet (1.5 m).

To exit east from here toward Soldiers Cove, go between Alick and Indian Islands, again watching for the spits.

The anchorage at the north end of Chapel island is easiest to enter from the north. Head south from red spar "QN10," leaving the buoy to starboard, and keep clear of the spit extending southeast from Chapel Island's northern end. The spit is well shown on chart 4275. This bay is a little open to the east, but it's satisfactory in the usual westerly weather. It is unwise to try to go between Indian Island and Chapel Island, as there is at best 4 feet (1.2 m), and I suspect the chart is not entirely correct. Chapel Island is part of a clean and well-kept Indian reservation. The native fishermen harvesting oysters always have a friendly wave for passing yachts.

Soldiers Cove has a clear entrance, and Macnabs Cove a series of spars. Both provide reasonable protection, but have rather a large number of

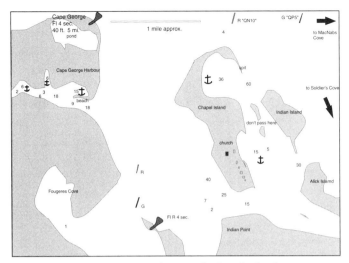

Cape George Harbour and Chapel Island.

between Poor Point and Militia Point. It offers perhaps the most spectacular scenery in the lakes.

Going clockwise around the bay, you first come to Morrison Harbour, which is completely open to the east. It's not a place I would stay in overnight. The shoals off Poor Point and MacLeods Point are marked by green spars that are not always easy to see. If you do not approach Poor Point within a half-mile, you will be all right. Pringle Shoal, a bit farther off, has more than 8 feet (2.4 m) over it, so it is not likely to bother you unless you have a big boat.

MacLeods Pond has less than 2 feet (60 cm) in its entrance, so is not suitable for yachts.

Pringle Harbour is best entered from the east. I have never used it, and it is a little exposed except in settled weather. The two entrances to Pringle Harbour are formed by the gaps in the fringing sandbars. Enter with caution, as you would any other lake harbor guarded by sandbars.

Farther to the west there are few hazards, if you keep a sensible distance off the shore, until you come to Dundee.

summer cottages on their shores, something not afflicting Cape George Harbour, which is uninhabited. The best anchorage in Macnabs Cove is the little cove to the northwest. You shouldn't have any difficulty if you have chart 4279 and keep in the middle. Soldiers Cove is perhaps a little exposed to the north.

Passage from St. Peters Inlet to Grand Narrows

Chart: **4279**

One of the few passage on the lakes where you cannot see your destination from your starting point is the run from St. Peters Inlet to Grand Narrows.

From Cape George lighthouse, steer 005°M for 2 miles to Kelly Shoal buoy "Q35." From there, a course of 026°M for 10.5 miles will put you right in the middle of the Barra Strait. There is nothing to run into, and I usually enjoy this two-hour sail.

West Bay

Chart: **4279**

West Bay is about three miles across, bounded by hills 700 feet (210 m) or so high, and is entered

Dundee ★★★★ [4] [A]

Chart: **4279**

Dundee offers a marina, a vacation resort, spectacular scenery, a delightful anchorage, and all the amenities of civilization except groceries.

Approaches. The entrance to Dundee is straightforward. Just leave flashing green buoy "D11" to port, and after passing the red spar on your starboard side, favor the Ballams Point shore. The marina is just round the little point, and if you dock there, don't stray more than 50 yards from the dock or you'll be in the shallows. It is also shallow

233

between MacRae Island and Dumpheys (Dunphee) Head, and I don't recommend trying to pass through there.

Anchorage, Dockage. All the usual services are available at the 30-boat marina. There is a rather forbidding list of "Don'ts" at the marina office. For instance, you are asked not to use your barbecue, or hang your washing in the rigging—but I'm not sure if this is meant to be taken seriously. Some of the characters I know to have tied up here take any regulation as a challenge to be overcome. Fees for visiting yachts are about $15 a night.

During the winter of 1994/95, the yacht *Elsie*, built in 1916, was being restored here. Elsie, Alexander Graham Bell's daughter, married Gilbert Grosvenor, founder of the National Geographic magazine, around 1916. The boat was built for, and named after, her at the Pinaud boatyard (now Cape Breton Boatbuilders) at Baddeck. *Elsie's* tanbark sails were a fixture on the lakes. I believe she will be available for charter.

If you don't want to avail yourself of the marina, and your boat draws less than 6 feet (1.8 m), there is a delightful anchorage in the little cove just behind Dumpheys (Dunphee) Head. It's also close to the restaurant at the resort. There may be a small dock in the bay just off the resort, where you can tie up your dinghy, but don't try to bring a big boat to it.

Ashore. The resort is about a half-mile east of the marina, but it is a pleasant walk. An 18-hole golf course reveals spectacular views of the lake.

There is a restaurant, but I have not used it myself.

If you have dogs or children, there is a sandy beach just west of the marina, in the cove, and a much longer one just to the west of Ballam Head.

West Bay has beautiful scenery, with high hills sweeping down to the lake, tall trees of birch and some softwoods, a multitude of small farms, and for this supposedly economically depressed area, a great number of impressive new homes. For my taste, the West Bay area has the best scenery in the lakes, and is well worth a diversion from the rush to Baddeck. I suspect that a hundred years ago, much of the province looked like this (apart from the new houses), but the marginal farmland has now mostly reverted to dense secondary-growth forest.

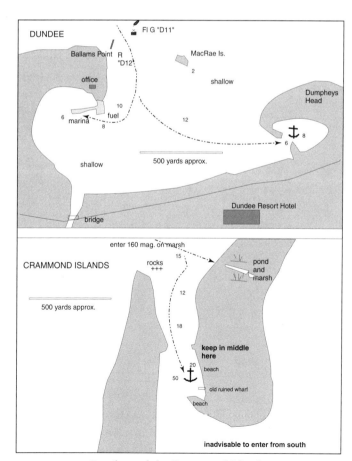

Dundee and the Crammond Islands.

Coves West and North of Dundee

Chart: **4279**

West Bay Cove, Ross Pond, and North Cove are small coves between Dundee and MacKenzie Point. They are pretty communities when seen from land, but I have never visited them by boat.

Crammond Islands ★★★★

  NO FACILITIES

Chart: **4279**

At one time there were farms on the two Crammond Islands, but the isolation engendered by the spring and fall break-up of the ice has caused this lifestyle to become extinct. I'm not sure exactly when ice forms in the lakes, but it is certainly before Christmas, and when I visited the lakes at the end of April, 1995, doing the final research for this book, there was ice as far as the eye could see throughout West Bay, and that was after one of the mildest winters on record.

Approaches. Entry from the north is advised: Steer 160°M toward the marsh on the eastern island. The marsh shows as a gap in the island's profile. That course will keep you off the rocks extending from the north point of the west island. When you get to the narrow bit, be sure to keep in the middle. The channel then opens into a little basin, and you can anchor anywhere, though some parts are quite deep. The remains of an old wharf in the southeast corner of the basin should be avoided.

The sandbars at the south end of the basin form a pleasant little beach, and this is a deserted, well-sheltered anchorage in any but extreme conditions.

Islands North of the Crammond Islands

Chart: **4279**

North of the Crammond Islands is a cluster of small islands, the biggest of which is MacRae Island. Unfortunately, they are all a little exposed and I have never heard of anyone anchoring among them, though there appears to be an appealing little cove, open to the north, on Calf Island.

If you're heading northeast between these islands and the mainland, pass red spar "DC2" on the wrong side and go between it and Low Island. Leave the buoy really close to port, no more than one boatlength away. To the west of the buoy is a shallow patch with less than 5 feet (1.5 m) at low water.

Marble Mountain ★★★★★

  NO FACILITIES

Chart: **4279**

This is one of the most picturesque anchorages on the lakes. It has fine views, wonderful walks, and honest-to-goodness warm water.

Approaches. From flashing red buoy "DA2," a course of 310°M takes you to the lighthouse on Cameron Island. Nameless Shoal is just to port of your track, and may have a rock, not shown on chart 4279, with about 3 feet (1.5 m) over it at low-water springs. It is marked with green spar buoy "DA3," and because of its uncertain position and existence, careful navigators will not approach it too closely. On the direct line between the red buoy and the lighthouse you are all right. All the other shoals off Cameron and George Islands have at least 8 feet (2.4 m). There are no longer leading marks into Clarke Cove, though they may still be shown on some charts; but there is a flashing red light on shore close north of Clarke Point.

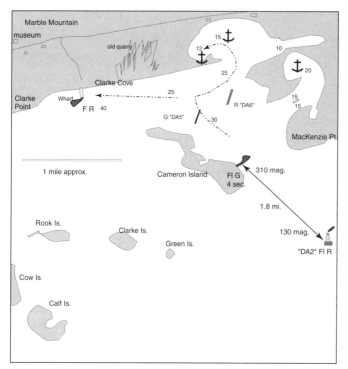

Marble Mountain.

here one July the water temperature was 70°F (21°C)—positively tropical by Nova Scotian standards.

The other coves between MacDonalds and MacKenzie Coves are also satisfactory anchorages, but most visiting yachts use the spit or its adjacent cove.

Ashore. A small government wharf lies a mile to the west of the spit. It has depths of about 8 feet (2.4 m) at its end, and it makes a handier mooring if you are visiting the village, which is 400 yards from the wharf and 400 feet (122 m) up in the air. Aerobics freaks will love the steep climb. They can also take the path right to the top of the mountain by going up to the main road from the wharf, turning right, and walking along about 200 yards before resuming the ascent.

As this is a near-vertical climb of 1,000 feet (300 m), you should have some confidence in the state of the arteries to your vital parts before you start. You are a really long way from any medical facility if they start playing up. If you don't get angina on the climb, and visibility is good, you will be rewarded with some of the finest views in the lakes.

There is a small museum just left of the junction of the main road and the road from the wharf. The museum displays artifacts from the time when this was a booming area with an operating quarry. The store, alas, closed a few years ago, and many of the large houses are now unoccupied, though the area is becoming popular for summer homes. However, as driving along the road in winter is nearly as heart-stopping as climbing the hill, I suspect new development will be limited.

Passage through the channel between Cameron Island and MacKenzie Point is straightforward, just keep in the middle. There is a pair of buoys at the northwestern end. You can close the shoreline to within a few yards here. The shore is very steep-to, descending in less than a half-mile from about 800 feet (240 m) to sea level. The big hole left by quarrying operations, which ceased in 1921, dominates the shore, and still can be seen for miles.

Anchorage. The most sheltered anchorage is found by running up to the northeast and rounding a spit seemingly made of tiny pebbles of pure, almost white, marble. If you keep about 10 yards off the end of the spit, you will have plenty of water. You can anchor anywhere in the cove, or put the bow of your boat ashore and run an anchor into the shingle. Unless a storm surge covered this bank, I doubt that anything could bother you here.

The road passes the head of the cove, and there are a few cottages, but little activity. When I was

Malagawatch and Denys Basins

Chart: 4279

Every time I pass the entrance to the Malagawatch and Denys Basins, I resolve to explore their inner passages, but I regret that I've never had enough time. The multitude of sheltered waterways, the almost complete lack of human habitation, and the general remoteness of the place, would make such a journey fascinating, and I therefore include a brief description.

I have gone all around here by road. It was still winter when I explored the almost entirely unpaved roads. There was not a single power pole or house for long sections of road, and there was certainly no cellular-phone signal. All in all, this journey was quite an adventure in itself.

Unlike much of the rest of the lakes, the land is low-lying here, and the scenery is more subtle than spectacular. I assume everyone will have a copy of chart 4279 aboard, so I have not drawn a map of the harbor. The chart shows sufficient detail for you to get around.

Little Harbour ★★★

 NO FACILITIES

Chart: 4279

The first thing that strikes you when you look at the chart is the narrowness of the entrance to Little Harbour. Yet I believe entry presents no difficulty. The best water is on the western side. The sandbars forming the entrance are larger than you would think from the chart, though, and there may well be less water than advertised. I would suggest caution in southerly winds of any strength. The harbor is completely enclosed but rather large, making protection indifferent unless you are in the lee of the shore. There is another anchorage in the bight of Pellier Island, just to the east, but I have never tried it.

Big Harbour ★★★

NO FACILITIES

Chart: 4279

Big Harbour is the site of the remains of the Malagawatch Boat Canal. In the 1890s roads were non-existent, but there was a boat passage from Orangedale, where the railway station was, though Denys Basin. The boat canal went from there into Big Harbour, and then there was a short portage into Little Harbour, thence to Marble Mountain. There are a number of similar abandoned Victorian waterways in the province, the longest being the Shubenacadie Canal from Bedford Basin to Truro. They're all but forgotten now that we take roads for granted.

Approaches. Entry is simple, between Sheep Island and Macrae Island. If you are coming from the west and go inside Militia Island, keep off the bar, northwest of the island, that extends halfway across the channel, and then swing quite wide of Pellier Point Reef, which sticks out a half-mile east from the island.

The best anchorages are either side of what is called Nills Point on the chart. The western bay is rather shallow at the top, and the head of the bay is navigable only by dinghy.

Denys Basin ★★★★ 5

C NO FACILITIES

Chart: 4279

Apart from a dirt road (part of which had degenerated into a sea of mud and was closed when I was last here), and the very small village of Orangedale, there is scarcely a sign of human habitation around the Denys Basin.

The only incongruous thing is the train whistle, as the railway to Sydney passes a little way to the north of the basin. The railway, formerly run

by one of our wonderfully efficient public corporations, had been slated for closure because it was uneconomic. But it has received a new lease on life under private management, and is now making a profit. You are likely, therefore, to continue to hear the Orangedale Whistle—as expressed in a song by the Rankin Family—two or three times a day for a while yet. The sound of the train, though perhaps not quite in keeping with the surroundings, will at least remind you that you are not the last person alive in this remote area.

Approaches. Denys Basin has to be entered between Lighthouse Point and Campbells Island. Apart from the little anchorage behind Fiddle Head and Malagawatch Point (MacRaes Cove), which the adventurous might like to try, a wide berth should be given to the whole shore between Malagawatch Point and Campbells Island. It is full of rocks and reefs, and you cannot go inside the islands.

To enter the basin, pass along the north sides of Campbells, Round, and Cranberry Islands, turn to the south, and then continue west along Boom Island. The spit at the west end of Boom Island sticks out nearly a half-mile, so don't try to cut the corner. Green buoy "C61" marks the end of the spit. Red buoy "C62" marks a similar, though shorter, easterly extending spit off MacLean Point. These are the only buoys in this harbor, though (ironically) if your chart is not up-to-date, more may be shown.

Anchorages. There are any number of anchorages in the various coves of the basin, including Portage Creek, just to the north at the entrance. Determined gunkholers can penetrate as far as Mahoneys Point, where there is a pretty anchorage just below the bridge. If you go this far, you will need to watch your depths, as the channel is narrow and tortuous.

McKinnons Harbour

Chart: 4279

A major port in the heyday of the quarrying industry, McKinnons Harbour is now closed by a shallow bar. When it's in a good mood (or perhaps when elections are coming), the Department of Transport dredges it out. There are now so few voters living here that this hasn't been done, as far as I am aware, for some time, and any approach to the entrance should be made with extreme caution.

Iona and Grand Narrows

★★★   NO FACILITIES

Chart: 4278

Grand Narrows marks the boundary of the upper lake, the Great Bras d'Or, and it is here that the twin hazards of the bridge and the tide have to be overcome. But the difficulties should not be exaggerated. It's possible to sail through the bridge. I've done it on a number of occasions—not I might add, with the overwhelming approval of my crew.

Approaches. The ferry is no more. It has been replaced by a modern box-girder bridge, attended (don't forget, this is Nova Scotia) by the usual degree of political controversy. In this instance, the bridge was designed to be built of steel, but the contract was awarded to a company that made it from reinforced concrete. I forget whether it was too heavy, or too weak, but for one reason or other its opening was delayed by more than a year. It did work, however, the last time I went under it. Those aboard a yacht accompanying mine were not so fortunate, though. The captain didn't believe the red light was meant for him, and his mast was 12 inches (30 cm) from being demolished by the bridge deck when the boat finally started going backward. He still gets ill thinking of it.

The railway bridge, which has a clearance of 15 feet when closed, was built in the last century and is still going strong. It's a swing bridge, whereas the new road bridge is a lift (bascule) type. They operate in tandem from the same control box. They have the usual red and green lights. Most of the time, you will find the bridge opening before you get to it. If the lights remain red, it is for a good reason, such as an approaching train. I presume they keep a VHF watch, though I have never tried calling, and there is no mention of it in the official *Sailing Directions.*

On the approach from the south there is a green buoy that should be left to starboard—buoyage throughout the lakes is orientated from the entrance at the Great Bras d'Or.

You can estimate the strength of the tidal stream by observing how it affects this buoy. Unfortunately no such aid is available if you're coming from the north. Whenever I have been here, the tide has been flowing in line with the Barra Strait, but you may experience a northwesterly set on occasion, which tends to push you toward the wall on the port side going toward Baddeck. I suspect, though, that the set would be more worrisome to the pilot of a 250-foot (75-m) cargo boat than to the skipper of the average yacht.

The tidal stream can run quite hard, up to 3 knots, and it is impossible to give any reasonable tidal predictions. The tide is much affected by local meteorological conditions, such as a difference in atmospheric pressure over the two lakes, or differences in the winds, and the like. You will need to be a much better sailor than I am to sail through here if wind and tide are against you.

If the tide is running south, a horrible little slop may arise for a mile or two south of the bridge. If you are heading south on the beat, it is wise to make sure everything is tied down before you get to the bridge, as it's darned difficult to do so once you are through it, and there is nowhere to stop.

Barra Shoal lies a half-mile north of the bridge. It has a minimum depth of about 14 feet (4.3 m), so it shouldn't be a major concern. Of more import is Big Shoal, 5 miles north of the bridge toward the eastern shore. It has only 4 feet (1.2 m) over it. Big Shoal is marked by green spar "Q25," and is best avoided by favoring the Maskells Harbour side of the channel.

Dockage. There is a small wharf on the southern side of the bridge, on the Grand Narrows side, to which you may tie up in an emergency. I did so once when I couldn't start my engine. The wharf was originally maintained for the ferry, and its condition may now be uncertain.

There is a much more substantial and protected wharf on the north side of the bridge, on the Iona side, and you can moor there if you want to visit Iona.

Ashore. Iona is a pretty village dominated by the large stone church. There was once a store and garage here, but they were both closed during my last visit in 1995. The Highland Village, a replica of a typical Cape Breton community of the early nineteenth century, is a brisk one-and-a-half-mile walk away.

Maskells Harbour ★★★★

 NO FACILITIES

Chart: **4278**

Boulaceet is the old name for Maskells Harbour, 4 miles north of Iona, and many sailors, particularly those from away, still use the old name. It is often said to be the most photographed and most popular anchorage on the lakes. I suspect this is a slight exaggeration, but it is certainly a pretty spot, and very sheltered.

Approaches. Maskells Harbour is easy to enter. Just identify Gillis Point lighthouse, and enter on a heading of about 280°M. A spit extends northeastward from Gillis Point, marked by green buoy "QD1." The spit has at least 6 feet (1.8 m) over it,

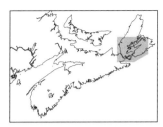

but most people will feel more comfortable if they leave the buoy to port going in. There is a second, visible, spit on your starboard side as you progress into the harbor.

The most sheltered anchorage is on the northwestern side of the spit, just inside it. There are sandy beaches nearby, and another over by the lighthouse. A boathouse at the head of this cove is the only sign of human habitation.

It's a pleasant diversion to row over to the lighthouse and walk up around it. When I first visited this harbor in 1978 there was a house here, but it has since disappeared. The high wooded hills provide perfect shelter, so you'll usually find a few other boats in this popular anchorage. I cannot conceive, however, that there would ever be a time when you couldn't find somewhere to anchor.

Baddeck ★★★★ [3] [A]

Chart: 4278

Baddeck is usually the final destination of boats cruising the province, as to go farther puts great demands on time if you have to beat back to the East Coast of the USA—or to western Nova Scotia, for that matter.

Approaches. When I'm coming from Grand Narrows, I round MacKay Point, and usually go between Spectacle and Bone Islands. Spectacle Island is a rock with a number of rotting tree stumps on it, having been attacked by cormorants. There are submerged rocks off Bone Island and it is essential to follow the buoys, which, going this way, are red to starboard and green to port.

If you're approaching from the east, stay in the northern half of the channel, as there are a few rocks on the north side of Spectacle Island.

Large vessels use the St. Patricks Channel that runs past Baddeck. They're on their way to and from the gypsum mine at Little Narrows, and though they're infrequent (once or twice a week), you should be mindful to keep out of their way. This is a very narrow spot for a 700-foot-long (213-m) boat.

While I usually enter Baddeck from the east, there are no particular difficulties in the western entrance.

Anchorage, Dockage. Baddeck is the major tourist town on the lakes, and most facilities can be found here. The town is dominated by the government wharf, where you can usually tie up. It is occasionally used by freighters loading pulpwood, and the wharfinger will shoo you away when one is expected. He will usually have extracted your docking fee first, this being the only public dock in the province at which I have ever paid wharfage.

A little way west of the public dock are the premises of Baddeck Marine—(902) 295-2434—a much better place to tie up. Unfortunately for me, they've never had space when I've been there. There is, however, fuel, water, showers, a laundromat, a sewage pumpout (don't ask questions about where it goes after being removed from your holding tank), repair facilities, charts, and marine supplies. I have found the owner very helpful when I needed some obscure spare parts.

Cape Breton Boatbuilders—(902) 295-2664—which used to be the famous Pinaud Boatyard, is in the cove just a little farther to the west. Moorings may be available there, but it would be wise to call in advance. This is a full-service boatyard that should be able to handle any vessel less than about 60 feet (18 m) long.

Most local vessels have moorings just off Kidston Island, and it is usually possible to find space to anchor there if you don't like the look of the wharf. The Lions Club maintains a children's area on the beach at the east end of Kidston Island, and a small swimming area is roped off in the hope of keeping out carelessly handled speedboats. There is a ferry service to the beach during the summer months.

The shelter at the wharf is indifferent if it blows hard, especially if you are on the windward side. I have had some real fun moving back and forth to the limited shelter on the lee side of the wharf. The wharf is also crowded with tourists during the summer, which may encourage the less gregarious to find a quiet anchorage. This is also one of the very few places in the province where I have been seriously hassled at a wharf, and the last time I was there, in 1992, there was a rash of theft and vandalism, including thefts from boats at anchor. One of my traveling companions later attended a court hearing to give evidence in a case involving a stolen outboard motor gasoline tank, so this kind of thing may now have stopped. I would not like to blow these incidents out of proportion, particularly in an area where income from visiting yachts contributes significantly to the local economy, but the situation we were in was most unpleasant, and someone could have ended up being shot. It would be as well to in- quire locally, and to be careful about leaving your boat unattended if you don't get straight answers.

Ashore. The best place to get groceries is at the Baddeck co-op store, west of the government wharf, on the road east of the Cape Breton Boat- yard. They will deliver to your boat, at least if you're at a wharf. The liquor store is a little way farther along—once again, quite a way with a case of beer. The Trans-Canada highway goes through Baddeck, and from here it's about a half-hour's drive to Sydney. Sydney airport is well served with at least a dozen flights a day from various parts, so it is a good place to have new crew fly in. There is a small hospital in Baddeck that might survive the present round of budget cuts, and there are also various hotels, art galleries, and the like. There is a tourist information booth on the wharf.

The Bras d'Or Yacht Club lies close east of the government wharf. The treasurer would be grateful for any pa- tronage of the bar. Showers and water

are available, though space at the yacht club dock is limited.

I can't remember eating any really inspiring restaurant meals in Baddeck, but I can certainly remember some bad ones. Maybe I haven't tried hard enough.

Alexander Graham Bell. The inventor of the telephone spent a good deal of his later years at Baddeck. He and his wife are buried on the fam- ily estate at Beein Bhreagh, the large headland east of Baddeck. A museum near the government wharf details Professor Bell's life, and many of his numerous inventions are displayed. Bell had interests in aviation, and naval architecture, as well as electricity. The first powered aircraft in the British Empire flew from Bell's estate, in 1908 I think, and the first hydrofoil vessel was developed there, too. A visit to the museum is a fascinating insight into those early technologies.

Baddeck Bay

Chart: 4278

If the bustle of Baddeck town begins to pale, or the weather is throwing a tantrum, a delightful anchorage can be had in Baddeck Bay. There are two good spots: one is in what the chart calls The Harbour, and the other is in what the chart calls Herring Cove.

Herring Cove is the site of the wreck of Irving

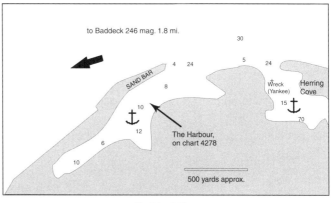

Baddeck Bay.

Johnson's *Yankee,* a 90-foot (27-m) schooner famous in yachting literature. She lies close to the shore at the northwest part of the cove, and it would be sacrilege to anchor on top of her. The anchorage behind the bar is perhaps slightly more protected, but both are good in anything less than a hurricane.

In the early 1950's, *Yankee* was being operated as a charter vessel in the lakes. She sank at her mooring.

Washabuck River ★★★★

  NO FACILITIES

Chart: 4278

The Washabuck River is 4 miles southwest of Baddeck, on the south side of the St. Patricks Channel. The hazards are well shown on chart 4278. It is best to keep outside of Stoney Shoal, which used to be a grassy island until the cormorants got it.

Care is needed at the entrance to the Washabuck River, as it is guarded by nasty pointy rocks, rather than the usual sandbars. If you stay in mid-channel and follow the buoys, you will be all right. Any of the coves provide satisfactory anchorage, but I have used the one called Deep Cove on the chart. It's deserted, and surrounded by low hills covered with trees. You are miles here from the nearest house.

Farther up the St. Patricks Channel

Chart: 4278

Most visitors go no farther than the Washabuck River, but passage to Whycocomagh presents no great difficulties, and is well shown on the chart. There are a few more obstructions here than there are on the rest of the lakes, but they are all well marked as far as the gypsum mine at Little Narrows.

There are good anchorages at MacNaughtons Cove, close to Cranberry Point, and at the entrance to Denas Pond, just before the chain ferry that crosses Little Narrows, both on the north side of the channel. There is a small store at Little Narrows, on the south side, but the wharf shown on the chart has crumbled away. A number of anchorages exist at the head of the bay, and they're quite spectacular as the hills here are over 1,000 feet (300 m) high, but I've never had time to explore them.

The Great Bras d'Or

Chart: 4277

The northern entrance to the lakes is the Great Bras d'Or. It's the one you must take if you're bound for Sydney, Ingonish, or Newfoundland. The passage is complicated by the tide, which runs up to 5 knots, though the rate is nowhere charted. You must have *Canadian Chart and Current Tables, Volume 1* to make this passage; it is not safe without it, as strong wind-over-tide situations in the entrance are dangerous. If you have got this far without the tables, buy a copy in Baddeck.

If you are entering this channel from the south, rather than from Baddeck, keep well away from Coffin Island (now an almost-submerged reef) a half-mile northwest of Kempt Head on Boularderie Island. It's marked by buoy "Q23."

While they're outside the range of this book, Big Harbour and Otter Harbour provide sheltered anchorages in the Great Bras d'Or.

St. Andrews Channel

Chart: 4277

Regrettably, again beyond the range of this book, the St. Andrews channel is another exit to the north, but is obstructed by a fixed bridge with a 20-foot (6-m) overhead clearance at the Little Bras d'Or. The tides at the entrance are even more turbulent and unpredictable than they are at the

Great Bras d'Or, and the original swing bridge is closed because the entrance is considered too dangerous for navigation. Determined explorers will find anchorages at Island Point Harbour and Long Island. But even if you have a powerboat that's able to get under the bridge, you'd be well advised to use the other entrance.

East Bay

Chart: 4279

East Bay is another area rarely visited by yachts, probably because the harbors on the south side are rather exposed and tricky to enter, and the ones on the north side are way off the beaten track. I have not visited any of these harbors by boat, but it's possible to anchor in a number of the coves around Eskasoni (the Indian Islands) and a rather pretty anchorage at Cossitt Point. Benacadie Pond looks interesting, but has only 5 feet (1.5 m) in its entrance. The entrance also is exposed to southwesterlies, and should be approached with extreme caution.

Eskasoni is the largest community on the lakes. It does not, however, appear as such in any tourist guide, or even on the province's road maps. It is the largest Indian reservation in the province. The problems of these places have defied solutions from generations of governments, and would fill many books larger than this one. Without being judgmental, I have to say that this is the only place in the lakes I have seen garbage on the shore. The packs of wandering dogs and obviously substandard housing conditions, regardless of the causes, may prove disturbing to visitors. Silver Donald Cameron says in his book that he quite likes this place, however. Perhaps the answer is to go and see for yourself.

Johnstown Harbour ★★★

 NO FACILITIES

Chart: 4279

There are a good number of summer cottages on the shores of Johnstown Harbour, 8 miles northeast of St. Peters. The harbor and the nearby road are busy by rural Cape Breton standards, so this is perhaps a less attractive place than Cape George, 3 miles to the southwest.

Johnstown Harbour is well sheltered, however, and has pleasant little beaches. Entry is from the north, and simple enough if you keep in the middle and avoid the ruins of the old wharf. Anchorage is possible anywhere, but is perhaps most attractive just inside the bar at the entrance. Hay Cove, to the south is blocked off by sandbars but may be accessible by dinghy.

Other Books About Nova Scotia

This is not an exhaustive list. Many of the books about smaller places are published privately, and you won't find them in library catalogues (there is usually a selection in local bookstores and pharmacies, however); others listed below may be out of print and a little more difficult to find. To help, I've tried to include as much publishing information as possible.

Canadian Hydrographic Service Publications

Canadian Tide and Current Tables, Volume 1: Atlantic Coast and Bay of Fundy
This is essential. If you can't find it before you leave, pick one up at your first port.

Atlas of Tidal Currents, Bay of Fundy and Gulf of Maine
Handy if you are going west of Cape Sable, but this is a computer model and observations in the water are limited.

Sailing Directions, Nova Scotia (Atlantic Coast) and Bay of Fundy
Covers the entire province except the Northumberland Strait and west coast of Cape Breton Island. It has a big-ship orientation, but has some nice aerial photographs, especially of Cape Breton. If you are going through the Canso Causeway, you need the Sailing Directions for the Gulf of Saint Lawrence.

Radio Aids to Marine Navigation, Atlantic and Great Lakes (TP146E)
Not essential.

Atlantic Coast, List of Lights (TP 395E)
The latest edition is 1995. Useful if your charts are out of date, or you are using U.S. charts.

All the above can be ordered directly from:
Hydrographic Chart Distribution Office
Department of Fisheries and Oceans
1675 Russell Road, P.O. Box 8080
Ottawa, Ontario, K1G 3H6
Tel: (613) 998-4931
Fax: (613) 998-1217

East Coast Marine Weather Manual
This is not published by the Hydrographic Office, but the Department of Supply and Services, 1989, Ottawa, ON, Catalog # En 56-81/1989E ISBN 0-662-16934-4. This is a handy little book, but may be hard to get outside Canada.

Other Cruising Guides about Nova Scotia

A Cruising Guide to the Bay of Fundy and the Saint John River; Nicholas Tracy (Camden, ME: International Marine, 1992, 1995)
This is a good book, but its major emphasis is west of Cape Sable, and does not go farther east than Lockeport. I think my coverage of the overlapped areas is a little more comprehensive, though Nick may have a different point of view.

Cruising Guide to the Nova Scotia Coast; John E. McKelvy, Jr. (Dedham, MA: Pilot Press, 1988)
This is a derivative of the original guide published by the Cruising Club of America, and edited by Charles W. Bartlett. The original has some delightfully idiosyncratic descriptions,

missing from the newer editions, one version of which is published by the Nova Scotia Government. There are no photographs and very few charts in this book, and many areas are left out. Coverage does extend to the Magdalene Islands, which are not covered in any other guide.

Yachting Guide to the South Shore of Nova Scotia (Halifax to Yarmouth); Arthur Dechman (Riverport, NS: South Shore Sailing Company)
This is quite a popular guide among the Nova Scotia yachting community, especially those from the more populated parts of the province, but again, it has large gaps in the coverage. There is nothing between Pubnico Harbour and Shelburne, for instance.

Cruise Cape Breton; originally by R.D. MacKeen (Halifax: Diversity Publishing Co., 1974)
This is a useful book, and its coverage of Cape Breton is more comprehensive than mine. (Dr. MacKeen lives there, and considerable government money went into its publication.) I am not sure how much updating goes into it, and some caution should be exercised if its information is largely that of 1974.

Cruising Nova Scotia—Marina Destinations for the Cruising Yacht (Halifax: Nova Scotia Department of Tourism, annual)
This has a useful list of telephone numbers, but the information in previous years has all too often been compiled by someone with no nautical experience at all (the list of facilities in our area, for example, usually being transcribed incorrectly). It is free, however at most tourism centres.

Natural History of Nova Scotia

Seashores—Summer Nature Notes for Nova Scotians Merritt Gibson (Hartsport, NS: Lancelot Press, 1987)
Encyclopedic collection of line drawings of seashore plants and animals, birds and fish.

Birds of Nova Scotia; Robie Tufts (Halifax: Nimbus Publishing Limited, with the Nova Scotia

Museum, a branch of the Nova Scotia Education Department, 3rd Edition, 1986)
A beautifully illustrated collection of every feathered beast ever seen in the province, unfortunately a little difficult to find outside the province.

A Field Guide to the Birds: A Completely New Guide to All the Birds of Eastern and Central North America; Roger Tory Peterson (Boston: Houghton Mifflin for the National Audubon Society, 4th Edition, 1980)
Slightly less comprehensive, but may be easier to obtain outside the province.

General Information, Travel Guides, History, and Novels

Fodor's Nova Scotia, Prince Edward Island, and New Brunswick; (New York: Fodor's Travel Publications, 1992)
The local version of this well-known series.

Nova Scotia; Sherman Hines (Halifax: Nimbus Publications, 1986)
Pictorial study by the province's best-known photographer. There are a number of other similar publications by this author available in local bookstores.

Wind, Whales, and Whisky; Silver Donald Cameron (Toronto: MacMillan Canada, 1991)
Describes a voyage around Cape Breton, with insights into the mores (a little too left wing for my curmudgeonly taste) of the place.

Sniffing the Coast—An Acadian Voyage; Silver Donald Cameron (Toronto: MacMillan Canada, 1993)
This one set on the Eastern Shore.

We Keep a Light; Evelyn Richardson (Whitby, Ontario: McGraw-Hill Ryerson, originally published circa 1938)
A classic story of a lighthouse keeper's family on Bon Portage Island, Shelburne County, won the Governor-General's Award.

Index

A

Abbotts Harbour, 62
Abuptic River, 59. *See also* Argyle River
Acadia. *See l'Acadie*
Annapolis Basin, 31–32
Annapolis Royal, 32
Anchoring, 14
Anchor lights, 15
Andrew Passage, 212–213
Andrews Island (Eastern shore), 210
Andrews Island (Mahone Bay), 132
Apple Cove, 107
Arichat, 225
Ardnamurchan Club, 61
Argyle River, 59–61
Argyle Sound, 60
Argyle Wharf, 60
Aquaculture, 25–26
Aspotogan, 144
Atlantic, Steamship, wreck of, 159

B

Baccaro Point, 85–86
Baddeck, 240–241
Baddeck Bay, 241–242
Bakers Gut, 114–115
Banking, 23
Barrington, Barrington Passage, 82–84
Bawleen, The, 186
Bay of Islands, The, 192–193
Bear River, 32
Beaver Harbour, 191–192
Bedford Basin, 170
Bedford Yacht Club, 170
Bell, Alexander Graham, and museum, 241
Bell Channel, 114

Belmont Resort, 220
Big Harbour, 237
Big Tancook Island. *See* Tancook Island
Blandford, 141
Blind Bay, 154
Bluenose (schooner), 169
Blue Rocks, 123
Bon Portage Island, 67–68
Borgels Cove, 140
Boulaceet. *See* Maskells Harbour
Boylston, 220–221
Bras d'Or Lakes, geographical features, 229–231
Brazil Rock (off Cape Sable), 10–11, 65, 85
Brazil Rocks (off Port Mouton), 100
Bridgewater, 119
Broad Cove, 107
Brooklyn (Liverpool Bay), 103–104
Buoyage, 19, 21

C

Camp Cove Wharf. *See* Argyle Wharf
Canso, Canal and Causeway, 228–229
Canso Harbour 212–214
Canso, Strait of, 229
Cape Breton, economy and culture, 221
Cape George Harbour, 232–233
Cape LaHave, 111, 113
Cape Negro, 81, 85, 88
Cape Negro Island, 85, 86, 87
Cape Roseway, 88, 89, 92
Cape Sable, 73, 74, 75, 76
Cape Sable Island, 69–73, 81–84
Carters Beach, 100
Carters Island, 94–95
Centreville (Digby Neck), 33
Chapel Island, 232–233

Charlos Cove, 208
Charts (of Nova Scotia) 4–8
Chebogue River, 44–46
Chedabucto Bay, 219
Chegoggin, 39
Cherry Cove, 107
Chester Basin, 136–137
Chester "C" Class Yachts, 139
Chester (Harbour), 138–140
Chester Race Week, 140
Chester Yacht Club, 139
Chezzetcook Inlet, 177
Clarke Cove. *See* Marble Mountain
Clark's Harbour, 70–72
Clyde River, 88
Cockerwit Passage, 64–66
Coddles Harbour, 207
Coffin Island, 104–105
Cole Harbour (Tor Bay), 208
Country Harbour, 205–206
Couteau Inlet, 227
Covey Island, 114–116
Covey Island Boatworks, 114
Crammond Islands, 234–235
Cranberry Island (off Canso), 213
Crane Cove, 210
Crawleys Island (Chebogue River), 45
Cripple Creek, 82
Crooked Channel, 113–115
Cross Island, 120, 124–126
Cruising Permits, 22
Cub Basin, 158
Current. *See* Tidal Streams
Customs, Ports of Entry, 22–23

D

Dan Blain's Cove, 152
Daniels Head. *See* South Side
Dartmouth (City of), 171
Dartmouth Yacht Club, 170
Davis Island (Negro Harbour), 88
Deep Cove (Mahone Bay), 140–141
Deep Cove Island (Tusket Islands), 49–50
Dennis Point (Pubnico Harbour), 63–64
Denys Basin, 237–238

Derabies Islands, 214
D'Escousse Harbour, 226–227
Digby, 31–32
Digby Neck, 32–33
Digby Pines Resort, 32
Donald Head. *See* South Side
Dover, East. *See* East Dover
Dover Harbour (Eastern Shore), 211–212
Dover Harbour (Halifax County), 151–152
Dover Passage, 211
Dover Run, Little, 212
Drum Head, 205–207
Duncan Cove, 165
Dundee (Marina and Resort), 233–234

E

Eagle Head, 105
East Bay, 243
East Dover (Halifax County), 153
Eastern Passage, 163
East Ironbound Island, 142–143
East Point Gut, 123–124
East River. *See* Argyle River
East Sandy Cove, 35
Ecum Secum, approaches from seaward, 196
Ecum Secum Inlet, 194–197
Ecum Secum Wharf, 197
Ellenwoods Island, 50–51
Electronics. *See* Navigational Aids, electronic
Entry, Ports of, 22
Eskasoni, 243
Etoile Island, 58

F

False LaHave, 114–115
False Passage (Ship Harbour), 181
False Passage (Canso), 213
Felker Cove, 193
Firearms regulations, 22–23
Fishermans Harbour, 205
Fishery, problems of, 45, 96, 147, 214
Fishing, vessels, types and regions of operation,
    23–26,
Flat Island, 55
Fog, 12–13

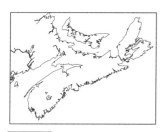

Forbes Point (Cockerwit Passage), 68
Forbes Point (Liverpool Bay), 103
Folly Channel, 114–116
Franks George Island, 147
Freeport, 35
French Village Harbour, 146
Frontal Systems, 13
Fuel, supplies of, 16

G

Gates, The, 187
Gegogan Harbour, 202
Gerard Passage, 186
Gifford Island, 134
Glasgow Harbour, 213
Glen Haven. *See* French Village Harbour
Glen Margaret, 147
Goldboro, 206
Gold River (Mahone Bay), 136
Gooseberry Island (Argyle), 60
Gooseberry Island (Chester), 139
Grand Manan Island, 10
Grand Narrows Bridge, 238–239
Grand Passage, 34
Granite Coast, The, 151
Graves Island, 140
Great Bras d'Or, 242
Green Island (off Yarmouth), 47
Green Harbour, 93
Gullivers Cove, 33
Gunning Cove, 93
Guysborough County, North Shore of, 219
Guysborough Harbour, 219–221

H

Harbour Island (Country Harbour), 206–207
Haddock Harbour, 226–227
Halibut Bay, 114
Halifax, 151, 160–163, 165–171
    Armdale Yacht Club, 167
    Approaches, 151, 160–163
    Anchorages, 165–168
    Cunard Wharf, 168

Explosion of 1917, 169
Facilities Ashore, 168–169
Local weather patterns, 163
Maritime Museum, 167–168
Narrows, 169
Northwest Arm, 166
Royal Nova Scotia Yacht Squadron, 166
Traffic Control, 151, 160–161
Harrigan Cove, 193
Harris Island, 49–50
Hawbolt Cove, 198
Hawbolt Island (Mitchell Bay), 194–195
Hawbolt Island (Marie-Joseph), 198
Head Harbour (St. Margarets Bay), 145–146
Hearn Island, 157–158
Heckmanns Anchorage, 129
Heisler, Ben, 139
Hells Gate, 51
Hermans Island, 131
Herring Cove, 165
Holland Harbour, 204
Horsehead Cove. *See* Beaver Harbour
Hospitals, 21
Hubbards Cove, 145
Hubley Cove, 146
Hurricanes, 13–14

I

Indian Harbour (Eastern Shore), 204
Indian Harbour (St. Margarets Bay), 147
Indian Harbour (Sambro), 164
Indian Islands (Bras d'Or lakes), 243
Indian Sluice Bay, 56–57
Indian Point, 133–134
Ingomar, 87
Inhabitants Harbour, 227–228
Inner Island. *See* Stoddard Island
Inner Sambro Island, 164
Inside Passage, The, 190–198
Iona, 238–239
Ironbound Island (Eastern Shore), 184
Ironbound Island E. *See* Ironbound Island
Ironbound Island W. *See* Ironbound Island
Isaacs Harbour, 205–207
Isle Madame, 224–227

J

Janvrin Harbour, 226
Heddore Harbour, 177–178
Johns Island (Cockerwit Passage), 65–66
Johns Island (Tusket Islands), 51
Johnstown Harbour, 243
Jones Island, 57–58, 60
Jones Ledge, 58, 60
Jordan Bay, 93

K

Ketch Harbour, 165
Krauch, Willy, Smokehouse, 185

L

l'Acadie, 36
LaHave Bakery, 118
LaHave Islands, 111–116
LaHave River, 117–119
LaHave Yacht Club, 118
Larrys River, 208
Ledge Harbour, 62
Lennox Passage, 226–227
Lennox Passage bridge, 227
L'Hebert, Port. *See* Port L'Hebert
Liscombe Harbour, 198–199
Liscombe Lodge, 201–202
Liscombe River, 200–201
Little Dover Run, 212
Little Harbour (Bras d'Or Lakes), 237
Little Harbour (Eastern Shore), 180
Little Liscombe Harbour, 199–200
Little Port L'Hebert, 96–97
Little River Harbour, 46–47
Little Tancook Island, 142
Liverpool, 102–103
Liverpool Bay, 101–102
Lobster Bay, 55–62
Lockeport, 93–96
Louse Harbour, 211
Lower East Pubnico, 63
Lower Sandy Point, 93
Lower South Cove, 121
Lunenburg Bay, 120–122
Lunenburg Back Harbour, 129–130

Lunenburg Harbour, 121–123
Lunenburg Peninsulas, 123
Lunenburg Yacht Club, 131
Luke Island, 147

M

Macleod Island, 192
Macnabs Cove, 232
Maders Cove, 132
Mahone Bay, Approaches, 127–128, 132
Mahone Bay Inshore Rescue, 127
Mahone Bay, town of, 131–133
Mahone Bay Wooden Boat Festival, 133
Malagash Cove, 187–188
Malagawatch, 237
Malagawatch Boat Canal, 238
Marble Mountain, 235–236
Marie Joseph Harbour, 197–198
Maskells Harbour, 239–240
Marriots Cove, 140
Mars Head, 159
Marshall Cove, 209–210
Mason Island, 131
Mason Cove (Tangier), 183
McGrath Cove, 154
McKinnons Harbour, 238
McNabs Island, 171
McNutts Island, 92–93
Medical Facilities, 21
Medway Harbour, 105
Meisners Island, 140
Mersey River, 103
Meteghan, 37
Meteghan River, 36
Mitchell Bay, 194–195
Molasses Harbour. *See* Port Felix
Moose Harbour, 102
Morris Island, 57–58
Morrison Harbour, 233
Moser River, 193–194
Mosher Island (LaHave Islands), 115
Mosher Island (St. Margarets Bay), 147
Mount Desert Island and Rock, Maine, 10–11
Mouton Harbour (Port Bickerton), 204
Mud Island, 54
Mulgrave, 221

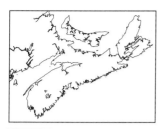

Mushaboom Harbour, 187
Musquoidobot Harbour, 177
Mussel Cove, 220

N

Narrows Basin (Mahone Bay), 134
Narrows, The (Halifax), 169
Naval Exercise Areas, 162, 176
Navigational Aids, electronic, 15–16
Navigational publications, official, 5
Necum Tech, 193
Negro Harbour. *See* Clyde River
Newellton, 71
New Harbour (Blandford), 141
New Harbour (Eastern Shore), 207
North East Point, 82–84

O

Oak Island, 135–136
Oak Island Inn and Marina, 136
Oak Island Money Pit, 135
Orangedale, 237
Outer Island. *See* Bon Portage Island
Owls Head Bay (Eastern Shore), 181
Owls Head Bay (St. Margarets Bay), 144, 145
Owls Head Island (Tusket Islands), 47

P

Passages
    Canso to St. Peters, 221–222
    East from Cape LaHave, 111–112
    East from Ecum Secum, 197
    East from Jeddore, 179–180
    East from Halifax, 175–176
    East from Sheet Harbour, 189
    East from Tusket Islands, 65
    False Passage, 181
    Inside Passage, The, 190–198
    Inside to Shoal Bay, 182
    LaHave River to Lunenburg, 119
    New England to Nova Scotia, 10–11
    Outside Tuffin Island, 196
    Rounding Cape Sable, 73–76
    Sambro Ledges, 161–162
    St. Peters to Grand Narrows, 233
Peases Island, 51
Peggys Cove, 147
Petit-de-Grat Inlet, 224–225
Petite Anse, 225
Petite Passage, 33–34
Petite Riviere, 114
Petpeswick Inlet, 177
Pinkneys Point, 46
Piracy, last conviction in Canada, 65
Piscatiqui Island, 214
Popes Harbour, 185
Portage Cove, 213
Port Bickerton, 204
Port Felix, 208
Port Hawkesbury, 228–229
Port Howe, 211
Port Joli, 98
Port La Tour, 84–85
Port L'Hebert, 97–98
Port Maitland, 38
Port Medway, 106
Port Mouton, 98–101
Port Mouton Island, 101
Port Mouton Wharf, 100, 101
Port Royal Harbour. *See* Leblanc Harbour
Poulamon Bay, 227
Prices Island, 209, 210
Princes Inlet, 131
Pringle Harbour, 233
Prospect, 155
Prospect Bay, 156
Provisioning, 16
Pubnico Harbour, 62–64
Pubnico, Lower East, 63
Pubnico, West, 64

R

Radio communication (VHF, etc.), 16
Rafuse Island, 130
Ram Island Passage, 94–95
Raspberry Coves, East and West, 210
Ratings (of harbors, etc.), explained 3–4

River Bourgeois, 226
Roberts Anchorage, 59
Rogues Roost, 156–158
Rose Bay, 120–121
Round Island (Mahone Bay), 134
Ryan Gut, 158–159

S

Sable River, 96
Sambro Ledges, passages through, 161–162
Sambro Harbour, 163–164
Sambro Island. *See* Inner Sambo Island
Sallys Cove, 184–185
Salvages, The, 85, 86
Salmon River (Beaver Harbour), 192
Salmon River (Jeddore), 178
Sandy Cove (Chester), 140
Sandy Cove (Princes Inlet), 131
Sandy Cove East. *See* East Sandy Cove
Sandy Cove Head (Eastern Shore), 184
Sandy Point (Shelburne), 93
Saulnierville, 36
Schooner Passage, 47–51,
Seabright, 146
Seal Harbor, 207
Seal Island, 52–54
Search and Rescue, 21, 35, 72, 100, 127, 175, 204
Shad Bay, Shag Bay, 154
Shearwater Yacht Club, 171
Sheet Harbour, 188–189
Sheet Harbour Passage, 190
Shelburne Harbour, 88–92
Shelburne Harbour Yacht Club, 81, 89–90
Shelburne, Town of, 90–92,
Shelter Cove. *See* Sallys Cove
Sherbrook, 203
Ship Harbour, 181
Shoal Bay, 182
Shore Access, Right of in legislation, 9
Shut-in Island (East of Halifax), 176
Shut-in Island (St. Margarets Bay), 143, 147
Sissiboo River. *See* Weymouth
Smith Cove, 198
Soldiers Cove, 232
Sonora, 203

South Shore Marine, 136–137
South Side (Cape Sable Island), 81–82
Southwest Cove (Eastern Shore), 179
Southwest Cove (St. Margarets Bay), 145
Sperry Cove, 116
Snows Cove, 158
Snug Harbour, 116
Spanish Ship Bay, 200
Spry Bay, 186
St. Andrews Channel, 242
St. Margarets Bay, 143–147
    Approaches, 143
St. Marys Bay (Western Nova Scotia), 32–37
St. Marys River, 202
St. Patricks Channel, 242
St. Peters, 223–224
St. Peters Canal, 222–223
St. Peters Inlet, 231
Stevens Cove, 136–137
Stevens, David and family, 130
Stoddard Island, 68, 69
Stoney Island, 82
Stonehurst. *See* Tanners Pass
Sugar Harbour Islands, 208
Sutherland Island, 192
Swims Point, 73

T

Tancook Island, 141–142
Tancook Island, Little, 142
Tancook Schooners, 141
Tangier Harbour, 182–183
Tangier Island Gut, 183
Tanners Pass, 126–127
Terence Basin, 159, 160
Three Fathom Harbour, 176–177
Tickle Channel (Canso), 214
Tidal Streams, 19–20
Tides, range of, 17–18
Tittle, The (Canso), 214
Tittle, The (Western Nova Scotia), 57
Tiverton, 33
Tor Bay, 207–208
Town Point, 45
Traffic Separation Zones, 24, 26

Trout Cove, 33
Tuffin Island, 196
Turpentine Island, 50
Tusket Islands, 47–52
Tusket River, 56
Tusket, village, 57

V

Voglers Cove, 106–107

W

Washabuck River, 242
Weather Forecast Areas, 12
Weather, in Nova Scotia, 11–14
Webbs Cove, 206
Wedgeport, 51–52
West Arichat, 226
West Bay, 233
West Bay, islands in, 234–235
West Berlin, 105
West Head (Cape Sable Island), 70–71
West Ironbound Island, 120

Westport, 34–35
West Pubnico, 64
Weymouth, 35–36
Whale Cove (Digby Neck), 33
Whale Cove (Eastern Shore), 210
Whitehaven. *See* Whitehead Harbour
Whitehead Harbour, 208–210
White Islands, 196
White Point (near Liverpool), 99
White Point Beach lodge, 101
Whycocomagh, 242
Wine Cove, 210
Wine Harbour, 204
Wobamkek Beach, 100
Wolfe Gut, 114–115
Woods Harbour, 66–67

Y

Yarmouth, 39-44
Yarmouth Approaches, 39, 40, 41
Yarmouth, Town of, 41, 42, 43
Yankee Cove, 209, 210
Young Island, 134

Waypoints and Notes

Waypoints and Notes

Waypoints and Notes

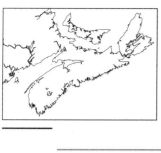

Waypoints and Notes

Waypoints and Notes

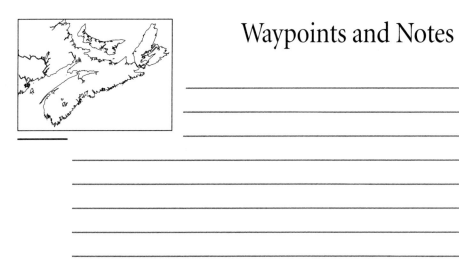

Waypoints and Notes

Waypoints and Notes

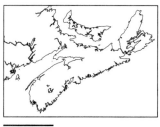

Waypoints and Notes